The Bardo of Waking Life

Selected Other Works by Richard Grossinger

Book of the Cranberry Islands
Book of the Earth and Sky
The Continents
Embryogenesis: Species, Gender, and Identity
Embryos, Galaxies, and Sentient Beings: How the Universe Makes Life
Homeopathy: The Great Riddle
The Long Body of the Dream
New Moon
The New York Mets: Ethnography, Myth, and Subtext
The Night Sky: The Science and Anthropology of the Stars and Planets
On the Integration of Nature: Post-9/11 Biopolitical Notes
Out of Babylon: Ghosts of Grossinger's
Planet Medicine: Origins
Planet Medicine: Modalities
The Provinces
The Slag of Creation
Solar Journal: Oecological Sections
The Unfinished Business of Doctor Hermes
Waiting for the Martian Express: Cosmic Visitors, Earth Warriors, Luminous Dreams

As Editor or Co-editor

The Alchemical Tradition in the Late Twentieth Century
Baseball I Gave You All the Best Years of My Life
Ecology and Consciousness
Into the Temple of Baseball
Nuclear Strategy and the Code of the Warrior
Olson-Melville Sourcebook: The Mediterranean
Olson-Melville Sourcebook: The New Found Land

The Bardo of Waking Life

Richard Grossinger

North Atlantic Books
Berkeley, California

Published by
North Atlantic Books
P.O. Box 12327
Berkeley, California 94712

Cover photo by Teijia Saga
Cover and book design by Susan Quasha
Printed in the United States of America

The Bardo of Waking Life is sponsored by the Society for the Study of Native Arts and Sciences, a nonprofit educational corporation whose goals are to develop an educational and cross-cultural perspective linking various scientific, social, and artistic fields; to nurture a holistic view of arts, sciences, humanities, and healing; and to publish and distribute literature on the relationship of mind, body, and nature.

North Atlantic Books' publications are available through most bookstores. For further information, call 800-733-3000 or visit our website at www.northatlanticbooks.com.

Library of Congress Cataloging-in-Publication Data

Grossinger, Richard, 1944–
   The bardo of waking life / by Richard Grossinger.
      p. cm.
   Summary: "The bardo of waking life is a meditation on the Tibetan Buddhist bardo realm, which is viewed as the bridge between lives, the state people enter after death and before rebirth. This book examines waking life and its history and language as if it were a bardo state rather than ultimate reality. Bardo is at once prose poetry, intimate memoir, and anthropological inquiry"—Provided by publisher.
   ISBN 978-1-55643-700-7
   I. Title.
PS3557.R66B37 2008
818'.5'407—dc22

2007042473

For:

Robert Simmons and Kathy Warner,
Elliot Spiker and Karel Weisberg,
George and Susan Quasha,
Andrew Lugg and Lynne Cohen,
Robert and Sonnie Goodman,
Charlie and Susan Halpern
Keith Karlson and Al Walker,
Pat Humphries and Sandy Opatow,
Ed and Sonya Mondazzi,

couples whose love for each other makes a difference.

Acknowledgments

I want to thank Mary Stark for reading, correcting, and commenting candidly and profoundly on this manuscript as I wrote it. Her influence is reflected throughout the book, sometimes in the words I use and sometimes in words that aren't there because she vetoed or at least frowned upon them. There are a few sections where, in truth, she deserves a "co-writing" credit.

I also want to thank Kathy Glass for doing the formal edit at the end. She not only caught a surprising number of typos and other errors but helped refine the tone by serving as a second conscience.

I will cite (or re-cite) a few others here: Rob Brezsny for his constant pronoic visioning, David Ulansey for his devil's advocacy, Rich Borden's Human Ecology class at College of the Atlantic in Bar Harbor for their feedback, Dusty Dowes for his wise snippets, Charles Stein for his brilliant wisdom always a step ahead of the curve, Esperide Ananas for her tour of Damanhur, Gerrit Lansing for having the references any time I asked an esoteric question, Gene Alexander for his radical insights, Patricia Fox for her teaching, Paul Weiss for the chi gung, Phillip Wohlstetter for keeping the politics honest, Miha Mazzini for his challenges from outside the grid and the chance to read from this book in Ljubljana, Slovenia, John Upledger for his transmission of healing, Cullen Dorn for his unsparing glimpse of infinitude, Steve Perrin for the trail, and Robert Simmons for the transparency and the crystals.

Thanks too to Susan Quasha for her elegant design.

The photograph of the swans on the cover is an image I held for over ten years, hoping to find a book on which to use it. I am grateful to Teijia Saga and his son Takeo Saga for granting permission, and to Hisae Matsuda for tracking them down and handling the correspondence gracefully in Japanese. I hope North Atlantic Books will be able to publish a book of Mr. Saga's remarkable swan photographs within the next year or two.

Contents

Second Cycle

Fourth Cycle

Fifth Cycle

"This magic moment,/so different and so new … /will last forever,/ forever/until the end of time...."

— JAY AND THE AMERICANS, "THIS MAGIC MOMENT"

"The human body is like a rootless tree and relies solely on the breath as roots and branches. A lifetime is just a dream, like an out breath which does not guarantee the in breath after it. And today does not insure the morrow. If life is passed aimlessly with death ever coming unexpectedly, the bones of the body will disperse, the four elements will scatter, and the deluded consciousness will transmigrate through another realm of existence without knowing what form it will take in another life."

— LU K'UAN YÜ

"I believe we can nowhere find a better type of … perfectly free creature than the common house-fly. Nor free only, but brave, and irreverent to a degree which I think no human republican could by any philosophy exalt himself to."

— JOHN RUSKIN IN "THE QUEEN OF THE AIR"

"The infinite future is before you, and you must always remember that each word, thought, and deed lays up a store for you and that as the bad thoughts and bad works are ready to spring upon you like tigers, so also there is the inspiring hope that the good thoughts and good deeds are ready with the power of a hundred thousand angels to defend you always and forever."

— SWAMI VIVEKANANDA

"The blues they come,/the blues they come./Nobody knows where/ the blues come from./The blues they go, the blues they go./And everybody's happy when the old blues go."
—LEROY CARR, "PAPA'S ON THE HOUSETOP"

"The Earth for us is a very bad place from the cosmic point of view—it is like the most remote part of northern Siberia, very far from everywhere; it is cold, life is very hard. Everything that in another place either comes by itself or is easily obtained, is here acquired only by hard labor; everything must be fought for both in life and in the work....

"If men could really see their true position and could understand all the horror of it, they would be unable to remain where they are even for one second."
—G. I. GURDJIEFF

"The pure men of old slept without dreams and woke without anxiety.... They did not know what it was like to love life or hate death. They did not rejoice in birth, or resist returning to rest. They came on a whim and went on a whim. They did not forget their origin, neither did they search into their extinction. They savored the gift they had been given and forgot it when they gave it back."
—CHUANG TZU, FOURTH CENTURY B.C.E.

"Who can explain it?/Who can tell you why?/Fools give you reasons;/Wise men never try."
—RICHARD RODGERS AND OSCAR HAMMERSTEIN,
"SOME ENCHANTED EVENING" (... *YOU WILL SEE A STRANGER
ACROSS A CROWDED ROOM....*)

"At the center of our being is a point of nothingness which is untouched by sin and illusion, a point of pure truth, a point or spark which belongs entirely to God, which is never at our disposal.... This little point of nothingness and of absolute poverty is the pure glory of God in us.... It is like a pure diamond, blazing with the invisible light of heaven. It is in everybody.... I have no program for this seeing. It is only given. But the gate of heaven is everywhere."

—THOMAS MERTON

"All up and down this whole creation/sadly I roam...."
—STEPHEN FOSTER, "OLD FOLKS AT HOME"

"If we destroy ourselves and our environment, the rock-eating microbes underground will in all likelihood endure, and over the next three billion years, species by species Earth's biosphere will repopulate itself with the same tireless industry and exquisite artistry. And if this regeneration is not decreed to happen here, it will happen on another terrestrial orb—if not in this universe, in the next. Sooner or later, here or elsewhere, we will inevitably find ourselves again awakening into existence at this very crossroads. Shall we once again succumb to hubris? Have we not perhaps already, in bygone ages, despoiled our nest and come to naught, cycle after cycle? Past and future converge in the choice that is before us in the present moment. From the heart of Nature, the divine mystery beckons."

—PIR ZIA INAYAT KHAN

"Bigotry is the sacred disease."

—HERACLITUS

"You twice attain the highest office of the land, and indeed the highest office on the planet, and you use a national tragedy to justify invasions of two countries that had nothing to do with an attack on our soil. To satisfy personal vendettas, ambitions and greed, hundreds of thousands of people are dead, and you do not have to say 'sorry' and indeed, you continue to manipulate simple people by telling them that millions of people have been 'liberated' from a dictator and our country is safer and freer now, never mind that you have imposed a more severe dictatorship on the people of the lands.

"Corporations are now free to pollute our skies and waters and send our jobs overseas and reap profits globally off the backs of people all over the world and to the detriment of workers here in the United States. Many free-trade agreements have the effect of harming the citizens of all the countries involved for the benefit of a few. Many people have lost their savings and retirement while the CEOs of these companies still 'rape and pillage' like Blackbeards and receive their enormously immoral bonuses. Atonement is not even possible in these situations because the wealthiest in our country are looked up to as people who are really living the 'American Dream.'"

—Cindy Sheehan

"One day when the secrets of the Sun/enlighten everyone,/the Universe shall shine."

—Donovan Leitch, "Universe Am I"

"the world, the mundus

        round—

no explanation

    all that happens is eternal

no examples, no proving

possible"

—Charles Olson

Preface

In this astonishing book, Richard Grossinger takes us on a layered journey of constant revelation, some measure of delight, and fleeting moments of despair, to a planet we dimly recognize for having dreamed it once. In fact, it's not just a planet but a teeming esoteric realm of conscious existence, the mooring place of a ghostly boat which embarks and disembarks in the sea of our inner life.

We feel we are traversing vaguely familiar waters, only to realize that it is indeed our home, our own blue planet—and the currents that carry us in our explorations are the very paradoxes of human existence and awareness.

If truth be told, it's the author himself who is the newcomer, not us. We are seeing things through his wide, startled eyes. Though it will never show up on any c.v., I suspect Grossinger is from an entirely different zip code in the galaxy and is lending us his outsider's perspective. This may not be his first go-around on the Third Planet from the Sun, but he has most certainly known the stirrings of an existence long ago and farther away. To his examination of our earthly plights he brings the freshness, curiosity, fondness, hope, and sorrow, suggestive of an old soul who may have "been there, done that"—but elsewhere in time and space. Of course, I don't know that literally; I mean it as a manner of speaking about something else, mysterious in itself. Then again maybe I do mean it literally. It doesn't matter.

His cover story is that, like myself, he was trained as an anthropologist, so he can stand a bit aside from the usual cultural blinders to observe the world around him. I don't dispute the formal credentials, but Grossinger's fine attunement to the vital flow of our inner tides speaks more of a time-traveler poet than an academic.

I am reminded of the words of fellow-anthropologist Loren Eiseley: "By this tenuous thread of living protoplasm, stretching backward into time, we are linked forever to lost beaches.... The stars which caught our blind amphibian stare have shifted far or vanished in their courses, but still that naked glistening thread winds onward. No one knows the secret of its beginnings or its end. Its forms are phantoms. The thread alone is real, the thread is life."

That is the subject of Grossinger's timeless yet timely inquiry, that and more.

In ancient Chinese medicine, much could be learned of the state of a person's entire health by reading his or her pulses, which have subtle gradations and meanings far beyond the Western clocking of our tickers. Sometimes, when the patient was a female, the doctor had to examine her from a discrete distance, from behind a screen. A ribbon would be tied to the patient's wrist, and from the far end of this cord the physician had to detect these same infinitesimally subtle variations of quality, tempo, and timbre, all indicating the ebb and the flow of *chi* throughout the patient's body.

This is what the author has learned to do, as a vigilant observer from another place and time, long separated from us by a screen of illusory distance. What's more, he gets the pulse right in its every nuance: the rhythm of a coastal marsh, the vibration of a helpless bug upturned on the roadside, the shudder of a nation at a crossroads, of a planet in the throes of drastic transformation, of a cosmos heaving with cataclysmic cycles of chaos, destruction, birth and rebirth, of coming-into-being and annihilation. The rhythm beating Time behind the dance of Shiva.

In fact Grossinger intuits the tempo at the very heart of creation, throbbing with what turns out to be a supremely simple force—Love.

This is the very pulse which the author knows how to feel—in fact has no choice but to feel with almost unbearable acuity. Through it he has touched upon the vastness of the universe and sensed how this vastness is curled up inside every detail, every sense, every motion here in this incarnation. It is the author's burden, but also his salvation and ours, to know that this bright, sensual, fleeting existence means something profound and not just in the short run, but in the longest run we cannot even begin to imagine.

The paradox is that the thread can only be accurately read when it is pulled out taut. The pulsations are transmitted through the art of challenging the fibers of the ribbon. And Grossinger spares no diligence, no expedient, no wile. He never gives up pulling, drawing out the stories twisted within the thread, sensing the tension, even creating the tension, but always to give the best and truest reading of the moment and every other moment that lies curled within it. The thread of life is a woven river of living consciousness winding its way from the elusive "patient" behind the screen to the eager, vigilant observer standing aside.

The traveler "come from aways," as they say in the Maritimes, tugs on the rope of his own bodily vessel, and pulls it through the currents again and again, terrified yet drawn by both the strangeness and odd familiarity of it all. Buoyed by unseen guidance, he sounds the depths of the unconscious, of material existence, and of the universal consciousness which beckons us all. His pilgrim ponderings, observations, and work-in-progress conclusions ring true. They are startlingly unique yet at the same time validating of something we all know somewhere inside us. They are obvious, but only after he has pointed to them and given them name. Naming is an explorer's prerogative, essential to the mapping of any route within or without. The salty living cord is safely pulsating in his hands, and he throws it as a lifeline for others who swim these same waters.

MONTREAL, QUEBEC, 2008

Foreword

ROB BREZSNY

The Honey and Vinegar Tasters

John Keats wrote that "if something is not beautiful, it is probably not true." I celebrate that hypothesis in my book *Pronoia Is the Antidote for Paranoia: How the Whole World Is Conspiring to Shower You with Blessings.* I further propose that the universe is inherently friendly to human beings; that all of creation is set up to liberate us from our suffering and teach us how to love intelligently; and that life always gives us exactly what we need, exactly when we need it (though not necessarily what we want).

Dogmatic cynics are often so mad about my book's title that they can't bring themselves to explore the inside. Why bother to actually read about such a preposterous idea? They accuse me of intellectual dishonesty, disingenuous Pollyannaism, or New Age delusion.

If they do manage to read even a few pages, they find that the blessings I reference in the title are not materialistic fetishes like luxurious vacation homes, high status, and a perfect physique. I'm more interested in fascinating surprises, dizzying adventures, challenging gifts we hardly know what to do with, and conundrums that compel us to get smarter and wilder and kinder and trickier. I also enjoy exposing secret miracles, like the way the sun continually detonates nuclear explosions in order to convert its own body into heat, light, and energy for our personal use.

But I don't take the cynics' fury personally. When I suggest that life is a sublime mystery designed to grow us all into strong, supple messiahs, I understand that's the equivalent, for them, of denying the Holocaust. They're addicted to a formulation that's the opposite of Keats': if something is not ugly, it is probably not true.

Modern storytellers are at the vanguard of promoting this doctrine, which I refer to as pop nihilism. A majority of journalists, filmmakers, novelists, critics, talk-show hosts, musicians, and pundits act as if breakdown is far more common and far more interesting than breakthrough; that painful twists outnumber redemptive transformations by a wide margin and are profoundly more entertaining as well.

Earlier in my life, I too worshiped the religion of pop nihilism. In the 1980s, for example, I launched a crusade against what I called "the global genocide of the imagination." I railed against the "entertainment criminals" who barrage us with floods of fake information and inane ugliness, decimating and paralyzing our image-making faculties. For years, much of my creative work was stoked by my rage against the machine for its soulless crimes of injustice and greed and rapaciousness and cruelty.

But as the crazy wisdom of pronoia overtook me in the 1990s, I gradually weaned myself from the gratuitous gratification that wrath offered. Against the grain, I experimented with strategies for motivating myself through crafty joy and purified desire and the longing for freedom. I played with ideas that helped me shed the habit of seeing the worst in everything and everyone. In its place I built a new habit of looking for the best.

But I never formally renounced my affiliation with the religion of cynicism. I didn't become a fundamentalist apostate preaching the doctrine of fanatical optimism. In the back of my wild heart, I knew I couldn't thrive without at least a tincture of the ferocity and outrage that had driven so much of my earlier self-expression.

Even at the height of my infatuation with the beautiful truths that swarmed into me while writing *Pronoia*, I nurtured a relationship with the awful truths. And I didn't hide that from my readers.

Yes, I did purposely go overboard in championing the cause of liberation and pleasure and ingenuity and integrity and renewal and harmony and love. The book's destiny was, after all, to serve as a counterbalance to the trendy predominance of bad news and paranoid attitudes. It was meant to be an antidote for the pandemic of snark.

But I made sure that *Pronoia* also contained numerous "Homeopathic Medicine Spells," talismans that cram long lists of the world's evils inside ritually consecrated mandalas. These spells diffuse the hypnotizing lure of doom and gloom by acknowledging the horror with a sardonic wink.

Pronoia also has many variations on a theme captured in William Vollman's testimony: "The most important and enjoyable thing in life is doing something that's a complicated, tricky problem that you don't know how to solve."

Furthermore, the book stops far short of calling for the totalitarian imposition of good cheer. I say I can tolerate the news media filling up half their pages and airwaves and bandwidths with poker-faced accounts of decline and degeneration, misery and destruction. All I seek is equal time for stories that inspire us to adore life instead of fearing it. And I'd gladly accept twenty-five percent. Even ten percent.

So *Pronoia* hints at a paradoxical philosophy more complex than a naïve quest for beauty and benevolence. It welcomes in a taste of darkness, acknowledging the shadows in the big picture. But it doesn't go as far as I will someday be able to go when I have ripened into my full powers. I'm not smart enough yet—am still on my way toward that more complete view in which both pronoia and paranoia have a place.

As he shows in *The Bardo of Waking Life*, Richard Grossinger is much further along the path I'm headed down. He trumps the cynics and the pronoiacs alike—even trumps the dialectical tussle between the cynics and the pronoiacs.

He simultaneously soars and burrows free of the us-versus-them clench so as to arrive at a transcendent subterranean vision that proves both of the following statements are true: Life is a bitch and then you die, AND life is a conspiracy to shower you with blessings. The unexpected fact of the matter, he suggests, is that everything is totally fucked up AND everything is perfect just the way it is.

Grossinger may bristle when I compare him to Byron Katie, whom he's nothing like in many respects, but the two of them are in my view the founding shamans of Taoism 2.0, a fresh spiritual tradition that doesn't know it exists yet.

After dancing all night at a Dionysian festival a few years ago, I had a vision of what it might look like: "Not just the old Chinese-style Tao," I wrote on a paper towel at 5:30 AM, "but the Oxymoronic Tao—a mutated, updated, Californicated version of the Tao: Tao with an attitude.

"Not the calm, abstract, passive, world-weary, everything-is-everything Tao of the ancient sage Lao-Tse, but the fragrant, shimmering, electrifying Tao of the outrageous now, where each discrete glint of individuated beauty is discernible amidst the mass of confusion, rousing us to revelry and activism.

"Not a Tao just sitting in cool unflappable contemplation of the ultimate unity of the wound and the cure, but rather a Tao that gets out there with an aggressive affirmative action program for artfully highlighting and rejoicing in the incongruous juxtapositions; a Tao that romances the contradictions with an exuberant experimentalism and whips up slathering throbs of ripe mojo.

"The Oxymoronic Tao will be a Tao that doesn't pacify and dial down our martial force. Rather, it will supercharge us, hooking us up to the elemental power that flows wherever opposites unite.

"Here's the bonus. With the Tao as our fuel, our vision will open to the reality that opposites are always uniting everywhere. It will make anything and everything we gaze upon turn into the philosopher's stone, the grail, the pearl of great price, the treasure beyond measure."

The Bardo of Waking Life aligns us with that Tao. It ushers us into a blissful abyss where we're pummeled and caressed by an erotic crush of screamingly tender contradictions. Our fixations crack apart. Our egos ache. We swoon with the stark elation that comes from knowing how freaking interesting everything is. We're shocked and healed, healed and shocked. Every terror is a source of wonder that rips us out of our ignorance. Every miracle blows our minds so mercilessly we can't help but cry out with a bewildered, primordial longing for more.

I hope to write my own version of *The Bardo of Waking Life* someday.

To do it, I'll have to master the art of being dead and alive at the same time; I'll have to learn how to be both here in my daily life and also over there in the realm I will be more naturally focused on after my body dissolves. I won't exactly be dreaming while awake or be awake in my dreams, but both simultaneously. It will feel like having a lucid dream with my eyes wide open, the sun at midnight filling up half the sky and the full moon at noon in the other half.

When I write my own *Bardo of Waking Life*, it will be because I've become adept at living outside of time, peering down lovingly at our special snatch of history with the liberated compassion that comes from being blended with the eleven-dimensional consciousness of the Logos—even as I exult in the curious sensation of being ground up by the wheels of linear time … even as I exercise my skill for joyfully plucking the essential teaching from each perplexing, glorious, shattering, victorious moment … even as I thrill to the majestic spectacle of my body constantly transforming into a different version of itself, all of its atoms regularly exchanged for new ones in the cyclical interplay of apocalypse and rebirth.

But that won't happen for a while. My wild heart isn't ready. I have not yet achieved the knack of being torn apart and woven back together a hundred times a day, every day, by life's wrenching insistence on cramming delight and loss into every single perception.

While I do have an ever-growing tolerance for, even a budding attraction to being seared by the way extravagant beauty and desolate longing are always arriving entwined, I'm not yet strong enough to surrender to being seared ceaselessly. And I will need to be able to do that in order to create my own personal *Bardo of Waking Life*.

I'm more than halfway there. I know what it's like to be annihilated by the pouring-out-of-my-skin empathy I feel for you and all the other creatures I live among. And I know what it's like to reel with rapture as I'm rocked by the yelping, visceral thrill of my blood resonating with your blood, of my nerves reliving the memory that they're made of the same star dust yours are.

Someday I will be able to hum in the grip of both those states simultaneously. Not just in rare fits of agonizing joy, but on an ongoing basis. As a constant meditation. As a daily spiritual practice.

I may be projecting or mythologizing in my notion that Grossinger is the person, of all those I know, who has most completely accomplished this triumphant crucifixion. But it doesn't matter if I am. *Bardo* is medicine pinched from the gods. It's a gift from the future, a magical artifact materialized out of a future dream. It's the smoking gun that proves the mutant archetype is ready to incarnate in flesh and blood.

For now, I'll call the archetype the Oxymoronic Tao, though if I'm true to its serpentine laws, I'll no doubt have to change its name frequently in the coming years. That's one of the secrets, I suspect, to making sure it will keep working for me, turning everything and everyone into the philosopher's stone, the grail, the pearl of great price, the treasure beyond measure.

MILL VALLEY, CALIFORNIA

Grace Before Meals

ROBERT KELLY

A Letter to Richard Grossinger

This book, this waking up between lives in the between life itself, the long shaping of the book, the appearance of it, its own peculiar *now*—all that makes a huge moment for you and the body of your own work. Following as it does *On the Integration of Nature*, it is the culmination of so many decades of study and exploration and telling about it.

But it's also a precisely important moment for us. Who is us? The ones who have been watching grow, return to the world, the possibility of meaningfully talking about what's around us [world—the word means the 'wraparound', what's around us all the time] hard, insistent, vigilant—without the convenience of narrative fictional or otherwise, without the lyrical packaging of poetry, without the comforting trusses and armatures of theory. To talk about the world as it happens to your head when you are in it.

Another age would have spoken of observation. As Goethe or Ruskin might have, *without prejudice,* observed the habits of an insect or the outgrowth of cotyledon towards plant. Watching things grow.

Grow. I see your work (this vein at least of your work, from *Solar Journal* on forward—journals without datelines) as a swelling in the vast conspiracy of alertness that threads through the noise of the world, waking us to this leaf or that galaxy. So I sense you as kin to some of the other great ones in our time who

have, in my ken, grown along hidden lines towards clarities—
Peter Lamborn Wilson comes to mind, Charles Olson, Robert
Duncan, Gerrit Lansing, Christopher Bamford, Guy Davenport
—each magisterially alert, each so different from the others, one
or the other of them at times prone to succumb to temptations
of political theory or narrative doodling or spiritual loftinesses

What you are doing makes me think of Montaigne, Burton,
the great Thomas Browne who could from a muddy old pot dug
up create the greatest piece of prose in English, just from looking at it and thinking about it, thinking it through. Where the
thinking-through is, becomes, the formal presence of the text.
The chastity of your texts makes me think of Ruskin, and especially of the diaries of our hometown hero, Henry Thoreau—
one of the great *watchers without theory.*

Literature is so rich nowadays. Its house has so many conve-
niences (fiction, lyric, drama, memoir) and like most rich houses
most of the stuff is never used, to much point. The bone-dry
Jacuzzi, the fourth TV that's never turned on. Maybe we need a
simpler house, a room where people talk to each other, gizmo-
less and at risk of each other's minds. That's what you're laying on
the line. No story to distract us, no theory of cosmic influence
or political shenanigans or psycho-conditioning. Just the clear
articulation of what wells up in the attentive mind—a mind you
know how to articulate.

ANNANDALE-ON-HUDSON

The Bardo of Waking Life

First Cycle

A dragonfly is more advanced than a human being, in dragonfly terms. Its swift, surveillant flight, stopping and starting instantly, likewise turning on a dime, is well beyond what human motility can approach—it is the evolutionary equivalent of language and philosophy. Plus, dragonflies have no use for speech or dialect; they are the mere embodiment of predatory flight. That is, they have nothing to say which they don't do.

Any plane that tried to carry out dragonfly maneuvers would tear itself apart.

Likewise, no Olympic muscleman, at scale of lifter to object, could out-press an ant. Not only would ants win the gold, the silver, and the bronze, but a crippled ant would finish well ahead of the most able Kazakhstani or Turk.

It took millions of years of nonlinear flux via proteins and neural nets to render a beehive, a masterpiece of apian art as well as an archetypal object.

It took millennia of stone tools, metallurgy, and cybernetics for humans to achieve its approximate simulacrum in a computer disk. For what it is and what it's supposed to do, a beehive is perfect.

An anthill is also perfect: tunnels of habitable symmetry from white noise, a billion vortices underlying stacks of organized chaos. It is the coevolutionary partner of the ant, its *sine qua non*.

A fish, exerting flaps against rods, enacts elegant design principles—propulsion approaching, even as it arises from, inertia.

In the Metropolitan Museum of the Milky Way Galaxy, a spider web plucked from Earth in the eighth millennium B.C. hangs adjacent to an iPod Nano. One critic from the Pleiades deemed it an *even more exquisite* representative of Sol carbon craft.

In this same exhibit hall, mites from Enceladus and Europa are exemplified by fractally pleated micro-fabrics.

Titan is not just an unrefined "Earth"; it is a tabernacle of methane philosophy.

We judge ourselves super-advanced by our own parochial standards, but we have overproduced, overpopulated, and megaconsumed. Look at this swollen anthill. We are ravaging one of the most beautiful blue and white globes ever made, like some horde of locusts.

Score a *full* point for spiders and the mites of Enceladus.

While we practice materialistic idolatry, we do not even take "matter" seriously, squandering ten molecules for every one we gainfully employ. (All manifestation is magical—nothing surplus, nothing waste.)

Aloof gourmands, in our macroeconomies we enact a parody of our carnivorous heritage. Real predation is so much more earnest and sincere. Most twenty-first-century humans are complaisant yuppies by comparison to voles and mantises, marlins and buzzards. Mortal balance is waged on a blade of *différence*: a talon, a fang; a dart, a sting.

Lichens sustain an entire multi-colored civilization, digesting minerals in the stones on which they breed. They are almost one hundred percent efficient—in a state of balance, aesthetic harmony, and contemplation of the void. Their "dirty work" *is* their culture, a footprint we seek now on Mars.

Andy Goldsworthy's sculptures are respectful of the universe in which they are set—temporal assemblages in collaboration with indigenous vectors and materials.

Gravity, tides, boundaries, shear forces, and melting points are sculptors without ego or mind. By accepting them as his peers—in fact the true masters—Goldsworthy raises planetary masterpieces rather than anthropocentric idols. It is not so much, as he puts it, that he gives a herm of rocks to the ocean as that the ocean takes his humble collation and makes more out of it than he ever could.

Behind nature's obvious munificence and beauty are starker, barer forces that cannot be dismissed or omitted from abstract equations. Gradients of atomic mass determine every vista, be it a garbage mound or an alpine sunset. Micro-mechanics of Golgi crêpes and ganglionic synapses set all internal parameters of art.

Landscapes are darker, Goldsworthy opines, than we routinely allow, though not in a malign way, merely in the sense that they are meticulously thermodynamic. They are not pretty or meant to be pretty—consider any so-called "pastoral" scene on the Moon or Venus. The sheep who share his farm may look playful and fluffy, but that is misleading; they are incredibly strong, willful animals.

A flower is not dainty either; it is a fire, an explosion of seeds in time.

Far off, cataclysms are unfolding in a peaceful sky.

When the collection of gravitational disparities and converging gradients known as Katrina came ashore in the Mississippi delta, residents in homes on tree-lined New Orleans avenues found themselves, in a moment or two, several miles out to sea, crawling onto their roofs to look back at coastline.

This is how peremptory Moon and Sun are, how instantaneous their expressions of relative position and heat. What is placid one moment can, from an imbalance in the flow of molecules that heavenly bodies govern, become cataclysmic. Heel-to-toe, whole cities are moved.

Ordinary things are not ordinary. There is no army that can stand against a whisper of air.

All creatures are little machines: Mushrooms and Mosquitoes and Mice, Muskrats to Owls—factories that make themselves *of* themselves, that run off their own syrups. Their fine moving parts are composed of materials we could never allocate so exquisitely: hydrogen, carbon, oxygen, nitrogen, manganese, copper. Man's machines, jury-rigged of metals, require synthetic fuels or external power sources and transmission lines to ignite and go.

It is unclear where a philosophical boundary might be drawn between the robots we concoct and self-organizing ones, especially in this epoch of miniaturized circuits. While artificial machines industriously reproduce behavior, alive ones are more adroit because they do not mimic but breed phenomenologies. Their internal landscapes and novel behavior, ignited in cascades of molecules, are coterminous with the inside of a universe from which they arise by an inscrutable process. As the infinity "without" melds into the infinity "within," they form a third, conceptual infinity that engenders the astonishing sensation of "being."

What is implanted in us without petition and at no apparent price we take for granted.

Creatures are sole expressions of the forces and gaps that underlie their genesis. Boundaries of streams and springs and wind-blown water hundreds of millions of years later become membranes and then cells; then fish, bugs, horseshoe crabs. Which points to another difference: it takes billions of years to design the template for a single living machine, run its alphas, imbed its index in a series.

It takes additional millions of years to program lineages of interdependent cells to invent mechanical objects.

Stray thermodynamics could never establish factories of metal and stone, sensors of amperage with mineralized appendages. It must first grate molecules into minds.

As our son Robin held newborn Miranda in his arms (Vermont, 1974, not yet five himself)—now, thirty-one years later, she cradles his baby Leo in hers. This is a family.

Exploring Webb Pond in a kayak on an autumn day so misty that there are intermittent ribbons of rain, I see other kayakers suddenly arise from fog and then disappear. There is no shore, no sense of location, just a floating scenery in which forms manifest, not as I might imagine but with dreamlike palpability.

Hooting laughter and catcalling issues from women at a mini-shuffleboard game on the table in Bettina's cabin which of course I can't see, so the sound seems to emerge from everywhere and nowhere across the lake, voices in séance.

Long Pond, several miles from end to end and more than a hundred feet deep in spots, is a droplet, full and burgeoning, as gusts carve ripples on its surface—brief persistences of goose bumps in ceaseless rills. Breezes scissoring waves reveal shades of blue, gray, violet, magenta; these form out of one another and shift, second by second, like the footprints of dust-devils.

Surrounding cliffs are stamped in a different chronology. A glacial horoscope is kept by talus: giant and irregular slabs and eggs of rock have been set atop one another in haphazard repose—a rough timepiece of planetary history.

Cloud formations roll across illuminated blue. Each giant cumulus is a clock, forming as a shapeless second-hand, circulating like soft crystal in prism. They are spun by fire and light, slightly contaminated and wet.

Sun draws a pellucid nimbus around the wingtips of the gulls as they come in bunches to bathe.

From my kayak the lake at moments smells as fresh as a newly opened watermelon.

Moonless night. Look in the nocturnal abyss—a Great Civilization seen from faraway! All those stars along the faint, infinitely thick hub of the Milky Way bespeak fabulous cities, every one of them a place strange and beyond conception.

There are so many Broadways and Main Streets out there.

Din of crickets and flashes of fireflies denote activity here at the bottom. Cosmic puddles have their own screeches, howls, chitters, plunks, and chirps.

The dilemma that space is infinite, that there are too many stars for comprehension (including ones we can't see), is not the predicament it would seem to be. The universe is *not* too *beaucoup*. We *can* take it all in. Consciousness is finally sheerer than any chunk of unconscious matter, can cut through its amplitude, however vast, to the camouflaged design.

Airplanes cross to and from Europe—flickering scraps of mineral. Fabricated from ore in sections and welded in hangars into compound objects, they arise on their bric-a-brac engines, push peremptory steel through the lower heavens—an indication that thought, operating long enough on matter (say two hundred thousand years), can cobble pelts and transport bodies across local space-time. Tough, malleable blimps, they brave the abyss of meaning to show how ensigns travel.

Creation is rough. It is unfinished. And it is immaculate.

The universe, which itself arose as a bright sap, or (some say) a pop, a rip in something else, is now unfurling brazenly. That stuff must have come from somewhere, from some prior cosmology. If you are going to spill that much mead, there has to be a pome, its stores converted by stars into dust out of which comets and other filaments sprout, dousing worlds with serum. There not only has to be a universe prior to the Big Bang but a reason for such a bold and declarative ignition—and not just our kind of "reason" but a real one.

Hydrogen is the transitional form of a molecule that lies on the nether side of the Boom, of materiality itself. As it spills through sluiced gates, it fords a universe of infinite energy, infinite possibility.

Think of all the energy released by the splitting of one hydrogen atom, and then visualize all the atoms that go into making up the tail of one squirrel. The microcosm is the architect of the macrocosm.

There is a sun far more luminous than those yellow-white bonfires parading in the night. That is why the landscape of the qabala is vaster than that of astronomy, Kether more candescent than Sirius, the Heart Sutra a mightier and more radiant river than the Milky Way.

How else to explain the surge of light, energy, atomized matter, and meaning that burst out of the reputed walnut of the Big Bang and covered everything, including itself, in a torrent of nakedness and complexity?

Water is more than a translucent syrup that bubbles up from its table and collects in streams across rockbeds, crystallizes in clouds and plummets back in tiny wet stones, smashing into puddles and sog. It contains premolecular seeds from another chart.

Air is not only breath but *prana*. In a rippling blanket across trillions of light years, the ether of occult oxygen feeds the third eye and crown chakra; its fine breath of nonmolecular air fans mitochondria, fueling consciousness.

Light is more than light. It is revelation.

Stone is not only inert rock but a dormant intelligence, sluggish in our zone, dreaming and metabolizing a molecule at a time.

Time is a labyrinth, a chimera viscid enough to accelerate particles across firmaments, opaque enough to retrieve worlds out of the debris of former cosmoses. Only where the universe is dense and gravid do clocks actually tick.

Objectified awareness is an integral aspect of existence.

"This is" is fundamental.

Swimming underwater near the northwest edge of Long Pond, I collide with a garden of lily pads—a zone of flat spiraling ribbons. The cinema is so unexpected that I revisit it from different angles. Submarine stems come into focus, distorted across their dimension like a cartoon of DNA twisting up from pond bottom. On the surface, brilliant white compages sport sleek green trellises; underneath, the data stream.

The oldtimers playing with the Skatalites need very little movement to present their ska. For such venerable t'ai-chi masters, it comes down to an economy of gesture, sending a much younger opponent spinning by a light but trained touch. The callow guys may do a lot of extraneous jumping up and down, waving arms and horns, exhorting the audience, but their sound is contained within the matrix of elders. *Ska, ska, ska; Jamaica ska.*

The songs are introduced briefly, understated, because anything else would be hype and no doubt they've "been there, done that," for decades in fact.

"This one's 'Occupation.' This one's 'Lonely Town.'" Barely a millisecond after the words are out of his mouth, the trumpets have made their initial blast. "This one's 'Trip to Mars.' This one's 'From Russia With Love.'"

Many musics intersect—reggae, Afro-Cuban, rock, jazz, dub—they come and go in harmonic medley.

"This one's 'Guns of Navarone.' This one's 'Eastern Standard Time.' This one's 'Nimble Foot Ska.'" Now the horns start like clockwork and are punctuated abruptly; now a ride on the keyboard, hint of a Kingston dancehall; now the thump of the drummer, a statement so loud it rivals my heart in my chest. "This one's 'Addis Ababa.'"

The old guys are Lloyd Knibb on percussion; Les Sterling, alto sax. The newcomers are Devon James, guitar; Ken Stewart, keyboard; Karl "Cannonball" Byram; Kevin Batchelor; Val Douglas; Vin Gordon. Halfway through the set, Les introduces, "The Queen of Reggae herself, fresh from Kingston, Jamaica: Miss Doreen Schaffer."

"Greetings, Bangor," she announces in elegant patois. "This one's 'Sugar, Sugar.'"

These days I feel empathy for every bug and spider; I try to steer or carry trapped ones out of the house. I go to some lengths not to disturb webs, changing course to avoid them.

Hard to believe that, as a child, I joined the crew with canisters of insect spray, racing around our bunk at Camp Chipinaw gleefully frosting hornets! I thought nothing then of competitively swatting flies, idly squushing bugs.

The more time you spend in a body on Earth, the more you get it. Each creature, even the most aggressive, the most austere, is a lonely, fragile, quivering gem. It is difficult to get born anyway, dangerous to live, as anything.

We all share a consciousness of this day on Earth. There is only one such consciousness. It is in every wild bug as it is in us.

I find myself more and more wanting to acknowledge affinity, extend good will, even though the motivations behind my acts are meaningless to spiders and flies. They do not share my impulse at any level except the most deeply unconscious. They do not even like or admire what I am.

I felt bad when I did not go back and at least turn over a beetle lying on its back in the road, legs flailing. The image of the beleaguered creature stayed in my mind for weeks and, when my next chance came, I was ready. I freed a butterfly from a spider's web; it sputtered frantically in stickum before gaining profitable flight.

The next afternoon, kneeling by a puddle off Long Pond, I floated a leaf to a cicada-like thing that was upside-down, drowning in the tiny lagoon. It wrapped its legs around my makeshift island and gradually pulled itself on. I lifted the raft out of the puddle and set it on a log. The creature crawled off, scrupulously dried itself, tested its wings, dried itself, tested its wings. I trust that eventually it flew.

What haunts me still, though, is how many such insects drown in anonymity—some of them around this very pond, others in lakes across the planet, in liquids on all habitable worlds.

I appeared inside an incalculably narrow window of opportunity to effect this single rescue. It was one throw of the dice in a trillion trillion—and now this being, this entity, in all its guises, through its transmigrations and metamorphoses till the end of whatever this is, will be waiting for me, lifetime after lifetime, wondering *where* I am, when I am coming back, not even remembering *who* I am or knowing that I really existed.

A gull striding on Sand Beach looks so much like a proxy person, or at least a personality, that I am reminded how the other animals *have to be* for us to be. We are not an accident or fortuity, nor is life a visitation by a reigning species.

When children marvel at birds' antics, as they preen feathers and peck at seaweed for odd vittles—when circus spectators laugh uproariously at the bear raised on hinds—they are responding to the multiple faces of creation. Animals are wizards and totems costumed in tissue layers, antecedents of a tribal codex—innominate and savage.

There is no advanced world anywhere in the universe lacking sundry critters, diverse in size and sort, except where humans or some other varmints have run them off.

The simplest unicellular animal recognizes photons, is photosensitive. A plant's consciousness, such as it might be, makes a quantum splash in phenomenology, tuning exquisitely into knowledge. Light defines both the bog of unconscious mind and the beachhead of consciousness.

Animalcules afloat in the microcosm know beyond fact that creation is a form of light. They feel their existences as vibration.

What physicists—even subatomic ones—don't take into serious enough account is that, without light passing through organelles, we would not know space, distance, and scale, or even that there are stars—or even that there is us. There would be no dice and no one to throw them, nothing to peel the void.

So, of what are we presently unaware because we do not have the equipment, the antennae or molecule towers to apprehend? What anneals the cosmos beyond light and vibration? What rare fibers compose its strands?

The main hope we have is that, while creation is rough and cataclysmic, it is graceful and precise. Yep, callous, predatory *and* vulgar just about everywhere, yet so gentle it cannot crack an eggshell.

We are brought ashore on amazing boats on which we were asleep. Our blankets are removed, and we are touched by a pagan hand.

It is meant to feel like this.

In August rain, spider webs are laced between sprigs of spruces and across low-lying blackberries and weeds. They form also in the grass and between the parked car and house, between the car's antenna and side-view mirror.

Intrepid arachnids, scurrying along girders in midair, string fibers of high-quality line. They drape strands between branches of trees, hoisting tensile networks like space-stations orbiting worlds of advanced civilizations—except that these are translucent and proprioceptive, their maker umbilically at their center.

It takes only minutes to expel a web, as I observe a zooid on the window, squirt coming out of its butt as it scoots in smaller and smaller polygons, each one congruent to those ringing it: an artisan laying down his crest.

Soft white tents, horizontal-like platforms and vertical-like sails, are filling with wind across fields and releasing it, holding to invisible studs that affix them to shapes so that they undulate and stretch to their limits.

Slugs crawl on the ripest blackberries, sometimes as many as three to a berry.

The trouble with latency as an explanation (e.g. he hates gays because he has latent homosexual tendencies) is that *everything* is latent. Recognizing latency of motive doesn't stop the worst wars or most heinous abuses and massacres. What is written into history are the acts themselves, not their latencies.

On Huckleberries

"You must try some of my huckleberries;/I've been eating them for six or seven weeks now,/haven't got sick once,/probably keep us both alive." Jefferson Airplane, "Wooden Ships."

Until the summer of 2005 I didn't know what a huckleberry was, though I had seen them without recognition. Black jujubes, they dilate on low-lying shrubs along the trails of Acadia and, in fact, throughout North America. Naturalist Steve Perrin named them after we climbed the ladders above Echo Lake onto Beech Cliffs.

I had thought that those ubiquitous dark drupes were cranberries or chokecherries or something poisonous. Steve's branding of them drew a fresh card out of the "berry" tarot. At his behest I took a cautious bite. The fruit had a subtle, cidery flavor, high on pulp and skin—intoxicating! Each was either slightly sweeter or more acrid than its predecessor. I enjoyed not knowing the sugar content until I crushed a pip in my mouth.

During the remainder of our hike I continued to sample, occasionally running to catch up.

"Pick away," Steve said. "What you don't get, the bears, foxes, and deer will be grateful for."

Either they were slow to the feast, or there was a cornucopia on Beech Cliffs because, over three weeks, I found enough to fill three quart-containers without reducing the *prima facie* density of the patch.

Blueberry-like in size and shape, huckleberries are almost black, have stiffer skins, and are crunchier in the mouth. The majority are as shiny as good shoes, but buff ones are more reliably sweet.

Mingling with low-lying blueberries and occasional cranberries, huckleberry shrubs are generally taller, while their fruits resemble the latter more than the former in size and color—though a quick bite proves even the sweetest cranberry astringent by comparison with a huckleberry. If a cranberry has been zapped long enough by the sun, one can still draw a bare nip of sugar before it turns bitter and dry.

At the height of huckleberry season, only a few late patches of blueberries linger, their fruits wrinkled and soft.

I discovered fatter huckleberries in abundance around Webb Pond, just north of Mount Desert Island, close to the water, emerging right out of the muck. Vibrating with nectar, some were as rotund as high-bush blueberries.

I also found them in the sun on the crest of Flying Mountain where I pointed them out to a family of initially dubious hikers whose two boys began picking and eating as soon as the parents ascertained they were not nightshade.

Huckleberries hold a distinguished lineage in colonial cookbooks and of course through Mark Twain. I asked Steve why they are not a popular eating berry anymore, and he thought maybe it was because they can't be harvested with rakes and also because their season is short; that is, they are just wild enough not to lend themselves to commercialization. He added that a friend liked to pick seven-berry pie at this time of year: blue, cran, rasp, black, huckle, partridge, and service. In more northern climes, the Viking cloudberry can be substituted.

Yes, some huckleberries can be a tinge bitter, but they clearly distinguish themselves from unripe berries of other purple-to-black varieties. There is an abiding wine-like piquancy to almost all of them, and the ripest, plumpest ones at direct solar exposure are more like an heirloom pear or apple than a berry—they are truly the Guinness stout of blueberries. Yet, even though they are abundant in fields and wetlands and advertised for free by Mr. Twain—or, down-market, "Moon River" and Huckleberry Hound—their fruit has fallen into disfavor or obscurity.

My relationship with Lindy began in October 1963 as a date with a college girl; it is a commitment to something that never stops changing. There isn't a break from moment to moment, but it evolves. We are always there with each other, in relationship. It is difficult to get located in a narrative when the story is everywhere.

"Who are you?" she accosted me once, years ago, in the midst of an argument. "You're just some guy I met."

So many years were rocky and filled with inexplicable acts, as we struggled to get perspective on something that time defied but that defined time (as well as timelessness). I feel as though I am pulling on a yarn that goes on forever, with every twist of its braid the connection itself.

The homonym is true: wife is life.

Universe: The universe is the astronomical All. It began with the Big Bang; yet the unknown realm that preceded it was technically "universe" too.

Creation: Creation is the aggregate of all universes, Big Bangs, and dimensions. As long as something is, it is in creation.

Existence: Existence is the experience of being in creation. It is the only part of the universe that we know from within.

Mystery: The mystery brings these realms together: the sensation of existence with the epiphany of creation with the spectacle of a universe.

1. Reality is determined solely by frequency of manifestation. All entities vibrating at the same frequency are stable, e.g. solid, within that frequency. The world is a tone, setting plants, animals, even mud, in a trance at its frequency. Pistachios, tangerines, and chocolate, however yummy, are made solely of vibrations and spacing. Because we are vibrating at the same octave, they seem real.

2. Provinciality is overcommitment to a transient reality. Any "reality," no matter how hardcore and imperial, is abandoned as soon as a new condition arises.

As it is, we hardly know how to tell reality from a dream. All we have is the testimony of our senses to octaves that stretch to apparent infinity or at least that far into the relativistic crust of light.

Fall inside any dream or bardo state, and its trackings burst with voltaic radiance and verisimilitude, shooting across mathematical scales to eternity in all dimensions. Sentience is a snare. The only escape is to untie its shoes and take them off while still on the prairie—to be awake while dreaming.

3. Trolleys of molecules alert us to the fact that we are here and something is required of us. Across the transdimensional bands, creatures tune in to any number of dramas, each with its own vibration of atomicity—each a caprice of materiality. Even for Einstein, this was never an Einsteinian universe. His juggling of numbers—sacred in the guise of secular ones—gave rise to the present starry proposition that rings our civilization. Yet, he conceded, there is "an intelligence of such superiority that, compared with it, all the systematic thinking and acting of human beings is an utterly insignificant reflection."

Elegantly put, but how could it be elsewise? The overall architecture is beyond discernment from any perspective inside it, which is why neither Superstring Joe nor Stephen Know-It-All Asshole Hawking has or will have a field theory rallying the attributes and laws of nature or can say what stuff is or ain't or how it got here.

As April confided to June, "May be."*

4. We answer to a reality we did not create, as least not knowingly, not by majority vote. This will go on lifetime after lifetime, or whatever occurs in their place.

What we actually *are* is up for grabs.

If existence weren't compelling and credible, it wouldn't be happening. If it didn't function as a seamless waking dream, then the lattice of cells wouldn't hold.

---

*Courtesy of Clint Eastwood played by Ed Dorn.

Once we get out of the background we can't stop the projection, so we have to embrace it, riding the bronco at our turn.

5. One dimension supervenes another, each resonating intrinsically—all of them equally real, equally transient.

That we are in the most precarious situation imaginable is, luckily, what makes life safe. If everything is still being signed and changing signs, there is no need to rely on one symbol system or another, one realm or another, one life-death or another. Just follow consciousness. Where it leads, go. Act. Where it doesn't lead, you don't have to go, enveloping as it is, 24/7/360 though it glows.

6. There is any number of realities, conceivably billions of dimensions or maybe just seven or thirteen, each fashioned by tentacles of thought. All it takes is waves of intelligence performing as existential objects, stoking vagrant particles into landscapes. It is all virtual. We would not know how to conceive a really real reality.

7. But this world is not make-believe, because there is nothing to replace it, at least nothing at this level.

8. Action is determined by circumstance and conferred by instincts, so-called evolutionary motifs ("I'm famished; gotta score some fructose" or "Here comes that humungous lizard; let's vamoose outa Dodge!"). You can't just resonate in place like tar. We are precedented patterns anchored by DNA, urgent flakes of ancestral memory.

Everywhere in the universe, acts give rise simply to one another. Situations arise and creatures respond. Worlds are born.

9. Time, or the perception of time, is caused solely by spirit sinking into density, putting on the robe of matter. Up high, near the ringhole, there is no time; stuff goes everywhen. Bagpipes play everywhere and nowhere.

10. Ontogeny *does* more or less recapitulate phylogeny—a string of meta-logic waged in molecules—and, together, they recapitulate the symbolic history of the universe as well as—*and this is the key*—the universe itself.

Our spiritual urgency exists literally and solely because of our mortality—the equation of life and death at which we arrive every moment, every day. The point of any serious practice is to re-remember our situation and develop a relationship to it.

The Buddhist view that everything results in disappointment and loss is not as pessimistic as it initially seems. In fact, it is reassuring. There is no point in trying to hang on to what cannot be held.

A successful person who deems that spiritual practice is not for him, a waste of his valuable time, faces additional disappointment and loss because everything fine and fancy will be taken from him. His cheer is dependent on opulence and fortunate circumstance, maybe good looks and cleverness. For no particular reason except the obvious, he will have to give these up and rely on something more basic in order to find his essence: the only thing he actually owns, the only thing that counts. He is just another beggar, another gimp. He has a longer journey than someone who has already forfeited ambition and is looking directly at the abyss.

The trick to being here is to participate and be a player without getting fooled that anything, including self, is more than a passing vestige. That does not yield a dismal zone of blighted phantoms but a sensuous world of imagination and love.

When we began living part-time on Mount Desert Island, I didn't expect to have a friendship with Bill Kotzwinkle, as he was notoriously a hermit, misanthrope, and snob. A mutual friend introduced us in 2000 after Lindy and I bought a house there. Bill and his wife had been on the island since the mid-Eighties when his novelization of *E. T.: The Extraterrestrial* gave them the down-payment for prime secluded shorefront. Because director Steven Spielberg had long admired Bill's fiction, he hired him for the task. In truth, novels like *Fan Man* and *Doctor Rat* and short-story collections like *Elephant Bangs Train* are among the twentieth century's great unacknowledged works of literature.

Fan Man is *John from Cincinnati* meets *Waiting for Godot* with winks of Burroughs' *Junkie*, *The Lone Ranger*, *Huck Finn*, *Major Hoople*, and Melville's *Confidence Man*. Horse Badorties, its East Village hero and default narrator, has got to be one of the top ten literary eccentrics of all time. Yep, take your place alongside Caliban, Queequeg, Billy the Kid, the Underground Man, and Humbert Humbert. As one reviewer put it, "An adieu to the hippie era and the summer of love … this is really about the crash, man. This is when people began to drop out without tuning in or turning on."

Once I was around for an extended period, Bill and I began hiking the small mountain range near Seal Cove. We traded writings, which is how I came to read his *Book of Love*, a fictionalized account of his growing up lower class in Scranton, Pennsylvania, before escaping to find his artistic calling—a feat that the narrator characterizes as a near miracle. The novel is set in a landscape of hazing, casual cruelty, nasty pranks (for instance, being forced to drink another's kid's urine), and fisticuffs. When the supposedly righteous Father O'Hora downed a bird with a bee-bee gun, the boys brought the wounded animal to a neighbor, Mr. Yacavola, for ministering:

"'Set 'im down,' he said.

"'It's alright now ... you'll be flying soon.'

"Old Man Yacavola reached behind one of the pens, came out with a brick and brought it down with all his might on the bird.

"'Bury 'im.'"

Bill turned out to be less a hermit or misanthrope than the invisible man, a trickster who didn't want to be seen, by anyone, anywhere; he was a Jungian conspiracy-theory paranoid meta-zionist survivalist anti-New Age hippie-neocon pseudo-tai-chi wannabe-superstar super-highbrow. We climbed Western Mountain many times together, off-trail to avoid tourists as was his wont. All the way up and down, and at the summit looking out over Blue Hill Bay with its isles and boat traffic, we gossiped Jungian psychology, Hindu cosmology, and the like, while debunking spiritual scams East and West (Bill's default topic).

One afternoon following such a hike Bill surprised me, as I set a teapot of dandelion root and cups on my living-room table, by proposing that we try to be *really good friends*. I wasn't sure what he meant by that or how it was done in our case but I said I was willing to give it a try: "Does that mean we should talk more candidly about things?"

"As long as they're real things. I have no tolerance for gossip."

"Like what?"

He clearly wanted me to go first.

"Okay. Well, we're both getting older. How do we deal with the potential for serious diseases and our mortality? When do we trust the medical establishment? How far do we go by alternative stuff? I mean I'm terrified of doctors, yet—"

He cut me off. "This is bullshit, Richard!"

Startled, I reconsidered my options and offered, "What about our relationships with our wives? We've both been married for almost forty years, and we're totally vulnerable. How do we deal with love and the potential for loss?"

I could see dismay, even disgust, creep over his face. I was looking at the creator of Horse Badorties, at Yacavola.

"I can't believe you. This is beneath dignity. We're sitting here, two philosophers, two shamans, medicine men, with an opportunity to speak the truth to each other, and you want to turn it into a men's group."

"I give up. What should we talk about?"

"There's an eagle out there, waiting on our deaths to devour our souls." His voice rose urgently in decibels of drama: "Soon enough we'll both be dead. Richard, how are we going to get past that eagle?"

He was talking about Don Juan's spirit eagle in the esoteric universe of Carlos Castaneda. I realized I was betraying a tentative grin.

"This is a serious matter, sir. This alone is worth our discussion, not such paltry gossip as you are proposing. The eagle is of the utmost concern to us as poets and magicians."

"But," I complained, "this bird is so powerful and the shamanic preparation necessary to outwit him so profound, that if he exists in any form resembling rumor, we're already toast. We should have been preparing ourselves short of age three to have any chance of making ourselves invisible to him or dazzling him with our art. I mean how do you zoom or sidle past the eye of the universe itself?"

Bill had on his game face, and I scanned it for any touch of irony or self-parody. There was none. Scraggly hair and beard like fire, he looked honestly terrified, perched there on the couch. "Richard," he screamed at me, "don't sit there like a fool. Answer me. Your life, my life depends on it."

I fumbled for anything that made sense. Then I said, "You got out of Scranton, didn't you?"

Fixing the Problems of Our World

Admittedly there are no solutions—not now, not in a hundred years. All we can hope for is a change in consciousness, the sort tendered, for instance, by optimistic proponents of a 2012 vibrational shift (pessimistic ones warn of Armageddon then).

I think it will take at least a thousand years to get socioecological metamorphosis on this planet—and we may not have that much time; certainly the current civilization doesn't. I can't imagine a burst of percipience making life on Earth see the bigger picture. It would be a profound harmonic jolt that could penetrate all human and animal psyches simultaneously.

Secular human activity occurs on a stage so far removed from its unconscious source that we would hardly know whether present ghastly events portend a coming quantum leap or total anarchy and catastrophe. On the surface we seem to be getting worse—more violent, brutal, destructive, further every hour from an economy of renewable resources and a world without war.

But conscious acts are not a measure of actual consciousness; they are the outcome of all that is working its way through unconsciousness toward a fugitive reckoning. The most vicious deeds and avaricious habits might be harbingers of awakening. Beheadings and genocides, aerial bombings and suicide retaliations, child armies, slaughters of herds of elephants for ivory, blowing up and poisoning of coral reefs for a fish or two are not optimistic signs, but they may precede a breakthrough rather than a cataclysm, for they let us experience as direct fact the impossibility of proceeding in this way. They notify—not men and women—who don't get it and don't care, but the psyche, which, by definition, always gets it, and is capable of radical shifts and u-turns.

Truly fucked-up behavior blows out the shit, clears the unconscious of its compulsion to express every dread fantasy and attendant guilt.

The impractical, privileged notions below cannot work. They are guileless, preachy, simplistic, and trite—but, in order to be ready for the changing of the guard, we had better start thinking about our stuff in radical or errant ways, because for sure the guard is going to change.

Of course, they are wrong: dead wrong and relatively wrong too. Yet we must put something out there—pipe dreams call them, utopian chimeras. We must exercise our daring and dire imaginations if we want to address—perhaps even survive—the tidal wave that is coming.

1. The one basic, comprehensive consciousness shift that could improve the planet (and also is within our present grasp) is to end inheritance in every culture in every form—or at least put an austere limit on it. This means no deeding of assets and commodities—it does not regulate personal heirlooms or sacred treasures. *Inherited material advantage* is what cannot be passed on to relatives and protegés.

The goal is to curtail dynasties and their hegemonies, to halt reigns of class by lineage or adoption, Caesar to Caesar, Bush to Bush; House of Saud, House of Trump.

Give each newborn creature a clean slate—the obligation (and benefit) of discovering who he or she is without a bequest. Make "earning your keep" a global incentive. Put such a taboo upon vouchsafing assets that the mere suspicion of it, like of cannibalism or incest, becomes abhorrent. A legal end to inheritance is at least conjecturable, whereas most of my other propositions are dozens to hundreds of thousands of generations from plausibility.

Even a dollop in that direction would be a dramatic reversal of where we are hurtling: a new millionaire every minute at the price of the impoverishment of the masses. Most people, especially wealthy ones, consider the deeding of property and rank their right (they even want their wealth to pass untaxed—a macabre aspiration if you think about it).

In America of all places, higher education and legal justice have become class privileges—and there are now more eligible blacks in prison than in college. In the world at large, talent and service are stymied big-time by corporate and royal appurtenance.

Ending inheritance would underwrite other changes, impose a subliminal nudge in their direction. If wealth were more fluid, wars would be less iconic, and industrialized nations might adopt greenhouse-gas limits more readily.

I suspect that at least half the planets along our present time-space continuum have arrived at this resolution. Either that or they, like us, are up shit creek without a paddle.

Yes, with all that estate capital pouring into mega-bureaucracies, corruption is inevitable—avarice being what it is—and any kind of wealth-distributing agency potentially sets up communist dominion on a mind-boggling scale.

That people will find other ways to control resources and manipulate power is a separate problem. It doesn't change the fact that the present automatic transfer of affluence and clout from generation to generation, usually within families, begets castes, underclasses, refugees, prostitution, indentured labor, and, ultimately, slavery. In league with the present global economy, dowries breed institutionalized ignorance, con artistry, and crime by bands of brigands and underclass soldiers, leading to jihads, revolutions, and terrorism. While belittling human potential, inheritance fosters disruptive and anarchic modes of reapportionment and all but ensures incompetent rulers.

If accumulation of stuff is inevitable, better to valorize a Polynesian "big man" or Mohawk chief who will scatter his wealth ostentatiously. Guardianship of property will not corrupt him, as his conceit and pleasure are to achieve a lofty stature, not possess trinkets.

On "big man" planets the most exemplary rulers are the poorest in terms of material goods.

Opulence is merely a code anyway, a series of signs to which everyone assents.* Money is a symbolic place-holder, a subset of

---

*This discussion arises in part from my 1966 anthropology course with Marshall Sahlins (see his book *Stone-Age Economics*, University of Chicago Press, 1972) and in part from my recent conversations with Charles Stein. Stein himself draws from the writings of Jacob Klein (*Greek Mathematical Thought and the Origins of Algebra*, M.I.T. Press, 1968). I hereby declare the weirdness in my version—Chuck's multiple notes conflating promiscuously and verbatim with my own surmises and meta-version of Sahlins here. *Mea culpa*—my mud!

"the Emperor's new clothes," as neither gold nor other currencies have any intrinsic meaning or province as value or function.

"Money" is a transcendent state that holds everyone in thrall beyond denotation or logic. It has become divorced from its own production since at least the early Renaissance, mutating as rapidly as people dream up new uses, new markets, and shrewd and shameless (if ingenious) principles of conversion to their own advantage. We have been worshipping numerical and mathematical artifacts, hoarding and trading signs in a weird global bazaar that now subsumes every acre, waterhole, insect, plant, and gene.

In the tribal world prior to the birth of quantification, goods were implicit acts of exchange and social signs. Money was in the first instance a thing of value: gold or tobacco, cowrie shells or women, chickens or what have you. A valuable object was taken as a medium of exchange for other things of value: synecdoche.

In the subsequent ancient world, numbers were thought of as specific instances of quantities: there were "sheep numbers" that counted sheep, "bowl numbers" that counted bowls, and, in a Platonic context, ideal numbers that counted ideal objects— monads. The Pythagoreans may have spoken about number being the ultimate principle of which things themselves were composed, but they were likewise thinking of numbers as something concrete, like the ratios that expressed the relationships between musical pitches.

In the modern world, money no longer has its basis in anything at all. It is no longer synecdoche. It has become an abstract term by which not only can all value be quantified but, becoming an absolute value in itself, transforms the ordinary circumstances under which we value things and activities, states of being, etc., into symbols whose sole senses are the cash value by which they can be produced or sold. No wonder we have an environmental crisis: the world has been abstracted from its roots in not only nature but society, in not only nature and society but meaning.

Numbers are literally nothing. They do not have substance. They are not things. They are distinct from even the numerals by which they are symbolized. They are pure abstractions for quantities, relations, magnitudes, orders. But in being removed absolutely from any concrete entity, they became fit to express that which all entities are presumed to be. Arithmetic made possible the quantification of substance, leading to money as the quantification of value.

Having divorced object from meaning, and valuation from real utility or worth, we have now monetized mathematics itself such that one layer of abstraction and arbitrage has been set atop another and then another in a ceaseless pyramid scheme beyond simple formality or regulation. Once we make these virtualized counts inheritable, the dead don't die; documents merely transfer, as they morph into their heirs. Death is indeed a scandal.*

Hedge funds are currently popular and successful because, once zero can be all and all is but another form of zero (and, miracle of miracles, less than zero can be more than all), then the slot machines crack open and pour out limitless golden geese, to be slaughtered at the beck and call of shareholders.

We have created the illusion of capital beyond diminution or risk and have separated the fruits of labor from toil itself so that while one class sweats and all but starves, another, magically

---

*In Western capitalist societies, death is a rude biological intrusion into the machinery of production and commodity accumulation as well as a disquieting anomaly given the seeming infinity of goods and imperative to acquire as many of them as possible. Death brazenly interrupts commerce and reminds us that neither credit nor debt is limitless.

elevated above fields and factories, propagates numbers by wands (and on BlackBerries), delivering an astonishingly painless cornucopia into its own castles, penthouses, and estates. Money alone now generates money, while labor bears the pain. Most people slave morning to night for mere codes and tags, struggling to acquire wage-worthy objects, while a few financiers receive massive, invisible surges of power and goods without duty or endeavor. Many of them get additional bonuses in the millions—the lifetime wages of a small village—for perpetrating these feats of money magic and capital diversion. We are truly lost.

Marxism may have failed in practice, but only because of Sovietization and Maoism; in the long run it is the better game. The alienation of capital from work distorts the energy equation of the planet and strips value from the precise modalities that yield long-term profit: sustainable ecosystems, just societies, earned power and wealth.

The drive for capital to centralize itself—for wealth-wielding institutions to expand without limit and to compete beyond statute—can only end in an omega point, as it were, when all wealth is concentrated under one subject. At that point the obviousness of the madness of the situation will rise like a god from the sea and become so fully apparent, that existence itself will (ideally) be able to separate itself from the thralldom that quantitative ontology and its capitalist offspring have forced on us.

As dominant as currency is today, it is not real; it can be dropped without the Earth's atmosphere or oceans recording the event, without the gravitational field flinching one iota. Wind and water still get to play their game, living creatures still arise to seek their destinies.

Money has an enemy.

2. You can't turn all a planet's rivers, seas, and oceans into dumps and sewers. Cumulatively over centuries, no fluid is going to be capable of matrixing life.

It took water billions of years to filter out its toxins and radioactivity and breed its alchemy—check Titan and Venus for something resembling the starting point. All the gunk and rust and grease and catshit; feedlot offal, plastics, estrogens, pharmaceuticals, and industrials can't just mix willy-nilly in a witch's broth or the result will be not only noxious but lifeless. Right now the reserve of vital seawater is huge compared to idle trickles and valves of contamination, but the soup is thickening. When it arrives at that invisible tipping point, god help us!

Along those lines, New Orleans should have been sealed off and quarantined to dry out in the sun. Pumping back water rife with the miso of factories, garages, attics, and dumps took at least two hundred and fifty years off the life of the Gulf of Mexico.

(A less ecological but more socially practical alternative: in the months after the next "Katrina," the nation should invite not just a few, but *all* the students on spring break to secure and then clean up the mess, grime pool by grime pool, nail by rusty nail, slab of sheet rock by moldy sheet rock. Let them party bigtime only after serving big-time. It will feel good in a way that nothing since Iwo Jima has, not only to the kids themselves but all Americans. There will be less drunken foolishness and indolent pranksterism in Daytona Beach and Aruba *et al.*, and, one way or another, egotistic lunkheads will return as planetary citizens.)

The denizens of Frank Herbert's post-global-warming planet understood that biological existence was finite. Every drop of sweat had to be captured in wetsuits if Dune's habitants wanted to have any H_2O to metabolize or drink. They recognized, as we will have to sooner or later, that water is the only real commodity, far more valuable than gold, more beautiful than emeralds. What other crystal is alive and vital at room temperature? Water is a shape-shifting gem.

More than that, water is us. Bad water in polluted seas and desecrated rivers is a sordid harvest, signifying profligacy and social disintegration: every critter for itself until each waterhole is a cesspool or desert.

3. Population must be regulated, though not by the draconian criminalizing of "extra" children or the slaying of infant girls. On a psychic level it is dangerous to kill: to restrain progeny and push spirits out of a world. It is more effective to address population regionally, holding communities collectively responsible for their young and local species balance. Given them responsibility and real power, they can do it; they don't need Big Brother. Just watch.

Death to the casual census! Death to murder by abstraction and algorithm! Life to morning outside the empire! That's what got the hominids and other monkeys out of Africa.

Zero population growth is a tall order, but the alternative is to chew the planet to a nubbin and run a global police state. I suppose bird flu, contaminated sperm, or full-scale jihad might depopulate the theater too; but it's either one from Column B or a Malthusian spiral from hell unless we solve the problem in-house.

ZPG requires more equitable distribution of resources than the present free-market-for-all. Don't you get it? If you reduce people to nothing, they will have children—offspring provide allies, workers, soldiers, as well as someone to take care of them when they are old and infirm. You can't stop animals from using their bodies as they will. Sperm and egg don't bargain or respond to statutory regulation. That's what populated Eurasia and archipelago Dreamtime and still does, on 168th Street as in Osh and Ogan Ilir.

We should entertain the disincarnate world on environmentally tenable terms. Everyone can't get a body on demand. The Milky Way is gargantuan, and there are untold numbers of Milky Ways. Spirits can hie elsewhere if they must be born, unless the point is to overpopulate this place and then blow it into the next dimension on a runaway bus.

4. Cooperation must become our intrinsic guiding ethic. The long war of nature must seek an armistice after a billion or more hellacious years. We are in this together, as consciousness: the lion, the mantis, the lamb. A strike against any is an attack against all. The universe itself cries out for this recognition, howls to survive, weeps for its heart and soul.

But oh, how quickly ideals are forgotten once the action begins!

5. Burn vegetable oils and feces for energy. This can be as impromptu as driving to McDonald's or Burger King and fueling up with dregs of potato oil or trekking down the avenue to the Indian restaurant and topping off a gallon jug from the puri frying vats. Yes, these establishments will continue to wreak more biological and meteorological havoc than they can repay in ergs (measured on some hypothetical Excel sheet), but we can begin to bias our economic and ecological formulas in the direction of reuse and sustainability. We can provide daily rituals and mudras for recycling as a fundamental act even as we have begun to mine "urban ore" and enfranchise fleets of anti-garbage trucks.

Take back as much as possible of what was discarded or incompletely consumed. Collect the poop of domestic cats and dogs (and people)—convert it to gas. If everyone saved all the shit and decay in their households, packaged it sanitarily, and hauled it to the nearest retrofitted power plant or composted it in their garages into fuels and fertilizer, we would begin to cultivate an understanding that energy is sacred, and we might stop squandering it in wide-scale manufacture of junk and mindless missions by SUV. Ultimately there would be less to reclaim.

We are transporting materials and citizens now heedlessly all over the planet at tremendous cost in energy, taking them some place and then bringing them back, usually with their stuff. Anything any day, based on whims and vain imperatives, could wind up anywhere. Picture us as great apes and you see how ridiculous it is to have pack members flying between continents, motoring down paved trails. Marketing is the biggest boondoggle of all.

By imposing themselves as middlemen to dip and overdip their beaks, the high fliers, the gentleman-C assholes who went into sales and marketing at six-figure salaries, have bullshit the rest of the planet that they are indispensable. Producing absolutely nothing, they hold gratuitous conferences at which they indulge in self-important power-point presentations. They leave gigantic carbon footprints. Why should a gorilla in San Francisco need to get itself to Tokyo or London to promote a product? Is that worth the molecules of oil and air it consumes?

Assess the actions of this civilization each second and evaluate what is being moved. Question why. We are neurotic and restless, our economy a displaced symptom of an undiagnosed pathology. Let's make businessmen (and women) into stewards, not just product-barkers. Let's calculate what the Earth and its creatures really need to be happy and at peace. If they can do it in the Orion system or as nearby as Alpha Centauri, we can do it here.

We must try to act efficiently, understanding that, on the physical plane, there is an energy cost to everything, and also that anything in a new position will release quanta, some of them redundant or exorbitant, most of them unnoticed and unwanted, many of them costly beyond reckoning or measure. And they are gathering, unreckoned, toward that tipping point.

Any house, apartment building, or office, with its planes of solar absorption, intricate baffle of wind resistance, gravitational gradients, potential synthesis of the urine and fecal by-products of habitation, and general indoor metabolism and breathing of CO_2 is capable of producing far more energy than it consumes, of feeding rather than draining the grid. Every skyscraper could leave a carbon-negative footprint.

Reverse the basic energy equations, change the direction of flow; intention will follow the isobars.

No assembly lines of doodads and chachkas! No joy rides! Skateboards and surfboards over NASCAR, Harleys, and jetskis. Burning Man, yes—RV armadas and ATVs, no. Dzogchen practice, yay!—Vegas slots, boo! Yoga class today (and tomorrow)—cancel all needless business trips. Does it really matter how much is marketed and sold if you are rendering yourself and the planet dead?

6. Wheels are the keynote invention of our species from which all others are derived. Wheels—from wagons to clocks to computers—transfer the subliminal impulses of gravity and inertia into motion: culturally applicable moil. We must free these circles to turn more fluidly with purer inertia, making use of their innate shape to receive the bounty and free disposition of matter and mass along curves in gravitational fields. Don't accelerate or override circles. Let them spin at no cost to the atmosphere or environmental collateral.

Creature-drawn vehicles and metabolically powered rigs—bicycles, stagecoaches, wheelbarrows, rickshaws, and shopping carts (one by one or coupled in long trains)—are the most energy-efficient ways to move goods.

On this very day windmills and waterwheels blanket the most successful planets in the Milky Way and Andromeda systems. Throughout the universe giant wheels are turning everywhere without evident impetus, moving economies and politics, flaunting eternal motion. Worlds are at peace.

Even on Earth, bacteria, volvoxes, jellyfish, bugs, and worms are using their own native wheels to run economies that dwarf the macroeconomy by more than a trillion to one.

Beggars, mendicants, and street people must be validated as the stewards they are, wheeling vegetables, bottles, rags, and papers, and recycling society's bricolage, by donkey, wagon, wire cart, and on their backs. They are not an aberration; they are the seeds of eco-transmutation.

Poverty is a harbinger of a different form of wealth.

7. Keep all lineages of plants, insects, amphibians, mollusks, fishes, worms, and mammals alive and happy. Every gene and genome will ultimately be needed. This indigenous information pool is our only reserve or archive of anything. Our urbanized lives bank on the unexamined quiddity that grasses and jungles, topsoil and silt, waters and air remain densely populated by uniquely adapted creatures of diverse size, scale, shape, and non-Euclidean investiture—filament by filament, droplet per droplet, molecule after molecule. This interwoven fabric of mites and monsters in mute communion and combat with one another is the living fiber of our planet. Extinguish it from neglect or gluttony and we might as well be walking on cinders and astroturf in spacesuits.

8. Global warming has so many separate causes and accelerating factors that it is already beyond political control. Even a worldwide Kyoto pact could not come close to keeping pace with the industrial expansion of a precinct of China, to which one can add the deforestation of South America, the wringing of oil out of Alberta's sands, the transactions of air-conditioners and hair-driers in Bangkok and Miami, roadside bombs and other incendiary devices, gratuitous explosions, and idle fires, and so on. Every piece of metal sticking out is a heat coil in the sun.

This crisis needs an unconscious shift at the same level as the primordial production of oxygen by bacteria back at the dawn of life. That fluctuation triggered a burst of molecular intelligence. A world which started under the canopy of volcanic ash exhaled into a blue sky and singing larks and lizards.

Are you listening, 3012?

Everything at a global scale is a collective manifestation already: hurricanes, nuclear bombs, glacial ice, war, coffee, cars, fashion shows, cigarettes. New forms manifest as we allow them into our collective unconscious.

9. Stockades may have once legitimately protected civilians from social menaces and enemy captives, but American's corporate bastilles provide neither protection for society nor lip service to rehabilitation. They are chambers of displaced retribution. Incarceration has become punishment, a ruse for politicized bureaucracies to yank people out of their homes and communities and isolate them in cages to be abused, taunted, dehumanized, and raped for reasons that are as obscure as they are craven.

The penitentiary system in the "land of the free" is a quasi-legal subterfuge to: i) boost industrial production; ii) export blame and guilt; iii) enforce class; iv) punish unregulated use of hallucinogens while discouraging commerce in *some* recreational drugs; v) house mental patients cheaply; vi) impart posturing points for politicians; vii) provide moralistic recreation for the evangelical hoi polloi and programmers of 24-hour TV; and viii) assuage unknown gods.

Commoditization of souls to serve a rapidly growing PIC (Prison Industrial Complex)—its bureaucrats, contractors, guard unions, and their service rackets—is a scandal and a crime in itself.

More than half the prisoners in the United States are social and racial victims and scapegoats, not real violators of life or limb or even property. A mere traffic error, toke, or vehicular space-out can lead to decades in detention camps. When a young man can be locked away for thirty years or more for selling a few joints of weed or robbing a grocery store because his family is starving, we have *Les Misérables* playing in our cities, the nobility rising to clap.

Jail is legalized slavery, as racially grubstaked as the trade in humans out of Africa.

When the goal is not justice but ritual punishment, chastisement of innocents is inevitable.

By then they are *all* the wrong prisoners.

"All prisoners," chanted Diane di Prima in her 1970 *Revolutionary Letters*, "are political prisoners: every Indian on a reservation, every junkie shooting up in a john, every pot smoker, the ancient wise turtle at the Detroit Aquarium, our own greedy minds, our own dull senses, our own tense bodies...."

Penning other creatures for crimes, real or imagined, or similarly indenturing them as cheap labor is a futile exercise in dominion. No group or category is ultimately tamed or curtailed, yet in the meantime enforced custody imprisons everyone, innocent and guilty, and haunts everyone's dreams.

People are forced into cubicles where they patrol the passage of meaningless hours and days, watch their lives float by as their bodies and minds grow old. Time itself becomes their enemy, and existence slowly seeps into waking death.

They are not left alone with themselves, as monks or zen priests, to seek meaning or redeem their deeds through the dark zazen of tedium and isolation. They are blatantly and sadistically traumatized; converted into not only objects but scorned and abusable objects, like cattle in stockades. Would that they were confined in solitary meditations, to be reconciled with their conscience and society and made whole again!

People are sentenced not only to time in cells but execution by the State. Transposed into satanic rituals with goose-stepping marches, these legalized murders seem camp parodies of cinema that imitates *them*. They are in the same entertainment genre as feeding Roman slaves to lions during Coliseum games and other hostage-and-beast divertissements, guillotine beheadings, staged quarterings, witchburning pageants, crucifixions, and civic killings down through *Homo sapiens'* squalid history. The fact that America's death performances are not viewed by cheering audiences in stadiums renders them no less populist or recreational. In fact, the unseen act without a palpable image (beyond occasional news footage), without the edifying catharsis of blood and pain, is all the more sordid and sterile. The government is making snuff films. Killing is thrill-killing, all.

There is absolutely no justice or reparation in capital punishment—maybe a temporary safeguard against reprobate offenses by hardened criminals and sociopaths—but no grand redemption, no functional amercement.

And the death penalty doesn't deter; in fact, at the level of the shadow, it abets the very crimes it is invoked to hinder. To unleash institutional violence on a murderer neither avenges his act nor assuages the demon at its heart. By the simple physics of action/reaction, the scrupulous karma of each displaced deed activates the next. Unbalanced energy cannot be eradicated or revoked; all situations must find their resolution in an outcome.

Our sentences invariably boomerang. As we feed cycles of fear and guilt, we implant crimes again on an unconscious level. Violations are given new power by the gas chamber or electric chair and take hold over the populace again, their impulse and thrill transferred subliminally. Only the façades are behind bars—to be electrocuted, hanged, and lethally injected. By the time the people arrived on death row, the actions that got them there had eroded into something else. These sorry specimens are dead men walking, zombies with their spells broken. They don't even know what they did or remember why they did it—not really. The firing squad is aiming at victims, not crimes.

In China, meanwhile, prisoners are executed so their organs can be extracted and sold for hard currency.

With each forced custody or execution, we enact our collective fate. The lot of prisoners across this planet (animal captives likewise) is a warning: As long as we are not a compassionate or a just species, no one is safe! The mind that is unforgiving and implacable, that flogs for its grim satisfaction, is a mind that can turn against us in the blink of an eye. It is our mind.

What keeps any of us from being boiled in oil or beaten to a pulp or drawn and quartered by some enemy, maniac, or fascist? Nothing but a web of individually sanctioned good will within society. Our safety rests on a thing more gossamer than a spider's thread—the collective Word. In its absence all hell breaks loose; it would not even be worth being born.

Kafka got it right: the trial could begin tomorrow, the police arrive tonight. Anyone—anyone!—could be arrested for any crime, real or imagined, is susceptible to finding himself or herself dependent on others' mercy.

CIA operatives kidnap strangers, then pack them off to dark sites in Central Asia or the Sahara, to cage them in deprivation chambers. There they subject the hostages twenty-four hours a day for months at a time to deafening rap and white noise; slice them with razor blades; waterboard them so that they nearly drown, again and again and again; deprive them of natural light; visit them only as masked, silent guards who bring putrid water and rancid food; make their rooms unbearably hot and then put them naked in refrigerators; carry them around in foul-smelling suitcases; chain them to metal rings in unbearable crouches and make them stand until their ankles double in size and their kidneys shut down; tie beehives to them; suspend them from the ceiling by their arms with their toes barely off the ground; lock them in compartments so small they cannot stand.

Eventually some of these detainees try to commit suicide by bashing their heads against walls. They then have to be tranquilized and immobilized in straitjackets.

And Americans, not Nazis, are running this show. Cavalier American doctors are orchestrating the science of human breaking points, torturing under Uncle Sam's banner of beneficence and the best hope for all mankind. If they aren't the good guys, who is? Who is running this universe?

Is it any wonder that the interrogators themselves start to go mad? Once they cross an unmarked line into an unknown place, they find it near impossible to come back. Inside the space desecrated by their own acts they cannot secure peace of mind.

When they pull the skin off the universe, they see something they didn't expect, much bigger and more ghastly than they could have imagined, staring back at them, informing them what *it* can do, how evil and grim it can be. It tells them that they are not in charge, not at all. It can lift a mere finger, not even a real finger but a specter of one, and do far worse, and for longer, and already has. Then they crack.

You cannot inflict something on someone else without it turning back against you. You can't be safe unless you keep those in your care safe. You can't accept love until you have confessed your crimes and been forgiven, but there is no one to confess to and no one with the authority to forgive. You can't be safe until you know what you are capable of, what you can still be compelled to do. Consciousness compels this attention.

Since we are all potential thieves, pedophiles, murderers, embezzlers (look inside yourself, really look!), we cannot suppress those comportments in society at large—so we must convert their energy into generosity and love. After all, they are not what they seem; they are scraps of failed consciousness, suppressed graces yet unborn.

Video footage shows a group of young black men in a New York State prison yard, debating Machiavelli's versus Rousseau's views of natural man—high-school dropouts who have been reading Hegel and Kant in German for homework in their cells. How could you not be moved to tears?

While they are doing time, these guys are taking college courses because only after losing their freedom did they realize what they wanted to do with their bodies and minds. Of course, society never taught them useful trades when it counted—not really, if you consider the modus and decorum of the average public classroom in America. And who could deny the allure of the street and its simple justice and easy pickins?

Almost anyone can be reclaimed; the thirst for knowledge and education are our only credible tools for rehabilitation, of committed jihadists too.

Every moment we live rests on the quotient of compassion in our species, in ourselves. Those who provide mercy create mercy. Those who spare others cultivate both local and divine forgiveness, for themselves too. And for the universe as well: this kind of stuff gets around and is somehow known among the galaxies. It travels through all consciousness everywhere, faster than cosmic rays.

Liberate and transmute the energy inside the thrill! Liberated people will find useful things to do, creative ways to transform their violence and passion.

What is needed is a new wave of abolition that strikes at the heart of human enslavement of sentient beings and of ourselves.

10. Although it is a leap to syllogize from slave ships to jails to slaughterhouses, in truth they are tines of one world-view. Prisoners are a kind of meat on ice, whereas the sentence of "meat" is a warrant imposed on edible animals. We may not initially see the parity between a convict on death row and a cow in a feedlot, but jurisdiction is jurisdiction; prerogative, prerogative; murder, murder; and consumption of body and consumption of soul come down to the same unexamined cannibalism. Even the corpse has renewed power; a dishonored body revives as a dangerous ghost. This is vintage Stone Age science:

"The greatest peril in life lies in the fact that human food consists entirely of souls. All the creatures that we have to kill and eat, all those that we have to strike down and destroy to make clothes for ourselves, have souls like we do, souls that do not perish with the body, and which therefore must be propitiated lest they should revenge themselves on us for taking away their bodies."*

We have a birthright to eat omnivorously, as all life forms do, but we do not have a right to imprison other creatures in grim citadels and then butcher them on conveyor belts by machine.

What self-respecting lion or eagle would oppress its prey in penal confinement for months or years at a time, depriving it of liberty and the pursuit of happiness? You may see hideous things in the eyes of the shark and the lynx, but you will not see this brand of cold depravity. Humans invented it.

Murdering living creatures on assembly lines is one of the more brutal acts on any planet anywhere. Earth's slaughterhouses are insults to creation; our gratuitous carnage is a mockery of God.

When we torture and butcher sentient beings, turn animal bodies into clothes and meat on an industrial scale, we are establishing the baseline of our own sentience and compassion, who we are and how we choose to treat ourselves. We are establishing the fate of all souls under our stewardship. We are declaring the type of universe that we are willing to tolerate and live in. We are sentencing everyone, almost forever.

This is a profound one, and it will take a very, very long time to work our way through it. Yet we might as well start now because time is a-wastin' and there is nowhere else to go.

We need to learn to feel, really feel, the pain of harried geese and deer as if our own. We must make it unbearable to harm other creatures gratuitously; it must be as if we were attacking ourselves. Empathy is outright essential to our evolution, our

---

*Knud Rasmussen, *Intellectual Culture of the Iglulik Eskimos*, 1929.

survival. We have to feel, truly feel, the separate, autonomous existence of each creature as a life relevant and internal to our own as much as "I" myself. Only then will we lance and drain the sociopathic boil inside each of us.

Let the ant live, let the duck fly! This does not mean that the peasants should starve. The duck doesn't even seek this, nor does the ant. Nothing in them bleeds that message.

It means that our inherent consciousness of the unity of sentient beings must transcend the predation of nature. If we kill for food, then we should kill with honor and gratitude, as tribespeople across the planet did throughout the Stone Ages, implicitly. Eat well, eat heartily, eat *them*, but do not debase their corpses or spirits, *our* spirits; do not spread superfluous voodoo that will feed off you and me and the rest of us for generations to come. Propitiate! Every time, pay homage to the sacred limen of life and death you are summoning by your fatal blow. Leave a marker of honor at the gate. Otherwise, you will deliver inconsolable grief and rage to some ignored god.

If we could take even the first steps of intention toward respectful and empathic slaughter of animals, even though we are going to eat them, we would alter this planet at its core. The glacier of our being would thaw toward what it must become.

11. The real test in Lebanon is not Jews and Muslims, is not Ruhollah Khomeini's Party of God versus the Israeli military machine, is not neocons against mullahs (by proxy), is not even combat and truce, is not (sorry, folks) whether we are headed toward smuggled Iranian WMDs and Armageddon or an international peace-keeping force. It is not finally a debate between Hezbollah's use of human shields and Israel's carpet-bombing of civilians. It is nothing less than a test of what lies at the heart of

this species, the human experiment. It is the divine audit: Are we good or are we bad?

Only one answer is acceptable because the other, the answer that feeds Dick Cheney and his kind, will lead us collectively to hell. If we are the bad guys, then even God cannot help us.

Offensive wars are collective acts of hysteria against the "other," attempts to change physics by razing forces in opposition to one's own agendas and desires. In the end, however, they breed only the karma of retaliation and distort the fate of everyone and everything on the planet.

"Peace now" doesn't mean just stop fighting and plan the next ambush, or seethe and plot in your corner. It means actual reconciliation and unity, something that never goes away. If we elevate rhetoric over action, Lenin is as much of a pacifist as Gandhi.

Those most stridently pro-peace or pro-animal-rights often spread hostility identical to that which they oppose in war-makers and killers. Likewise, those who are violently pro-God and pro-life are unwitting agents of the one they vilify as Satan. Their God becomes the henchman and lackey of their terror of the darkness in their own hearts, in all our hearts, the shadow that the entire material creation was breathed into being to address.

Achieve real peace at your core as opposed to slogans that ignore the source of all discord.

What is passing for religion in most of the Earth now is its opposite: xenophobia and road rage.

12. We must begin to utilize nonlinear paraphysical energies: the mental, the psychic, the psychokinetic, the radionic. Civilization is already (though few recognize it) idioplasmatic: an act of pure mind employing raw molecules to erect a skyscraping edifice, to give material shape to an ancient and archetypal dream. It is also,

of course, on a secular level an incremental tinker-toy hoisted by Maglemosian potters and Neolithic masons imparting their designs to guilds of chemists, physicists, and engineers. But that doesn't mean that it is not a projection of mind into matter, a predisposition of atoms to the collective brunt of our mentation.

Slowly but surely the unconscious mind penetrates stone and constructs civilizations, siphoning molecules and grinding history out of volcanic rock.

The city and civilization of today are the unconscious realization of the Paleolithic shaman's deepest magic, the blind apotheosis of his most fervent desires, the invocation of his most feared ghosts. This is his paradise and his nightmare.

It was a long time coming, but he took a very long breath and quaffed out a profound conjury. As he exorcised the beast, he put a spell on all society to follow. But he did not get the heart of the beast; he did not even fathom it beating *inside* his ceremony. That is the work left for the shamans of today: to complete his task. A major piece has been done; the city has been realized, and we dwell within it. The roads and tarmacs have been laid.

What we conjure now will be the planet of tomorrow.

Depending on human intention and invocation, anything could still happen—*anything*.

If we put as much attention into mindedness and breath as we do into machines and metals, then we could transcend technology itself and—slowly but surely like cell colonies over the next million or so years—become creatures of light and love. We could finish the shamanic work.

At the ashram, zendo, and yoga class, you see the bare beginnings of this act.

In simple terms, the wish of Stone Age man and woman was this: give me a method for turning signs into functions (e.g. language) and utensils with which to tame nature (e.g. machines), to protect me from great storms and cold and merciless beasts—to feed me.

They dreamed shamelessly, without (of course) knowing it, of factories of steel and towering caves of stone; of marts packed with fruits and fishes, warm cloaks and sharp blades; of self-propelling carts to penetrate the incalculable forests; of tractors and shovels to clip trails through the brush and thrash it down; of vessels to traverse horizonless waters; of wings to invade the kingdom of the hawk and turkey vulture. What we entertain now are realizations of the unknowable shapes behind Palaeolithic sorcerer's ceremonies, the templates driving primeval life and Earth itself.

It was the destiny of Stone Age hunters to have children who would have children who would realize these totems, who would wrench them out of absolute darkness by their lives, epoch by epoch, until now, at the pinnacle of the age of materialism, we inhabit the planet of the wizard and the minx.

There is another dream, as obscure in us as the dream of the City was for Pleistocene man and woman. We can no more intuit it concretely than a Stone Age seer and hunter could imagine an apartment building or jet engine, but we know as well as we know anything that it is there, different from this, at the bottom of our bottomless dreams—that objects, realizable forms, ways of living and being await us on the other side of the abyss. In the tragic vividness of what we see in legion before us, we know only that there is an other.

We will have children, and they will have their children and, though they will suffer as much as ancient peoples did, maybe more, through many fruitless congresses and failed meditations and acts of war, they will gradually give birth to our obscurities, and it will be as vast and unforeseeable a civilization as this one, made of light and empathy and fully telekinetic.

But the purifying jihad of the Vandals comes first.

13. There is unlimited untapped power in the world already, but we are addicted to only its crudest, most concrete forms. We are not even trying to hone our birthright as creatures with radiant mindedness.

We are as oblivious of real energy as we are of the meaning of the night sky.

Our local star is brimming with nuclear and meta-nuclear energies, bursting into the cosmos, overendowing Mercury and Venus with its wealth. A few small flags in this Third Orbit capture quanta of solar wind and here and there photosynthesize it into green molecules, fashioning a garden amicable to life. Lacking mind, plants know what we can't.

Light is pure neg entropy, flowing out of Sol into our sink-hole, which solves an unlikely equation, weaving a Dreamtime of meadows, mountains, and seas, while radiating useless heat back into the universe.

Electrons flow through gates to weave chlorophyll lattices. Vide vegetation and its intricate blossoms. Calyces and calypsos are unfolding of themselves, without human agency, out of sheer light.

In under fifteen minutes the Sun provides more than enough energy to run our entire civilization for its duration, with negligible contamination. We don't yet understand how to sip or conduct this river of light. Quite obviously we don't. It rushes out into the Galaxy as torrents of pure nutrition, an unadulterated form of the thing we are. To fair terrestrials, sadly, spilt milk!

Our minds are even more powerful than the Sun, and we certainly don't know how to use *them*.

The interior lei lines and batteries of the Earth—as well as its huge electromagnetic core—feed the vestigial megaliths of an extinct civilization with a current that we neglect because we have no terms or measure for it. We do not see it; we do not feel it; we run flimsy devices right next to ancient machines that are still operating, but for which we have divested the dashboard and manual and cannot read the stones. For so long have we favored gross over subtle energy that we have lost the capacity to discern and conduct the free cosmic machinery or even our equally free human torso.

Let a starship of extraterrestrials attain Earth orbit and scan the local terrain. Its pilots will not long overlook that there are fueling stations everywhere. This planet is a cornucopia, while its inhabitants blindly fight and starve. The visitors leave with full tanks but in sorrow, as "ignorant armies clash by night."*

A gigantic etheric device sits before the Alps, esoteric instructions engraved into its morphology. Built by an intentional community of a few hundred Damanhurians, the Temples of Humankind are linked by nine hundred tons of copper wiring interlaced with filaments of gold and silver—a vast radionic sending and receiving circuit like an activated crop circle or Martian monument; a primitive but noble attempt to get us back in touch with the universe.

The Temples are also networked by "wireless" globes of dissolved alchemical salts, each illuminating a distinct spagyric color. These flasks synergize with the wiring to receive and amplify transgalactic, interdimensional whispers, heal trenchant diseases, and prepare consciousness for a quantum leap.

The machine was assembled according to a reincarnated map, the template for which was realized eons ago in another galaxy.

---

*Matthew Arnold (1822–1888), "Dover Beach": credit him also with the couplet that serves as the epigraph for modern woman and man: "Wandering between two worlds, one dead,/the other powerless to be born."

Reaching so far beyond the limits of terrestrial culture that it is all but invisible, this sphinx taps the alchemical properties of metals without reference to ordinary limitations of protons, relativity, or the speed of light.

Earth culture may have dabbled in alchemy and internal (Taoist) alchemy, but it has never evolved past Bronze Age science, a technology whose limits in mechanical engineering, supramolecular chemistry, quantum dots, and fiber optics we now subtend. Lead, tin, mercury, platinum, and the like were captured and alloyed by humans primordially and archetypally to make tools and vehicles, hence have been trapped in a lesser metallurgy via the molecular memory of each element's intrinsic shape—e.g. its capacity to hold patterns and transmit kinetics in the form of electricity and magnetism. But all metals are *also* individually intelligent in another, more animistic way at a level we have not yet discovered. One does not have to run voltage or data through them to get them to transmit information and force.

The possibilities of light and gravity are for all intents and purposes boundless. Pure physical energy is moving continuously through the jetstream six miles up at 250, 300 mph. Forget retrieval systems as tenuous or metaphysical as lei lines and alchemical modules—loops of rotating kites on helium balloons attached through carbon nanotubes to turntables and generators on the ground could transmit conventional energy along aluminum or copper cables. Drawing down these monstrous winds would provide power for civilization across this entire planet and still leave 99% of it free to dance and dissipate in the sky.

In a single tide the equivalent of thousands of Katrinas roll down the Bay of Fundy, providing potential electricity and fuel for all of North America and Africa—kiss it goodbye today; kiss it goodbye tomorrow. Meanwhile Niagara's daily gradient fritters the equivalent of all Eurasian civilization, by heat, evaporation, gravity, and friction.

Check out the many bays, lagoons, and cataracts on this planet, large and small, fractally imbedded in one another. For that matter, every puddle and icicle is a battery. You don't have to move supertankers of oil to drive a civilization.

As a symbology, as a world among many worlds, we have missed the point. We are blowing off the operating manual inside our beings for our own planet. We are running a vulgar gas station when the living alchemical depository and free-energy mill are at hand.

One day we must build true power plants and open actual energy gates.

For now, move consciously like a chi gung master. Transport a tiny module of cosmic energy. Squeeze it, sip it, pump it, play with it, bathe yourself—paws like a cat. Let it splash all over. Splash it onto everyone else. There is so much extra that, in being generous, you gain everything.

14. The dead must be consulted. The dead can no longer be allowed to slip away. The dead *must not* be neglected. Despite what has happened to them they are still members of our community; they are creating our present, and it is not even safe to ignore their meddling or sway.

Life on Earth is characterized among cosmic worlds by the fact that spirits come from nowhere to dwell in bodies and then vanish from hence, leaving only corpses. And we accept that! We bury or incinerate them and say bye-bye, in our hearts and minds. We go on like zombies, letting it happen, day after day, offering cover stories and alibis, pretending that it's okay when it is anything but okay. We don't protest; we don't either wage the riddle or log the crime.

Without a forwarding address, we think we cannot track or query the dead; we do not heed their lessons or read or understand the difference between where we are and where they are. And most important, we do not see how the dead are trapping our civilization in its present crisis; not because they are against us and want us to fail—not at all, in fact the diametric opposite: because the very act of *not seeing them* leads us to misinterpret and abase their powerful influence, to refuse their counsel and their astonishing gifts.

We make wrong choices almost every time primarily because we do not understand the field of play.

The dead have not ceased to exist. They are vibrating at a higher pitch than our senses can read. They like we are imbedded among rivers and skies and mountains, but theirs are of light emanating translucently in hues unfamiliar to mortals. While no ontological barrier separates us, just about everything dissuades us from each other's existences. We are wraiths to one another, and that is tragic. More than tragic—it is the whole game.

We cannot lose our friends and family members simply because we are too noisy and distracted to hear their calls.

This is the greatest failing of our species, the central truth we have forsaken, the sapience we are most pathologically evading. The lost tablet of the universe is at hand, and it contains evidence regarding our condition that, when it comes to us whole and explicit, will break the stranglehold of all fundamentalisms and materialisms. It is the wakeup call that the rest of the universe wants to witness us receiving.

The dead are transformed, even as the living were in order to get here—the womb is a fibrous vehicle for transporting life pods. We do not see the sarcophagus arriving; we certainly do not see Charon's dory, filled with waving passengers, departing. We literally shut off the channel and ban others from listening or watching. We hold our hands over our eyes and ears to avoid the blasphemy, to avoid being shattered by the radical nature of our situation. The result is a planet-wide stupor.

We alone have the opportunity to heal the cosmic breach because in us it has been most fully incarnated, indoctrinated; jammed somehow into our code, our collective psyche and cells. It is no minor interdict, for it has been inveigled subtly and unconsciously, all the way back to the first carnivorous eels, and before. It is the ruling doctrine of the planet and its cosmology—ramified, fish by fish, cat by hunting cat; church after ramshackle church, king to ordained king.

But some have been able to peer behind the veil, and their reports form the flank of the great occult: the sacred teachings, the illicit gospel, the gossip of the spirits. At most, fragments of it eke out in channeling sessions, brief encounters with ghosts, and a growing cadre of books and films about other worlds, dimensions, and realities. These melodramas disguise while spilling the truth.

We don't understand suicide bombers or their radical means of death. They are conducting politics by other means—cosmic politics. They are trying to blast open the bubble around this world and expose the true dimensions of all acts, political ones immediately, the rest later, because, at that level, there is no distinction. Most of these avenging jihadists, despite their committed ideologies, don't have a clue why they are doing this. In fact, they experience it as something else, equally powerful but far more sentimentally valorous than it really is.

Their sense of mission, the sublimity and the naïve conviction they salute, the sacrifice they make, horrifically though it resonates through the present clime, horrific as they intend it to be, is meant to serve the planet, to carry all of us, apostles and heathen alike, on the turtle's back through the hole in our creation myth.

Because they do not know how to be truly horrific, because they do not know how to do what they think they are trying to do, they effect the thing they would most singularly renounce as apostasy. They are creating the future, beyond Muslim (or Darwinian) law. They are bodhisattvas, servants of Allah, the real Allah.

Yes, they are doing the work of angels, but even the angels do not condone it. Like us, the angels are appalled, disgusted by the inhumanity and callousness. Yet the angels have no choice but to accept the offering and turn it to their own ends.

It is so barren and ingrate, so futile, that they guide it into the sole meaningful path it breaches. They must. They must use it because it is what the Earth is giving them to work with—people throwing back the bodies, the libations they were granted. And anyhow—sigh!—it's where humanity is at. Revengeful, melodramatic, spoiled humanity—so-called King of the Beasts, stamp of the divine.

You can't get where you're going unless you start at where you are. You can't wake us up to the dead unless you demonstrate what is actually being done by surrogate to the living, in Palestine and elsewhere. This late in the game, you can't have political and social justice without having cosmic justice. You can't have satori without infitada, infitada without satori. Each liberation hinges on the other. You can't do the work of the angels without first making the angels weep.

If Osama bin Laden taught an esoteric tarot, he might "communiqué" to the effect that, when lightning in the form of his hijacked jets struck the tower of ignorance, tyranny, and habit, it released seeds of conscious possibility. It incinerated and crushed many innocent people (and caused others to leap to their deaths), but it cumulatively spawned a healing clan on the other side of the veil; it rewrote collective karma—and what came back on the wind was (and still is) an inaudible hymn. The choir of the martyrs of 9/11 is singing to us, all of them, but we are not listening. In fact, the present conviction is *not* to listen, not to risk knowledge and transformation, but to go to war against a mirror.

Despite themselves the suicide bombers are saying: "The universe in which you are conducting politics, are arbitrating the fate of peoples and nations, does not exist. You cannot solve any of your crises of resources and national identity unless you see what they really are, who *we* really are. The winners are not really winners; the losers are not ultimately losers.

"Here, now play this game. You may not like it at first but, in the end, it is the only one in town."

15. Madrasas, Aryan Brotherhoods, Crips, Bloods, Malditos, Neighborhood Dukes, Dreamboys, Bratz, Mara Salvatrucha 13, and the like should do the real job for which they were brought into existence. They should initiate warriors and samurai, become guardians of the vision-quest instead of its assassins, form shamanic guilds rather than crime gangs. So much real courage and gallantry and mortal training should not be squandered on cheap bravado and petty theft. Such a gauntlet, when run victoriously, should yield more than street cred, prison power, and fancy tattoos. The Earth is already filled with empty military rituals and wasted soldiers. If you have earned enough status and clout to intimidate, to make others quake and bow before you, then be a prophet, teach the real lesson, become a bodhisattva, a true avatar. Release by grace what you have bound by terror.

16. The "United Nations" should rent the North Korean army indefinitely and deploy it in trouble spots like Sudan, Somalia, Iraq, Oaxaca. The Koreans historically play no favorites between

Christians and Muslims, Arabs and Africans, Shi'ites and Sunnis: those idolatrous drama queens have been purged out of them by their own privations and struggle. Plus, they have a different fundamentalist theology, a Korean "Koran/koan."

A great opportunity was already missed—Kim Jong-il's troops would have been quite disciplined and proficient in halting the slaughter in Rwanda. So transport them to Darfur at once; give them the basic mission and a free hand. They will force those janjawid militias and various rebel factions to cool out. Faced with a bunch of well-trained, incorruptible Koreans, the vigilantes will eventually turn tail and go home.

The North Korean army should have been airlifted to Indonesia after the tsunami. They would have restored order and rescued the injured in New Orleans post-Katrina faster than FEMA—the loss of life would have been mitigated. They could still be parachuted into the mountains of Pakistan to erect villages for earthquake victims. They could stare down narco-terrorists in Badakhshan, Cali, Juarez, wherever. They could enforce nonproliferation of nuclear weapons, break child-enslavement camarillas and other mafias, and contend for the Earth's oxygen balance against Amazonian and Kenyan vigilantes. They could protect the elephants of Chad against tusk-poaching bands with automatic weapons, defend the snow leopard and the frog too. They could sentinel the rainforest at key points, push back illegal clear-cutting, and spare some carbon tonnage for future generations to breathe. They could keep a quota of the remaining species and their niches alive, the fields and waters minimally habitable, because our danger is great and the time is short. They could express their doctrinal purity for the entire planet rather than one delusionary provincial cult.

The Earth needs them far more than Kim Jong-il does. And we have got to start somewhere; Gaia has got to get its own army—I mean, who else is going to do the job? Certainly not America and China, certainly not Monsanto, Halliburton, or Exxon. Certainly not ambitious yuppie environmentalists with their green yoga and "50 [more] simple ways." Yes, it has got to be all of us together in a wave of obscure intimations hitting everyone uniquely, moment to moment—off-the-grid permaculturalists and new rave musicians leading the way. But it would certainly make things easier if we had a few troops on our side.

Al-Qaeda, Hezbollah, and their minions are likewise begging to be enlisted in acts of ferocious love and healing, even if they don't realize it. The servants of Allah know how to recruit and train and die selflessly for honor.

Hey, bad boys, make it the honor of the whole planet, the defense of all sentient beings—and we will be right there alongside you, halfway home.

I sense that the North Korean leaders are pleading for the world to help them on this—to save them from themselves. They are building nuclear weapons to get us to force them to stop, stop the madness, stop it all, on both sides of the DMZ, to protect them and us, before it is too late.

If al-Qaeda would switch to the agendas of Earth First!, Oxfam, and Greenpeace, we'd be a hundred years ahead of where we are. They could still do their suicide bombing under a different protocol if they had to, but it would make even more sense to put their bodies at the service of life rather than paradise. I doubt that Allah would mind or, for that matter, even notice the difference. No god wants his biosphere to die. This sharia transcends all others.

Guess what, would-be martyrs and pilgrims; there has been a change in game plan, and this is the real jihad of our time.

The cost of renting Kim's military would be food and medicine for the North Korean people along with investments and micro-loans to jump-start their economy.

Maybe Pyongyang, presently outside the global economy, unsullied by either late modernism or New Age fantasies, could become the pivot for alternative technologies, Earth's capital of ecological design. They wouldn't have to tear down too much infrastructure to substitute solar homes, electric cars, and wind factories. They would only have to invert—not renounce—their belief system to turn it into *prana* and *psi*. They are already practicing dharma.

Americans should recognize an achievement for what it is and not libel it prematurely or get turned around by their own ideological biases. The truth is: the West would love to have such an army. The neocons don't stand *against* North Korea; they would like to make their own North Korea. That is, they dig the sanctitude, the suppression of heresy, the well-drilled standing army in the service of the Idea. They just don't want it playing for another team. Remember how neocon forerunners bribed and enlisted Nazi scientists and Soviet security experts once their polities collapsed: "Come right over here," they said, "and do the same stuff *for us*." Well, how about for the United Nations this time, at least until we make something better!

There is no Axis of Evil anyway; there is only axial power to be conducted toward the common good.

The Korean army has been created at enormous expense and consequence; it is a great military and industrial force in working order, trained and regimented, directed toward ideals. Redirecting it toward calamities and real needs in the world would be a blessing for everyone, everywhere.

In any case, the world must use this engine to serve a positive goal while there is yet time. Either we tame these warriors, or they will, sooner or later, erupt across the Peninsula and beyond, in tsunamis of destruction.

17. Osama bin Laden, Ehud Olmert, Sayed Hasan Nasrallah, Mahmoud Ahmadinejad, George W. Bush, and the various fascist hirelings in their employ must be forced to compromise in a way that serves humanity rather than their corporate ambitions, macho pride, fascist ideologies, inflated theocratic egos. If they really want to assist God on Earth, enough of the petty bullshit; let's have it!

18. All the arguments and policies of the world are in language, which warps toward blatancy and sophistry and does not reflect the tough realities of people's existences—e.g. when someone tells scallop-draggers that there won't be any more scallops tomorrow if they keep using computers to scan and scour underwater shoals, just as there aren't any cod today, they won't hear it or they will hear it as something else.

We are still reptiles, governed by electrical bursts of fear and appetite in the brainstem. Everything loftier is a projection of those emotions onto the cortex, a fleeting puppet theater.

From deep within, we still want, we hunger, greedily; we huddle in danger, ruled by alarm.

A man whose social and financial security is tied up in his boat is not going to give up dragging scallops because of a word. A logger, however short-sighted his chain-sawing of ancient redwoods, is not going to stop cutting trees after a rousing eco-speech. Does he care that he is pissing away good soil and polluting salmon-bearing streams? Lip service aside, he doesn't give a fuck. He just wants to get through to evening in one piece ... and the next morning and evening ... and so on, over the March hill. He doesn't want professors telling him what to do.

In 2005 salmon fishermen and loggers in the Northwest spent five days in powwow, talking past each other and the attendant environmentalists, but at least they were talking. We can start with words instead of weapons, but it is going to take a lot more than words. Reason forever runs into rationalizations and counterarguments. Change—lasting change—finally comes, usually when it is least expected, from another place entirely.

19. The world must exist for some reason, innately and energetically, and certainly psychically—it is not about the accumulation of goods. In that sense and that alone, the Rapture is what we are moving toward—not as an Ascension or Second Coming, but as the ineluctable destiny of mind in matter. This entire cinema projected in molecules is coming from somewhere, and we are either its lens or the dreamer.

There are no country clubs in the sky or male-privilege paradises. How would such a place function anyway? Stasis turns into hell.

Quick, warn the mullahs and preachers: all stasis *is* hell. You don't want the paradises you are hawking.

As badly as things are going here now, it is an honor to be part of it; that is, to be in a body. In the great experiment of the universe to stream into matter and live out its primeval dramas, we are here, among them, on board.

In the long run, the simple fact of placing spirits in bodies on worlds will win. There is no other way for things to unfold. Once creation got going in this fashion, ninety percent of the battle was over, though the rest of it will stretch over billions of years of the illusion we call "time," and it will be a cliffhanger all the way because that's what spirit in matter needs to encounter in becoming itself.

The first questions of pre-Socratic philosophers were actually the lingering questions of the Stone Age and still are the questions. They were the incipient questions of marine worms and lizards and remained unanswered at the dawn of mammalian consciousness. It is not as though squids and possums don't ask; it is just that, in order to do so, they must pass their molecules to chattering monkeys ... and then Babylonians and then Greeks.... Everyone is asking, "How came we here? What want ye of me? How doth the oracle at Delphi speak and conceal in riddles? How cameth night to be separated from day? What is the nature of sky and its signs? How were war and strife made? Of what is the thunderbolt hurled by Zeus? How do I bathe again in the same river? Whither shall I go?"

Somehow Bob Zimmerman figured it out. Hundreds, no thousands of kids in the early Sixties wanted to be guitar-wielding, songwriting saviors, hipsters in an Elvis or Woody or Joan Baez mode—but this dude went out and did it, simple as executing a pancake recipe. When he departed Hibbing, Minnesota, for Greenwich the Village, he was just another hitchhiking wannabe homeboy with a second-hand suitcase and an axe. Two months later he returned to Minnesota, the voice of his generation. And it wasn't as though he underwent some heavy-duty training or dramatic initiation in old New York. During his stint he hung around clubs, witnessed the scene, improved his skills, made himself a general pest. Then he declared, "I can do this" and went home and wrote songs that no one could touch.

When he landed back in the land of lakes, recalls Tony Glover, a fellow musician, "he was playing at some party or something, and it was like a whole different guy. You hear these stories about the bluesmen, and they go out to the crossroads and sell their souls to the Devil and come back able to do stuff ... that old mythology; it was one of those kinds of deals, almost. When he left Minneapolis, he was just average, you know. There were five, six other guys doing the same thing. When he came back, he was doing Woody, and he was doing Van Ronk, and he was finger-picking, he was playing crossharp. And this was a matter of a couple of months. I mean, this was not like he was gone a year or anything. It was a couple of months."

Dylan himself acknowledges these essentials: "That's when I went to the crossroads and made a big deal, you know like shewww, you know. One, one night, and then, uh, went back to Minneapolis, and it was like, 'Hey, uh, where's this guy been? You know, he's been to the crossroads.'"

He changed his personality; he changed his identity. He reinvented his history, laundering himself from a middle-class Midwestern Jewboy to an outlaw musician from New Mexico. Fellow Village-scene folksinger Tommy Clancy saw it happen: "In old Irish mythology they talk about the shape-changers.... He *changed* voices. He *changed* images. It wasn't necessary for him to be a definitive person. He was ... he was a receiver. He was ... he was possessed."

When his name morphed grandiosely from Zimmerman to Dylan, you might have thought the runt'd have no chance of making it stick ("... *don't speak too soon/for the wheel's still in spin....*"). Yet Dylan, not Zimmerman, is who he became, even as Cassius Clay became Ali. Both went the full fifteen rounds. No one nowadays questions rapper tags or shamanic trim. Metamorphoses have become tribal. We are allowed to throw off the ancestors and re-name ourselves.

"*And* [T. Clancy again] *he articulated what the rest of us wanted to ... but couldn't say.*"

"… wanted to … but couldn't." Refrains and lyrics, unimaginable beforehand, were drop-dead obvious once garnished in Dylan's voice. Simple rhymes with a quirk of inversion and bravura here and there became folk canons: *"Far from the twisted reach of crazy sorrow … /let me forget about today until tomorrow," "but I was so much older then…," "break just like a woman," "Ramona, come closer…," "'There must be some way out of here,'/said the joker to the thief."* Yes, he wrote and sang what *everyone wanted to write and sing,* a music every guitar-toting dude and his brother, every chick and her sister was on the verge of, yet somehow, for some reason, couldn't grasp; even after Dylan demonstrated A, B, C how it was done, because by then they were half in awe, half still resisting or—"Positively Fourth Street"—outright begrudging and cussing him. He read the vernacular and he read the metaphorical; he found the lost melody of his era and he caught the time's casual but portentous jive: *"… dimestores and bus stations,/people talking situations…."* The songs were *that available,* like plums on a low branch, and Dylan stepped over some invisible moat—trickster dangling on the brink of infinity—and said, "Folks, I think this here is what you're looking for."

It was caterpillar to butterfly—an overnight initiation in which the student takes the whole lesson from a teacher who doesn't even exist, and makes the communal quantum leap. His lyrics were daring, light; facile, passionate; flashy, matter-of-fact. He was John Keats strumming "Ode to a Nightingale," Dylan Thomas seething "Rage, rage, against the dying of the light," Ira Gershwin, and Chuck Berry, Upton Sinclair and Sherwood Anderson too. He was a cross between Woody Guthrie and Jack Kerouac, Jean-Paul Belmondo and Georgia O'Keefe.

In the early Sixties, most everyone in the Village crowd was political in a sort of idle left-wing, anti-war, procommunist way—

Van Ronk, Pete Seeger, Baez, even one-time Copa outsider Bobby Darin. But Dylan couldn't be bothered by allegiance to ideological fashion; he didn't *really* care about the politics behind his songs: "*'There's too much confusion,/I can't get no relief.'*" He was listening to a timeless and ultimately more radical reverie "*and a hard rain is a-gonna fall.*"

"We thought he was hopelessly naïve," Van Ronk mused later. "In retrospect, he was maybe a bit more sophisticated than we were."

"Hey, Woody," Dylan in effect called, "you don't just have to sing about working people and dustbowls and preachers and vigilante thugs. You don't even have to be pious or good. You can lay down cosmic buzz, capitalist trysts, pawnshop trinkets, misty mountains, '*everybody must get stoned,*' '*the handmade blade, the child's balloon,*' '*Spanish boots of Spanish leather,*' '*forever young,*' the whole freakin' universe. Add a little Broadway, a nip of Nashville, a scry of Elvis, a pinch of Scotland, a little post-Yid burlesque. Go exactly where you're riffing but hit everywhere and everything with it."

It was mediumship; it was poetry too—raw and improvised with the grit and ad-libs still hanging on: from "*Hold it, Doc, a World War passed through my brain*" to "*How many seas must a white dove sail…?*" to "*wiggle, wiggle, wiggle.*"

Dylan was also a conman and unrepentant liar, an appropriator (in Minnesota before he went to New York) of others' phonograph records, a master of fake insouciance, a lifter of songs and arrangements, for instance Van Ronk's "House of the Rising Sun." But he wasn't a mean-hearted or a selfish thief; he was more a jackdaw, a friendly bandito, the ultimate changeling and, as he told Van Ronk, after being requested by him *not* to record that one because *he* (VR) was about to: "Uh-oh." Because he had already done it. It wasn't about loyalty or propriety—things were way too far gone for that—it was about getting it done finally, so everyone could move on. "Uh-oh," for sure.

How does the sacred gangster get made, and how do any of us get made? And what is in the air, and what of it do we actually hear, and what do we know without being taught? How do we get in our own way and how do we soldier on through?

An artist has a unique capacity to remove the blocks, to become who s/he already is: "… *in the darkness of my night,/in the brightness of my day*…." I think you have to want it a lot (but not desperately, definitely not desperately). You have to want it the way one wants two and two wants three, merely and undeniably. You have to want it enough that it becomes ordinary, that what would be desperation in another person is nothing at all in you. Dylan wanted it so badly he did it.

At roughly the same cultural moment, Allen Ginsberg became the spokesman for his generation too. An advertising copyman who got bored with shilling products, he signed on as his own client. His jingles weren't the usual Madison Avenue tripe—they were the grandest, boldest words anyone was speaking then. They went from *"I have seen the best minds of our generation destroyed by madness*…." to *"Reborn forever as long as Men in Kansas or other universe*…." A one-time commercial hack became an internationally honored bard chanting Blake songs, crowned May Queen of Prague at the fall of communism.

The extravagance of ad copy and commodity never left Ginsberg, but he wrote blarney truth instead of blarney gibberish. It was advertising copy still, advertising copy forever, yet the best goddamn ads anyone ever composed—ads from the cosmos, ads that angels themselves might have penned from the debris of sorry mortals.

Ginzy was also a morally marginal pederast, a slippery apologist for his own seductions of boys and freelance debauchery. Even as a revered elder, he was a narcissist, hedonist, and carny vamp.

In the end it matters not a whit. If you sing, truly sing, you can get away with just about anything human.

In 1945 at the age of thirty-five, Charles Olson—a politician, a Roosevelt man, and highbrow academic historian—began writing poetry. The dropping of A-bombs on civilians at Hiroshima and Nagasaki at the same time as the discovery of stacks of bodies at Buchenwald convinced him that the progressivist, humanist experiment was over. The answer could only come from before the Greeks, beyond the zodiacal figurations of sky, at the scale of Titans—no Europe, no Asia. Rooting himself north of Boston in Gloucester, he set the Earth in the Galaxy, its long axis through the landscape of a Holocene fishing port. "Don't be fooled," he told an audience seventeen years later, "by the universalization of the present. The work, the real work, of the future, has already been done, and the future that is proposed for us is a lie."

Hankering no debt to post-modern clichés, Olson drank directly from the Sagas and the lost texts that preceded Norse and Phoenician eddas and Mayan runes. He scorched past what hard-working poets had been politely rehearsing for decades, reaching over those younger, more avant-garde, and even more articulate, and spoke gruffly, before anyone else could, "I, Maximus ..."

When the dean of the San Francisco poetry renaissance, Robert Duncan, first heard from this historian back east, he encouraged him to send his "amateur" attempts, expecting them to be the stumbles of a stiff man at a new calling. Instead they were proto-Hittite Homeric fragments: *"Hail and beware the dead who will talk life until you are blue/ in the face."* You don't have to understand the drift exactly; you can all but hear the echoes of Tartarus and the Cyclops, and Cro Magnon priests: *"And you will not understand what is wrong,/they will not be blue,/they will have tears in their eyes...."* Ordinary words, yes, but drop-dead syntax.

The truth is, despite this "winner-take-all"/"American Idol" society in which one clueless person is anointed spokesman or spokeswoman for the masses, we are in it together. We are all capable of great ballads. Paris Hilton is faintly echoing Paris and Helen—Britney Spears a lost Druid spriggan.

Some almost-Dylans and almost-Faulkners became drunken bums and street addicts. Some near-Ginsbergs ended up boozey whores and predators. Others became serial molesters, serial killers instead of serial poets. It's that close.

"I never knew exactly what was happening," confessed an older Ginsberg, "even when I was alive." And Dylan: *"The answer, my friend, is blowin' in the wind ..."*

When I look back at my early prose, it seems artificial, overwrought. I realize now that it has only ever been a matter of quieting my mind and getting out of my own way. That was awkwardly so in my first gambits of *Solar Journal* and *Book of the Cranberry Islands,* their moments of magic clotted with cautious, derivative posturing and elaborate imitations of fellow writers that I tried but was unable to disguise.

I was young; I was ugly; I didn't want it enough. I only half wanted it. I found it more convenient to bluff—though I certainly thought I wanted it as much as, say, Dylan did. I really only wanted a wife and a safe calling; I was fine with teaching in the boondocks.

I couldn't have hitchhiked from New York, "*... a complete unknown/with no direction known*," to some Navaho village to find my calling. I was scared shitless. Dylan wasn't; he was determined to put himself on the line, to get—"I was born far from where I was meant to be"—home. So, soon as he could, he headed for the crossroads with "*nothing, nothing to lose*."

I never had the freedom inside myself to be as brash and unfettered as Zimmerman, as unabashed and heathen as Ginsberg, but I do understand the crossroads; the gesture is at last familiar to me.

If you give yourself to everything that you adore and want to be, if you do it selflessly and with a generous heart and spirit, willing to embrace creation, risking all, even honor, even love, even happiness, certainly safety, then you get your songs for free, without any hoops to jump through, ranks to crash, elders to serve. You get there naked and forlorn. I admire this vocation. I think it is the only one.

There are two sequences of nouns in which English behaves like the Hopi punctual and segmentative "aspects," e.g. changing a manifestation of character through time and space or both by modification of a stem:

Vigil, a spiritual watch, turns compulsive, *Vigilant*. A *Vigilante* escalates his or her anxiety into an ideological crusade.

Despair, a plateau of mourning, gives rise to *Desperation*. A *Desperado* imposes his grief on others.

"Once you are born," proposes a Zen saying, "nothing can help you. Once nothing can help you, you are born."

If Superman inherited the collective wisdom of 280,000 or 2.8 million worlds, what of our one? Or was the point for him to learn those systems in order to enter our backwater world and apply their greater truths?

The imprint of all things on this planet as it gyres through space is a sound or sight: clouds piling up, clasping the global thermostat in their nebulae; infinitesimal shades of ocean, of chance, revealing differential chemistry and biochemistry, deviating herds and flocks, roar of traffic, the screams from man's factories and slaughterhouses: cacophony from the Great Flask.

If the thunders of all the waters and winds and life forms and metals could be heard simultaneously, it would be a din beyond imagination. If all the collective perceptions of every living creature, mites and insects, fish and mammals, could be fused into one emanation, it would be a light of devastating intelligence.

This is how the Earth howls and what it looks like in naked space, swishing visionary robes through the zodiac.

Chakras and lei lines stream downhill across galactic fields into vital worlds everywhere; all meridians come home to the single cry and tangle of existence.

A planet gives off a tone, a hue, a vibe, a meaning and cry, and those elsewhere in the creation hear it and feel it and know in an instant who and where we are and what must happen.

The Mendocino coastline—Pacific waves flushing its coves and disintegrating against gigantic rocks, cold fog and bare fields, fake modernity and pot farms and redneck drivers—is a landscape trapped between life and death: profound, advanced, and terrifying. By contrast, eastern Maine, lichen-covered and tattooed with cottages and moraine, is old and habitable.

It must be right, all of this—beauty, murder, madness, joy— because it is anything at all. However crude, it is made of the subtlest light, advancing toward the next apotheosis ... then the next.

It is what it is supposed to be. Anything we imagine in our wistfulness or idle speculation, whether utopian or progressive or biblical, would not get us there, would take us nowhere. That is why we are here, in the shit-hole.

At three years old I heard doom on my Nanny's radio. I was playing on the kitchen floor; she was standing over pots on the stove. I was in a daydream reverie. Then suddenly the words, unmistakable and malign, went splattering across the world: "... *down the dungeon stairs, into the darkness forever.*" I heard it and was stunned, a child's simple consideration of what it meant. I felt my mind balk, the universe come apart. A bottomless abyss shattered any artifice or façade.

I understood my situation. The feeling was something like: *this is real in a way that nothing has ever been before, and I am in it, forever.*

That smudge on the horizon was not just a suspicious inkling but exactly what it looked like.

I ran into the hallway and, finding no way out—no other condition or world—I stood there in terror. Vertigo took over, tossing me back to the beginning of time itself. I knew it was over, had always been over.

It was futile to think I could outrun it merely by being alive, a boy. Sure, I could pretend to be safe in a family, but that camouflage didn't protect me. "They" could come at will from where they had always been, put an end to such paltry means.

The adults, not knowing the cause of my fright—not that it would have made any difference if they had—at first yelled at me to stop and then tried to console me. They were rote and irrelevant.

I began to shudder, the throes turning into sensations that I didn't even know existed. I kept picturing the dungeon, the stone stairs leading down, a shadowy figure at the top. I was frantic. I began to scream. That got the idea across, more or less. I was tucked into bed in a straitjacket of sheets and blankets and they put Vick's Vapo-Rub on my chest. Its camphor was both reassuring and sinister, imbuing me with fumes, slowing me back into the sad, dense world. I lay there, comforted by the aroma and the covers, sobbing as my body sank into dirge. I gave up. No point in fighting, I might as well relent. I fell asleep. Eons later I awoke. But the hangover would last the rest of my life.

Most people would have mocked the theatricality of the voice: dramaturgy of little consequence. A different kid might have thought, "Wow, that was scary!" and writhed in delight.

Not this three-year-old! I heard an omen pretending not to be an omen; a ruse to win my compliance under a tactic of spooky entertainment. And I knew I was not going to allow them to trick me in that way again.

The voice expressed something I had always dreaded without knowing. It was not the dungeon *per se*, which was like other threats on television and at the theater. I had seen Peter Pan and Flash Gordon. I knew about evil vicars, wicked pirates, Ming the Merciless. I read horror comics, Grimm's fairytales. Those were make-believe—this was real.

There was an authority behind the voice that neither its hack author nor grandiose narrator recognized: a prophecy seeping into a vague room in an obscure city, a witch cooking poison while her chattle waited and obeyed, waited and obeyed.

The radio woke me from a sleep deeper than my life.

Children go to horror movies all the time to experience *"down the dungeon stairs into the darkness forever."* They even declare how they *love* being frightened. They practice bravado and artificial courage. They pretend that the good guys—Hopalong Cassidy, Tarzan, the Fairy Godmother—rule the universe, arrive always in the nick of time. They don't recognize ghoul and slasher deeds for what they are. Heedless and stupid, they don't understand how vapid, how brief their solace.

Beyond the borders of candyland, of fun-and-gamesville where they intend to hang out forever, protected by the distracted elders, is a warning. If they truly heard it, they would not recover so easily. They would not flaunt it or toy with arousing ogres.

Because the actual peril is so great, they have to caricature it to refute it. They comfort themselves, lampooning unimaginable deeds as if they were "camp," which is putting a ridiculous amount of faith in the notion that the composers of horror stories are benign instead of in the service, perhaps knowingly (likely unknowingly) of the darkness itself.

Victims of sexual predators and murderers learn all too soon that those in costumes are not all actors, that anathema does not stay forever mannered or go "Boo!" Children in Nazi concentration camps couldn't leave after the movie. There was no reprieve from jailers and executioners. Hitler's minions may not have tossed people into dungeons, but they came as antipathetic guards, fake "doctors," wardens of gas chambers. The doomed heard the voice, and it spoke German. Boys and girls were alone in the universe, at the mercy of captors who were neither human nor within the range of diplomacy or petition.

The radio posed a primordial and metaphysical problem to my nascent consciousness, one that I had little notion of how to resolve. I struggled with it all through grade school and adolescence—the voice behind the voice, the threat from outside meaning, the tumble down some other stairs into a far more final dungeon—the ultimate oblivion and dismemberment.

Three years later, a cataract of overly white water pummeled the porcelain of the tub as I was being undressed for my bath. I tore from the room half-naked down the hall. It had looked like an ocean, a cancer in which I was to be drowned. More than an ocean, it was a whirlpool of acids, of cripples and blind men, of letters without an alphabet, like the shower of needles into which the Mongos forced a frantically struggling Flash Gordon.

The real crisis could not be articulated; it had no symbols to mediate it, to get it safely into the world. It represented what I knew beyond words—though, once language held it, it was words to which I returned over the years for a confirmation of the terrible thing that was going to happen … the original dungeon, the true "down the stairs, forever."

After all, if words didn't mean exactly what they said, why did they exist? What else could they mean, except something even more terrible for which there *are no words?*

I couldn't evade one hideous interpretation of the dungeon: it was about malevolent forces' final, lasting victory over good and kind ones. This is a thugs' universe, and they own us because bad is fiercer than good. Consider the "real" dungeons—jails, torture chambers, death camps. *And there is no other universe.*

Just look at the ordinary behavior of locusts and hawks. Or gangs in prisons, bartering the weak like cigarettes. Or Thai villagers selling their daughters into brothels. Or rebels recruiting children into militias at gunpoint, after killing their parents and raping their sisters. You think that voice at the dungeon stairs isn't real?

Not only is life under a grim, insatiable force, but every other possibility is even worse.

I found no solace except to do other things and increase my overall capacity for survival here. So I lived, more or less, like everyone else.

Gradually the event's impact wore off. Yet the effect, as I said, was permanent: a gauze over everything. I remained vigilant. I eventually took a calling. I found a partner. I made a family.

Over time, I came to understand that having a punishing and cold mother gave the radio voice a measure of legitimacy. The portent may have been far more menacing than she could ever be, but it somehow felt like her, was associated with her domain.

The Mother *is* the Universe, certainly to a child. The ambush might not have nailed me so acutely if, in her stead, there had been a parent who was reliable, who at least liked and protected me, who hugged me instead of getting angry or going for blankets and Vick's Vapo-Rub. Such a one would have changed the rules of engagement. I might have been trained for cosmic battle before I was asked to fight. I might have been prepared for the world's searing beauty before being shown its dazzling glare and heart of darkness. I might have been taught honor and magic, given a kiai for breaking spells. I might have been allowed to become conscious before my consciousness was shattered.

There *are* symbols, chants, mantras with power equal to any hex.

But when the elders don't take horror seriously, they don't mollify the demons that break the minds of children, they don't teach us ways to soothe ourselves, to make us laugh, to sail us into restful sleep with Wynken and Blynken, nursery-rhyme figurations of our own bodies among okay stars and a friendly moon—"a wee one's trundle-bed." They don't initiate us into the protection of the totem or the lodge of elders; they don't encourage us to seek a guardian animal. Aliens instead wait outside our courtyard window, to scoop us off in rockets to their machinations. And when the elders taunt and frighten, when they *try* to make children afraid, the line between monsters and parents is crossed in a profound and traumatic way.

When there is no shared burden, no pact to protect each other—no nets of silver and gold or snug wooden shoe or singing Mom—parenthood becomes pretext. And this is even when there is no flagrant abuse.

I was robbed of something precious, something every mammal needs for survival—I gradually came to understand that.

My mother's suicide, plunging with a pillowcase over her head from a sixteen-story window twenty-seven years later onto lower Park Avenue, made my childhood ring true in a whole different way. Its long latency was over, and I could see who had been my keeper. My brother's stabbing himself to death thirty years later spoke volumes to our clan malady. I consider that my susceptibility to Nanny's radio was partly a response to deeds beyond memory, parental neglect more than hoodlums at large. The domain before language for me was not Nazi molestation but a confrontation at birth with Medusa herself, a merciless hag who meant to seduce her children into her order of malevolence, a tormentor who was going to make us torment ourselves and others—who was going to lead us to the fatal staircase, again and again, forever, until we walked down it of our own accord.

I now see what happened, not explicitly but at a slight angle because no one can look at an absolute. The moment the voice spoke of the dungeon I experienced a recognition at the border of consciousness, a recognition *of consciousness itself*, its presence like a wave swelling over an unformed ego. This recognition was intrinsic or became intrinsic. Not every person would have allowed it to happen, except I didn't allow it. It was there before I knew what it was. Then I *knew* what it was, what consciousness was, way too early. It was unrescindable, located in my memory as I grew.

As to where the recognition came from, I don't actually know. Either it was innate and in some fashion defines my being, or, like the worm milk of *Dune*, entered from my mother's bloodstream, crossing the barrier between her psyche and mine to meld with existence.

Though I don't feel the initial shock of the radio voice any longer, it carries a dull pang, a conviction that it is always right, that I have encountered nothing since with such primal and authentic power. I may be older and wiser, but I can't be older and wiser than it. Its subpoena, like my mother—her eternal "no"— is the stuff of which the world is woven.

I was a child of the dark goddess, the unseen real. I had to develop an antidote or be overcome by her talisman.

Only recently, nearly sixty years later, have I begun to rethink the dungeon voice.

Riding my bike home from work covers three and a half miles, the last one and a half uphill, so I am exhausted at the final push. Catching my breath as the stitches in my side subside, I set the bike in the garage and troop up the pitch-black stairs into the kitchen. The passage from the basement is euphoric, though I have to be alert to punch in the code before walking past the motion detector or I will trigger screeching and a call from Sentry Alert for my password.

Yesterday, climbing the dark corridor from the dungeon, I realized that there always was an alternative. It is not as strong as The Thing, and it certainly is in language. But it did remind me that we can fight back and perhaps even save the universe—or at least gain tolerable lives for ourselves. I told myself that it was all in our hands, as I allowed an equally bottomless cosmic joy. A triumphant, goofy smile disclosed a part of me that had always been safe, cheerful, and defiant, as I whispered: "Up the stairs, into the light forever."

Computers are the epitome of banality. Not that they aren't useful (hell, they *define* "useful"!), but they have taken literalness and obdurate platitude to a new level. It is like being trapped inside a chess game while pretending you aren't playing chess.

The early twentieth-century Russian philosopher P. D. Ouspensky proposed that we use *all* machines at our peril, because for every external convenience and conveyance we gain, we cede an internal one, something we need in our psyche or soul. Exteriorizing transportation, manufacture, calculation, even meals; allowing ourselves to be entertained and mesmerized by photokinetic semblances of real events, we forfeit our depth and memory and surrender our power to metals, plastics, artificial rays, and synthetic carbons. The price exacted ultimately outweighs any temporary boons. And yet computers store and access esoteric wisdom; planes fly lamas to sites that would never witness the dharma otherwise.

Machine reality is an issue to be resolved across tens of thousands or even millions of years. In the end we will have to give up this technology to become what we are. We will have to pray, for real. We will have to befriend the cold and dark, the inconvenience of things—plain old things—and make ourselves open to transubstantiation, to the true meaning of being flesh and blood in a place of rocks, barriers, and rugged edges.

Back in the mid-Seventies when I taught at Goddard College in Vermont, the Marxist anarchist philosopher Murray Bookchin was on the faculty. One of the first eco-activists, he started the Social Ecology program there. A gruff, old-fashioned New York intellectual, Murray liked to advance radical communal lifestyles and utopian societies, while continuing to live and eat in retro ways and argue combatively at the drop of a hat. One evening during a party at our house, I overheard him regaling a circle of students with a proposition he called "California dumb."

"What's that, Murray?" I asked, joining the group.

"'California dumb' is: you just invented it yesterday, nobody ever thought of it before, and it's going to save the world."

I nodded, then added playfully, "By that token you're 'New York dumb.'"

The students glanced uneasily back and forth at us.

"What's that?" he finally barked.

"You think you just have to say it and write about it; you don't have to do it."

"Then I'm 'New York dumb' and proud of it."

Second Cycle

Three Meditations on Grief and Bitterness

1.

I can't help feeling that the damage done to me and my brother and sister opened us to a complex sensibility, a vision-quest that could not have unfolded in any other way. Our mother was a defrocked shaman, her wings broken by her enemies in another place, another time. She was given a body, sentenced to be born again.

The universe is a zone of damage, and I have come to wonder if, in fact, that is the point: not *doing* damage but using "symbolic" damage to redeem a deed far more ancient than we can imagine, to heal a gash that was made in something more real than this molecular landscape.

Grief begins at the core of the deepest happiness; in fact grief is the only bliss that is not a fragile mood or contrivance, that can be trusted to last. Unless we live among predators, as both predator and prey, eater and eaten, unless we travel in heartbreak and remorse, we will never understand how to journey across the true desert, the mottled void that is consciousness, and find our true home.

Every devious torture enacted on me in childhood, though irreparable, has tended to find a resolution in an exquisite image or insight.

Pir Zia: "Pain may be the most compelling song of invitation in the divine repertoire. An open wound is an aperture between the outer and the inner."

2.

The thing I was in childhood—drab, gloomy landscapes; raindrops finding random paths down dirty windows; eternal melancholy in all directions—is how what I am now feels like underneath. It is no longer my daily imperative, my involition, but it gives my life breadth and meaning.

Yes, it is irredeemable and morose, but it is emotionally real and confers texture and joy on the world.

3.

As a boy I loved to suck flavored charms and guzzle bright-colored ades. I didn't know that their rainbows were fraudulent, but I suspected that they "weren't good for you," as my mother habitually warned. After a while sugars burned the tip of my tongue and deadened the roof of my mouth; their tang faded, and attempts to restore it by puckered lips and palate only disappointed.

Tansy and thistle, mullein and burdock root are bitter tastes I cultivate and crave. They do not vitiate, they restore. They go beyond taste buds into cells and organs. Without corn syrup or artificial sucrose, cranberry and grapefruit seed enhance not only metabolism but thought. Neither sweet nor sour, in fact irrelevant to such a distinction, they are rendered shallow, even repugnant, by sweetening.

Three Meditations on Dreaming

1.

Dreams are never dreamed by accident. The brain replicates ontological existence. We are creatively fooled into participating in reenergized fragments of who we are and what we are, whatever we can't or won't let ourselves know. We experience the forerunners of all that unconsciousness holds in store for us, in a form that is bearable. Without dreams, waking life doesn't happen.

2.

Freud had dreams about 85% right: they are libidinal vestiges, wish fulfillments converted by sublimation, introjection, and condensation into brief hallucinatory discharges experienced as real while they are firing.

Dreams are all that the universe is bringing into being that may not initially be bearable or is too amorphous and primitive to jell. Their labyrinths are designed to guard sweet sleep, to keep the dreamer unconscious and enchanted. Using strings of symbolic logic, they exalt contents that have fallen into or arisen from depths, wrapping them in forms in which the conscious mind can tolerate and engage them (although sometimes even those regalia are too graphic, so turn into nightmares).

One big piece that eluded Freud was recognized by Jung— dreams carry not just personal contents but everything lodged in our cosmic memory: the transpersonal artifacts of atoms, cells, species, and cultures. What transcends our egos also precedes our individual existences.

The unconscious is a paradoxical notion anyway. If something is not conscious, then it shouldn't exist. If it does, it should have as little relevance or relationship to us as a snowflake falling on a moon in the Orion system. Yet unconscious forms obviously do exist. They not only exist, but they cast a deeper shadow over consciousness than consciousness itself. They are not only everything that we have forgotten, but everything that is lodged in our being and psyche below a threshold of activation—by anything, anything at all. The unconscious is vestigial, phylogenetic, *and* ontological.

There is another piece: dreams are complete bardo realms in themselves, equivalent to life. Lives, conversely, are imaginal constructs, long dreams. Agencies of transference flow both ways, between waking and dreams, between internal and external landscapes. It is not so much that dreams are life epitomes as that both dreams and lives are tropes through which bursts and distortions of energy (desires) pass under exigencies of a central ganglion and trunk-lines. All of this traffic charms the dreamer/lifer across legendary kingdoms of illusion.

3.

That we have lucid dreams betrays the depth of this world. What is inside us continues to create realities, integrally and unconsciously. This is true when we are awake too, but dreaming demonstrates its commutability.

A dream is an exercise in how we are put together, whereby our affairs are internalized, their pain and surplus leached. They show us our real depth and what is being done whether we know it or not or want it or not. Dreams are our actual wishes and desires, the sole experiences we *cannot not* have. They absolve us and make us day-ready. Even a leopard must dream.

What Freud discovered and mapped is also his blind spot. Dreams are not subsidiary to reality. They are artifacts, albeit fragmentary ones, of a higher reality, synopsizing and condensing and pointing toward source.

When I dream of flying, using previously unsuspected leverage in my arms to alight, aeronautics is easy, like something forgotten or merely overlooked. I *know* I can fly; I could *always* fly. It is just a matter of ratcheting myself up a bit off the ground and then levitating. I ease myself up an invisible staircase, a step at a time, until I am sure I can do it. From there I climb precipitously, float above trees and houses, ascending ten, twenty, thirty feet. Once I am fully confident of the method, I propel across the sky. I soar above the city. I do not fall and do not expect to fall.

The dream knows what I no longer know.

Colors are not words. There is no reason why they should mean anything. But they do. Phonemes of photons, they zip at 186,000 thousand miles a tick.

Yellow is my favorite, but what is yellow? Handmaiden to white, it is a slight tarnish of pure light. Take away a bit of white's absolute luminosity, and what remains is yellow—sunlike, golden as a crown, buttercups in a field, marsh marigolds, a finch's wing, a plastic flute. The two reasons that yellow exists are: 1) white is too brilliant to be seen, so yellow is its filter, its costume, revealing that pure light has not only brightness but emotional resonance and depth; 2) yellow is what happens when the complication of a world intercepts the pure output of a nearby star; witness the daily sunset, a clash and fusion of wavelengths at the world's horizon.

Blue is my second favorite—sky as prism, water when it is translucent. Azure, cyan—blue is often inedible. Its degrees toward sunset—magenta, violet, mauve—are harmonics of creationary energy. But blue is simply yellow's antipode, what is reflected when yellow is at the core. Water is actually yellow; sun blue.

Green is botanical, photosynthetic, transformation of yellow through blue into algae and vines—rainforest and shamrock, Eastern Woodlands and kale.

Red is a stream of knowledge—iron and blood, bird belly and Chinese flag. It is the cushion in the queen's chamber, the carpet of war, a vermillion pillow case, a barn, a fire engine, to-matoes on a vine.

Three Riddles about Infinity

1. Physicists "solving" quantum equations by alternate universes have proposed that every time a new physical possibility is explored, the universe splits at that junction, much as "superposition" states of subatomic particles have simultaneous "up" and "down" spins, or appear to be in different places at the same time.

Insofar as there is an infinite number of possible alternative outcomes, each one gets played out, in its own universe. For instance, a motorist who manages to pull his car out of a spin just before it crosses the center strip into oncoming traffic might feel relieved at his narrow escape. In a parallel universe another version of that driver will have been killed. In yet another universe he will be rushed to the hospital and recover after weeks of treatment. The count of alternative scenarios is not only endless but endlessly branching off into new ones, mathematically following a map created by matter itself, as Julia and Mandelbrot sets radiate out of one another to form a humungous cosmic bush of universes.

Only parallel versions of events splitting off from themselves can account for the probabilistic nature of quantum law.

2. Where does that crumb of bread I toss aside go? Will a bacterium digest it? Or will it just disintegrate and join the nameless soot? Do I encounter its molecules again? Whence goes its breadedness?

I am overwhelmed by possibility, as I pick out and follow a speck, or watch a feather descend and rise in the air. What is patrolling and protecting the universe? Where is the sentinel, the chaperone? Who mourns or inters each mouse and wren?

A scrap of sticky paper captured by my bike tire and worn off several days later—at what precise point in the road did I acquire it? How did the rotation of my wheel in seamless circumferences meet gradients of wind, water, and stone to deposit the scrap such that it adhered to the rotating rubber? Where did I distribute it in subsequent revolutions? What became of its disheveled whole?

A parallel and damnable concern: Is it true that in eternal time of universe after universe everything must eventually happen, some vehicle must pick up and consign every imaginable scrap at every conceivable angle from all different sizes and shapes of objects on all worlds?

What a lot of stuff in every version and variation, every possible alignment and sequence! You'd have to run each single event over again, changing minute factors, one by one—and then every event arising from each of those re-runs. You'd have to generate every potential result, however one-in-a-trillion absurd.

Every photograph would have to be taken with slightly different framing and focus, snapped again and again and again. Every piece and pattern of dust and pollen in the air on every world would have to form every array and pattern.

Just as an American President with the name of my high-school history teacher, William Clinton, took office during my lifetime, so would there have to be a President with each of my other teachers' names, and a Vice-President too, and one with all of my classmates' names, and one with every other name, and possible name, in every country, and so on. You'd have to elect George J. W. Bush and George Q. Bush, etc.

Every wave on every shore on every planet would have to crash again with foam and particles in a slightly different array and salinity, and then a slightly different array from that, until every possibility and subset of every possibility had been rendered.

That would have to be true of every body of water, every field of flowers, and all of them in relation to all others in every different combination, not only on this world but all worlds in shifting tandems. Every vat of rice or quinoa or extraterrestrial seed would have to vary as to each of its grain's fractional and fractal position, size, and micro-shape and the relative size and relation of their container to its axis. The same would have to be true of grains of sand on every beach among the many worlds.

Even in a quantum universe, that is not only inconceivable but *de toute l'impossibilité*.

Yet there are those maddeningly inept monkeys at keyboards in our minds, not even trying to type the whole of Shakespeare, nonetheless bound to the task until they accomplish it. And "forever" is a long time.

Unsupervised infinity is the ultimate obsessive-compulsive disorder, both sterile and absurd.

How will this dilemma get resolved, will any of this get changed into something else except by the collapse of the universe itself?

But in "forever" the universe could endlessly self-destruct and recreate itself from scratch at some future time, after intervening universes, with variations, or not.

3. I do not think the universe has to bubble through an eternity of every lot being drawn, every token called, every possible event and variant elapsing somewhere. It is not infinite or eternal in that sense. It is infinite in its intrinsic expression, which looks to us on its quoin (with our flimsy equipment) sometimes like the other kind of infinity. Both are beyond our imagination—the former quantitatively, the latter qualitatively.

Every molecule in the universe is doing something, reacting to its existence and position, all of them simultaneously—and, even if this interpretation is mechanistic and tyrannical, it is tolerable.

Or, put otherwise, the opposite—complete freedom—is intolerable, yielding a universe of swarming dust in clouds larger than galaxies.

If the cosmic machine is meticulous and uncompromising, then it is accountable; it has some basis—and we, the one seeming anomaly, the usurper of entropy known as life, have a seat in its operation.

Consciousness must be as precisioned as atomicity, as flawless as a collie moon shepherding grime into Saturnian rings.

It is devastating to imagine how many molecules every motion we make sets into further motion, let alone all the molecules activated by creatures on the myriad worlds, plus all those moved by stars and turbulent gas giants. Yet there is a saving grace: every one of them is sewn gravitationally to every other. They make up a whole that, in its unity, is undulating and evolving.

As overwhelming and irreconcilable as the destiny of particles might be, it is encouraging that they comprise an open system.

Anything stuck in place, unable to escape its own identity, would be truly damned.

What pessimism misses is the fact that life is going somewhere.

The loudest sound I do not hear is that of my own speech. While I focus on the thoughts behind my voice, a noise resonating inside me is being put into the room—squeezed out of my lungs, puffed through a conduit as nerve-impregnated as a river eel. Its meaning is driven by my heart through my lungs, wind pipe, and throat; its gusts are carved by my lips, tongue, palate, and teeth into Indo-European phonemes, as brain-distilled meanings pulse through my cells.

Horns and woodwinds replicate and distort this anatomy into types of music.

My own voice is an electronic speaker; yet it is strangely mute because I am so used to hearing it.

A dog barking is a cellular megaphone, an amplified biology shot into the landscape—from hormones of frustration, from synapses of rage, from plain old canine reality, the incomprehensible prison of body being.

Whenever one's own voice is noticed, it is hard to speak or think. One cannot participate in a conversation in which oneself is a conversant. The sound of self is hollow. It performs a flat meaningless parody like the reverberation of an overseas phone connection.

To ourselves we are *always* gratuitous.

Three Animals

Dogs are social beings who regard the appearance of a canine interloper as possibility. Two tails wag, and heads lock into conversation, even if the exchange is:

"Hi, Mr. Fuck You!"

"Yeah, hi Mr. Fuck You too!"

Fights are gladiatorial more than raptorial.

Cats, on the other hand, do not tolerate feline mirrors. They have no use for their kind. Sublimely territorial, they view every feline transient as an intruder. Their response is approximately: "Who the bejeebers are you? Die, will you!" They see no possibility in encounter, except when drawn there by the goddess of desire.

I read in the paper this morning that the groundhog is an especially nasty and pugnacious animal. A zoo-man whose job it is to train these guys to act cute for Groundhog Day commented on how difficult it is to get them to play the part.

"Their aggression is unreal," he told his interviewer. "The bastards wake up in a bad mood. From the moment their eyes are open, and probably a bit before, their attitude is: kill it all and let God sort it out."

Dialogue with a Neighborhood Raccoon (raccoon speaks first)

"Why do you give vittles to those scrawny, sneaking felines when you could be feeding a magnificent stealthy creature like me? How do they gain the privilege of your caves while I, so much more stylish and godlike, with my cosmic striping and t'ai chi fluidity, am forced to quarter in drainpipes and culverts? Why do you tithe to them like royalty while I must scavenge your garbage and mulch piles for my scraps? You shoo me off, while you protect those arrogant, quarrelsome sissies!"

"We think they're cute."

"Cute! They're nothing but con artists and whining hams."

"Well, they have us over a barrel. We've been parleying with them since Egypt, before your Raccoon Clans sent their delegates to our councils."

"Are you going to hold our Turtle Island lineage against us? We could have evolved in Libya or Italy, you know. If we were native Euros, you'd respect us. We'd be way ahead of those glorified civets. Egyptians and Celts would have bred us into their most intelligent campfire pets; we'd be show animals by now.

Instead, the Eastern tribes cut us into totems, smoked pipes with our astral beings, hunted our beautiful bodies. Their descendants abandoned us and the sweat lodge and ceremony itself. Now we are homeless junkies, roadkill for crows."

Three Cats

The cat is counting. It feigns sleep in the sun, as humans move about its position, altering the objects that make up its context. It will only allow so much of that. "That's one. That's two."

The cat seems barely to be attending, but it notes exactly where the pawns are, how the chessboard is playing out. It knows what its threshold is.* The humans think they are getting away with their intrusions, but the cat is thinking, "That's three. On six I'm out of here."

Animals are by force of nature content to be what they are.

The cat, after sleeping all day, wakes and finds itself still a cat. It walks off in its cat body to do cat things.

For cats the great existential question is: How did they get all the catfood? And why them?

I mean by smell and movement we're animals too, and we show no sign of doing the work or having the talent to produce that much kill.

*Of course, we play the same game with each other, using more abstract gestures, more devious rules.

The summer of '65 Lindy and I lived in a cabin in Aspen. We lit fires of crumpled newspaper and kindling in an old woodstove to get the place warm enough to rise from the covers, when we barely knew each other, forty-one years ago. The aroma of that wood, the smell of bacon and coffee, the Roaring Fork River will never go away, because we made something of it: we made this life and raised a family.

But it wouldn't go away for other reasons if we hadn't, if we had drifted apart. Romantic loss and romantic gain hold us forever in their spell, probably longer.

We know each other so much better now than we did then, but in another sense we knew everything then, and that's why we married and had children and live in a pool of shared memories.

All of it is real, as none of it is real.

Creation is a mammoth affair spread over many venues and taking a huge amount of time. It is a chance for nothing to get somewhere and everything to get somewhere.

No scientific explanation is complete because all derive from facts under duress. Axioms are excuses, rigged arrays, didactic parables.

Stone Age philosophers understood profoundly what physicists with cyclotrons fail to grasp—life is an awakening, world is magic.

Even a fish or a badger has an inkling of cosmic truth.

Why most of us are infidels is beyond me, except that that must be part of the journey, to keep us going, kingdom to kingdom, dimension after dimension.

Throughout the universe all manner of species know crucial facts about what *this is*. If their perceptions could be gathered together and organized into an intergalactic physics and biology, we'd have something approximating true science.

Life is the same daily activities night and day, day after day, on this jinni's orb under gravity's charm. Most people want to be in bodies, tenaciously so. However, the coronation does wear thin with age. One tires of it because stuff never really changes. What goes around comes around. Even if we had eternity to be here, eternity would be the same. It is terrifying to die, but also terrifying to live.

Eternal life would be eternal death.

Dying may be our greatest and most successful trick. It is our ace in the hole, our guarantee of escape from a life sentence, as wonderful in its way as getting born. It is our only way out, our only way to consolidate karma and reduce it to its bare essentials. It is how we keep our core from gathering so much moss that we no longer exist. It is how we regain our ground. It is how we simplify things so as to become really real in the end. We vamoose like a great trickster mage. And no one can find us, not even ourselves.

As I grow older, I become more suspicious of life's status as the single go-round, the one story. If this is but a flicker of radiance amid the eternity of darkness, a single awakening from Socrates' dreamless sleep, why is it happening now? Who is dreaming?

It is not just sour grapes at using up my allotment here. I have been working on death since the day I was born—life has forever been a stream that cannot be entered more than once. Sure, I wouldn't mind being sixteen again, April love ahead of me. I wouldn't mind joining the ranks of those who must resolve this "fossil fuel/global warming/terrorism" quandary—my grandchildren and their children and grandchildren—because it is shaping up to be one hell of a century or two.

Yet for the first time I have a bit of hesitant excitement and curiosity about the end, about what is next, what the universe is. Death has been hanging around my whole life, giving it context and meaning. I am preparing to be bounced where the fates will bounce me, depending on what—other than nothing—I am.

The 9.5 years that it will take a spacecraft to bust out of Earth's gravity well and be slingshot by gas giants to Pluto, out at the edge of the Kuiper Belt, must be measured against an event barely the size of a ball-bearing out of which the *entire universe* detonated once into a state so protracted and sticky it continues to fulminate and distend.

If the engineers had delayed in launching their craft, Pluto and its companion Charon might have gotten so far away that Earthlings could not hail them in their lifetimes. It is already a remote orb, the only so-defined dwarf-planet/moon not visited by automated craft in the last quarter century.

Space and time are provisional. They exist nowhere. Consciousness, the measure and mirror of all things, obeys entropic prerequisites within space-time, but it views the Big Bang from timeless space and spaceless time.*

Clanging as a bell in Original Mind, the Cosmic Thud is an echo of something else, postered on the wall of creation, world by world. It is not creation or the skin of the cosmos. It is a false

---

*A note to artificial-intelligence mavens: you know damn well there is zero congruence between a holograph/scan of the brain and the subjective experience of being/identity.

bottom. Fine organisms within the explosion, within the mathematics of their nervous systems—crickets and crabs—develop relationships that propose, without acknowledging, the evanescent in the elephantine.

Life on Earth inhabits but a skin around a mantle that contains more than 90% of the planet, itself congealed around a bubbling nickel-iron core, a dollop of original solar pudding.

The Moon incorporates a substantial whorl of the virginal dust and minerals in Earth's primal orbit. Jupiter, thousands of times larger than Luna, has vacuumed the junk in its path around a relatively tiny rock, using gravity—nothing more sophisticated than rolling a snowball or suction-sweeping tool back and forth over a track—to make a gigantic methane magnet. But even a planet as chubby as Jupiter falls well short of the hydrogenous bulge of the Sun and its amigo stars. Those objects can burn their own bodies for billions of years, and they stretch seemingly forever across the majesty of their own girth, yet are tiny pinpoints in night. This speaks to the enormity against which we are smashed, the cavernous field of our existentiality.

Consciousness, while intangible, is as profound as the ocean or starry night, immense as the universe itself, for it is the glaze in which the hubbub reflects. It is how matter discloses its character by illuminating from within. As I have written elsewhere, embryos are the medium whereby the universe inscribes itself on its own body—through which it expresses its esoteric nature and provides a clue to its origin. Embryogenesis is what the universe knows how to do, intrinsically and lineally, without instruction or prompt, sans blueprint, lacking any explicit agency or extrinsic quality control. As molecules and cells knit and aggregate into sheets around cavities, holograms develop idiosyncratically, phylum by phylum, planet by planet. They repercuss the underlying fabric and re-kindle its projection. Honoring local thermodynamics, they manage to defy entropy and propose hypersphere and tesseract.

The textures, the tangled complexity challenge us to turn their very vastness and turbulence inside-out, in cultural acts, as proof that the parcels the universe has sponsored are its own children. We must adorn the skin of the cosmos even as tribal artisans embossed wandering daemons from night's canopy onto caribou hide—first texts—to generate meaning itself.

Our basis is completely mysterious—don't try to tell me that the impetus holding fetal phases together, gluing tissues into functional sheets, transmuting meridians into metabolic series and fractal organ fields, sage to each lineage and life form, is mere DNA flow, valence, and shear force twirling randomly under gravity and heat. There is a template, somewhere. Beyond thermodynamics, an esoteric intelligence is mirroring, lasering two and three dimensions back and forth through one another until crystals cake into banks of nerves.

Doth a ghost dwell inside the living machine? Absolutely.

From the homunculus of the fertilized zygote through the chrysalis of the blastula, cosmic energy is sucked onto this frequency. Each layered folio of complex carbon, each involution and synaptic synchrony of thickening strata of carbons, each gastrulation of multi-cell regalias cloning more layers and new exteriors, each fractal impaction, each differentiation of what is already integralized, is a deepening of the carbuncle whereby phenomenology is wrapped into a mummy-like figurine in a blue-oceaned luminous world.

There is no other train schedule, guys.

The DNA/cellular matrix is either cosmic script with local dialects or a dialect of some greater cosmic language. No one holds the pen that darns its trajectory, nothing programs the rapid needle of its ink and autograph. So when I said "inscribes itself," I meant not only finned marine pods and shaggy, tail-wagging mutts but an embryogenic blueprint whereby those frescos are daubed, anointed, and robed with the integrity of a master copyist billions of time a day.

Before the middle of the last century the Indo-European mystic George Ivanovitch Gurdjieff proposed that the role of humans is to convert molecules to consciousness, to raise raw untutored elements, which in this dimension originate in the cores of stars, to subtle states and, by that process, accelerate our own and creation's evolution.

Hidden within the extant landscape, G. taught, is a transaction whereby stuff molecularizes solely to be converted up the ladder from sub- to super-conscious awareness. This is as axiomatic for stray hydrogen and nitrogen atoms as for Greek philosophers and sea "mammals" in the Aldebaran system. To this end, the universe needs dumb rock and predatory fish as much as it needs the yogi and the Christ. Its entelechy is matter, matter and *work*.

Exquisitely ontological threads of being underlie even dust-devils raging down empty corridors.

Love, humility, and bravery, when practiced consciously and sincerely, are incised on something far more indelible than cells or caribou hide, yet paradoxically only insofar as we be constituted of molecules and cells. The way out of this stew is to live and change our essence, literally to metamorphose our own juices into sublime nectars.

Just as dreams comprise the figments and debris of waking life, so is life composed of the residue of other lives, albeit in subtler, more cryptic packages. We do not perceive our past lives because they have been rendered pellucid so that this life can be conducted through them without interference.

What good would any of this be—this world, this embodiment—if it weren't consummate and final, a chance at ultimate rapture, ultimate loss?

No life would make sense or seem real if other lifetimes were equally vivid and accessible while it happened. We need to be each place fully and undividedly. When we are here, there is no place else and no thing else, and never was.

So we don't get to postpone issues for other lifetimes or transfer urgent concerns to future bodies. Life and death have to be *life and death* to us, to every wildebeest fleeing, every tiger in pursuit. Otherwise, there is no point.

Search not for memory bridges; you will not find them. If there are transfer stations, we will arrive at them soon enough. But, for all intents and purposes, this journey in fog is it.

God will not allow us to break his spell. God, that sorry personification/projection of human authority onto unknown design, is the collective intelligence from which our individual existences are rent. If God were not perfectly camouflaged from us in her thousand manes, each more subtle and opaque than the next, then the trance would end and this world would no longer exist. God must hide to keep the world going, the enchantment real.

His disguise is foolproof, and we are the fools. If his beard fell off, if he appeared in any form, the jig would be up.

Who would live, who would stay here if he could see God through the gauze of reality? Everyone would say, "Oh, you're God. Well, I'm out of here." It would be a joke, or worse, a bad play.

The universe was not created by God or gods but psyches shaping differential layers, most of them below (or above) the Freudian unconscious and Jungian archetypes. We cannot, no matter how good a flam we put on, hide from ourselves.

This is one of the least publicized canons of the human condition. We may deceive others—hook, line, and sinker—but we always know who we are. Even a sociopath's true nature is disclosed to him, elude it though he does through his charm, through trying to charm himself. He can twist and turn somersaults and conceal all but a smidgen of his internal dialogue, but that smidgen is always there, nudging at him. The more he ignores it, the more he empowers it—the more insistent it becomes.

He too is part of the God that can't be known.

The secular world *is* the spiritual world. If this creation had been made sacred and spiritual through and through, it would not have been spiritual at all. It might have been sacristical, a theocracy into which fundamentalist Muslims and Christians want to shoehorn us. That would have been a sorry creation.

A secular world is the only kind of world that can be spiritual. A secular world is an abundant world, revising its meanings as it unfolds. Creation bursts chimerically beyond the dull premises that subtend it.

All gods are attempts to impose man on creation, not spirit (which is already there) but man. Anthropomorphized divinity is not devotion to God but evasion of divinity. God is greater than any imagination of his covenant, immeasurable and multiform, as much a beaver as an old man.

Only Gnostic and pantheistic dakinis have anything to do with nature, as their dalliance splashes into matter. The rest is religiosity and politics—beasts primping on thrones.

We are only possibility, and God is no one but the background against which possibility rests.

As Meister Eckhart put it, more or less, God wouldn't have carved open a world in this fashion if it weren't necessary as a way to get to him. He has interred us in matter whereby to track the abyss and transform it in his name (and absence) into light. Bodies let us do things that, as spirit, we could only imagine.

Spirit has to go this far into matter to realize its nature as spirit.

Karma is not control, not destiny; it is continuity. As energy is transferred atom to atom, molecule to atomic molecule, so are disposition and instinct transmitted cell to cell. Otherwise, how would a cell know what position it was in? How would it even know it was a cell?

We exist in a precinct where we can lose everything and all knowledge of everything, become a babe again, and still be who we are.

Something else is transmitted from lifetime to lifetime, something that knows what and who it is without knowing anything at all, something that must even learn to walk and talk all over again.

Ego is not consciousness but *of* consciousness. When body/mind perishes, ego is toast.

The dead return to the ground of consciousness, not the beings they once were but the timeless void out of which those beings awoke.

Reborn in infant bodies, they separate themselves into time. It takes a while for mind to realize that it has come into dichotomy and movement, into horizon again. The child sunders from eternity, picks up its toys, and gets a job.

That's the way it works: all paradox, no certainty, lifetime after lifetime: an inexorably karmic universe of the broadest dimensions and depth, of which we are the creator, across whose desert we now convoy.

Sit on a zafu and imagine this: the stream of sensations that make you up, your very "I," is a candelabra sourced in a flame. Go to the flame's root, not its fire. Experience conditionless radiance pouring into you.

Every indigenous mindform is fused to its existentiality by a torch, as leaves high in a tree feed off subsoil roots.

Imagine the wick feeding your flame, the light at the source of your mindedness. Can you find it? Sort of? Where does your awareness, your life-reality originate? How do chance molecules enter your eternal flame?

The Thoughts of Hugh Selby, Jr., Scribbled During a Movie Interview

◆I love the AMA. My doctor said, you've got no lungs. Go home and die. Then he sent me his bill. Yeah, I love the AMA. I was going to live just to prove him wrong.

◆Resistance to the natural pain of life produces enormous suffering.

◆You can't encounter a problem without an answer. It is a spiritual impossibility to have a problem that has no answer.

◆I'm back from the dead. I've died many times.

◆How you get from darkness to light is through emotional experience. Emotional experience alone leads to compassion. That's wisdom. The intellect doesn't have anything but a jumble of facts. To save our selves, our souls, this whole bloody thing here, it's wisdom that we need.

Heard on the Path to Inspiration Point While Riding a Bike Through Stray Conversations of Walkers

"Brokeback Mountain," "his name is Short and he's short," "incredible painkillers," "all I ever wanted from her," "becoming virtual reality," "a.o.a., any old asshole," "over the hill," "on the spot," "was multi-tasking," "prefer movies at the theater," "the last thing I want is power of attorney," "but I told him," "sucks," "mushroom hunting," "postponed till the first week in February."

Women use the word "fuck" in a sexual sense more easily than men do. They are more comfortable with its snug claim on their bodies, not only its suggestion of intimacy but its implicit power of veto over pleasure, its aggression fusing with submission to desire. Not only do they not mind, they cultivate it.

They say "fuck" endearingly, seductively, combatively, provocatively, insultingly. They understand its innate charisma, *their* innate charisma, the capacity of the word to shock, compel, strip away pretense, to establish candor and connection. They say, "Stop with the sweet talking, babe; you only fancy me, pine after me, because I'm fuckable."

As much as men are drawn to both the act and the word, as fervidly as they preen its bravado and strut its rap, they are subservient to it. It has a dominion over them like a charm uttered during a voodoo dance, a spell they cannot keep themselves from obeying. What is both irresistible and incendiary is a gift, and a curse.

Of course men are afraid of the word, of allure itself, because even though they stand to gain from it, in fact *everything* (they tell themselves), it proves that they are not in charge, have no control finally over their own gendered bodies and minds. They are pawns of a primeval, impersonal yen working identically in snails and mice.

Women are more comfortable with "fucking" because they don't need it as much, thus can take a step back and experience what it is, even *that* it is, just a thing. They don't have to neutralize *its* warrant to keep their own, hence can ask, even as a real question, "Do you want to fuck me?" They understand the primacy of those pronouns, the logarithmic tension maintaining their gaps, the provocation of space between any two organisms, 'twixt here and there.

"Do you want to fuck me?" is a shamanic pronouncement in the shape of a rhetorical question.

On Sexuality

1.

Sexuality is a driving force of nature, a seminal energy in terrestrial biology, no doubt cosmic biology too. Inculcated at a subcellular level in all zooids that must mate to produce progeny, it is transduced into tissues and emotions. In the less cortical realms of the animal world, sexuality remains, like predation, its own existential fact. Animals are at the service of drives; they are forces of nature individualized. In simple vertebrates the primordia that instigate cell syzygy and conjugation are rigidly prescribed, unsullied by pornographic thoughts, in fact any critical thought. Where there are no symbols to reflect ambiguities, desire and sensation are absolute. To a heron or newt, touch is its own event, to be drunk like wine.

In mammals the same cell-based energy gets embroidered by symbols of the higher cortex so that, by the human phase, it is infested with rules and customs and incorporated into plans. In the framework of society, sex is reconceived as its own fact again, developing iconographies and rigorous etiquettes and stances of normality. Language causes acts to be named and totemized, but it does not alter their primacy or unexamined zeal.

Only among humans, on Earth at least, does desire seek a resolution in lexemes; thus, only among humans are moral and other epistemological ambiguities waged in sexual acts.

2.

All manners of deeds, impulsive and contemplative, unconscious and conscious, declared and undeclared, are carried out in the name and service of human sexuality, from ordinary romance and courtship to recreational lust and sex-play (sometimes euphemistically deemed "lifestyles," e.g. the title of the condom section at Wal-Mart).

Everyone experiences his or her sexual nature and its urgency uniquely, is attracted to some things, blasé to others, repulsed by others. Sexual hegemony embraces simple heterosexual and homosexual acts as well as a spectrum of fetishes directed toward children, animals, dwarves, giants or giganticized organs, corpses, prurient toys, images, smells, sensations, and even indefinable gaps between forms where nothing seems to be but people squeeze themselves into an idiom of desire incomprehensibly. While sexuality itself travels along recognizable nerves with the blood and hormones through the body, accumulating in erogenous zones, its objectified targets are psychologically, culturally, and idiosyncratically selected, and often represent fusions of neurotic or psychotic cathexes into libidinal charge.

Sex also autonomously crosses into violent, nonconsenting, compulsive acts in which one person imposes his or her (but usually his) will on another creature. Bodily and emotional violation runs a gamut of mischief from sodomy and rape to sexual murder. Those who initiate such acts claim (by name or otherwise) to be expressing irrepressible and primordial drives. The notion of "abuse" is irrelevant—even sissy—to them. Sexuality thus declares itself a desire without a reason or avenue of deconstruction, an act that is its own sole explanation, imposing its prerogatives at will.

Transgressive deeds occur throughout the rest of the animal world too, somewhat arbitrarily in relation to phylum or species; for instance, sadomasochistic snuff dances among insects and combative courtships by felines, crabs, and chickens. Love, gentleness, and fidelity are likewise expressed unpredictably, from geese to manatees to monkeys. Biologically, however, desire has no meaning or satisfaction other than its successful expression and, even then, it is only temporarily discharged, instantly regathering and mutating, hungering for new validations of its drive.

Although predation is an extreme, usually criminal mode of sexual expression among humans, I believe that, to some degree, most people covertly think of sex as biological in its imperative and beyond their control or capacity to bridle—suppress maybe but not abolish. In even mild transgressions (unwelcome advances, callous teasing), sexual predation betrays the inherent belief of the aggressor that his incursions are legitimate, justified by innate desires, and involuntary. Passion, even in the form of injurious violation, is worshiped as its own god. Pleasure is considered an inalienable right, and the sensibility or even separate existence of another person becomes incidental. A sexual predator is no more concerned about damage to a fellow sentient being than a lion is about the welfare of a zebra. A stalker's urgency to express his sexual drive—sadomasochistic, pedophiliac, necrophiliac, whatever—privileges a lust that recognizes no amelioration or irony, a compulsion that creates its own context and permits no other, let alone that of morality. In this form sex is a fire that consumes everything in its path.

Luckily, a relatively small number of sociopaths totally lack empathy for others or reflection into their own unbidden fantasies.

3.

One day at lunch an otherwise uptight, corny business associate whom I had known for years—a married person of high left-wing convictions—without warning began narrating his "exciting" visits to child brothels in Thailand and then recalled his fling with a high-priced prostitute in Australia, all from a sense that he was establishing intimacy, describing the good life, and confessing luxuries at the heart of human existence. He evidently meant his sharing as a sort of gift—a tale of colonial yuppie recreation, to be admired in male company.

Nowhere in his outward personality did such acts reside, although thereafter I could see them subsumed in his clownish narcissistic gestures. He did not evince even the slightest cognizance of the ethical implications of his deeds or shame at telling them.

Under the taboos and sanctions of society our true sexual natures are masked, sublimated, or displayed symbolically in overperformed poses and quasi-sexualized (or perversely desexualized) personae. Sex is conflated with other intensely cathected functions such as power, religious dogma, and social authority; it becomes a crutch for devalued and neglected functions such as touch, friendship, conviviality, the general need for intimacy, relief from loneliness, and brotherly, sisterly, and parental love. Most technological societies are sexualized beyond people's desires or needs, even as material goods, from hamburgers to cars to homes, in these same societies are exotically supersized, leading not to fulfillment but depression and inertia.

Depreciated, otherwise healthy functions get rechanneled through eroticized projections. Translated into sexual strategies, at core they remain different unfulfilled hungers for which sexuality is a distraction. Displacement is a primary source of sadistic, masochistic, and exploitative sexual behavior, as constantly priming the pump of genital urgency and abstact pleasure yields sterile, futile acts that seek to discharge any stray sensation.

In a parable so familiar as to be stock comedy, an older man feels attraction toward a much younger woman and worries that his feelings will go unrequited because of their inappropriateness but also because the woman does not feel their equivalent for him. What is rarely explored in such instances is the degree to which sexualization has tainted or taken over the guy's fatherly protec-tiveness, empathy, Platonic love, and sheer admiration of another's charisma and spirit. He sexualizes from laziness rather than de-sire. He has so valorized and reinforced erotic fantasies his whole life that he has not learned to signify other needs and capacities.

The character played by Kevin Spacey in *American Beauty* comes to a key revelation toward the abrupt end of the film (and his own life): his sexual obsession with the cheerleader friend of his daughter, after whom he hungers the entire movie, actually holds his damaged feelings of compassion and paternal caring plus his own fragile sense of beauty. Only when the girl responds and they are stroking and undressing does he realize not only that he can't follow through on this act but that he has traveled far from his own desire. He has been tricked by the commoditi-zation of erotic feelings into glitzy signposts of nirvana.

This distortion of human life is a tenet of the Islamic critique of the West; yet sexual projection and abuse are universal, and many Muslim cultures foster equally brutal regimes through reverse tactics (the veiling and clitoridectomy of women and treatment of them as male property).

4.

Meanwhile touch itself has become such a depreciated and ta-booed function that its pathologizations are more acknowledged than its naïve expressions. Pure touch is soothing, reassuring, and, most of all, healing. It transfers primal energy, good will, and companionship between two people. Yet the sexualization of mere contact, often ironically by ideologues in vocal oppo-sition to sex, has contaminated and tabooed it into a "dirty" or sterile act.

In the early '80s I volunteered at our daughter's Montessori school during lunchtime. My "job" at Bright Star was to monitor,

referee, and amuse preschoolers. I engaged in activities ranging from story-telling and wordplay to wrestling and imitation
t'ai chi. A favorite game for the kids was climbing around me
on the play structure while I sounded out their first and last
names backward and occasionally turned them into Pig Latin.
My daughter became Adnarim, while a Korean girl with a similar name became Adnama; a cute little boy, Eoj. Many times I
tussled raucously with them, throwing them over my shoulder
and carrying them around. These games roused mixed feelings
in me: *déjà vu* of my own childhood, ancient aggressions, snippets of animal horseplay and teasing, even love. Though I recall
being passingly disturbed by some of these, I didn't take them
seriously or as anything more than they were: currents and sensations of being in a world.

As the decades passed, my attitude toward those rough-
housing sessions darkened, not in their interpretation but their
relative cultural danger. I would never dare such a thing now, not
because of what I felt but because of how "touch" has been re-
interpreted. One cannot be sure how any act will be characterized by the "sexual correctness" police. In a world of *Capturing
the Friedmans*, ordinary feeling and improvised physical play between adults and children have become not only shameful but
potentially criminal.

For several years after Bright Star, I called Joe's parents, maybe once a year, to check on how he was doing. Seven or eight
years into the '80s, I experienced a distinct shift in these friendly
exchanges, either a reticence and discomfort on their part or a
projection of my own unease. My interest in Joe and my long-ago
relationship with him no longer had the same innocent tenor.

On the heels of the highly publicized archaeology of a seeming epidemic of child abuse, our culture arrived at a vilification
of touch, placing under suspicion almost any unofficial adult

interest in children. The violative coach of the novel/movie *Mysterious Skin* became a collective representation of the norm; the bogeyman was suddenly everywhere.

I stopped calling Joe's parents and, with pedophilia rampant on the Internet, things have gotten far worse since. I'm afraid, for future-time readers of William Blake's printed page, "love sweet love" is once again a crime. People are not permitted to discover or explore diverse bands of sensual energy; every flicker of it is tabooed from the first hint of youthful charge—except (ironically) for its most casuistically sexualized forms: these are set off, often with tongue in cheek or smug winks, in allowable rituals for unwelcome courtship and prostitution wherein they are statements of class and the exercise of the power of gender and wealth. Sexual exploitation under evangelical or tribal dispensation, whether Muslim or Christian (or Hindu), is its own self-parody.

5.

Medical palpation is a traditional modality for relieving not only headaches, depressions, anxiety attacks, and muscle tension but also serious organ pathologies. Yet, with the molecular robotization of biology, manual medicine is now considered quackery. Doctors relate to patients through machines and numbers generated by machines rather than their own touch. The poor hands have become embarrassments both scientifically and socially, base and imprecise instruments as well as potential violators of personal boundaries. Meanwhile the outsider disciplines of cranial osteopathy, Polarity, Feldenkrais, and Chinese and Ayurvedic medicine continue to cultivate forms of touch to heal conditions for which standard allopathic medicine can only employ expensive, invasive surgery and/or drugs.

The Upledger Institute, where one lineage of craniosacral therapy originated, has developed a protocol for teaching therapeutic palpation to very young children. The program itself has been formally titled Compassionate Touch; some of the pupils euphemistically call it "Happy Touch." In a number of schools in Wisconsin and Indiana where this technique has been taught, first-graders learn to dissolve their mother's headaches, "make nice" each other's bumps and bruises, and comfort and heal a pet that has been injured. In later years graduates of this program turn out more cooperative with one another and adults and generally less angry and aggressive.

"Happy Touch" should be taught in every school in the nation, every country in the world. Who knows how its practice would radiate positively into political, economic, and environmental spheres!

Yet the opposite has occurred. Virtually no schools in the United States will chance teaching children a system that has them touching one another, not because of any legitimate fear that it is harmful or transgressive but because of a near certainty that some parents will raise holy hell and accuse those running the program of homosexuality and anti-Christianity or begin quoting the Bible and Nancy Grace. The besmirching of touch orchestrated by fundamentalist Christians, lawyers and police short on emotional intelligence, and hanging judges is complemented by other, related prejudices throughout the world. "Happy Touch" would have just as little possibility of acceptance in an Islamic country. Tribal cultures and those practicing Buddhism and Hinduism might be more tolerant.

One of the shocks encountered by the "lost boys of Sudan," Darfur orphans raised in refugee camps in Kenya and granted residency in the United States as teenagers, is that boys can't touch each other here without being considered "fags." On camera these young men playfully grab and hug each other and declare they will not give up this mode of interaction because they know it is a fine thing.

Sexual feelings arise sporadically with any kind of touch; they are ineradicable and harmless. After all, sexual energy is a channel of multiplex somatic energy from which it cannot be sanitized.

During the early '90s I was invited to join a three-year course in bodywork at an offshoot of the Lomi School across San Francisco Bay in Corte Madera. There were three of us amateurs in a group that was otherwise limited to health professionals—altogether five men and fifteen women. These were, for the most part, accomplished women who had developed healing capacity and projected their own charisma and empathy through it. In the best sense they were dakinis and witches. I was attracted to a few of them to the degree that the intimate techniques we practiced made the exercises provocative for me.

For the entire first year into the second I couldn't refine the quality of my touch. I felt clunky and pedagogical as I tried to put my hands in the right place and carry out correct moves without violating my partner's personal space. I wanted to be beyond reproach. Most of all I tried not to feel anything. So that was the result: I didn't feel *anything*.

At some point early in the second year, frustrated at being unable to experience what everyone else seemed to access effortlessly, I came to the eureka: Energy is energy and, if I was blocking erotic sensation, I was blocking sensation itself.

While doing the techniques, I began to risk letting myself feel attraction and even the beginnings of genital arousal. To my astonishment, the sexual component passed quickly while its vestigial charge in my body turned into the missing sensation of melting and heat that I was seeking in my hands. I could feel its waves coursing through me, and I could transfer them and track my partner along gradients of tissue tension.

I never would have gotten there if I hadn't allowed sexual energy, so-called, to initiate it.

Erotic attraction comes and goes, even these days when I practice palpation. I am not sure it is even sexual; it is more like a misperception imposed by cultural attitudes and shame in early adolescence when we hardly knew what we felt, what it meant, or what its licit range of expression was.

6.

By Darwinian logic, the requisites of species fertility and gene sorting are built into nature and summon humans (particularly high-gamete, fertilizing males) to seek as much dispersion of seed among as diverse a variety of eggs as possible, so the existential self-justification for lust takes on a biological patina, much as apologists for capitalism excuse greed and exploitation by the presumed built-in survival of the fittest in nature: kill or be killed; accumulate or have others get the goods; fuck and hoard women or become extinct.

Whereas I don't mean to oversimplify or minimize our repertoire, I do think that, whatever else sex is, it is a biological drive that continues to impose impulses that translate into forms of desire, all with the goal of enticing the male into using his seed to fertilize more female seeds, the female to get her eggs activated. This is true at core even when a particular desire is not heterosexual or conjugal.

Beyond that, sex is either the libidinal energy of cells translated into meanings and insatiable nostalgia for itself or, if not, then a sophisticated figment of the same, an illusion foisted by cellular meanings onto their tissues and ganglia to dupe them into mating and continuing their lineages in new cells. Either way, sexuality is a mystery and ontology that is beyond ordinary analysis and interpretation and, while rooted at our creature origin, contains within it not only its own existentiality but the existential fact of being, of being alive, or, as classicist Norman

O. Brown well named it, life against death ... something against nothing.

That is why it not only feels so good but causes so much trouble—and also why it feels so bad. If we don't know who we are, how can we choose something over nothing, let alone every time? We do, though, again and again, romantically, erotically, socially—and at the heart of each psychosexual act we sense a more ancient passion, the surge of "being" against its own mortality and the mysterious and central urgency at our root.

Of all the episodes of the 1950s TV show *Amos 'n Andy*, the one that comes to my mind most often involves the sale of a bogus house by the Kingfish to Andy. As was often the case, Andy unexpectedly came into some scratch, so Kingfish busied himself scheming how to relieve him of it. In this episode he decided to sell Andy a property, and the particular real estate he hoisted on his unsuspecting friend was actually a piece of cardboard deployed on an empty lot, a photograph of a house with a cutout door on it.

I don't remember what gullibility led Andy to fall for such a flagrant deception, but he made the purchase. He then brought dim-witted Lightning to view his new domicile. The trouble was, whenever they tried the front door, they stepped into the backyard. After a number of such forays, Lightning finally was inspired to investigate further. Circumambulating the structure, he declared, "That's one mighty thin house there, Andy."

I may not recall the details exactly, but you have the basic plot. It stays in my mind because it was hilarious then and remains hilarious: Br'er Rabbit tomfoolery at its most artful.

It also stays in my mind because it holds a figure of speech for vital energy. When I am sensing the interior of a body by osteopathic palpation, these words occasionally come to mind: "That's a mighty thin sheet of tissue." While rotating and distributing the chi gung energy ball during Dragon and Tiger, I draw it long and thin so that it is hardly a spheroid anymore. "That's a mighty thin ball you got there, Andy!"

I find it naïve to presume that preparers of food do not slip up in their hostilities and deposit their neuroses, pranks, counter-phobias, and other obscure perversities on plates delivered by waiters and waitresses. If nowadays an insult or highway lane-change leads to gunfire and militias routinely blow up neighborhoods to avenge collaborators, why not suspect that each of us has been fed sputum, offal, urine, blood, sperm, dingleberries, and other unguessable turds by deranged and sociopathic food handlers? We can't guess at what restaurant it happened, whether a five-star or a Denny's, but (by a corollary of Murphy's Law) it was likely when we least suspected it, in an appetizing, reassuring display of vegetables or scrumptious meringue.

An unacknowledged fear of defilement, of being defiled, drives the defilers. Under the collective ambivalence imposed by society, under repressed awareness of their own contradictions, vandals invent acts of ritual corruption, in part to immunize themselves against pollution.* Also for recreation and out of boredom, often innocently, sometimes not. That, plus some folks are noodlebrains, and others enjoy being assholes.

---

*Check out Kevin Smith's *Mallrats* for a stunt involving feces-coated chocolate.

And this is not even taking into account that most of the vittles we consume are prepared and packaged by unknown others whose states of sanity and projections of good or bad will we cannot begin to guess. Already, the FDA regulates permissible adulteration of food products by dead-rat fragments and various other animal corpses and excretions (defined by parts per million).

We behave more prissily than our situation warrants. We are processing venoms, microbes, and contamination all the time. As we swim in a conflation of mind and molecules, in the stream of everything, inexplicable crimes of bodily invasion are committed.

None of this matters. None of this makes us dangerously sick or kills us; it is just additional carbon and nitrogen.

Undoubtedly the twenty-first century will belong to China and India. Iran, Pakistan, Venezuela, Somalia, Nigeria, and Indonesia will be heard from too. The notion of Mssrs. Bush, Rumsfeld, and Cheney that the United States is some sort of lone superpower is ludicrous. The birthrate alone decisively stands against the West, in Malaysia and Oaxaca as much as Egypt and Gaza. While we have something left to offer them, we should be making the best deal we can.

This here nation is a sham, a thrown-together republic, a polity without closeable borders, without native clans or indigenous continuity, sustained by imported resources and debt to foreign banks, maintained by increasingly shrill, moronic, and self-righteous rednecks riveted to domestic dramas, setting standards of international policy by sectarian moralities and taboos. They engage in oversimplified, grandiose geopolitics like the dry drunks and closet cocaine addicts they are.

Borrow more money (presently five billion dead presidents a day)—soon all we'll be able to afford is the vigorish to China, and foreigners will start dropping our currency faster than Albanian gold futures. Send more troops into bottomless millennial conflicts and civil wars; try to drive all the illegal Mexicans out of what was once Mexico; chest-thump; carry your Second Amendment arms; crow, "Shock and awe, baby! Get my shock and awe!"

Already China owns the mortgage on the house. Arizona, California, New Mexico, and Texas are, at most, on another century or so's loan from Sonora, Chihuahua, and Baja.

Frankly suicide bombers and other terrorists, past and yet to come, pack far more shock and awe than the entitled arsenal of those zealots who lead us now.

As bankrupt as they are, when these idiots in suits periodically decide to consolidate their power, they use a thimble of imagination to ratchet up the fear level of the constituency to orange or red. It takes but a counterfeit stone to scatter the pigeons, to set the mice scampering. The President and his crew are the terrorists, for they have strategically woven terror into the membrane of American life.

Guess what: we have already surrendered.

Black Magic

Neocon is code for fascist magician. Ann Coulter's outbursts are satanic, resembling those of the demon-infested, hissing damsel in *The Exorcist*.

The President himself is delusional, with low-grade Tourette's and Attention Deficit Disorder. He has converted his rage against us all into a sham vendetta against "terror." It is not "them" but "him" who hates us for our freedom. Plus, he can't tell the whisperings of angels from the ministrations of hungry ghosts. He behaves as though his enterprise in Iraq lies somewhere between a patriotic sermon and a fraternity prank gone awry. This is that ADHD disconnect.

What about the Internet rumor that W's mother, Barbara Pierce, is Aleister Crowley's illegitimate daughter? Apparently Barbara's mama, Pauline Pierce, traveled through France with the Luciferian magician in the fall of 1924 and gave birth nine months later. That would make our President the Master Therion's grandson.*

The rotating disk of stuff that made up the primordial Solar System is still rotating, even where motionless, in every particle, hence in every cell and Golgi of every creature. It continues to distribute quarks and neutrinos, yin and yang, shedding its own colossal *ba gua* body. Gas giants like Jupiter and Saturn billow and swirl with undifferentiated energy. Icy worlds like Uranus and Neptune spin vast electrometallic robes.

This original spiraling drum is mirrored in every person, rotates multidimensionally each time a plant or animal moves, collecting and dispersing yards of energetic silk with its appendages. Every creature, talented or not, does chi gung, is a sword master. By example every creature trains every other in authentic movement. Spiders and sun jellies; tigers, snakes, and hawks teach sword and *xingyi* forms, as well as modes of touch for yoga and medicinal dissemination.

The life body is but the congealed core of a greater torso, its fine currents extending yards beyond it, even as magnetic fields

* http://www.rense.com/general77/acrow.htm at the time of writing

of planets and stars extend billions of miles beyond their carapaces. We are all still planets, conducting radiation through auras, transmitting it discretely.

It makes no sense to quarantine us, as doctrinaire science attempts by fiat, from the universe, to declare us manikins without
spirit or resonance, *chi*-less blobs. To pretend to be nothing and
neutral when we are giving off so much voltage is irresponsible,
even criminal.

The primal event was sacred and enlightened, and everything
that has followed, no matter how fucked or casually profane, is
still conducting magic.

Without inherent torquing, none of this would exist. There
wouldn't be a skunk or a worm.

What we feel in our happiest, most expansive moments is the
mead of existence, the ember that sustains the rest of it, the
strand connecting us to causation, even if such times include the
ballpark, the hop, a birthday party, a pretty dress, a nap in the
sun, the smell of rose petals, *the way you look tonight....*" "First
love" overcomes all subsequent loss and is passed on to eternity.

Morning. Banks of lower clouds moving against higher ones,
Earth. Eye will miss. I....

Buttercups. Wind chimes. Brook water. Carrots. Watermelon.
Clover purple. Hay.

Over my life I go through a cycle from secular to spiritual, and each swath back over the spiritual I grasp something slightly deeper. One part of me lives the life as given—desperately, unforgivingly—as the other part keeps trying to dead-reckon where it is in time and space, from beyond time and space.

Notes on *Grizzly Man*, a film by Werner Herzog

"Now the longhorns are gone/and the drovers are gone,/the Comanches are gone,/and the outlaws are gone,/now Geronimo's gone,/and Quantro's gone,/and the lion is gone,/and the red wolf is gone,/ ... and Treadwell is gone."—"Coyotes" by Bob Mcdill, from *Grizzly Man*, last line ad-libbed by the pilot.

Lindy and I watched Werner Herzog's *Grizzly Man* tonight. What an amazing, profound, chilling thing! The film is completely over the edge into something else. It is like a documentary that gathers the unseen footage of the universe—a gaze into what should never be seen or heard (even as Herzog withheld Timothy Treadwell's death screams from when the camera was running with the lens cap on).*

---

*Sometimes, though, Herzog does ring a bit false to me here, as though the ham in him is running away with itself. When he blubbers, "Dear, you must *never* show this to anyone! You should destroy it!" it can sound something less than ingenuous. I feel like shouting, "Werner, please, stop! You're not Hamlet."

Grizzly Man is everything "America's Funniest Home Videos" and *The Blair Witch Project* aspired to be, yet is so much more real that it shows them up as overwrought frauds. It is funnier and spookier—more like a *Truman Show* of the Earth itself: A fox crosses the stage, mosquitoes surround the lens, ursine hind-pads disappear and reappear in swirling black waters—hungry old guy searching the bottom for salmon carcasses.

Wilderness blokes bearing their own photographic equipment—gun-toting "we're in Alaska, dig our high-end watercraft" touristas—presume that *they* are the barrel-of-the-lens but don't realize that a far more sustained eye, trembling with rage, is filming *them* as they hurl rocks into the void (toward the omniscient "camera") at a young bear to amuse themselves ... occasionally bonking it. The passive eye of nature that we never see is watching us, witnessing the hapless meddlers that we are.

Behind nature's camera, cursing the invaders on monitor, is the movie's subject and "star," lawyering as best he can for his bears—Timothy Treadwell. A self-appointed wildlife protector, he recorded more than a hundred hours of himself and animals in the Katmai National Park, Alaska—his legacy after the fatal mauling (and consumption of his body parts) by an unamused grizzly.

Herzog knew exactly what to do with this footage, how to select and cut, pace and edit, counterposing his own voice, overriding the sound track now and again with measured critique. Warhol-like, he sometimes stuck with Treadwell's camera after the narrator exited stage right or front—that's when flies and bees in their erratic mimeses, gusts of wind in vegetation became the actors ... like some random satellite view of a day on Mars or Titan.

Treadwell was an innately brilliant film-maker who, by the mettle of his camping out in no man's land, rendered the camera transparent in a way curators of Discovery Channel and

National Geographic can only dream of: fox paws on the see-through fabric of his tent; baseball cap stolen by a baby fox who scampers away with it to his den (Treadwell cussing in pursuit); snapping musculature of male bears on hind legs in combat, one of them dropping loads of shit; Treadwell's own hand in bear poop, his wonder that it has just been inside his *idée fixe*, that he can feel the heat of her body still. He documents the daily activities and conflicts of nature as they unfold, without Nature Channel voiceover and story-boarding, substituting instead his own goofball myths and Prince Valiant pageantry.

The actor may have been his own cinematographer, but he needed a conductor to arrange the cinema, to interrogate what it really was ... to edit for text, subtext, and hypertext, running "bad" scenes into "good" ones so that various self-conscious Treadwells and elaborated "aliases" flowed seamlessly. Treadwell couldn't make this movie, in part because he was dead and in part because his own rushes were as random and shapeless as his intention and existence.

He could not have chosen a more appropriate director—Herzog punctuated and staggered the sequences like a maestro nuancing a philharmonic orchestra. Under his steady, calm hand, Treadwell's multiple takes of scenes—variations of the same monologues against the same background—become esoteric revelations of obscure and bizarre acts. The self-declared Grizzly Man no doubt imagined a hypothetical PBS crew splicing only the most heroic and flattering portraits into an upbeat environmental drama. That is not what Herzog did; thus, this is not really the film Treadwell conceived or wanted. If he could have foreseen the final product, he might not have bared his fucked-up mind and wounded heart so compliantly.

Afterwards, as an inspired touch, the director invited world-class musicians to improvise a sound track while they watched the soundless projection—and then, over the ending and credits, he put the peerless Don Edwards yodeling "Coyotes."

Treadwell was already a Herzog character, much like Kasper Hauser awaking without a name, Aguirre leading an army across South America, Fitzcarraldo dragging furniture through the jungle with "opera house" inclinations, and Dieter Dengler fleeing the Pathet Lao through monsoons and brush, all of them cursing whomever are the gods. By the same token, Treadwell backpacked through Alaska, discoursing with gigantic bears as if they were people wearing bear costumes. He wanted to put himself back through the eye of the needle, the evolutionary tunnel, into the very souls of these animals.

Substitute glacial tundra for generic rainforest and you've got a classic out-of-control Herzog landscape.

Before he went into the outback, Treadwell was a guy who couldn't make contact with his fellow humans, who messed up just about all his romantic relationships (as he confesses throughout with a candor that is both admirable and arrogant). He couldn't live in society, period; the wilderness alone made his existence tolerable. So he used the bears to redeem himself: to expose his wounds, to quiet his mind, to ease his grief, to confront his traumas, to unleash his compassion on something real.

Treadwell reveals the animals' simple "joys of being ... their grace and ferociousness"—in short provides a glimpse into the lives of bears. He does it in a way that only a live-in bear impersonator could pull off. He does it so guilelessly that he speaks for all our guilt and aspirations, to be accepted still, despite everything, by the primitive psyche that we have ravaged.

In moments of near "primal scream" delirium, Treadwell croons, "I love you—I love you, fox that I have named Ghost;

I love you, bears that I call Mickey and Saturn and Sergeant Brown; I love you, bee expired in the flower. I love you, all and everything." Still clutching his childhood teddy, tentbound in nocturnal wind and pouring rain, he is about as alone and alienated as a middle-class American can get on this planet.

The he broadcasts equally manic "planet news" to the gods and denizens of this creation, to Allah, Jehovah, and what he calls that "Hindu floaty thing": "Am I fucked up; is this a fucked-up planet or what?" and again: "Fuck you, everyone."

But he is not some New Age death-wish eco-lib. Maybe he was blind to his own excesses and grandiosity, but he wasn't a madman or klutz. He is a guy who lies just beneath the surface of regimented populations in cities where were-bears and were-wolves wait to reclaim us from our symbolic reign into the original real that birthed our primordia and casts yet the arras of our minds. Even if we kill them all, the totems and souls of these untamed animals will stalk us till the end.

This aspiring actor (who allegedly came in second to Woody Harrelson for the role of bartender in *Cheers*) was a self-taught naturalist, survivalist, and animal trainer. It's not often that a recovering alcoholic and delusional emcee gets to make it in nature, let alone the Bering wilderness, for thirteen whole summers, as a confidante and chronicler of feral beasts. Yet he somehow survived year after year, while exposing the depth of our spiritual and ecological crisis. No one—Treadwell demonstrates—not even the guerrillas of Earth First!, is saving bears or the Earth or anything. Looking back at us all from the Alaskan wilderness, he shouts every variant of "fuck you" he can: "I came here in peace and love … you fuckers! Fuck you, Park Service. I beat your fucking asses! Animals rule! Timothy conquered!"

He shows us to ourselves—braggarts, slobs, bullies, poseurs, and despoilers—all of which he was too, though he was different in this way: he set himself before the bears for judgment. He was willing to be a humble ursine groupie rather than an inflated human goon. He had already sat in court in Van Nuys and witnessed criminals being sentenced to hard time. He put his butt there specifically to reintroduce himself to what life-and-death in the zone is about. So when he submitted himself to the bears and their verdict, he knew that he had come to the Great Hall of Justice and was going to be convicted.

But at least he was engaging the cosmic battle, casting his lot with furry demons rather than voodoo in robes. He chose Mesozoic shamans as his magisters, those clear-hearted pre-symbolic predecessors of the human regime, who merely deal out the law of survival: no retribution, no self-righteous posturing, no unnecessary gloating, no cruel twisting of the needle, no broken hearts. They are in fact nothing except ontologically sentient stacks of meat.

Yet at the same time, Herzog dashed Treadwell's delusion of himself as selfless friend to the animals of the North, diplomat from the Grizzly Maze to the schoolchildren of America. He exposed him as what he also was: a provincial bullhead, a yuppie imperialist crossing a sacred boundary between bears and humans that native Alaskans had respected for thousands of years. Treadwell intruded recklessly on ursine space, initially from his own narcissistic need to embrace the primal beast, later from his greater desire to be embraced back.

Remember, from the standpoint of the grizzlies, even the coolest dudes are blubbering assholes and officious nerds, not witty studs, not stars of anything, certainly not guardians or medicine men. Ultimately they are prey, to be cuffed and eaten.

Treadwell wanted nature to forgive him, but he was way beyond that. He wanted the planet to forgive *all of us*. That mission is what drove him and what makes *Grizzly Man* a sacred

document and not just a puff piece or YouTube upload of indulgent pathos.

Despite his hopeless provinciality and fatal anthropomor-
phism, Treadwell was so thoroughly initiated by the bears and
foxes and Kodiak country that he transcended his neuroses and
took on their stunted voice. By admitting his crimes ingenuously,
he eclipsed them and became a default shaman, commuted into
a spokesman for nature on the planet. Even while still a bombas-
tic, pretentious, suicidal lunatic, he gave an Oscar performance
of "life on Earth."

Grizzly Man, Herzog tells us, is about "not nature but our nature." It shows what consciousness and culture have done to
nature. It reveals raw nature shining back through Treadwell's
own damaged psyche, so much more brilliantly than culture
ever could. The errant bear-tamer performs a brilliant and
effective act of psychoanalytic transference, the animals his
shrinks and confessors, the camera his conversion device (because bears don't speak English and don't ordinarily do therapy). The act of filming transfigures the beasts into the best kind
of Freudians—dumb sentimental ones—as well as into "crazy
wisdom" kukurajas and Treadwell's jury (ultimately, they deliver his sentence).

The trope of the film-maker cum eco-warrior allows
Treadwell to be analyzed without an actual analyst, to receive
holy unction without a priest, to project his madness into a
saner, emotionally simpler, and more primitive other, to engage
in a dialogue with himself, bear by indifferent bear, to the purpose of his own liberation and perhaps even cure. The grizzlies even deconstruct his sex life for him, the essentials of his
repressed jealousy and longing, as they model lust, male competition, and mating envy in their absolute forms. They are,

after all, the id—living giant hulks of it, oversized passionate empaths.

If *"le transfer"* weren't "the enactment of the reality of the unconscious"* (to bring Mr. Lacan on set here)—the cross-species fling of analyst and analysand in the *quaestio*—Treadwell wouldn't have lasted a day in the Grizzly Maze. Yet he carried out his maneuvers, "expeditions" as he called them, for thirteen years—so the dialogue was real, the cure was real, the initiation was real, the acts of dissidence were real, the indictment of the world that made him crazy is real, and his representation of the politics of foxes and bears is also real.

I don't agree with Herzog's anti-moralistic conclusion that Treadwell's film shows that the universe is chaotic, predatory, and antipathetic. While I see the frustrations of unreflecting consciousness and thwarted empathy in the predators, I also perceive their innocence, their ordination as nascent buddhas luminous in their own right—but it hardly matters, because the presentation is vast and neutral enough to encompass every possibility. I do consent to this: when I look into those grizzlies' eyes, I don't see humanity or psyche or any possibility of reconciliation; I don't see people in fur; I see only raw, antipathetic hunger and restless rage. I see the violence of the sun itself.

The day after I watched *Grizzly Man*, my cats and even the spiders on the walls looked like bears. It is a film I will never get out my mind.

"la mise en act de la réalité de l'inconscient."

Corollaries of Creation (yet again)

1. Big Mind is not intellect. It is a reality-generating, molecule-sourcing turbine subtler than matter, telekinetic from its actual shape, not a thought-stream. In fact, it doesn't think. (See Flower of Life and associated sacred-geometry DOS.)

2. Stuff is empty. The dead bird does indeed look like a fossil of a spirit that once passed through this realm.

3. Life is a state sans context. Reality outside our lives is a different thing.

4. Without cellular enforcement, memory is a vacant storage bin. As the Real roots in itself, dispersing mist, everything fades into dream before vanishing beyond memory entirely. Yet, paradoxically, none of it is ever lost; it is always subtilizing itself en route to becoming what it is.

5. Buddhism tells us to recognize our nature at all times; i.e., thoughts arise only from other thoughts.

6. There hardly seems enough space—space inside our minds, gaps to pry open—to make ourselves safe by looking at things as they are.

7. Body is not an organizer of experience as much as a filter, to let in just enough sensation for this to work. Sensory pathways tune vibrations into stuff.

8. Profundity is all that matters—to feel something deeply and intrinsically, without a mediating idea. The universe is not after our allegiance, our success, our knowledge, even our happiness. It does not handicap our sorrow. It has no particular use for our edifices or technologies—here today, gone tomorrow. When we feel creation's depth through our own, then alone does the universe acknowledge and guide us. We can't force, charm, or calculate our way into heaven.

9. The heart cannot be erased as easily as the mind. Thus, keep all true things in the heart. Vet all truths through the heart first. That other stuff we have learned and then committed to cultural vocabulary—mathematics, philosophy, behavior—will disappear, a slate wiped clean. But if something was experienced deeply and wondrously, with awe and compassion, it will endure. It melds with karma. It is who we are.

Let science also pay homage to the heart. The pure curiosity that drives empirical inquiry is a sublimated function of the heart.

10. Whatever we find here on the Earth, good or bad, benign or malign, is what we have chosen. When someone has an unfortunate birth into physical handicap or poverty, finds himself/herself in a village about to raided, kidnapped from a slum to a brothel, this is not fair and also not just desserts for some former misdeed or sinful incarnation; but it is not a punishment. Only the entire universe can work to alter these conditions and bring justice to individuals. Until then individuals must stand in for the rest of us and help the world make it through.

The innocent are truly innocent; yet on some level everyone volunteered for his or her condition, even if they didn't, because it is up to them to illuminate the circumstance in which they are embodied, illuminate it through the beacon of their own being. What cannot be ascribed to karma as a sentence for deeds committed in past lives *must be* ascribed to karma as destiny—the goal of liberating the thread of all lives and individuating the universe for everyone.

We are precisely where we wanted to be, doing what we wanted to do, for reasons we intended and planned down to the last detail long ago, reasons we can't recall because they are too big.

11. We are *of* consciousness. Nothing else counts. Nothing else matters, literally.

12. After death, in the next bardo, the lights are so much brighter because they are not lights. The sounds are so much louder because they are not sounds. Outside of time, nothing happens because everything has already happened.

It is good to have non-time, but it is also good to have time because many things occur only *on the clock.*

13. Nothing is more terrifying, more painful, than passages between bardos, but they are the orbital jumps that make the universe what it is. The sole grace is that a newborn instantly forgets.

Yet this isn't a leniency because amnesia leads to rebirth.

Naked after life (e.g. without a body), we find the brightness and sounds unbearable. To get out of their din, we flee, scuttle back to a safe, conditional world; put on a robe.

What Is a Gene?

Before there was life anywhere on Earth, some spots heaved irregularly from volcanic heat, chemical interactions, shear forces under gravity. There was no metabolism, just fermentation and bubbles. There were no hearts. Mud simmering in sunlight was the closest approximation to a cardiac device, and it wasn't all that close.

Okay, take that a gob of that popping, oozing mud, put a daringly thin elastic pellicle around it. Photogram it down to each and every molecule and their positions in relation to one another. Stipple the specs onto a filament; make a rosary of such pebbles; fission it into a subfile. Cut a serial gem of it. That's a heart.

Actually it's not a heart; it's a chromosome. It's not a heart until a chain of ribosomal transmissions extraverts the two-dimensional draught into macromolecular architecture and oscillates it into metabolizing agency. A heart, like any organ, is a nonlinear projection of a linear map of nonlinear events. Every facet of every plant and animal, virus and bacterium was once, primordially, a motif in soil or puddle. A gene synopsized and digitalized it, and a conga of genes sewed its pattern into a shape.

On the other hand, there is no such thing as a gene for a trait. There are no discrete genes for any part of a cardiac muscle or blood pump, only genes for potentials. Genes transmit raw disposition prior to design. Contentless in the human sense, they speak in a babble that precedes actual meaning, in numbers that trump mathematics. Microbes, daisies, cobras, eels, and hominids are forged by cells, extracellular ingredients, and their matrices.

But how did pumps originate prior to genetic convoy, to accept DNA's summons? *"What the anvil? What dread grasp … ?"* cried William Blake, foreshadowing the modern conundrum.

When scientists at the Jackson Lab in Bar Harbor recently isolated something in proto-diabetic mice that somehow protected them from diabetes, they named it the Yi Factor after an associate of theirs and expected to be able to isolate it, if not promptly, then in a few months.

They knew a lot about what this Yi thing was from the get-go, and even more about what it wasn't. They eliminated all the obvious stuff; it wasn't albumin. When they still couldn't find it, they couriered a sample to Harvard whilst they continued to beat the bushes for that part per multimillion.

A system this old takes hundreds of thousands and sometimes millions, sometimes billions, of Earth orbits to organize, to go through the subprogram of building itself, imbedding and implementing its hierarchy of operations, geneticizing them, and refining their networks by creature. Over time it gets rid of as much surplus matter and information as it can afford or, more precisely (and with respect to Darwin), the loss of data, even critical data, that somehow does not impede performance, is acceptable (and of course efficient, given that a creature is a condensed algebra conducted upon and multiplied by the whole of nature). When you're cloning at this scale in a closed biosphere, you can't waste molecules. And if you have no deadline or budget, you can search for the system that packs the biggest wallop at the least material cost and interface.

So most of the goop and structure used to construct and run the Yi is divested—it didn't matter. What was once essential is replaced by something lighter, discarding its forerunner's superfluities. As long as the system continues to go, more and more ordnance can be deleted, and the operation will merely become sleeker, subtler, quicker, more savvy—and leave space, materiel, and energy for other operations, within the creature and in the environment at large. The Yi is there, somewhere, but it is also not there, except as a trace—less than a trace: a whisper of a voice no longer speaking.

The technicians at Jackson Lab are going up against an intelligence that has been working far longer than they have, are deconstructing an instrument much older than they are, even older than the *sapiens* species, in fact far more ancient than the epoch when their germs and those of mice were hatching in the same progenitor.

How many ticks of a cesium clock, cycles of sunspots, have they spent on their meager deciphering? How many hours of interrupted workdays separated by weekends and holidays? How long, for that matter, are their entire lifetimes or the lifetime of their species? A pittance! That's how long compared to the perpetuity it took to deposit the Yi, unnamed, into cells.

It takes unimaginably deep watches of time to enfranchise a living utensil. Nature is never interrupted, never takes a vacation, never stops ruminating over its systems and tinkering with them. It works beneath a nano-level with the intelligence of entropy aimed at infinity. That's a lot of hard drive, a lot of gigabytes, a vast span, a wide plane of action, and all of it at a speed far greater than that of light because it effectively combines the velocity of all its operations at once.

You might say that entropy is not very intelligent and assemblage by trial and error hardly sophisticated, but you miss the point. Entropy is both intelligent and sophisticated because it omits nothing, no possibility, even if it works with the acuity of a moron in mud. It randomizes because that's where the Oracle and the Sphinx are concealed, that's where Trickster Coyote reaches into his bag of illicit tricks.

The intelligence that Jackson Lab is applying is merely a subset of a greater intelligence that made them all—the genes, the mice, the Yi Factor, the source codes, the Yi family in Palaeolithc China—that imbedded them one in another, in operations encompassing cells and laboratories, cultures and ecospheres. A mosquito can't respond to the call of a whale nor can peacocks parley intellectually with snails.

Some fortnight or two hence they will no doubt find the footprint of the Yi Factor, not unlike a neutrino in a cloud chamber—but its meat and potatoes, the hinge of life, will elude them forever.

You have to have a body to be here. You need to be sewn into a suit. A shape, whether human or butterfly or cow, is the entry ticket into a world. It's the vehicle, the price, and the password. Get a body, live as a swamp bundle.

You are here until the zipper is pulled and the fumes depart.

The risk of hell—that all must go through its degradations, punishments, and sublime tortures—is antidoted by one simple mantra: *I am something.*

This imperative issuing from me, my spark of free will, is shaping the event. Unless I want it to happen, it won't.

Everything doesn't *have to happen.* It needs my permission, in the Freudian sense—the profoundest Freudian sense; it cannot be happening unless I not only think but capacitate it. It cannot enslave me unless I allow it.

Ah, but find "I" and you have the pass-key.

An atom is a resonating odyle that Einstein's heirs, bombarding with secular algebra, could not crack.

A cell is a gnarl of buzzing, magnetized electrons, an oilslick on the film of night.

All the caterpillars dropping from their nests onto the world, onto stones, onto effigies of monkey Buddhas, must carve their way from darkness to light. Every caterpillar must find its own true nature, crawling as viscera over rocks, in order to get to the next surface.

That there are so many of them cannot preclude their individuation.

I adore watching them in action, destructive as their reign is to the trees, because they are alive. They do not harm the rocks, and they worship and name the Buddhas in their own way, forming a tiara or beard on the head of a statue from China in Rowe, Massachusetts.

It can't be like this, and yet it is like this—problematic, unsatisfying, sufficient—in the gravity well and sunfield: propitious births all.

The First Lesson in the Power of Advertising

When I was around thirteen years old, a new brand of soap called Zest debuted with a flurry of television ads that showed people bathing in waterfalls amid orchestral crescendos. A voice-over described "the Zest feeling"—a whole different kind of sudsing action that made you downright ecstatic: *"For the first time in your life, feel really clean."*

I was curious what it would be like to use something other than our house brand, Camay, so I convinced my parents to buy me a bar. After unwrapping its parchment, I held a marbled bluish-green amulet like some discoid chocolate bar imprinted with sacred letters.

When I washed myself with Zest that night, I became as exuberant as the people in the ads. The soap felt liberating, slaphappy. I couldn't identify the precise source of its energy; it wasn't the foaming action, but there *was* something rhapsodic—perhaps its subtle fragrance, vaguely like Queen Anne's lace, which reminded me of wildflowers.

When my spirits needed a lift thereafter, I took Zest into bath or a shower and was transformed.

I told my school friends about Zest, but to a one they laughed, and the few that tried it reported nothing special. Although I knew it was ridiculous to ascribe joy to a bar of soap, I still sus-pected that they were missing something: *"They are not letting themselves feel it."*

For months thereafter I looked forward to baths and show-ers. I used Zest to get myself happy, to bust out of melancholy.

To my mind I had discovered something important that oth-ers were either too uptight or too snotty to get, something big and magic about the world: the Zest feeling.

The following summer I packed a few bars of Zest in my camp trunk and produced the jade ovals for my bunkmates. Since at Chipinaw we showered together, I got a chance to watch the soap in action.

No one in my bunk experienced the Zest feeling, but they mercilessly spoofed it with dances and paroxysms that left them writhing in fake ecstasy on the moth-littered floor. I blushed but was undeterred.

I continued to feel the ebullience of Zest. A shower with its lather made me less homesick. It turned the Chipinaw sky bluer, the flowers deeper yellow and red. I raced from the mess hall to my bunk, body zooming. I flew across the outfield.

A compulsive enthuser, I kept touting Zest. Yet from bunkmates I continued to evince only blank looks and goofy cutting up. I insisted they were wrong. So they sought an arbiter.

Our counselor took their side. "There is no Zest feeling," he declared. "That's what ads are supposed to do—convince you to buy things. It's all in your imagination."

If it hadn't been the Fifties, if it hadn't been America, if we had been initiated into some sort of inner life rather than told (in effect) it didn't exist, if we had been taught chi gung instead of Capture the Flag, if baseball cards had been revealed as icons behind their players and insignias, then he might have been able to report: "The imagination is a powerful tool by itself; it can turn ordinary things into magical ones and unleash boundless love. We each have the power inside us to be happy and experience miracles every day. We each have an innate desire to be generous and serve others. And that desire is also contagious."

He would have encouraged me to find the source of the Zest feeling in myself, in the native beauty and enigma of the world; to cultivate and spread Zest's compassion, even to practice a better poetry than Zest, as Wordsworth did, as Buddha did: the "visionary gleam," the "splendor in the grass," "empty essence, primordially pure." Not a soap, but a measureless lumination beyond wind in branches, beyond the night ablaze with stars, as we sang Taps, swaying and bundled together in the cold. He might have invited me to turn the Zest feeling into art or prayer, which we were taught under other names. In fact, we earned little felt stripes to sew onto proud arms of our Chipinaw jackets: red for arts and crafts, blue for religion, white for service, yellow for sports, green for nature cabin.

They thought they had better stuff than Zest, but all they offered were banners and slogans, soporifics and zest-killers: mirth that wasn't mirth, play that wasn't actually play. Life at Chipinaw was orchestrated cheers and games back then, and most of it wasn't much fun.

Of course, not only couldn't my counselor have said such things but, if he had, none of us would have understood or believed them. I would have made fun of him, just as my bunkmates did in the latrine. I would have turned chi gung into the heebie-jeebies.

I was in a Zest world, and it would be three long years before I purchased my first tarot deck and began to explore sacred images and the quintessence of the Zest feeling. Two years after that I began reading books on qabala.

Instead, the guy succeeded in setting me straight. He made me ashamed of my gullibility. The Zest feeling went away. I became cynical and modern again. After all, it was just soap.

I didn't buy any more Zest. Every now and then I came upon a bar at someone else's house, tried it, and, despite myself, felt a glimmer of the old Z jubilation—but I dismissed it as suggestibility.

The next year in high school I read two books that raised my consciousness about the relation between puffery and products. Their author, Vance Packard, a pop sociologist, scoped out the seductive influences in ads—in particular, the subliminal messages behind effigies that make us want to buy things.

Borrowing ideas from his *Hidden Persuaders* for my English term paper that spring, I decoded a series of Old Gold cigarette ads, showing how the placement of objects in each still-life affiliated the product with either happiness or success. The particular campaign I chose ran in *Life* and *Look* and involved little cameos as if by Dutch masters. Each put a pack of Old Golds among personal items like an astrolabe, an expensive watch, a bottle of imported brandy, pearls, a fountain pen, a denim jacket, etc.

My stepfather was in the advertising business, and I had hung out at Robert Towers Advertising long enough to know that his agency didn't design subliminal ads. They were into straightforward spiels—postcard landscapes and chic designs, "classics," Bob informed me. He would go through the Sunday *Times*, find one of his productions, and crow, "Look at that layout. It's Johnny Mercer; it's Rodgers and Hammerstein; it's Hemingway. Richard, you don't need the Vance Packards of the world to make effective ads. Lose that bum!"

He insisted that I was reading things into the Old Gold ads, that the point of the advertising business was to show something opulent and attractive—no one hid symbols in ads. But I assumed he was too small-time and regional to do the really advanced stuff.

Being in midtown, he was able to drop a carbon of my paper onto the desk of the Old Gold guy at a nearby agency. A week later he reported the man's telephoned response.

"He said it was a good piece of work for a high-school student. Your teacher should give you an A, and he'll have a job waiting for you when you finish college; but he also said to tell you to forget the subliminal crap. It's a load of malarkey."

I couldn't know it then, but I was about to be swept into the rapids of adolescence; I was on the cusp of owning a Waite tarot and signing up for the Builders of the Adytum correspondence course on Tarot Fundamentals.

A year after my flirtation with Vance Packard, my friend Chuck Stein introduced the poetry of Charles Olson to our creative-writing class, reading aloud "The Moon is the Number 18" while setting on the table before us the blue and yellow trump with its lobster emerging from a pool, its baying wolves and twin battlements on either side of a winding mountain path, its lunar face dripping yummy golden embers. A month later, Chuck led me on the subway to lower Broadway: Weiser's Basement of the Occult. I picked out my own deck.

I set the matrix of cards on the floor: the upside-down Hanged Man; the Magician with his table of sigils; the High Priestess with her rippling robes and pomegranate-embroidered veil; the Cube of Space; the Tower with its toppled king and knave; the lantern-bearing Hermit; the Charioteer, Devil, and Lovers, different angles of the same celestial emanation. I loved the exploding fields of many-rayed stars with their hermaphroditic angels, sacred birds, and goblets of five-sensed rivulets. I visualized their landscapes until they opened into a montage of symbols. Like "hidden persuaders," they held a subliminal message; only it had not been loaded cynically by executives at agencies but was transmitted esoterically, perhaps by entities in other realms.

Set in three horizontal rows of seven with the Fool at their helm, the Trumps came alive as a diagram of creation. I saw a river of blue energy begin to flow from the Priestess' robes through the Chariot and Wheel of Fortune to the sea of cosmic consciousness in the Judgment card. I felt a new euphoria, quite different from Zest. A transdimensional event showering worlds with divine embers was a lot more audacious and cardinal than soap suds. This was truly "old gold": a matrix of living minerals as well as the sign of manifestation.

The naked horned couple chained blindly to a half-cube by some fixed-stare, bat-winged Devil became comely Lovers in a garden, Satan their smiling angel—but only once they realized the chains about their necks were loosely hung. To be in heaven or to languish in hell was their choice, just as Zest had been my choice, my touchstone to throw off the shackles of my family and America, to convert gloom into happiness—to accept a subconscious field of divine operation. That same male and female pair comprised black and white Sphinxes, bowing before the Charioteer under a curtain of stars at the birth of the Symbol.

The cards didn't go away like soap. They matured in me and gave me a sense of my own existence. Zest returned and stuck this time and, even better, I was able to transmit it to others by laying out the deck and telling fortunes. My subjects were mesmerized by the Mediaeval images, the backdrop of gypsy wisdom and unauthorized knowledge, and I was their earnest ventriloquist, a wise teenage Fool. As a budding oracle, I was in demand not only at school and camp but among my stepmother's friends.

They brought their domestic and financial quandaries, though I kept explaining that they weren't supposed to tell me anything, the cards were larger than any story. Still, they laid it right out there—wayward husbands, stock portfolios, troubled children.

The readings I did for girls I liked were my first successful act of flirtation.

I turned to self-divination during my own crises large and small, through the remainder of high school and into college, especially when my existential situation seemed most bleak and hopeless. The cards provided direction at the crossroads, guidance through the miasma, like the rising trail from the crayfish's pool through the mountains to the Moon.

The tarot understood summer jobs and sadness and love, romance and destiny better than I did. It turned situations into opportunities. Its magic showed me that I was *never not* among sacred things. It anointed me a lay Hierophant, a master of Pentacles, a hero on a grail, always, even when riding the subway, even when playing leftfield or studying for a math exam. It gave an ordinary boy a sacred alphabet and symbols, a way to glimpse the hidden universe. It made me serious and worthwhile to myself.

It is *all subliminal*—that is, latent and iconic. The world is a giant, uninterpreted tarot. Soon enough I read Carl Jung's *Archetypes and the Collective Unconscious* and *Psychology and Alchemy*, Paul Radin's *The World of Primitive Man*. I became a disciple of Egyptian priests, Maori elders.

By then I knew that Zest could be the Philosopher's Stone, that a bar of soap could also be a Star.

Last night I dreamed of a UFO. I wish I could remember the part of the dream that preceded the spaceship because it was far more portentous. In fact, by the time the UFO slipped into a dark sky it seemed merely a cover image, an intentional distraction that now blocks my memory of the greater dream.

The ship was kind of gold-yellow, and it moved as though it was going to cross the arras and disappear like a meteor. Then suddenly it changed course and flew right at me. I initially dismissed this blitz. It was so obviously a pretext, a hoax, no better than a homemade disk dangled from an undetectable string.

Then my dream car began shaking and I understood at once that, though chintzy and far too yellow, this saucer was the real McCoy. As it circled again and zoomed in on me, it demonstrated beyond a doubt that I was of interest to its alien intelligence, that it could search me out even within my own dream on a remote world.

I began to get scared, and I tried to evade.

There was actually a word on the craft's outside, curving along its contour. I tried to read it, but the letters, though surprisingly my own alphabet, were upside-down. I caught a few of them at each pass, but never the word itself. It began "pla ...," but it wasn't "planet" or "plane"; in fact I gradually felt that it wasn't really "p," but a letter that didn't go with "l," like "x" or "r." It was trying to call itself "planet" so that I wouldn't know what it really was, so that I couldn't get back to the rest of the dream—except now I see a great boat, for a millisecond, and already it is gone, but I know that the boat is the real dream and carries the true word. The letters are alien; their transliteration bogus, the best that can be done.

The UFO emerged out of the extraterrestrial boat in an occultation of scenery to delude me with a tinny alien-ness and hide the import of the dhow, or whatever it was—forbidden tidings within this dream.

The Meteorite Crater in Arizona was punched out by a huge rock—and I mean huge—traveling through space at ten times the speed of sound. When it encountered the Earth, it shot from Paris to North America in two minutes and then slammed into the ground, steaming off H_2O and fragmenting into pieces, some of which landed hundreds of miles away. It left a mile-long, round basin.

Such events are an existential fact in this dimension. What is where it is does what it does, and the results are meticulous, consistent, logical, and have almost infinite territory to express their force and scale. Whole galaxies sometimes invade each other, all the stars and worlds in them colliding into one another and exploding with the force of the Big Bang itself.

This is a dangerous place.

Christ didn't just come here. He was potentiated long before Bethlehem, in the archetype of a fish and through Piscean gods. When he chose to enter our dimension as a spirit descending into matter, he realized he was giving up a lot of intelligence and grace, but he came anyway. Whatever, whoever he was, he manifested through prior Christ symbols and became the historical Christ.

What an illuminated world it was back then, a world in which a thousand, two thousand years before he arrived, Christ was prefigured, foreshadowed, *known!*

We no longer comprehend or respect the depth of the universe. The sea, the abyss from which the Fish arose, was populated once by nascent shapes: mermaids and dragons. Our projections into it gave rise to whole tribes of Oceanids: sirens, sylphs, shimmering undines, blue-haired nereids protecting sailors, future-telling naiads, cattle-stealing water-horses.

The oceans and lakes can never be that profound again. Science objects, declaring: "I am the full explanation of all that abides. Everything under, everything beyond the Sun, I know and cover, forever. I am Law. And by the way, thou shalt have no other god things before me."

The presumption is that science has corrected our imaginal organs, our means of divination, and projected them outward into the pure mass and interstice of things, item by item, fish by fish, now cell by cell and molecule by molecule, down to superstrings and quarks, substituting utter exposure and the steady progress of mechanical borers for spirits and mysteries of the void.

What an arrogant premise! Science deludes itself that it is parsing and assaying a real external, objective world. Physics, chemistry, biology, and the like are actually just layers of another internal world, swarming with as intricate myths as an Egyptian coffin lid or Mediaeval carpet, albeit nano-strings and mitochondria instead of fauns and unicorns.

It is all projection, all consciousness, and even cameras propelled into so-called outer space do not leave the precinct of internalized consciousness. By photographing Mars or Europa or a nameless galaxy, they merely transpose iconography into new zones of spirits.

Christ is barred from such a world, our modern one. There is no way in. There is no access for him, even among so-called believers. If he walked the streets of a contemporary city, cameramen and skeptics would follow him; they would look for his sleights of hand and enlist debunkers to erase his miracles. They would arrest or kill him before he could commit an act of personal sacrifice on a divine scale.

Science is now our religion and Christ is either a sociological object or a beatified apocalyptic tale. He cannot really be here, even for those who obsessively scan the world for signs of his return. They are not looking for him; they are looking for Tim LaHaye or for nuclear bombs in Jerusalem.

We have replaced the possibility of gods and transubstantiation with exiguous histories and biblical kitsch, linear time and technologically wired landscapes, and kidded ourselves that the circuits and objects in them are actual and confirmed. It is *all inside us*, the instruments as well, and, as we lurch from world age to world age, we are also traveling inside a yawing rubric of invisible and impalpable constellations that determine our civilization and fate. These wireless networks (birth charts, crop circles, *chi* bodies) are far more powerful than any weapons, more perspicacious than any microscopes, because they are absolute, self-existing, and sewn into the system. They are not made of anything and were never fabricated. It is they who are brewing the next epoch, the next dimension, who are sorting, have already sorted, what is to be.

Maybe Times Are A-Changin'

On WERU, "*We've been b-b-bamboozled and buffaloed by b-b-bubba Bush …*" And the bumperstickers in front of me read, "When evolution is outlawed, only outlaws will evolve" and "Rapture them up already."

During a summer-solstice ceremony on the marsh by Ripple Pond, a campfire is built and people sing show tunes like "Somewhere Over the Rainbow" and "Old Man River," Buddhist and Hindu mantras, and Seneca prayers to the Moon afloat in the universe: "*Neesa Neesa Neesa; Neesa Neesa Neesa; Neesa Neesa Neesa—Guyweeoh.*" A cake with candles is produced because it is Lindy's and my fortieth anniversary.

The stars are nigh, the Milky Way exposed through a dark cloak by the rent that consciousness makes in absolute space-time. Scorpio is rising with its semi-spiral torque, and the Dipper is positively glittering from handletip star to bowl.

Frogs are galunking in the marsh, so concertedly that they seem part of our ensemble, though they are out of tune and sequence. It doesn't matter. Their intent, unclouded by herme-neutics, is expressed so plainly and generically it could have just as easily been the chorus of a show tune, a Navaho chant, puffs through a didgeridoo, or damn near anything at all. Frogs ex-claiming their unconscious minds are the proof that conscious-ness is visiting the marshlands of the Solar System. They are sufficient hiatus in the dumb brutality of stone.

Turtles cross the yard, occasionally pausing by our cars to stretch their necks and gauge the situation. They make no sound at all. But their mummery is another refrain to our mantra. Carrying serrated shells that make their species a denizen of the Osage sky, bearing knowledge they cannot read or tell, they are just as eloquent as frogs or people.*

---

*"The rising sun emits thirteen rays, which are divided into a group of six and a group of seven corresponding respectively to right and left, land and sky, summer and winter. The tail of this species of turtle is said to have sometimes six and sometimes seven serratures. Its chest therefore represents the vault of the sky and the grey line across it the Milky Way." Claude Lévi-Strauss, *The Savage Mind*, translated from the French (The University of Chicago Press, 1966), p. 59.

What shelled creatures in a starry firmament demonstrate is that, across such enormous distances of transparent night as we suffer, silence is equal to a multitude of voices or many chirps. Though intention is mute, it carves a shape more vocal and phonetic than words.

Turtles are an adjunct to our gathering, delivering the great space between words, the prior universe of unlanguaged things, which allows anything to be spoken at all.

Men and women during the Stone Ages witnessed the Moon as a many-phased chalice, not knowing what it was—so what! Their observance was not any less clued-in to the nature of things than modern science's dissections of the orb's astrophysical character.

For as long as we don't know what we are, what consciousness is, how mind comes to root in bodies on worlds, we don't know shit.

Scientists act as though taking stuff apart is the thing to do—and, in a certain sense, it is—to see how the gears work. But taking a thing apart tells you nothing about what it *is*. If you go in with the prejudice that everything about anything is mechanical and spiritless, then that is what you will find—dead tubules and filaments made of molecules and radioactive rocks. (And the Intelligent Design people should stay out of this one because an anthropomorphic god is just as idolatrous, just as Golden Calfy as an atom.)

Better to see sylvan spirits and lunar demiurges than molecules, better to raise intelligent energy out of the Moon's reflection in a pool and pour its silver over our bodies as mercurial *chi*, washing our bones in it, then splash it back into the sky. Better to draw vital elixir, better not to stand alienated in Eden.

In the end we have to turn it all in for amnesia and Lethe. Might as well be everything we can until.

In my previous life is a city or a kingdom. It lies on the outskirts of memory, tinged with fairy tales and ballads—*"among the leaves so green-o."* It fades and then vanishes, as this ephemeral zone establishes its polities, as did other lifetimes, in their hours. The many existences of us accumulate like peridermal layers on a hedgehog's back, blubber of which he is not aware, though fibers in his density.

It is the accumulation of lifetimes that makes up a Great Life, a universal Man/Woman in the cosmos. One might detect these existences in us as a sort of isinglass of energy, invisible pellicles karmically imposing personality.

The landscape of forever illumines each life in every world.

The color of the late-afternoon sun on this Maine island is irreplaceable. Fleeting aromas enter the garden; cool salty breezes encroach from offshore. Two nights ago thunder and lightning performed a deluge of rain. Morning smelled like mint. Then there was a full orange moon.

What this adds up to is: if you were going to fashion a world out of atoms and make it round and thick enough to hold and be something to the ghosts who must inhabit it, this is a brilliant start.

Lindy and I were just twenty when we visited film-maker Stan Brakhage and his wife at their home in Rollinsville, Colorado. Over goat's milk cheese and wine Stan set before us his singlemost question, asked first by his friend Jim Tenney at a supremely happy moment in their youth, "Why can't it be like this all the time?"

I guessed the answer but was shy enough to wait for him to speak, which, after a moment's silence, he did: "It *is* like this all the time. We just don't know it."

Synchronicity is a far more powerful force than thermodynamics, but it can't all be synchronicities or this world as it is would snap. Synchronicities infiltrate reality now and again. We can never explain them, never solve them; they are in fact insoluble. We must accept them because the universe is linked across its higher dimensions by meaning alone.

There are not even six degrees of separation across the galaxies; how can there be more among tribes and miracles on planets?

A tantalizing hint of this cavorts in the sun: grasshoppers whistling, then taking flight.

"Michael row your boat ashore," nothing to do about any of it, just exploding beyond like a dandelion head or sands blowing into another dimension, rivers rushing into rivers into sea, bubbles crashing onto the shore in the cream light of a new dawn....

Third Cycle

I come back to an image of a year ago—a shape that dangled like a wasps' nest from a tree. Only there were no wasps, there was no tree, and it wasn't a nest. It was the latency of the whole universe that hung, unrealized for eternity, from a crooked branch of something or maybe nothing, no girth at all.

Imagine a cyan bug matriculating for eons in the trunk of a tree in which it has been deposited by something else, a juicy glassine beetle made of space and time.

It is the image itself, inside me, inside those bugs inside the appletree, inside all of us on Earth, whether in our DNA or the configuration of our electrons, that grasps implicitly what "this" is and where we are in it. The pouch is made of something that *knows* but does not know why it is hanging there, what it is, what else it could be. The blue slimy beetle who doesn't exist, him too.

That time is long past. Now the nest has been split open, and it is pouring across time and space and we are in it—"Us" a realization of its latency, us and everything we are and think and do, everything that natively is, everywhere.

There are billions of histories and chronicles on all the planets in all the galaxies of all the levels of the universe, but there is only one wave, one thought, spreading in all directions from every point, unconfined (except by itself) in any dimension.

This is what I intuit as I plunge into the pond on Bliss Road in East Montpelier, currents that are first icy, then warm.

This site used to be a marsh but the Biggams dammed it and the spongy ground hydrated to the brim. Spring-fed, it is just large enough to be a body of water rather than a wading pool. It's roughly the size of a baseball infield, embroidered with reeds and frogs. The temperature fluctuates from tropical to glacial, a characteristic of Vermont ponds I remember long ago.

Not only are we traveling through the universe but the universe is traveling through us. It needs to feel us, what we are feeling, our marvels and infatuations and heartaches; *Oh Danny Boy, the pipes, the pipes …*, and *Greensleeves was all my joy …* to know what that stuff is, how it came to be and find its instrument, the source of its music; to experience itself in us or through us. But most of all, and forever, the mystery and the wonder.… To record and memorialize that, why we are here at all.

From the first droplet of anything against the first bare surface, we were essential to something vast, rough, ahead of and behind us. Our present struggles and planet-wide dangers are no accident; they are an actual contour of creation.

We are charged with a huge responsibility to bring it home. And this is not just some insoluble crisis or a daunting array of dire contingencies. Nor is it a game for phony spiritual saviors and self-appointed gurus to grandstand, for soldiers to march to victory, on any world accompanying any star.

We have chosen this—that cannot be said enough. We are trying to rescue the "real," and we are neither its victims nor its paragons.

Yet, it is okay to be this happy, this afraid, this alone, this once. It is more than okay; it is an obligation. For it will all turn into something else, in fact can only, can only become, in exile in these amazing shapes, what they are.

When I open my eyes underwater, what I see is muffled light, everything suspended in a brown haze. This is Creation for the protozoa and fish and frogs matriculating here, unfettered by philosophy.

The swim evokes childhood lakes in the Catskills and Plainfield of the 1970s when our kids were young, and big and little bodies dipped in tandem. I feel how stunning it is to be in a wetsuit on such a world, qualms and nostalgias purling even as the waters flutter cold and warm.

I am alive.

Sometimes, thank god, one can't think; one just is—primordial and absolute.

Roadtrip

Vermont

I have to reach beyond photorealism to say what this landscape is. Outwardly, it is rolling hills with ponds, cows on unkempt fields, teepees and geodesic domes, windmills and microsodas (lavender lemon with ginger, citrus hibiscus), glacial boulders strewn in millennial haste, seitan factories, bumperstickers and graffiti hinting that this has become the bluest of all blue states, anarchist pastoral and countercultural, even as it was thirty years ago.

At night the Milky Way Galaxy flows inaudibly through starry black, a river of cosmic transport and deeply ciphered messages, bearing ghostly travelers along the truss of creation. It marks the hub of the gematria of our location out on the fringes of the medicine wheel. But Terrans do not know it as a medicine wheel or even that such wheels turn on high.

Vermont doesn't care, as it parts misty curtains into apple vapors and another shimmering violet dissolve.

On Sunday morning we are invited to breakfast on one of the dirt roads above Plainfield, near where Robin went to New School.

The phenomenology of those fields is eternal. The air is so hot that the flowers and grasses perspire like sages in the desert. You can almost taste their mints and raspberries, tomato leaves.

So many bees luxuriate that their collective sound mesmerizes, recalling that Australian Aborigines heard as well as saw the Dreaming and carved the didgeridoo to render its tones.

The barn astride tomatoes and squashes is collapsing, a snake of rotting black hoses and loose hay strewn. Shade under the apple tree is Robin before Miranda was born, when he ran down a nearby hill at Halloween in full tiger costume.

Gloucester, Massachusetts

Gloucester discloses a nineteenth-century industrial fishing village, something out of Melville or Pessoa. Houses, many of them Victorian with cupolas, wrap around cuts, hills, estuaries, and grace the harbor, nano-packed in snaking Euro streets.

Using a mapquested menu, we pick our way from 95 along 128 in and out many baffling traffic circles down an alley to Henry Ferrini's quarters on Wall Street. Henry is a documentary film-maker working on a Charles Olson opus. In an earlier docu-poem he set Jack Kerouac's *Doctor Sax* to jazz and montages, celebrating Lowell, Mass. Henry's uncle, still badgering the muse in his nineties, was Olson's buddy, and rival, as the two men slandered each other in poems when both were in their prime.

On Henry's emailed suggestion I squeeze into a nonexistent parking space so deeply under a catalpa by boat trailers that I have to claw my way out the driver's side. On the way up the stairs I hand a copy of our publishing company's book *Little Lord Farting Boy* to his four-year-old son Isaac.

"How do you like that, dude?" Henry exclaims. "You got thanks?"

On my next trip I bring *Walter, Canus Inflatus.*

"Another Walter. Your favorite dog, dude."

Isaac doesn't say boo. We learn soon enough that he is preoccupied upstairs with a cloverleaf of trains, cars, and trucks—on brief safari to check out the visitors.

The day is scorching so, when Henry points through the window in the general direction of the shore, I decide to check it out. Drawing an overly hopeful premise from the ease of his gesture, I presume that the beach is, like, around the corner. In bathing suit, a towel around my neck—no wallet, keys, or phone—I charge into the bustling afternoon and promptly get lost. Twenty minutes later, vaguely anxious and feeling under-dressed on a busy thoroughfare, I manage to ask a woman and then a man the way—a good twelve or fourteen blocks more, it turns out. The woman actually offers to drive me, but I thank her and run away like a shy teenager.

River meets ocean around islets of sand, intersecting in a complex topography whereby multiple beaches lie between estuary and Atlantic. I carry my sneakers so that my feet soak up hot silica granules, crunchy seaweed; then I set the shoes by the shore and work my way along the estuary.

Packed with children and inner tubes, Little Good Harbor River is as working-class as the subway at rush hour. I cross its lukewarm current into the frigid sea, there let waves crash me until I am dizzy.

Feeling like a kid who might next pay a quarter for a cherry popsicle, I stroll in the general vicinity from which I came, drying in the hundred degrees F.

I lose my way again, leading to minor adventures with local characters, as I solicit directions, engage in gruff banter, mostly touching on my being wet or lost in a bathing suit—old grizzled guys like what Olson was when he died in 1970, what I am becoming.

In the morning, Lindy and I, together with Henry, wheel Isaac in a wagon to the same beach. We sit on the sand, sharing literary gossip while the universal boy rock-climbs over LGH, occasionally disappearing behind boulders so that either Poppa or I must hop to and lug the sack of kicking child to safe ground. (Henry and his wife Susan adopted a Guatemalan child, making them harried parents in their fifties.)

We work our way gradually down to the ocean, bearing shoes and towels, leaving the wagon to faith. While Lindy and Henry continue the conversation, I plop alongside Isaac in whirlpools among the rocks where ocean is trapped and warmed. Water spinning in declivities and basins is too turbulent to make tide-pools, and Isaac is fascinated by their motion, its emptying and refilling leading him to shout: "A bathtub with waves!"

"It's a no-rent amusement ride," Henry calls out. "He's obsessed with the tidal action."

Two Lights State Park, Cape Elizabeth, Maine

Little shells are inhabited by scuttling crabs so that, snatch up almost any underwater whelk, and fragile outraged claws poke out and then retreat.

A girl has covered her legs up past her pelvis with mud so that she is a mermaid. The river entering the sea smooths her tail.

Slaid Cleaves Concert, South Berwick, Maine

We head down Maine 95, out of Portland, exit at Wells; Route 9 to 4, through North Berwick; long stretches of woods and open fields—just past Sarah Orne Jewitt's home, we pull up (5:30) at a lawn in front of a middle school where a makeshift sign declares: Free Slaid Cleaves Concert.

Slaid is a songwriter/folksinger originally from South Berwick and the Portland club scene. Fifteen years ago, he migrated to

Austin to hang with the pros. His early Maine work had bits of Dylan, Dion, Donovan, Springsteen, young Leonard Cohen plus a goodly dose of Aroostook garage rock: Dick Curless, "Drag 'Em Off the Interstate" and "A Tombstone Every Mile." (Slaid loves engines and motoring songs just as much as the eye-patched king of the Hainesville Woods did.) These days he is more bluegrass, Woody, cowboy swing—having fused Maine country & western with Texas yodeling, Louisiana blues, and Mexican border reels. We discovered him last summer, playtime on WERU, community radio out of Blue Hill, leading to his September homecoming concert at the Grand in Ellsworth.

Slaid is a balladeer of disaster, jail, alcoholism, premature death, broken dreams, broken hearts. ("The difference between folk and pop music," he notes wryly, "is pop's about sex and money; folk is about death; my agent said it's a happy Slaid Cleaves song when only one person dies.")

At the Grand, Lindy and I took to Slaid's deadpan lyrics and unexpected melodies: *"Broke down, cracked and shattered;/Left in pieces/Like it never really mattered"** and *"She drew me a little picture/of the lonely rider's grave."*†

Now, having nursed all year the two signed CDs we purchased from him in the Grand lobby, we are stoked to see Slaid again in person.

Quite early, we put down jackets to save a place and then hang out till the show begins. We visit Slaid's wife, Karen, as she is setting up a CD and t-shirt stand, talking about "the road" (14,000 miles in six weeks).

*"Broke Down."
†"Quick as Dreams."

First, there are opening acts: a just-graduated girl and then a freshman guy from Berwick Academy, both performing Amateur Hour folk rock. Then Slaid, a bit of stock-car driver, lumberjack, and grad student in him, comes on with a band he has thrown together for Maine and Vermont. While the guitarist has traveled with him and Karen all the way from Corpus Christi—Oklahoma to Pittsburgh to Long Island, New York, Berwick tonight, and tomorrow, Rutland Prison—two local musicians from Slaid's "growing up" days, those times he *thought would never end*," are improvising.

Slaid's nostalgia soon becomes everyone's. Referring to South Berwick as "the Ber," he dedicates ballads like "Last of the V-8s" and "Race Car Joe" to his favorite auto junk dealer and local mechanics (with waves to the crowd):

"Cross the road down at the bottom of the field/there's a rusty tractor/used to read John Deere."* You recognize the people, even though you don't. You feel eternal glimmerings and loss, won'drin' like Neil Diamond ("Brooklyn Roads") where in god's name did it all go?

It is a fine band for the evening: stocky bearded guitarist all Red State but cool; the professor on the pedal guitar, eliciting notes like a fisherman tossing out line or video-gamer trying to fit a camel through the eye of a needle; drummer guy a little loose and dopey for old times' sake.

Slaid is, Lindy comments, his down-and-out lyrics notwithstanding, such an affable performer with an easy-listening voice: *"November ski-ies,/smile down on me./Let the winds of change/Come set me free...."*

At first the crowd is sparse. But, as homecoming boy belts and loudspeaker summons, it fills up, and soon the lawn is hopping.

---

*"November Skies."

Yes, it *is* delicious to hear live again songs that have become so familiar to us: *"But there's more than meets the eye;/You didn't leave us when you died;/Your spirit will live on/In what we do and who we are."*

Lindy and I hold hands, smile at each other, in a state of general enchantment, and Slaid accords some of his best lines: *"This is real life brother;/This ain't no reality show"* and *"I've been chasing grace;/But grace ain't so easily found."**

Almost as riveting as the band and vocalist are the little kids, age two on up, acting out their fancies in what serves as an aisle, also in front of the stage. As twilight sweeps past normal bedtimes, they are tumbling, prancing, goofing, composing jigs, puffing out pig ballets, clogging up in improvised circles. Some l'il girls post their attention right before the stage and stare up at Slaid in fixed trances. Other kids form rows that snake and spin and then collapse. *"I've got nothing/but a Ford a barnful of hay./If it weren't for horses and divorces,/I'd be a lot better off,/why I might even be a millionaire."†*

There are so many children and bits, different personalities and improvs, all piquant and jolly and in utter contrast to the doleful lyrics, that the affair has propelled itself beyond an agro-folk concert; it is now a Fellini carnival: *"Each year the world gets lonelier/And uglier with sin./You'll never see those blue skies/Through young eyes again."§*

---

*"Wishbones" and "One Good Year."
†"Horses."
§ "Wishbones" again.

Sunrise from the Penthouse at Broadway and 83rd, New York City

In the purple light of dawn that has been landing on Earth since the Stone Age, and before, New York City opens like a giant bat cave or rabbit warren, something very complicated and molded irregularly of stone, but always from within, like an embryonic labyrinth, the lights left on overnight still luminescing in little rectangles, the water towers and penthouses and cubical cupolas atop roofs reaching to a heaven that no longer exists in a civilization that has been emptied by the voice of unnatural commerce and deity of soporific love. Little strings and sparks of light, like things that might be on a Christmas tree or in a Hopi Fifth World sky, mark the detail disclosed by the soon-to-appear sun, as daily revelation, all too neglected and even unseen (or worse, regarded as no more than another enormous apparatus in a venue characterized by appliances) pours into every cavity and cranny, lighting alleys and avenues and exposing the homeless blanketed on stairways.

The light steals the universe back from manmade electricity, divulging how complicated and unique the effigy, tower after tower, portico by portico, roof gardens and ornaments and grills and walls inside walls; how this is the work of a jeweler not a mason, and how the collective action of masons and construction teams over generations, using the planet's delegated energy from the depositories of Wanamakers and Rockefellers and Carnegies can only create a giant crystal or a single bat awakening and opening its wings, as it wonders, "Who am I? Who made me and placed me here?" Only to discover that he made himself and that the answers lie cloaked among ancestors and cubes of another light, an esoteric light, that cannot be opened, that holds the secret of not just this but any universe.

Planes circle like underwater fish with sonar, early flights originating elsewhere.

Now the voice of the fire engine, the howl of humanity's creaturehood, bursts through a deeper metallic circuitry, a spiral from inside a spiral.

High in the altitude, streaks of clouds, like long rumpled sheets, have turned into a kind of glowing wheat with the fire of the much brighter sun. The sky behind them is no longer gray but turquoise oozing through bluish gray. Soon a full rainbow will arrive, but the vehicles I hear below tell me that the urban metabolism has already revved full force, and the creatures of twilight will scamper for yet another day in the paradox of existence.

Mount Desert Island

Mount Desert is a scrabble of moneyed rusticators and dying fishing communities, some of them barely maintaining their original piers and habitants—all of it interpolated with Federal parkland. While Rockefeller and Martha Stewart estates rule the island's northeast side, Southwest and Bass Harbors and Tremont celebrate Appalachia-hood: trailers, abandoned cars and boats, old tires, other yard junk.

At a level well short of Rockefellers, *nouveau riche* outsiders are teeming in, the locals vamoosing. No longer able to afford the place, fisherman-supreme Wendell Seavey is now a greeter at a Wal-Mart outside San Antonio, while yachts of Texans grace the wharves where he went out handlining as a teenager in the 1950s.

The signature lobster dealerships have been taken over by urban money: yuppies, arbitragers, fast-buck artists, New Jersey associates of the Sopranos, who use the F-word liberally to show how tough or casual or downhome they are, though none of them have earned that right. They are weekend warriors in their SUVs and Hummers.

The only place which has the ambiance of F. W. Thurston's when Lester Radcliffe was running the establishment, October '69 (that incredible blue and gold fall when the Mets were making a run to their first World Series) is Gordius Garage where Big Al somehow finds working engines and credit for everyone, even those so far down on the luck they will never make it up and over the March hill.

Using its mountains as chakra-tuning forks, the island retains an incredibly high vibration, throwing a jagged mindedness through its glacier-runed topography and eclipsed light.* I have felt for a long time that this place is a consciousness vortex, its geomancy functioning as an acceleration of karma. Come here and get nailed on whatever it is you are avoiding and hiding, whatever you don't want to feel. Get pushed where you are stuck, where you least want to budge.

On Mount Desert I feel in an elevated dimension in which the less evolved parts of me are prodded, badgered, and enjoined.

At the top of Flying Mountain I recline on a slab of moraine and osmose its slow mineral pulsation, down into the igneous base at the sublime judder of Somes Sound. On this crude but exquisite Solar System device the astral sun x-rays me, imaging my third eye, heart, and guts.

The situation has a dangerous edge too: wild bears and mountain lions, ravenous fishers, the sheer drop from Valley Peak into the frigid currents of Fernald Cove, an eagle in steep glide who interrogates my swimming too cogently. The deceptively picturesque scenery is untame and doesn't care a whit about us. Waves follow

---

*MDI is almost to the Atlantic time zone, so it gets an early evening, and even before that, the mountains begin degrading the light.

gravity, and creatures follow waves, on land as at sea. Sometimes we get in the way.

My dreams fall to the heart of darkness. I awake from a trauma that happened so long ago it is cellular. I cannot shake it off the way a dog rids its fur of rain.

Norumbega and Beech Hill fashion a silent note of redemption, cradling an intimation it might take lifetimes to acquire.

Not only does Mount Desert have a bigness to it, but it evokes a forbidden archaeology, as though offering a glimpse into Dreamtime and past existences, an inkling of ourselves before Pithecanthropus or Neanderthal—shades of Atlantis and Lemuria, which I don't think were actual places on Earth or even in this dimension but exist nonetheless in our past. That's why so many colonists buy properties and erect mansions here, and five million or so tourists troop through, each annum—in search of something crucial but beyond gone.

In this land of atoms, of blood and guts minced through vortices of light, of mountains and rivers, gluons and electrons— there is still enough durable history for there to be maps, newspapers, magazines, encyclopedias; veritable libraries of them, computer disks and digital files. Carbon and silicon replicas. Much more sustained is this record, this chronology, than most dreams.

But only for a time. Only for a time for us. Only for a time for worlds. Only for a time for the whole extraordinary, horrific expanding, contracting phantom of a universe.

It will be crushed and erased, scoured down past its neutrons and bosons, stored in the Akashic Record of something or, if not stored, then needled in some way on the absolutely invisible, inconceivable fiber of All-That-Is, the source parchment of Dreamtime itself.

Yes, our chronicle is being etched in a script tinier than atoms or quarks on a papyrus LP of wave-lengths brighter than light, more subtle than sound. Its "factoids" are engraved in light without photons, runes without meaning, sound that is vibrationless, quanta that exist only on throws of dice that are never thrown.

We are in the Whorl of Whorls, not merely the Milky One but the Big Enchilada, where there are no clocks or wheels, no chronologies or spiraling galaxies, no relativity either. What yet holds us to the urgency of being is the same thing that makes the backdrop utter and indelible, reality real though stitched of nothing at all.

We are corkscrewed into ourselves, compelled into meaning by fabrications, days and nights, wars and their flimsy treaties. History, girl, is such a fine, fine brocade.

Money can't buy any of "you can't take it with you," so this astonishingly, brazenly charming, tragic and unreclaimable place is a grape to be clasped once, profoundly and exquisitely, and yet to be given up in the snap of a wishbone because that is how it happens. Great Gazpacho Ghosts! No warning. No choice. No reprieve.

There is one currency and many coins. There is one language and many dialects. There is one world-view and as many world-views as there are vistas on creation, from whenever, wherever any bug or goose lands. There may be a trillion or more inhabited planets and vibrational nodes in the dazzling chimera of a night sky across which comets and asteroids travel at hellacious speed while standing virtually still in a gravitational suspension so immense and galloping that, by contrast to its motion, all other motion is motionless—gears and motes of atoms inertially spinning while not moving at all.

Or there may be nothing at all up yonder, and we are hypnotized by a gush of light and shadow positing landscapes of extraterrestrial ilk. This downhome microcosm may be the entire Theater of Celestial Alchemy and Astronomy, the rest an affiche of a fake universe. How would we really know, instrumentation freaks that we are?

From the grandstand at the Full Circle Fair in Blue Hill, I watch the denizens hoedown before a stage where performers strum wires and waft horns, as melodies are launched: some cajun, some folk, some country. Children parade and ogle in the mud, slosh about. Young couples undulate mimetically, mirroring each other, as unpartnered women gyrate in place by willowy twists, sinuously unzipping the axes of their existence. Smaller chilluns hold hands in loops or line up, giggle, and spin. A little girl dashes and hops, pirouettes and poses, doing combinations of cheerleading and ballet.

Given bodies, they use them. Given carapaces, they prance. Given liquid, they splash. Given shapes, they vector. Siphoned into male and female worts, they flirt and embrace, even without touching.

And yet it remains tenuous, against a vivid indigo sky whose impalpability of pressure and light is gorgeously stacking up cloudlike shapes.

Why pretend? Why equivocate, either way? There is no other song to sing, no place else to go. The hieroglyphs and urns of other cultures, here or on some Rigelian archipelago or Antarean moon, are mere scratches on the veneer of the Great White Way, which is also black.

We do our stuff with the conviction of converts, the conversion of convicts. Life leaves tracks. The tracks reflect character and hem—the whole fucking morphology of the backdrop—for there would be no anything without it, no pharynxes to babble, digits to tincture glyphs onto vellum or beast-imprinted cave walls circling double-suns. No fulcrum at all.

We are the drop-cloth's alphabet; breathe as it breathes, hope on its behalf as it exudes a vapor that might become utopia or love or some lesser thing, held by its stem to a source.

Write chronicles if you want. Enact histories. Serious, serious, serious. Goof, goof, goof. Either way, all that we can be is it, sweet and sorry, agony and euphoria the same to the abyss as it cries out to us, through us, *as* us, to move in stillness and bring it home, baby.

The Benefits of Shitting in the Woods

1. A natural posture for extrusion is more ergonomic and efficient than a toilet seat. Squatting is a fine yoga for evacuating the contents of the intestines (like squeezing out the emollient from a tube of toothpaste).

2. It always helps to remind yourself you are real, not a statistic, not a commodity or demographic. When excreting waste in the woods, a human is like any other biont, feels some of what they all do—the leverage among digestive tract, low-hanging butt, and exit hole. We unload like a squirrel or mule, crossing species lines and addressing the universe humbly—not reigning from a plastic throne.

Of course, animals-made-of-cells is all we are, creatures whose esophageal and excretory colonies process streams of carbon, nitrogen, and metals, percolating their waste down a living tunnel of peristaltic fingers out an asshole. We cart this heavy stuff around until we can dump it. Even a paramecium sphincters out the by-products of metabolism.

3. It is ridiculous, when there is another viable option, to pollute bowls of clear, purified water with feces and turn it into raw sewage.

4. The smell of dung in the wild is lush and agricultural, sweeter than the same deposits in a bathroom. Public stalls stink—an airport bathroom, for instance, emanates the by-products of international junk food, ammonia, and suppressed anxiety.

Maybe someday airports will provide composting fields or eco-toilets to convert dung into energy.

Pretty much any dump outdoors, no matter how runny or hard, gives off a woodsy vapor. Human mulch is a cousin of hay.

5. Shitting should be a prayer and a meditation rather than an inconvenience or imperative requiring strenuous activity and minor diplomacy. In the woods, shitting provides relief without compulsion or aim: no guilt, no withholding.

6. Turds make a John Cage adagio—a sound of rustling into leaves or plopping onto dirt, not a sterile plunk or tinny splash. Amid ferns and other leaves, they suggest a chipmunk darting. Crows, busy with their own mishigash, call from the surrounding branches.

7. Shitting in the woods does not entail splattering the anus with cold droplets contaminated by other shitters.

8. Poop is warm, an envoy from inside one's body. Shitting outdoors is like taking one's own temperature without glass or quicksilver. On cold days, dung satisfyingly steams.

9. The composition of feces reveals how fast corn, sesame, flax, beets, goji berries, and the like have passed through us. Kernels and seeds remind us that what we drop can be only what we 'et.

10. Shitting in the woods is a kind of cosmic positioning device and forensic laboratory; it makes you aware of where

and what you are, raw and cooked, in both nature and culture, mind and matter—meanings that you forfeit mentally as well as physically in the latrines of civilization. Beyond the anonymity of turds into toilet-bowl abstraction down the drain, each cache is a sculptural object, an Andy Goldsworthy assemblage, to be whittled by nature back to soil.

The after-image of shit breaking down in the woods is fertile, as though you have done something lush rather than merely poisoning a septic system. Poop is delicious and gratifying to *think* as well as to do: your little pile on the ground, still there, cooling, drying, discoloring, decomposing. It came out of you.

11. Shit in the woods with the knowledge that you are taking a load off some sewer system and returning to nature what you borrowed. You are being generous in both a political and an ecological sense. You are engaged in a commission of ecological activism rather than obediently discharging into a grid. In the absence of a composting toilet, composting in the wild is the most generous and poetic choice for all.

12. The leaves of a stripped fern or other weed are smoother and damper than toilet paper, more lubricating to an anus. Those thin rolls of industrial parchment, even when advertised as squeezable and luxuriant, basically unscroll into dry sheets of sandpaper. Of course, leaves present their own problems—they disintegrate, are often too small individually, and can let particles through onto the hands—but these characteristics are organic and close in nature to shit itself.

Yes, leaves come apart, and they may surprise with a pin-like bite, but even the flimsiest apply a dab of herbal cream. And, on cool mornings, they are tallowed with droplets of dew. Toilet paper, by contrast, is a dead, denatured rag.

Note: if your leaf cache crumbles, you can cinch off a rosette of other leaves to wipe your hands and, however neat or sloppy the job, the lingering cumulative smell is not acidically perfumed but gamily botanical.

13. The scenery can be delightful. Accompaniments of beetles and birds in early-morning sun set your day in a tabernacle rather than on a pot.

True, some indoor bathrooms have engaging broadsides, Uncle John readers, psychedelic posters, and the like, but the woods cast three-dimensional holograms everywhere. While you are shitting, you can watch a spider working its construction of fibers on a leaf or rotating on a pinhead, maneuvering its body around invisible hubs. You remind yourself that what you are doing is not materially different from what he is doing; both of you are exuding paste.

That pink caterpillar-worm undulating over the lip of a bark crater, poking into space and then contacting substance as it folds and twists around it, is a perfect visualization, a palpable stimulation for your own acrobatic expulsion.

14. Picture the treasure that you are leaving for untold numbers of ants, mites, and other diverse insects that rush to the bounty. You donate your entire paycheck to them. Perhaps a mouse or fox will also sniff and partake.

You depart with a sense of accomplishment, without false dignity, having fulfilled the forbidden wish Freud diagnosed as "anal retention." In fact, anality (shit attachment and compulsion) is better aired in the wild, where there is juicier stuff for the mind to work on.

You "retain" your product as a palpable marker, an object you can hold in your imagination and whose gradual decay you can modulate in thoughts. It is that kind of retention: a managed deficit of guano instead of mere product hoarding—social justice instead of bathroom capitalism. You practice Stone Age economics rather than adding to industrial consumerism and national debt.

This is the basis of money in shit. Your droppings are prayer bundles and mulch, symbols and coins in the squirrel and bobcat world.

There are some downsides: mosquitoes, thorns, the risk of stepping in your own mess, poisons ivy and oak, inaccessibility of good leaves, chance hazards from an unfamiliar routine, a new genre of stage fright.

Remember: go deep enough into the canopy that neighbors and passers-by can't glimpse you, don't shit near a stream, and don't grab anything sharp or poisonous with which to wipe, and. Despite the honorableness of sylvan shitting, there is a strong taboo against this act and, if witnessed, it may make you a pariah on your road.

I don't espouse a pure conspiracy theory of 9/11; that is, a scenario that would have the U.S. Government, or more properly, rogue elements associated with either Br'er Bush or Cur Cheney (or both) responsible for clandestinely orchestrating the attacks. I might be willing to concede that they knew something about the strikes ahead of time that they are not disclosing and/or that they chose to ignore information chary to their docket—in fact, the converse: ignoring it promoted their agenda.

These two possibilities have developed contrasting acronyms online: LIHOP (Let It Happen on Purpose) and MIHOP (Made It Happen on Purpose).

MIHOP is unlikely for a variety of reasons, not the least of which is that Osama seemed to have sufficient motivation *sui generis*. American troops in Saudi Arabia and Somalia, the interdict of Iraq, and Israeli brutality in the West Bank and Gaza were more than enough agitation. Plus, he has spoken to this matter directly: "This innocence of yours—boasting of the rights of man and freedom while displaying arrogance and indifference for humans outside of America, committing war crimes in Iraq and Afghanistan, waging unjust and unnecessary war in Mesopotamia—is like my innocence for the blood of your sons on the 11th, were I to claim such a thing."*

While LIHOP is plausible, it suggests a different "house of pancakes": the thugs in the Executive branch may not have caused it to happen (by pure treachery), they may not even have let it happen (except by neglect), but they sure were happy when it did.

I find it totally believable that, at some point soon after 9/11, a bunch of these quislings ("morons and lying sacks of shit" in the words of political comedian Bill Maher) caucused behind closed doors—Bush, Cheney, Rumsfeld, Rove, or some combination thereof, perhaps even minus Bush—and praised the Lord. They realized that the implementation of their entire shameless platform had been handed them on a silver platter and they could now run roughshod (Halliburton, Iraq, Patriot Act, extraordinary rendition, black sites, wiretapping, Guantanamo, Iraq reconstruction contracts) without an actionable center-to-left peep. They had been bestowed—hallelujah—a strong, imperial presidency; termless domestic-surveillance and wiretap warrants; marching orders for the Bush family vendetta against Saddam Hussein; an American base in the Middle East; reversal of the New Deal and impoverishment of just about all social

*9/06/07—by the usual means of delivery. This one was substantially untranslated in the West and caricatured only by its last sentence urging Americans to convert to Islam. (See also the Notes for a vehement rebuttal of my argument.)

programs (except those benefiting the defense and pharmaceutical industries); fabulous enrichment of the military-industrial complex and its contractors; transfer of millennial chunks of wealth from the middle to the upper class; photo-ops for Mr. President in military attire, the so-called Commander guy; an almost unimaginable bounty of patriotic sound bites and stump propaganda; and the opportunity to start a new "cold war," one without limits in time or space that could keep the Republicans in office for a generation or more.

Transnational corporations and defense contractors were suddenly rolling big-time over the graves of Dwight Eisenhower, FDR, and TJeff. Political cronies, Republican apparatchiks, environmental scofflaws, and Blackwater mercenaries were guzzling at the public treasury like the Beagle Boys and Al Capone. Compared to that, the loss of life at the World Trade Center and Pentagon was a Tootsie Roll.

These bums also must have deemed that the casualties from a second Iraq war could be written off in a heartbeat: a few clockwork tears, some well-phrased oratorical lamentation and xenophobic hoopla. It's just that they didn't plan on so many dead and such a humiliating performance on the field, though they hardly wept any more despondently for the extra cost in life. Maybe for themselves and the inconvenience to their plan but not for the heroes and dupes who gave their lives for the cause, who took it on faith that the terrorists were over there and it was their patriotic duty to fly halfway across the world for payback and to save the American way from perverts in robes and camel jockeys.

A global war on terror was even proposed in a late '90s document entitled *Rebuilding America's Defenses,* sourced out of a neocon think tank, "Project for a New American Century": "The process of transformation, even if it brings revolutionary change, is likely to be a long one, absent some catastrophic and catalyzing event—like a new Pearl Harbor." Symbolically at least, that is the smoking gun. The real smoking gun will never be found.

Clearly George W wanted to invade Iraq well before 9/11; he badgered his subordinates (it is reported), "Go find me a way to do this!" He said that his patience had run out. Like some amateur actor playing Marlon Brando playing Don Corleone, he used the Spanish ambassador as an errand boy to squeeze other nations, citing the economic and political consequences of opposing Uncle Sam. This fraternity bigshot wanted to be Emperor of the East. It comes across in his pomp and attitude, what he and his cohorts communicate in the subcode of their behavior. At no point, going all the way back to W's ignominious rendition of *The Pet Goat* for Florida school children and his lame, though still admired, attempt to hit a note of Lincolnesque oratory with construction workers in Lower Manhattan, does one feel an appropriate response to 9/11 from this Administration. And Cheney seems like a pig in hog heaven—or more to the point, a mean drunk in a bar full of sissies.

It is hard not to feel that the Bushies are in full gloat mode, savoring every excruciating moment of this, their pretty-boy Caligula talking head with electrified mouth goading the masses into sentimental patriotism. These folks sure don't look or sound like custodians of a national tragedy; they evince no qualities of grief counselors or Churchillian war-time leaders. They seem like scalawags who dig their roles and are trying to shove their heaven-sent or LIHOP political advantage wrapped in the American flag down their opponents' throats. They have to cry to keep from laughing, which is why they are so good at crocodile tears. Nothing the Commander guy says sounds as though he means it—for a good reason: he doesn't. The things he actually means can't be said.

Whether the Bushies conspired to cause 9/11 or simply allowed it by conveniently ignoring the warning signs is hardly the point—their actions come out to about the same: MIHOP all the way. 9/11 was the answer to their prayers. The post-9/11 world is their kind of theater. They know it, and we know it. And no amount of posturing or pretending is going to put Humpty-Dumpty back on that wall.

On Healing*

1.

French anthropologist-priest Pierre Teilhard de Chardin spoke of an inertial power equivalent to gravity, more transmogrifying than any weapon or machine. "Someday, after mastering the winds, the waves, the tides, and gravity," he wrote, "we will harness for God the energies of love. And then, for the second time in the history of the world, humankind will have discovered fire."

An actual force like those of physics, this kind of love cannot be minimized as a mere attitude or mood. It is as core to the evolution of the universe as molecular heat; in fact in its guise as Eros (check Hesiod's *Theogony* for the baseline), it is heat's source, straight from the loins of the gods. Love, not entropy, is the driving engine of creation.

Switch the locus from physics to medicine, and the same invisible engine confronts us among lasers, ultrasounds, magnetic resonance machines, and molecularized drugs: we await their

---

*This piece is adapted from my preface to *Calm Healing* by Robert Newman and Ruth Miller (Berkeley: North Atlantic Books, 2006).

actualized state in consciousness, and it will be something akin to the direct transference of selfless love, e.g. pure radiant energy out of one body into another, a focused drive with the charge of eros but transpersonal and nonlibidinal.

In the early 2000s radical osteopath John Upledger discovered that, when therapists treated sick clients while accompanied by dolphins in ocean-water tanks, these sea "physicians" nuzzled the entry points to lesions and aimed their sonar through blockages, malignancies, or (in Upledger's nomenclature) "energy cysts." They knew how to transmit active, potent love, even though they don't particularly "love" us (and are not cuddly animals in a Fido sense).

The difference between an intuitive, living radiation and a laboratory one betokens the distinction between minded, directed elixirs and unminded, machine strafes. In the former, the prayer and love (and aliveness) of the sender transmit an activated force, even when generated by dolphin "meanings." In the latter, the target is hit, quite hard in fact, but no transference occurs, no synergistic ripple spreads, no internalizing cell-by-cell lotus unfolds; there is only budging the mule with a rope. The mule may move, but not much and not for long.

In a 1972 interview Freudian parapsychologist Jule Eisenbud proposed the negative voodoo or hexing aspect of this same physics: "Thoughts alone can kill; bare naked thoughts; isn't all this armor of war, this machinery, these bombs, aren't they all grotesque exaggerations? We don't even need them. To put it schematically, and simplistically, and almost absurdly, because we don't wish to realize that we can just kill with our minds, we go through this whole enormous play of killing with such—, of overkilling with such overimplementation; it gets greater and greater and greater, as if … it's a caricature of saying: how can I do it with my mind? I need tanks; I need B-52 bombers; I need napalm, and so on, and so on."

Substitute "heal" for "kill" and make the equivalent substitutions throughout this polemic, and you have the First Principle and Axiom of a new model of medicine. In a flourish concluding his colloquy, Eisenbud indirectly honors his mentor: "All science has produced cover stories for the deaths we create; it's streptococci; it's accidents, and so on. But, what I'm trying to say is, there must be, I feel, a relationship between this truth, which we will not see, and this absurd burlesque of aggression that goes on all around us, as if we're trying to deny that the other is possible."

The response from the 'hood in a not entirely capriciously imagined future—that is, after crime clans, drug cartels, and street gangs have graduated into healing societies and shamanic lodges—hopefully is, "Right on, late brother!"

2.

We are now mostly clueless. Throughout the civilized world, human beings allow themselves to be processed by appointment in assembly lines at body-shops as if they were objects, pistons and chassis in need of retrofitting. If our clinics are automotive, by the same metaphor our doctors are engineers; our hospitals, garbage transfer stations.

When the tools for diagnosis and treatment are robots, the individual being treated is also a robot or, more precisely, only the part of a person that is mechanical is being diagnosed and treated.

Overseeing this metaphor is a pantheon of industrial druggists, HMO managers, and insurance-company vultures (and their lobbyists), and there the situation gets even worse—much worse. Patients are tokens in profit-loss equations, as transnational drug pushers conflate the worst of Aldous Huxley's *Brave*

New World (pills conferring lifetimes of artificial health and bliss) with the bleakest of George Orwell's *1984* (an authoritarian state run by royal elites and pharmaceutical-industrial lobbies and their captive politicians).

Once people have been rendered commodities, to themselves and their physician overseers, they lose their innate vitality and its web of meanings. They become corpses, their existential lives nullified—all they are good for is generating capital for beancounters; after that they are one-hundred-and-ten percent expendable.

It is hard enough to cure people when the goal is health but when it is corporate profits, fergeddit. The only good patient is either a disqualified or a deceased one. Everyone else hemorrhages company cash.

The medical system has so turned around since the Reagan era that its main goal now has become not cure but denial of coverage.

This is truly the march of the living dead.

Plus we cannot much longer afford the sort of prosthetic medicine that self-serving bureaucrats now propose for everyone, extending lives of organs and organisms artificially. First and foremost it is not medical treatment from good will or beneficent intention, not at all. The primary agenda of the system is to suck as many of the assets of society as possible into the pharmaceutical coffers and pockets of its shareholders. Its credo is to conflate the illusion of absolute machined health with the chimera of cheating death. By promoting this hoax, Big Pharma has now surpassed its petrochemical rival in gross American dollars—but then they are different departments of the same corporation, the same confidence game and, if left unchecked much longer, will pull the house down on all of us. The cost of Medicare alone will bankrupt the U.S. Government by the middle of this century and leave the nation unable to afford anything except the interest on its national debt.

Transnational pharmaceutical and petrochemical guilds insolently export this pyramid scheme and its accoutrements to the poor in the developing world. Medicine travels in a trademarked CARE package, with Hollywood movies, Monsanto chromosomes, petrochemicals, the American dollar, and neocon propaganda about democracy.

The AMA* monopoly evinces nary a clue of the complex reality of living creatures, trapped as it is in socioeconomic dockets and corporate agendas and schemes too vast and devious for even its denizens to unravel. Like hooded birds, captive docs see only what they are supposed to. Myopically they assume that they *must be* well-intentioned; their way, the only way. In rehearsed Hippocratic sanctimonies they camouflage their greed, even from themselves. The result is a technologized system ruled by reductionist, fundamentalist preachers and hegemonous trade associations defending dogmas funded by drug companies.

Academic medicine is taking away not only our basic health but our hope, our compassion for our own bodies (and those of others), and our destinies as angelic, alchemical beings.

As the drive behind our innate healing capacity is suppressed and usurped, we suffer a spreading epidemic of iatrogenic and agrogenic diseases (pathologies caused by, respectively, physicians and food). While pretending to be educated consumers, we are downing poisons, treating with toxins and heavy metals and radiations. We are renouncing life and going for the death rays in a desperate attempt to cling to our zombiized existence. We no longer want to do the real work, or expect our physicians to do the work, of healing.

---

*American Medical Association, for those who don't know.

3.

Yes, material medicine has earned its spurs; it has achieved cardinal breakthroughs in the biophysical, biochemical, and genetic auspices of life: our *in utero* development, operating system, and the etiology of some (but not all) of our breakdown predispositions and disease loci. Along with this knowledge has come a hyperconcrete, vector-specific delivery system.

Therein lies a paradox, for at the same time, this great medicine machine is failing. It is failing socially because health is not a commodity and cannot be parsed and calculated into therapeutic acts, let alone (as noted above) under the squeeze of profits. It is failing economically because its proposition—the defeat of death by money—is impossible and will bankrupt any nation that attempts it as political sophistry. (Death runs on both sides of our family tree and rarely skips a generation.)

It is failing ethically because it is tied to a criminal insurance maze that has as its primary goal generating profits, patient by sick patient and invoice by invoice, at the price of real medicine.

But, *most significantly,* modern medicine is failing at an ontological level because it is tied to a scientism which premises—nay, demands—that existence is mechanical and molecular in a static, linear way. Even its famously dynamic physiology and microbiology are static and linear, for they leave consciousness and "being" out of their equations. How can you ignore the elephant in the room that is actually squatting on the whole planet?

The problem is that Western medicine AMA-style is *jurisdictionally defined as an enterprise* by keeping all supposedly metaphysical influences out. The term "quackery" snatches in its multi-octopus grasp anything that intimates that 1) mind can influence matter; 2) life is a synergistic process that includes intelligence; or 3) states of being translate into states of health or disease.

Doctors want their patients to be passive and *acted upon* and not to *act* upon their own conditions, even in complementary procedures that are offered alongside the dominant treatment modes. Physicians are aware of the role of lifestyle, diet, emotional states, etc., in health and disease, but even hip ones have predetermined a material context for these and use them, relative to their actual potency, at a level equivalent to—borrowing science's own metaphor—stone tools vis-à-vis cyclotrons. That is, their real efficacy is squandered—or demeaned by timid application.

While science has bravely and shrewdly investigated each and every cellular apparatus and their combined circuitry, that achievement is itself framed by the goal that researchers and physicians pre-set: to reduce life and its functioning to naked material parameters and then to address these in technological, patentable terms. Under this regime a cell must be a monolithic entity into which the vector-specific delivery system is funneled. The items delivered are almost always drugs and surgeries. And both of these have side-effects that dwarf the original "cure" as they radiate throughout nonlinear biological space.

A cell is actually a fluid field through which matter and energy flow and are transmuted beyond ordinary considerations. Each living unit in us is a node oscillating in a field of nodes.

4.

While the materialist paradigm is in ascendance, a new paradigm, both post-modern and ancient, is spreading like wildfire—"Planet Medicine" is what I christened it in 1978. It is based on precepts of shamanic healing and psychic projection, most of them as old, probably, as the original massage, divination, and herbal sodalities of the Palaeolithic epoch—and as multicultural and diverse as *Homo sapiens* itself. These Stone Age guilds and medicine clans were flourishing for tens of thousands of years before Egypt, Greece, and India formalized their precepts. Their pagan offices relied on herbs, pharmacohallucinogens, vibrations, vorticized water, acu-thorns, crystals, curative chants, energized hands and feet, and vision-quests. And if they combatted virulent pathologies with virulent potions, these were homeopathically prepared ones, microdoses of insect and fish venoms or plant and mineral essences, poisons that shed their toxicity while transmitting vitalized data in potentiated molecules that transduce crude substance into pure energy.

Their hermetic legacy includes archetypal processes we have inherited subconsciously: totemic projection, symbolic abreaction, sympathetic magic; yoga, chi gung, organ palpation, visualization, disease narrative, sand-painting, and shamanic botany.

"Planet Medicine" also caches a potpourri of simple but dynamic techniques for actuating cures: brushing, tapping, blowing, conscious breathing, Kirlian touch, modulated sound, drumming, hot springs, ice caves. Each of these praxes, if performed correctly, has unknown psychosomatic and mitochondrial/enzymatic effects, both inside cells and across extracellular matrices.

"Planet Medicine" may be ancient and primitive in its industrial technology, but it is post-modern in its application of scientific principles to meditation, prayer, and faith healing (all nonsectarian, of course); placebo effects; and psi (including telekinesis, telepathy, and transmutational conversion).

"Planet Medicine" is post-modern in another sense: the provisional paradigms more or less holding together math-physics' meta-model of relativity theory, quantum mechanics, superstrings, and dark matter provide a better paragon for understanding what is happening in organisms than traditional rubrics of Newtonian thermodynamics and Solidist anatomy.

Body-minds were never clarified physical objects. They are clairvoyant charismatic embryologies nested in non-Euclidean fields, encompassing chakras and meridians and dozens of other elusive, unnamed pulses with their own psychophysical control centers and homunculi.

The new paradigm also circumscribes a wide range of recently developed (or reconfigured) paraphysical and vitalist modalities such as *Reiki*, Bach Flower remedies and Australian bush essences, homeopathy, polarity, biofeedback, and cranial osteopathy. These systems mostly rely on homeostatic and nanopharmacological principles.

Craniosacral therapy (CST), a modern phase of cranial osteopathy, is a way of tapping into the body's many layers and matrices, using educated hands to sense and adjust subtle pressures of fluids and tensions of fascia and viscera, revitalizing organs and restoring underlying rhythms toward their natural states. Osteopathic medicine, the field out of which CST matriculated, is a legacy of the pre-technological epoch when palpating tissues was the primary scientific mode of investigating and treating health and disease; yet CST is equally the forerunner of a kind of meta-technological science of healing that parallels quantum physics in its capacity to weigh virtually imperceptible cellular vectors, use mindedness and breath to track and influence tissue systems and metabolic processes, and translate probabilistic and hypothetical events into real ones. It is a modality that entertains paradoxical, even contradictory, possibilities at the same time.

CST is also a full-fledged paraphysical art using light but intentional touch to transduce mind, matter, and energy back and forth into one another. I think of it as a fusion of a mild, noninvasive surgery—more delicate than any massage—with a wordless psychoanalysis whereby palpation releases cysts of trapped emotional and somatic energy.

Nonmaterial medicine is not a rival to material medicine, even at this contested moment. It is truly its lost partner. Matter can't always be influenced or transmuted by mind or vital essence, so drugs and scalpels are necessary too. But, in the long run, taking economics, ecology, and societal well-being into parity, we will do far better to forego technological medicine than we will to ignore these diverse syncretic modalities along the mind-body interface. Quantum practices, not "Bones" McCoy's hand-held doctoring device in *Star Trek*, are our most hopeful tools for a future medicine—after the melting of the glaciers and the decline of global petroleum civilization, when the Earth will likely experience a reinvestiture of regional and local healers and eclectic medicinal traditions.

Material preemption or intervention is always—*always*—an option, and the manual for it, now that it has been written and refined, will probably be locked into the human enterprise in one form or another for its duration. The art of healing, however, is more fundamental; it is our birthright and, for the long haul—again, the haul past the age of petroleum and climate change—it has the greater potential for healing not only people but people in environments, environments themselves, and trans-species, e.g. whole ecosystems. In a sense we barely begin to understand, it even has the capacity to leap every imaginable demarcation and heal whole galaxies. That is, acts of sincere healing bring man and woman into synchronicity with consciousness itself and the singularity of the universe.

The only alternative to becoming no one and nothing, a prisoner of arrogant and despotic cabals, is to become someone and something, an incipient Jedi knight, a magician able to heal not only himself or herself but others, someone able to change the course of civilization.

5.

In whatever direction our species matriculates from here, if men and women are to benefit from centuries of scientific knowledge and technological development without, as a by-product, becoming trapped in a cybernetic gulag subjugated by imaging devices and oracles of genetic determinism, without—in short—being buried by their own implements, they must begin to understand that they are warriors: their bodies are their own, their health is their own, and they are their own best physicians.

We must break autocratic medical authority and its biophysical algorithms and learn anew to self-heal and heal one another. Healing is neither a commodity to be auctioned nor a profession to be franchised; it is an *apanage* and an obligation.

As long as we profess and practice ignorance about our own creature manifestation and do not develop our energetic potentialities, we forfeit the crux of our astonishing existence. We play possum while the universe is calling for us to wake up and fly.

Yes, we know implicitly how to heal; karmically how to use disease, even the most debilitating pathology, for personal and spiritual transformation. We know how to turn self-curative capacity into active therapeutic symbols and medicinal acts. As cosmic power stations, we know how to transmit hologrammatic energy, We are self-organizing entities and damn good ones, not to be trifled with.

Without any help we unfurled from a mere bean, cultivating a helpless zygote into a multi-layered hologram. Without formal education we made all our own tissues and set our molecular-reaction cycles and differential equations of metabolism going; we assembled minded organs from a single cell.

We still do that kind of stuff. Through the blind commitment that got us made and birthed in the first place, we keep our machinery running and, when necessary, repair it ulteriorly. In invisible sessions, keeping no office hours, twenty-four hours every day, even while the outer brain is asleep, our inner physician applies the same magic by which it once upon a time convoked and autocatalyzed cells into tissue congeries and interdependent organ networks.

Do you really think that Golgi bodies and fasciae could keep from running amok and crashing under entropy without a Big-Minded embryogenic intelligence pouring like a dream through body-mind at every instant? Something is working us, playing us, emanating us, something profound and invisible and unconscious and pagan, something that had to be here, inside, for us to be here.

We must get down with ourselves anew and honor the radical ceremony of our lives.

6.

A true "healing" model proposes, among other things, that mind is neither a mere epiphenomenon nor a feeble hostage of body; it is the necessary and absolute activator of the embryological process by which a body-mind overrides entropy and propagates itself into Boolean space.

The original healing modality is Big Mind—a configuration-space of phase transitions expressing the core gene-cell-cosmos function and generating a biosphere of coevolving hypercubes cascading epigenetically.

Mere thought can be the most powerful medicine of all, for mindedness and cellularity are different octaves of the same original state, vibrations of the same wave form.

Big Mind is always present as an activating force in organismic state change (transpersonal intelligence as opposed to the mere monkey chatter of gossip mind). Big Mind is as much a fact of nature as water or *roches moutonnées*, those immense glacial boulders on the tundra of little mind. Big Mind is the source of Big Medicine and the Archetypal Medicine Man.

The hex that stands against Big Medicine is modernity's tunnel-vision genetic determinism—the belief (and despair) that we are no more than elaborate, flawed carbon-chain machineries, malfunctioning cyborgs barely able to repair a few instrumentally prescribed vectors. This is the Law, and all creatures, from lab mice to King Doctors, must bow to its jurisdiction.

But it is neither the cosmic law nor the law of our hearts. It is not the law on all planets or in all dimensions of the universe.

The notion that mind over matter is, by definition, futile "wishful thinking," is a ludicrous misjudgment and underestimation of the paraphysics of thought. Disease is first an idea, a mote in Big Mind, embryogenic mind, the unconscious body-mind hologram.

An individual's health crisis is virtually always aggravated—and often initiated as well—by wishing *too little*, by shutting off the force of invocation, of prayer, of hope, of joy, of vibration, of intention—sabotaging them through faint-hearted desire.

No, a mere wishy-washy wish is not going to cure or dislodge serious disease. Sorry, preacher man. It is only the kind of dynamic wish that a shaman or faith-healer trains to conduct which zaps and mutates disease with the accuracy and impact of a laser beam, e.g. the atomized force of a sun-star or focused sea mammal. The science of this mode of projection lies somewhere in the unprobed zone among traditionary magic, telekinesis, and chaos/complexity dynamics. Biblically it entails the delivery of prayers by the Christ entity: restoring sight to the blind, enabling the lame to stand, and reviving the corpse of Lazarus. These were (and are) acts of spontaneous transubstantiation.

Quantum touch and tantra infuse the narrative of Jesus of Nazareth, though most modern Bible-goers glide through the Scriptures without getting it.

Through observation, through metonymy, through inculcation in his/her being in (sometimes) fifty thousand or more disciplined repetitions,* a shaman concentrates, packages, and delivers a wish. He literally transfers it, in a manner Freud rediscovered in a Western context as the therapeutic art of psycho-induction. A true medicine man or woman accomplishes this transference probably instantaneously, if not (mirabile dictu!) at a speed even greater than light in a measurable sense—or, more accurately, in a mode that has nothing to do with either speed or chronology.

When the Everly Brothers sang, "Only trouble is, gee whiz, I'm dreaming my life away," they were serenading the troubadours of

---

*Not all healing modes are this active, of course, only those that gain power from sincere repetition. The rationale is this: a magician/martial artist who knows what it feels like to be in the ring with a dangerous opponent will not get stage fright and tremble at the presence of spirits or equivocate at the moment of truth. She will have learned her movements so profoundly that she will just do them, no matter the opponent, no matter the fog of cynicism all about her.

passive dreaming, of unrequitable longing, of lukewarm prayer.*
There is another kind of dreaming, active and lucid—active, lucid praying; active, lucid visualizing; active, lucid transference. Activated wishing is to dream one's life back, not away. It is the way that planets were "dreamed" into being by Big Mind.

We need to wish more sincerely, more sustainedly, with more specificity and on a more discrete trajectory. We need to subtilize and entrain our mindedness so that it can tune to the mirror zone of lysosomes and Golgi functions—what Upledger calls "cell talk" and matrilineal therapists Bonnie Bainbridge Cohen and Emilie Conrad execute in the form of internalized choreographies that, at least symbolically, intercept the signaling of tissues and organs down to their organelles and extracellular matrix. It is Big Mind talking through language mind to mitochondrial mind.

If you find it an absurd exaggeration to imagine refining your meditation to the point that you locate, address, and interest individual busy cells and their components, remember that all you are is a river of cells and organelles, millions upon millions of energetic centers flowing together in matrices to make up tendons, muscles, organs, blood, neurons, mind and ego, etc., all/each living, moving, effusing and diffusing mind.

You are a confederation of zoans melding into brobdingnagian apes. There is nothing and no one else.

---

*See Carl Dreyer's 1955 film *Ordet* (*The Word*) for the epitome: After the futile praying of sanctimonious and feuding bible-thumpers, Johannes, the mad brother, though seemingly cured of his "delusion" that he is Christ, demonstrates the real puissance of prayer (and the Word) by summoning his recently deceased sister-in-law from her open coffin back to life. I will go on record as calling it the single most unexpected and stunning moment in the history of cinema.

Maybe real Cell Talk can't happen, but what a waste it would be not to explore the possibility and see what all—and even what else—you might come up with.

Even a million repetitions will accomplish nothing without concomitant internalization, which means gradually cultivated and deepened awareness. Otherwise, the most devout multi-thousandth repetition is no more than slavish service to an idea.

Activated prayer triggers a quantum cell-repair element in the sense of both uncertainty principle and the quantum leap that can, in a moment of pure, intentional faith, go straight to the illumined meaning of one (or every) thing.

But don't be fooled that there is some sort of miracle balm accessible on demand. Healing is work. Pacifying and conducting consciousness takes focused yoga and committed attention/intention. It cannot happen idly or because we are nice people.

It is not a matter of a wish; it is a matter of the subtle, subcellular vibration set in motion *by the wish* and manifesting through its mantra or maintained unconsciously by a gifted inner physician. That's what carries the meanings of Big Mind through Shaman Mind into Cell Talk.

The most ethical and sustainable choice now, the only real choice, is for people to begin to learn how to take responsibility for their own well-being—in short, their body-minds and lives—to reclaim their inborn capacities for transduction and transubstantiation, for cell internalization and teleportation. It sounds ridiculous. It *is* ridiculous. It is also verifiably, as demonstrated by double-blind tests *ad nauseam*, impossible. But we are not being asked to explain it. We don't have to believe it. And we certainly don't have to satisfy the experimenters and skeptics. We just have to *do it*—just like we did it in order to get made in the first place from pond scum.

7.

Consider for a moment a planet, a United Nations, that permitted and nurtured love bombers instead of breeding death and suicide bombers; in which al-Qaeda, the base, trained guerrillas of therapeutic transformation who immolated disease-causing cysts of all kinds. I mean, ultimately, a planet at peace from the bottom up and the core out, wherein sea squirts and roundworms secrete medicine for other creatures, an Earth across ecozones of which dolphins and bears teach healing rather than predation, in whose skies and fields hawks and mice exchange mantras as well as DNA. This could be Gaia in a million or so years, once we get out of the second Stone Age, once we break into Big Mind and part the illusory veil of difference and mortality.

It was never in the cards for us Earthlings to transform nature by intellectual fiat or political correctness or to deliver a truce to the oldest primeval combat, but instead it was possible long ago (and still is) to mutate nature totemically in men and women clad as warrior beasts, accoutered for curing in the guise of killing. The death stroke has to be dealt, almost to the point of death, before it becomes the trident of life.

It was always in the cards for lions and coyotes, for bad guys and witches to do good by bad—to transmute karma, even at the kill. This is sort of why the word "bad" now marks a conjunction of "good" and "bad," at which, alone, "good" has any gumption.

Words must change meaning in times of high danger (or sophistry) in order to regain their primal power. "Sick" likewise means "wonderful"; "far out"; "right on, surfer dudes." Disease is an opportunity for change, for enhanced immunity and gurgitation of internal medicines tailored to our systems and situations, transmittable through intention.

Trauma is also sacred, a tool of soul redemption.

As the chi gung master/reggae priest is wont to chant, in these words or others, *"I'm gonna put on an Iron Shirt/and chase Satan off o' Eart'."*

Of course, mullahs and terrorists aver that is the very deed they are enacting on the cancer of the blasphemous crusader West: they are incinerating its tumor off the Earth. If you could hear the voice from the purity of their hearts, it attests that they are no longer able to be our friends or physicians, to act like altruistic herbs or needles because our malignancy is so bad it requires chemo. They must be fierce Bear doctors in order to excise and cure.

But murder is not the way. That will become clear for reasons having nothing to do initially with altruism or mercy. Whenever implacable machineries or chemical explosives are employed in place of minded subtlety and compassion, only tragic things happen, only dread diseases result, and those diseases escalate into worse and more globalizing plagues. You can't bludgeon or blast your way into paradise; you can't bribe the gods or force their hand.

8.

This brings us to a Second Therapeutic Principle of Healing: Whatever a healer, or the person acting wittingly or unwittingly as a healer, carries in his or her energy field—his propensity to his own illness, also his vitality—is transmitted in some fashion to the patient and back insofar as patient and healer occupy and jointly activate the same "mutually containing field." I am drawing on the words and concepts of the late Edward Whitmont, a Jungian analyst who also practiced homeopathy.

Universalizing the language of homeopathy, Whitmont postulated that the symbolic awareness of the healer (or destroyer) potentizes his or her "disease" (that is, its healing potential) and transmits the medicine of his being, his divine wound to the patient. He either enhances the power of a sick organism to reorganize through the opportunity of its disease, to grow beyond its transient symptomology, or, when s/he is an incompetent or hexing doc, further undermines the patient and deadens both organisms' synergistic potentiation, the physician's as well as the patient's.

This is why the life experience, emotional depth, healed wounds, and active traumas of the doctor play a crucial role in treatment. An allopathic doctor who is simply a superb technician may lack a spiritual quality necessary for true healing. Because this is a material world, his exterior skills succeed at the level of overt disease manifestation; he even projects unconscious clarity or karmic energy into the pathological crux. But, all other things considered equal, one is better off being treated by a physician who has been burnished by disease, who has internalized capacities of empathy and transmutation.

A shaman or doctor, even a terrorist or suicide bomber, stands in a role (again, wittingly or unwittingly) that requires him/her to become either a further ratification of pathology (by overmaterialized beliefs and treatments) or a homeopathic simillimum, a vitalization of the disease through subtle energy, the succussion of substance into information, and a reinstatement of the original morphogenic capacity of the life field. That is why healing can change not only sick people but history itself.

9.

This Second Therapeutic Principle leads to a Third: the universe—all the star-ridden, quasar-ringed, black-hole way to its limitless limits in this dimension, beyond even the furthermost telescopically, radiationally magnifiable galaxies—is a field of life energies. These are available and assimilable.

While we clearly arise in a maelstrom of bleak supernovas and runaway asteroids and comet seeds—exploding stars, superhydrogen bombs, colossal colliding rocks, entropy-entropy-entropy—we also are receptors of a very high and esoteric octave of energy. Beyond the random violence and debris of astrophysical space are sacred, *prana*-packed, *chakra*-channel traceries and bodies. We emerged from the swamp, true enough, but as simultaneously Darwinian and theosophical beings.

These two versions of the cosmos defy and contradict each other, but they also meld into the single domain in which we reside. In us physical and vital universes, macrocosm and microcosm ravel and converge. Sacred geography becomes sacred anatomy. Just because toxic radiations eruct from stellar objects, just because humungous, out-of-control mass predominates everywhere does not mean that healing energies, alchemical mutations, *chi* puffs, astral waves, and orgone do not also exist everywhere too, at a subtler and ultimately more profound level.

Picture a great moebius network of spirals spewing out through a spout, much like that of a ciliated microorganism, into the physical universe. An externalized domain explodes from the fat end of the conduit like a flood from a fire-hydrant spigot. At its tail, the spiral quoils down into the finest, most gossamer thread, which winnows below the realm of atoms, quarks, and superstrings, into dimensions of pure energy as well as something even purer than energy. Outside what we can perceive is just about everything—just about everything we are.

Outside our ordinary senses, beyond our dominant view of quasi-stellar space, we are already in another universe, another illumination, an outsider thermodynamics that, unlikely as this sounds, dwarfs the perceptible one by a factor of more than ten billion to one. In fact, matter is the flea that mind is scratching into existence.

It is from this transdimensional universe that the élan of *Reiki*, faith-healing, microdoses, prayer, shamanic invocations, and billions of other practices across the diverse worlds of the universe is summoned—the great common vat.

The difference between the exoteric energy pool circumscribed by scientists (thus far) for their various fleets and Star Wars, and the diaphanous energy field activated by healers and lamas is that the latter is not explicit or gross; it cannot be accessed by brute force or tyranny; it is cultivated, siphoned, and decanted only by meticulously disciplined techniques. Subtle energy is inaccessible, thank goodness, to the galaxies' soldiers and industrialists, as these would surely, if they could, harness it to the ends of subjugation of sentient beings, making the history of life the history of slavery. The real, enduring energy of creation is protected by a password, a code that can never be faked because it must be lived, is never merely provided, cannot be blackmailed or bluffed, yet is always available through the grace and sincerity of intentional practices. It is alchemized inside creatures, not factories.

Its fruition is the key to life on Earth, what ancient wisdom told us this planet is about: working through consciousness to change the universe and do the work of God in the house of woman and man.

I tend to go on quests. I have searched for embryonic beginnings … for the first living cell … the first human … my real father … where the dead go … for the beginnings of the universe. That impulse in me likely has a karmic origin, a beginning in itself that reflects a mission beyond all quests, a quest that is not even really a quest. Without knowing why, I act. Along the way I concoct excuses, invent cover stories, as if the goal of my curiosity were rooted anew in each puzzle, each lost person.

A cryptogram becomes its own mystery and, though none in the end get to the bottom of the real cipher, it would be far worse not to have their provisional solutions.

Your reply: "I have been deeply touched at some level by your search for me and that you saw something in what I had written back at a time, forty-two years ago, when I was so defended and out of touch with myself. It seems to me like a *terma* (how the Tibetans planted certain teachings to be found at a specific time when they would be needed). You have brought something to me that I needed right now in my process. I have been experiencing a kind of deadness of desire, no passion to do anything. Since feeling searched for, sought out, wanted, a happy, excited child-like part has shown up and the deadness is gone."

I invent roles because I do not understand the role I actually play.

Our science bespeaks an ontology in which it is assumed that the ultimate nature of things is quantitative. It is quite as if material reality were made up of symbols for which numerical quantities were the meanings. Science searches for the concepts to which numbers might be attached; scientists do this quite universally. It is decided in advance what things really are and—guess what?—they are the quantities attributed to appropriate general concepts for which things themselves, in their empirical appearances, are the superficies.

We have fallen into a trap set by language, and symbol—eidos—having created facsimiles to be inhabited only by aliases. The age of this sort of literalist science requires chewing off our own paws. In fact, we are well on our way to gnawing through our entire body. Its mandate presumes, idly as well as compulsively, that the point of existence is to dissect, to take apart and get to the bottom of things. To solve the crime and convict God.

From the hustle-bustle of DNA to the silent screeching of electrons to purrs of radiations of diverse, mystifying sources, we have arrived at a planet-wide sound and fury signifying only itself. Born into it, we die penniless, without suspecting a façade. The actual source is undiagnosed, the sphinx unfathomed.

Particle physics is the ultimate riddle-solving operation, sailing a ship right up to the void where matter itself dissipates, where the molecular sea drops off the edge of the Flat Earth, also known as three dimensions.

Scientists scoop down beneath atomic and subatomic levels, exhuming charges and space only, for substance has no base or bottom. It is position and vibration alone. The interior of an atom, in truth, looks more like a Sufi dance or a Navaho sandpainting than the contents of a pried sardine can. Where quantum physics meets sacred geometry, stuff is another form of emptiness. Physicists don't find anything because *there is nothing there*, only a turn in the road, beyond the stipe or navel holding matter to this dimension. Where particles bind the trance-state of existence, our Dreaming attaches to the source of all Dreams.

I have written elsewhere that the universe is infinitely dense and infinitely transparent—so, no matter how digitally and otherwise sophisticated the instrumentation becomes, hypothetically tens of thousands of years from now, physicists will find more (or less) stuff, and it will still only get thinner and thinner until there is nothing to measure even with the ultra-refined nanoscopes of the future. Yet it will not disappear entirely because the kernel inside all substance has neither a temporal nor a linear nor even a quantum relation to our locale. Whether its fragmentation nanoizes forever, leading to kernels inside of kernels, or merely baffles onlookers in other circles, the consequence is the convergence of density and transparency, its own infernal riddle.

Physics is just measurements anyway; the more refined the device, the more profound the provisional explanation—yet also the more quixotic the so-called law.

In late 1971 I wrote:

We weep for the cities of Antares as we do for the Minoans. We weep for our own loss, that we were there, and now we are here, and the next still on the bobbin, and the treadle still on the great interregnum sea. We weep for how deep in our own body we feel it is we know. Not what we want. Nor what we desire. It's what we know. What we know we know. To set it square, right; to come out of this undiminished.

My work since has been an attempt to explicate this passage.

Lying on my back on rocks in the cove at Hunter's Beach, my eyes shut, I hear the hiss of streamlets filtered through stony eggs of the seawall. Ah, it is the anthem of the primeval brook playing a full calliope of stones, rubbing on the untuned rocks of the nonlinear universe, grinding out a vast and mysterious music as it delivers runoff into the sea. Clackamores, aquaggaswacks, rainsticks, Nuna whistles, and udus tune themselves into a giant nonlocalized player piano whose scroll is Hunter's Brook. Chimes, theremins, kotos, and marimbas can also be heard; in fact any sound can be discerned if one listens carefully enough. White noise, like white light, bears all components within it.

As though from a different orchestra the ocean crashes, thunder of a billion nonlocal drums, a din as soft as a feather. As they lay their boundaryless symphony on the cove, the two concerts are connected by the gap that connects them in an accidental spin network.

I smell seaweed of tidal rocks, a draught of the hydrogen nectar of the Third Planet.

Using rocks as a mattress is not as miserable as one might think, for the body's soft tissues and vertebrae slide into available spaces and rest in axial repose. It is a massage and a yoga. In fact in the comics of my childhood, yogis and fakirs reclined on beds of nails and, the point was, they were perfectly comfortable—flamboyantly unperturbed.

It takes decades of conscious breathing to shift from such antics to an actual yoga of being.

Hiking above the cove, I come upon a stand of red and white pines. The sounds and recesses here are mostly breezes through branches and leaves—the rough, irregular oboe of complexity theory. Tree rolls are accompanied by sharp yawps of crows, an impulse to language as exigent as our own, though bounded by anatomy (the shape of their esophagus and the proportions and pitch of their lungs), not to mention the standing capacity of their brains. Each crow is unleashing unhewn alphabets into the sky, their letters never coalescing into noun- or even verb-ness.

Bird organs cannot sculpt or fashion explicit meanings, so they cast the source of all ontology. They clamor and cry, they intend. They intend everything—everything that we will ever say, everything that we will never say. They express the awakening of matter, its urgency upon discovering that it is embodied. They call to the heavens to feed them because they are hungry—in fact hungrier than all others.* They mean meaning itself.

And this is how organs evolve in nature and begin to announce their plight—and joy. This is where psyche and civilization originate among feathers, where molecules find letters in beaks.

Congresses of such cells, gulls and crows and seals *et al.*, squawk—Little Tommy Tucker, ever wanting supper.

The songs of the extinct forerunners of crows, Palaeozoic corvids and jackdaws of the Iron Age, are what we seek in our discourses and chants, in all Indo, Tibeto, and Uto dialects, in the wit and ungrammatical nuances that spawn new meanings, as one symphonic melody morphs into another and another, one rule of verb endings or pitch of vowels mysteriously shifts governance and tone. It is all random, and it is anything but random, and it will never find what it is looking for, but it will always look and get tantalizingly close, as a theme or a rhyme brings back a hint of what the crows were calling for on an August day in 2006, and on August days before and to come.

This is but a moment in the history of the universe.

No, this is but a moment in the history of the universe.

---

*An echo out of an old poem by Robert Kelly: *"because I am alive & make noise/because I can crack the cheap bowl of your sky with my shriek/because I care/because I am hungry/& cry louder than any other."*

Sometimes the cry of a wild animal will tell you everything you know and can't know, everything you want to know and don't want to know, about the vast and recondite universe we share.

In its proximity to language, it is a companion in exile, a solace, a clue to the origin of our own proud intellect.

In its remoteness from language, it is an omen of the perilous and lonely place we both come from, the primordial beast we yet are, the dark trail we each are traveling and have yet to travel, the ever-present threat of feral attack.

In its yelp of pure emotion and instinct, it speaks to its affines, the atavistic and non-human polyps throughout our body: the lizards and seals and jellyfish we harbor who do our breathing and digesting.

In its desperation and powerlessness to mediate its thoughts in symbols, it is a bellwether of how adrift we really are.

When Osama bin Laden and Sayed Hasan Nasrallah say that their forces will prevail because "You love life, while we love death," it takes on its real meaning only when we understand that the converse is also true.

I shouldn't have to elucidate, but I will if you care to hear it: The jihadists believe in a living radiance that is beyond life and death—and they do not consider the walking death of industrial capitalism life at all. They do not want to be bionic consumers or TGIF party-goers or upwardly mobile yup-yups. They spit on the lottery and give back the prize.

People who kneel, who heed the call of Mecca, may have their own shibboleths—rigid patriarchies, glory in brutality, ritual bullying, and stoning and slaughter of women under Sharia Law not the least of them—but clinging to lives of vapid luxury or indulgent fripperies is not their particular albatross.

I think often about my brother's suicide. How could I not? I will think about it for the rest of my life and possibly longer. I was already dreaming about it forty years before it happened. I would awake in the morning, amazed that Jon was still here. Not only had he died in my dream, but he had been dead so long that, when I traveled back to childhood, he wasn't there. He was a phantom of someone who might have been. I would find myself in the aftermath of some cataclysm that no one would discuss.

Was that because this was not the first time? (I won't try to guess the options on that one.)

He was never quite real, never of this world age, more like a figure from centuries ago, a bard of the *chanson de geste* in ninth-century France, a Civil War Rhode Islander, crossing Kansas Territory, matted hair and wild beard, plinking melodies on a beat-up lute. Now he seems a wraith of those things as well as the Manhattan kid, the handsome young Elvis and Mickey Mantle.

My younger brother—that is, my half-brother, Jonathan Towers—was born four years after me in 1948. He shared a room with me during my childhood and adolescence. I knew his sour, sweaty presence so well, his tuborous smell; I grappled for eons against his all-too-familiar rubbery body. Day by measureless day I watched him grow from a cross, smarmy child into a tennis star and class president into a wild hippie into a haunted preacher. A rowdy provocateur and street brawler in grade school, he became an honor student and star athlete, the varsity quarterback in junior high, then captain of the track team at Horace Mann.

During high school he also made his first forays into Harlem and the Village, to listen to music. In college (Madison, Wisconsin) he became an unrepentant stoner; a shaman without portfolio; later, a warrior without an army, cause, or code; an Indian without a tribe or Injun blood; a mental patient—the ultimate Seventies radical, though we called it the Sixties. His icon was Van Morrison, not Dylan, never the Dead. The lyric with which he identified most was *"Brandy, you're a fine girl … ."* He lived the vision-quest, in Wisconsin and Colorado, in New York's Central and Van Cortlandt Parks (where he once played ball and ran track), and (ultimately) suburban Connecticut.

I kept up an intimate if infrequent commerce with him during our adult lives, as he settled into vagabond status, a nomad without a job or family. At the end he was a lonely guy with a room in a run-down house off the Old Post Road, street poet of Westport, known locally as "The Walking Man" because he loped through town and over fields all day, from the marshes to the libraries to Chinese restaurants where he greeted the proprietors and over-praised the food, cruisin', driven by anxiety and myth. A committed Luddite, he used a manual typewriter and refused to take a bus or get in a car. On principle he avoided television and movies and spent days making alchemical collages and tarot cards and researching obscure pastoral and frontier histories like the Western writings of Ernest James Haycox. He spurned the internal combustion engine. He held up a hand to block the exhaust of each passing vehicle, making a spectacle of himself as he peered and bolted ahead.

He lived just past fifty-seven.

In May of 2005 he stabbed himself in the neck and abdomen multiple times (according to the official report), not an easy thing to do. It probably took more than courage or desperation; it took being partly dead already.

I talked to him on his next-to-last day. He had water in his ear and was so frantic to get it out that he wouldn't discuss anything else. I told him to lie down and breathe—it was the last thing I said to him and in retrospect it seems rather cavalier of me. I was in a car on a cell phone, crossing the Bay Bridge to San Francisco, while he was standing in a boarding house in Westport, Connecticut.

It was often a knife with Jon. In the early '70s outside Boulder, Colorado, he practiced stiletto warfare with Mexican kids whom he was supposed to be tutoring in English. He held a switch-blade to our mother's face when she confronted him during one of his college-dropout escapades. Then a few years later he waved it grandiosely at Lindy and me in barely contained fury and self-aggrandizement (Cape Elizabeth, Maine), before I called a neighbor. Several incidents later he was consigned to Sheppard Pratt in Towson, Maryland (1973). There he had his mind reamed by almost two years of stelazine and thorazine.

There is always rage in suicide. Violence against self, with a shift of attention, can latch onto someone else. Jon could have turned on me in my last visit to him in Westport (2003) when he got agitated and took on attitude, though I doubt he would have—*could have* maybe, but not *would have*. He wanted to prove to me that he was a man of the people, a revolutionary poet and warrior, that I was a pompous fraud. "You write well, that's all," he said, "but I'm a real man." The more he boasted, the more aggravated and menacing he seemed to have to become. He meant to terrify me. He enjoyed seeing me afraid of him. He thought his bravado could triumph over the family lesion.

I never visited him again after that and, when he begged me to come east to rescue him just before the end, I admitted, "I'm scared of you."

"*I'm* scared of me": his response.

For a long time he had considered jumping off the bridge into the Saugatuck, he confessed a week earlier, but didn't because the water below looked too dark (a compelling statement on the link between life and death). A blade was less spooky; it also allowed a Viking departure: warrior pose (more or less), sword in hand, dancing at the edge of his fragile audacity on a tether of magic. Committing *hara-kiri*, he exited defiantly, honor intact.

Insofar as I was even in his mind at that moment, I believe his stabs were meant not in fury against me but to impress me with the direness and inconsolability of his situation, the reserve of bravery he could still call upon in Apache moments—rash and urgent flails maybe, but not displaced enmity. It was desperation, unwillingness to face one more sleepless night. He couldn't shit or sleep, and he wandered under the moon like a banshee.

He didn't want to endure chirps serenading another drear and ridiculous day. There were too many eager birds; the world's foliage too thick, the sun more insistently "rise and shine" than he could bear. He refused the summons "to be." Life had lasted too long and none of it, he now realized, was going to stop, or speak to him. He had been abandoned; he was lost beyond salvation. (I know these things because he reported them, night after night in chilling detail, phoning me in both our AM hours. It was the first time he had allowed himself to use the long-range technology in decades.)

He probably dared his hands, breath by terrified breath, to aim the dagger and impose its terrible cuts, the abstraction of pain—a determined mind grasping a sharp object and slashing at its own belly and throat like someone fighting off an armed intruder. He was trying to excise and oblate the terror. He was finally taking existence apart, cutting open his overblown manikin of flesh and then blood, breaking the pact of the living and going right to the shit.

The ferocity of this piece is many things, but it is mostly at attempt to reclaim Jonathan's alive presence, not to let him die unmourned and unseen, trivialized or merely pitied. He *was* a street-fighter, a minstrel till the end. I cannot let him become a victim or a phantom, before I have proclaimed his incredible existence, his capacity for suffering and exaltation, his sacred madness, his betrayal of me and mine of him. I cannot let him go till I have found him. I have to get as close to his fury as I can, to embrace him once and then release him for good.

My apologies, Jon, for fearing you; for telling your secrets now that it is too late; for waiting till you were dead to publish your poems. I couldn't see them when you were alive; you were so vivid and distracting, such a truculent presence. Only your passing revealed them for the incredible documents they are. You were right; I was wrong. I hope you know that now, know that I know. I hope you somehow can see your book with the words of praise that Robert Kelly, Cecil Brown, Charles Stein, and Tek Young Lin provided on your behalf. They acclaimed you a poet in their company. Take that with you and never forget it. Sorry again for being late.

My apologies too to our sister and your cousins. My truth is not a pleasant one, but I intend no ill will. Writing is ruthless and prophetic, and if I still its oracle, I lose its prerogative. It is not a civilized or gallant voice, but it speaks without compromise or doesn't speak at all.

As far back as in grade school Jon dared himself to challenge bullies in the schoolyard. He issued foolhardy gauntlets and had to back them up before a loyal mob behind the auditorium. He fought on when defeated and bloody. He would never relent or surrender, even as his friends shouted for him to give up.

He would pound at ghosts in the middle of the night in our room, breathing heavily, dancing like a boxer, punching away at forms invisible. He had that much passion, that deep a rage.

Or maybe *he* was the bully. In the space we shared I felt as though I was under the regime of a humorless proconsul. Oh, we played our child games and had our monkeyshines, but at the same time he was judging me, manipulating me, taunting me, bumping into me on purpose. Eventually our smolder would boil over into scuffling and swinging. We pummeled each other; we stabbed heedlessly with scissors and metal toys. Then for a week or two we would be at peace with each other's bodies.

I disliked him so much back then that his mere existence tainted all my happiness. Having this boastful firebrand as a room-mate and broheem was the worst thing in my life, and the ancient name inside me for that feeling is still my true and se-cret name for him. He was bane and rival, dandy and swaggering peacock. It was lucky for me I was older and bigger, at least until early adolescence when he shot up past me, well over six feet. By then we had outgrown fisticuffs but not the battle, even as we turned into poet allies and metaphysical friends.

More than thirty years before the cataclysmic knife he slid a blade along his wrists in a Vermont halfway house—the proximal act that got him into the mental hospital. He said he did it because he couldn't feel any more: no delight, no nostalgia, no sadness, no attraction to women. He scored his flesh and released blood to find out if he could at least feel that.

His final thrusts sliced through the cumulative torpor, irrita-bility, fear, and emotional deadness, unlocking a torrent of grief and ire that must have poured over him in death throes.

It no doubt hurt like hell. But at least it was real.

When you think you've run out of possibilities, you still have an infinity of them, even if you don't know it at the time. Even when there is only one possibility left, that opens a universe of paths, because when one realm closes, another opens, another bathed in prior darkness-absolute. There is always a different "next."

That is what I tried to tell Jon on the phone, before he got obsessed with the water in his ear, what I try to tell myself in bad times. Find something else that is happening … and breathe. Thoughts are a dime a dozen; acts are for real; sticks and stones can break your bones like in the rhyme; violence boomerangs at about ten times the force that you put into it.

Conceive what else is possible, *right now*. And go there, before it is too late.

Since the early '70s I have written hundreds of pages about Jon's vagrancies and sacred quests, for both of us and whomever else it may concern … our cohorts now and then and again among the worlds.

I won't review those old stories. I will merely restate the obvious but say it more frankly this time: Our mother cut us off from our true nature as brutally and effectively as any inquisitioner. She obstructed, all but severed, our link with the core radiance that is each creature's birthright. She refused to let us become who we were. In its place she imparted a terrible talent and trade: to scare ourselves. She broke our minds and lit a dull terror in our souls.

Ordaining only the world of her limited and niggling imagination, she intercepted any and all communications from inner guardians. In their place she substituted harpies from nameless night—doubt, superstition, undifferentiated fear. She opened Pandora's box big-time and then watched us squirm. She taunted our potential graces and gifts and made them shameful and ugly and then used them to goad us into battle with each other.

She forbade calm or wonder, censored fantasies and imagination, assaulted daydreams, loitering, humor, or buffoonery—anything that challenged her totalitarian regime. We were permitted no slapstick or cut-up; all ribaldries were deemed indiscreet.

She sabotaged our sibling love and fashioned hatred of it. Like a trainer of fighting dogs, she bred us like combatants for household battle. We were supposed to despise each other but call it by other names, to protect her from complicity. She of course outlawed considerations of rage against her and enforced that curfew more effectively than most dictators. She did it by making us believe our thoughts were windows for her to peer into our souls.

She turned our compliance against us, our innocent deeds against us, and she turned our words and, most of all, our happiness against us, so after a while we didn't know how to be. That was her genius, to drive the demons out of her into us, to make herself blameless and lay the responsibility for her agony squarely at the feet of those ingrates pretending to be her children, especially Richard.

She obviated faith in human nature. We were blandished out of giving alms to beggars, having empathy for doormen and elevator men, appreciating strangers, admiring any human being except those she put on pedestals—they were perfect—everyone else was a crook or a phony or a molester. "Nice" and "kind" were inapplicable pieties in her domain, things for her to mock, that couldn't really exist.

She abhorred nakedness, bareass; made our bodies disgusting, curiosity about her or anyone else impermissible. In that weirded household, we lived in privatized cocoons, unable to allow each other's quirks and odors. Aloofness and intolerance were craftily imposed, as we collaborated in contempt and disgust for what is most intimate. There was no way to neutralize one another's farts and burps, b.o. and acne. These became points against us on each other's scorecards, and proof that we were vile. They were crimes against the Queen's glamour, her prophylactic presence, so they didn't exist and certainly could not be atoned.

Jon and I got lost in tangles of simple emotions and the sanctions against them. We were unable to abate trivial annoyances, so these grew into grotesque effigies of ordinary feeling for which we had no compass, no path that didn't take us deeper and deeper into weirdness and loathing.

That was her genius and it made her more dangerous than a Mom on crack or booze. She was viral, working her way inside us and turning our own minds against us, putting our thoughts at her service. A weaver of double binds within double binds, she got us to clone her again and again as variants of ourselves until we didn't know what was us and what was her. I still don't. Allegiance to her dominion continues to rule the nether half of my life.

This old conditioning used to come up for me in bodywork classes when my third eye rang with an almost unbearable flinching sensation, to turn away from another's hairy, bony body, his layers of fat and smell. My mother inside me demanded compliance, adjured loyalty to her primeval regime, which was my regime. Soon enough it was me who was proud and contemptuous, who couldn't tolerate humanity's gaffes and foibles, blubber and stench. But I gritted my teeth, dug my nails into my own acupuncture points, and forced myself to stay and finish the palpation with a modicum of clemency.

Petty more than powerful, shrewd rather than bruising, she was, if anything, thorough—thorough and vicious—and she did a job worthy of the Gestapo. I use this term with full awareness of its resonance for a Jewish woman coming of age in France during the years before World War II. I pick it because so many Jews of her generation continued to invoke the Nazis as proof that they themselves were beyond reproach of being cruel. Hitler became the cover story for her sadism and crimes, her alias for her supposed innocence.

While remaining a presentably fashionable woman, admired in Park Avenue society, she maintained an unrelenting attack on us behind closed doors that brooked no escape, no expiation, no time off for okay behavior. She never let her guard down. I can't remember a single moment when she didn't turn out to be monitoring me, inspecting me, plotting against my confidence. Even when charming me with her charismatic Mummsy smile, she was the inquisitioner, trying to catch me off-guard, to get me to slip up and give her ammunition with which she could ambush me at some future perfect moment when I might actually be happy.

During our "growing up" years she declared aloud so often that she loved Jon insanely, that he was her perfect son, that I was "rotten to the core," the only option for either of us was to humor her and play our roles—certainly not to refute her warrant, on this matter or any other. Any hint of betrayal would ignite her frenzy. She would scream hysterically and, during the worst attacks, kick us and stamp us with her shoes and claw at us with supernaturally long fingernails that made her seem like a wild beast beyond supplication, or she would go for a belt which she swung in reckless spasms until she exhausted her cursing and sobs.

The unspoken rule was that I could never be good—but it was really deeper than that: I could never love, I was a born criminal, I could never forgive or be forgiven, I could never have authentic fondness or generous motives.

I was the "instigator," the "big mischief," the evil one—to use her terms. I didn't know what decent behavior was because I was "constitutionally incapable of it."

She didn't mince words. Many, many times she called me "Hitler's boy" and "the devil incarnate." I don't know what she meant by that or thought she was saying, and I barely heard it after a while: "Dev Illin Carn'ate." Only as an adult do I consider the horrificness of such slurs from one's own Mom.

But then I was also forbidden to hate, even though I was, by my very name, hate. *Everything* was finally against the law.

Jon's good and my bad turned into the same thing—for we persisted according to code. We both became the monsters she said we were.

While I was my brother's designated playmate, I couldn't be his buddy because he was the prince and I was the wicked jester from the other family, the rotten, conniving ingrate, the double-dealing clown.

At least she gave my monster a script. She cut a path through the jungle for me, and I wended my way along it blind.

But she made it impossible for Jon to know who in god's name he was.

Good? What was "good" in such a kingdom?

I could at least be a rebel and reign over a territory of thought she was exempt from. She may have forbidden me to be complicated and hence to elude her that way, but she gave me another opportunity by making me her "other," by offering me the role of the eternal outsider. I found a vast realm of thoughts that she couldn't know—that with confidence I knew she couldn't know. I went beyond my sector and found a whole other universe.

I warred against her both openly and covertly. I was as sneaky and bad as I could be, so I ransomed some of my nature, at least in tattered form. It *was* my nature to transmute whatever was thrown at me and refract it back at a different angle. A Scorpion by my November birth, I do two things well: resurrection and negative capability. We Scorpios strip matters down to their crux and raise phoenixes, enact both functions ruthlessly and involuntarily. We know how to salvage the impossible, reclaim from ashes, turn hate into love, terror into epiphany. And we can go the other way too.

The deeper the inscription of the sign, the more intense the Scorpionic behavior. And I had every planet and moon in my chart below the horizon line, so I was truly the dark hooligan, the devil incarnate. I became my mother's succubus and parody; her exemplar but her traitor.

In a way that I hardly understood, let alone planned, I was the one who would not let her pass, even when stepping obediently out of her way. I knew how to leave my seal even on my surrenders, committing the perfect crime again and again, its weapon melting like a telepathic icicle: Trickster Coyote and Dennis the Menace supreme.

I met her precisely on her battlefield: savagery, panic, madness, hysteria, impugnment, violation. Of course I was bad—I was a bad, ungrateful, misbehavin' boy, worse than she even knew. I felt devilish to myself, and my pranks, my acts of resistance and treachery grew more and more uncanny and ingenious as time went by. I gave her the chills.

At age four I purposely rode my toy fire engine into a hydrant and cracked open my skull, so I could ring the doorbell and hand her my bloody head. A year or so later I filled her bathwater with books, dozens of them afloat like barges. I wet my pants; I wandered off and got lost.

Equally ingenuous and disingenuous, I made it so that she couldn't read me, even though she automatically attributed all her own motives and strategies to me and assumed I was guileful like her. Of course I assumed that too and couldn't read myself. So we engaged in a folly of fake interpretations of each other, believing stuff we knew on some level wasn't true but considering the variance trivial until the damage was beyond undoing.

My panics were my ultimate acts of disobedience. I became something neither she nor I could abide. Step by step I consecuted the crime, past mere trauma into a state where I cracked the entire universe. A persistent uneasiness and vague loss of context inside me would suddenly catch hold and burst into a swell that gripped my guts and blanketed my flesh.

Suddenly I understood what was going on. I saw it all starkly for what it was. I couldn't abide, so I was freed to do the dance, St. Vitus', to move in ways it was decreed we shun. I had no choice. I threw my body on the floor and writhed and let loose any sound that I could find in me. I succumbed to the force of it until I gave my seizure every last whimper and gasp and paroxysm. I heaved in reckless terror beyond solace, presenting her with a jig of hell in the vestibules of her own home.

I acted out the real haunting, but I simultaneously acted out what was going on in our household, mimetically and metaphorically, even as I paid no attention to it, for I was responding to demons that dwarfed our paltry apartment and its melodramas, in fact eclipsed the world itself.

I could see the dark hole at the center of all creation, the one that was forbidden, to even imagine existed, let alone look at unfalteringly, especially in my mother's company. I spread it through the family like some communicable disease. My horror made her glimpse it too, the one thing she least wanted to see. And she never forgave me or the child I was.

What other option had either of us? She had driven me out of all other places. So I executed a kind of cosmic chorea that went beyond her most dread fantasies of how bad it was, so that she could only stare at me in abomination and, yes, tremulous awe.

I put on a goblin's theater of what was going on among us, beneath the façade, in not just our apartment but the universe. Of course, I didn't know that's what I was doing. I assumed it was me, that I was the only one who was that crazy and frightened. I didn't understand that I was parodying everyone's dreaded fantasy, performing the proscribed play.

Jon complied; he wanted so much to be admired, adored by the Ice Queen, to be as handsome and wonderful as she told him he was. He was polite, entertaining, supercilious, righteously cheerful, abjectly sane, and even more law-abiding than her laws required. Whatever I was, he trained himself to be the alternative. So he became the better athlete, the infallible honor student, the articulate dinner companion—his parents' appreciative protegé and fan.

He was even the star of the synagogue, and his father hired Leslie Uggams to sing at his Bar Mitzvah ("What, a Shvartzer?" the rabbi complained). She was eighteen herself; her agent was my stepfather's friend. (Recently I heard a track of her singing, *"You'll find Shalom/the nicest greeting you know,"* and it all came flooding back, that day in 1961, her big melodious voice, how we thought our family was special and important, and had so much hope for the future. In her graceful lilt I recall the oft-expressed family dream that Jon would be "the first Jewish president," which, as she croons, turns into something else, both haunting and tragic and also macabre in a kind of sweet and sad way that opens the original wound and mystery of the universe forever.

"It means a million lovely things/like peace be yours, welcome home." Because this never existed and could never exist, something else, borne in the song, unrequited and essential, is allowed into the universe, and it is beautiful too. It was beautiful then, but no one could see it. All we had was the rigid charade of Jon in his suit chanting Haftorah.)

And why do we do the whole thing anyway, did we carry it out so relentlessly instead of ordinary life? What god did we serve? What virtue or pleasure did we gain for all that we surrendered forever?

Barred from any possibility of being my real mate, Jon served as our Mom's lieutenant and double agent against me until, as a teenager, to both her and my consternation he switched sides, a treason she assumed I finagled and for which she condemned me always: 'Put it on the docket, at the bottom of the list of all his other crimes!' She considered Jon's apostasy my final trespass against her, my ultimate, inexpiable reprisal. That, and the fact I went home from college (and thereafter) to my father and stepmother. She handled my disloyalty by cutting me out of her will, even though most of the money in her bank account was my father's child support for me. She left it to my brother and sister.

But I didn't lift a finger to prosletyze Jon; I didn't like him well enough to enlist him or waste my time teaching him—it was more that as an adult he began to teeter toward his own nature. He became a jive guy, a blues aficionado; he adopted Jung's alchemical drawings and Waite's tarot, wore rainbow-vision shirts, let his hair and beard grow, and attended countercultural festivals and ghost dances.

Over time, sadly he lost the hippie gentleness of the young hermetic devotee and poet. He couldn't square his adult life with his haunted childhood, and he didn't even know he was particularly haunted because there were so many other spirits and totems at large then. He incubated a rage that soon turned against everyone except her, and finally her too, with the knife, and then she got spooked and had him put away. So much for loyalty to her prince.

After his release from the mental hospital he was continually piqued and aroused to no useful end; he had no lifestyle or protocol to soothe himself. He followed whims: he preached Luddite and shamanic sermons to small gatherings in the parks of Baltimore; he read tarot for street customers.

As noted, he cultivated in himself our mother's contempt for all true healers, by refusing to be healed. How could he submit to psychoanalysis when she told him all through childhood that the doctor I went to, the one my father paid to send me to, was not a real doctor but a charlatan who taught me "only how to be more evil"?

His last shrink, the first one he allowed near himself in the thirty-three years following incarceration at Sheppard Pratt, a guy whom he picked from a newspaper ad, was a pretty decent analyst, but as Levy told him, "You'd rather defeat me than let me help you. You're willing to die to prove me wrong."

Our mother was likewise willing to die rather than be bad herself or guilty or anything less than one of the most meritorious ladies in Manhattan. She was willing to kill her own maternal instincts and herself before she would let anyone, let alone herself, witness her demons and imperfections.

She was fifty-five when she jumped out her window onto the courtyard. I heard that my stepfather, arriving on summons from his office, screamed at her corpse, "You can't do that! We're Jews."

Her claim that she loved us bent the words "love" and "mother" out of any recognizable shape until, without realizing what had befallen us, we had no idea what either name really meant. If what she was sending our way was "love," love under the aegis of mothering, then we had to redefine the territory, organize ourselves to receive her energy under those names. It was easier to invent games with baseball cards on the rug or just play another round of Monopoly, Clue, Scrabble, Sorry!, their endlessly reenterable landscapes, the variant distribution of wooden letters or yellow and green properties and cards with iconic numbers, making up our endless private histories, lotteries of the imagination: the landscape of our childhood. We could run Sherwood Forest and Sparky and Casey Jones and Bozo on the victrola. That's how we kept the afternoons and evenings bearable—that and baseball cards and Yankee games on the radio, boxscores in the newspaper—through many years of torpor and wistfulness, until rock 'n' roll and magic came along.

Of course we were bathed in her simulacrum of concern. As my stepfather often remarked, "No one ever loved her children more!" He was right: no one ever more effectively destroyed her children's minds in the name of love. And did she ever declare that love theatrically and melodramatically, in fact all the time! I now understand it was the kind of love the lion has for the carrion of the deer. And it felt like that.

She wasn't a mother at all.

The word "mother" gradually developed an ugly aftertaste for me, like those plaudits in ads that you know contain more than ordinary hypocrisies: insidious lies. "Mother" was like "Himmler" disguised by its primordial humming "m," a comforting "uhhhh" with an affable voiced "th." I began to cringe inwardly at the word, as though everyone confidentially meant by it what I did: a witch covered with Noxzema cream.

I mistrusted love for a mother from then on, so I don't know today how to access the concept, except uncomfortably, even in this piece. It was forfeited by me, along with the charity and tenderness that accompany it selflessly throughout the animal kingdom, a thing I now know intellectually but not in my heart. Jon never realized that there was something missing in the world, something he would never get to experience, something totally delicious; that there was actually love and that it had been taken from him, *pro forma*, by the queen.

My salvation was submission to saints. I learned very early to surrender to compassionate teachers—my childhood psychiatrists, friendly camp counselors, and especially my charismatic and daffy stepmother Bunny, a relationship that drove my mother bonkers, as if I were having an affair with a slut. Later, I yielded to poets, Reichian therapists, martial artists, Buddhist lamas, and, of course, my wife and children. I learned the relief of giving up control, the grace of bowing, the tearful ecstasy of confession, and the boundless jubilation of throwing down my weapons and walking off the battlefield.

I let Bunny, my stepmother, be my mother, and then I let Lindy be my mother as well as my lover, fashioning a second childhood in the orphic springs and autumns of Michigan, Maine, and Vermont, regressing through them to become whole. I got to experience a glimmer of what I had lost and how vast it could have been. I understood that, with love, simple love, we might have been a real family instead of a travesty.

Jon never ceded to anyone, even his women; he fought, belittled, and derided sincere reaching out, so in the end, when he needed help, he didn't begin to know how to ask for it, how to receive unction.

He was isolated and alone, not because he was "The Walking Man," but because he was his mother's child.

His confusions about bodies and touch, attraction and repulsion became so warped that he lost any criterion for his own desires or behavior, any way to dead-reckon where he was in the universe or with women. Outwardly he was a handsome charmer, and the girls loved him, a teenage guise that he kept a long time past twenty. Inwardly he knew he was a fiend and a pervert, so he developed an arsenal of deft performances— from a Brando sneer to a super-bashful sweetness. He could be Whitey Ford, Eddie Fisher, or Rickey Nelson and, after the mental hospital, he could be Jesus. But he rarely stayed in character for long.

According to our sister, Debby, he sexually abused her numerous times during adolescence. I was astonished I could grow up in the same household and not know about such acts until more than thirty years later. No wonder he used to read the same paragraph over and over in his schoolbook, unable to let himself move to the next, as he dared himself to read it one more time. He became so frantic on occasion that he would plead with me, his sworn enemy then, to come over and turn the page because he couldn't, wouldn't.

No wonder I also had to remove his hand from the desklamp light bulb because he wouldn't do it himself, and it hurt. No wonder at the end he asked me to help get water out of his ear from three thousand miles away. Can you imagine scalding your fingers because you can't allow the alternative? No wonder he could dare himself to touch his sister, to put a knife into his neck. Courage was loyalty to the queen. Courage was the antidote to compulsion (and guilt masking itself as compulsion). Courage was the sole redemption for failure. And what else could either of us do but fail?

When there is no love of any sort, and love is what everyone most craves and would give anything for, and the path to love is broken for good, and the knowledge of love is lost, then one's convulsive approaches to love and feints of love become only what love isn't, what love pleads for you not to do, because you won't turn the page.

Just as our mother could not be sweet or maternal but demanded everyone acclaim her as a dish, a broad, so Jon could not find brotherly affection or care for his sister, and what he did feel for her he misread and nursed into its antithesis. (People used to ask me what it was like to have such a beautiful and sexy mother, but I could never get what they were seeing; it was like some sort of diabolic riddle. To me she wasn't pretty at all; she was an ogre and a crone, and her face looked embalmed and mean. As a teenager I would try picturing her just like any other cute girl, have sexual fantasies about her, but I felt nothing, no tingle or wave. Later I realized I was trying desperately to feel anything about her at all, even love. That was what Jon was doing with Debby, in his own way.)

By the time my half-siblings stopped talking to each other in the early '90s, Jon had broken his sister's ribs alongside their father's deathbed (in a fight over his money) and thereafter she actively prayed for his demise, telling me more than once she hoped he would be found dead in some gutter.

Debby turned into a grouchy, imperious Manhattan waitress, a job that belied her Mount Holyoke and Middlebury pedigree. The year before Jon's death I called her on duty behind the luncheonette counter, shocking her by breaking an inviolable rule because she wouldn't answer her phone at home. I said we needed to talk about Jon; he was going downhill fast. "Good," she declared with the faintest trace of irony; "I hope they find his body soon."

When I broke the taboo again to tell her what happened, her first response was, "Omigod!" We exchanged empty words for a moment, and then she put me under interdict; she stopped talking to me altogether. She refused to see us the next time Lindy and I came to the counter, until the owner asked us to leave—we were disrupting business.

The logic of her response still eludes me, though I understand it emotionally. I don't think it was merely guilt on her part. It was more like "cider house rules" ... colored by exasperation at me for forgiving Jon, hence making her seem ungenerous by contrast, not taking his crimes against her seriously enough to merit the death penalty. Or maybe she didn't distinguish between us; she just wanted that Jonathan-Richard creature out of her life.

For her *I* was the one who never really existed. Jon, unfortunately, she could not negate or amend because he made himself irresistible; he was the family golden boy, the one who ran the four-minute mile for all of us, the Jewish president in waiting, "The Mick." He also didn't vanish periodically into another family.

I approached him once about the matter of incest, soon after hearing about from her, years after they stopped having anything to do with each other, and decades after it ostensibly happened. He responded with childlike outrage: "She blamed *that* on me? It was her idea."

I did not pursue it again with either of them.

What I see is that in the end he could not tolerate his own body and what he had done with it, though most of it was normal stuff, and probably even the incest began as old-fashioned horseplay tainted with fantasy. But there was never a line between "I think it" and "I have to do it." The fist-fights proved that. The light bulb proved that. The coroner's report proved that.

In most people's inner dialogue, thoughts initiate acts, but the barrier between the two is a firewall. When you relinquish it, you lose this world.

Jon had no vocabulary for the healthy intersection of prurience and love, fantasy and kindness, sexual strategy and conviviality, no boundary between those obsessive-compulsive thought demons with their dares and his own actual desires. So he turned his imaginings into fetishes because he didn't know what else to do with them and assumed he had no other options; that is, he assumed because he thought it, it had already somehow happened and to not meet it on the battlefield was to violate his original oath and be a coward.

He was like the Senoi dreamer who has to act out a nightmare in order to keep it from occurring but, in his case, the protected ritual with its sanctioned community participation and immunities was shot to hell by his never seeking or knowing how to seek symbolic mediation. Instead, he performed the literal dream so that, by happening, it would not have to keep happening in another, more nightmarish way. That is, he would mold what cannot ever be wrenched into daylight into a ghastly shape to avoid the phobia driving it—to do it in order not to do it—or more precisely, to violate the boundary between thought and action bearing down on him so as not to be violated by its allure and ambivalence forever.

He could never pardon me for having broken the unrecognized vow of family solidarity, for having taken my body elsewhere (he and my sister shared that fealty to Mom). He could not tolerate that I had done something so intimate, so repulsive as to marry, have children, and have those children turn into adults. Yet he wished he had done the same.

He had intense love and hate for me, an untenable blend of admiration and antipathy, identification and envy, affection and murderous ire. He always wanted to be me and yet was vexed by my style and acts. He would mock me as a sellout, a preener, while he claimed to be a man of the people.

("A real trust-fund homeless guy," our sister remarked on one occasion, "a working man who never held a job in his life, the kind of man-of-the-people who breaks his sister's ribs over a twenty-dollar bill next to his dying father.")

My brother wanted me to embrace him, and he wanted to wring my neck. He wanted us to be the best of friends and to fight to the death of one of us. He told me how every day, sometimes (he imagined) every minute of his life, he thought obsessively about me and pictured me, us, doing things together, brothers of yore. He wanted me around him always—yet we saw each other at most once a year, and not at all some years, because he never traveled (being religiously opposed to the internal combustion engine and its applications) and pretty much put in his time on the street or in the marshes so that he was hard to track down. Twice I drove to Westport and left without finding him.

Long before either of us had full language or identities, our mother hammered the first commandment into us: Richard is evil; Jon is good … until it became our mantra and paralyzed any authentic feeling we could have for each other, or anyone. It squelched empathy and compassion in us and, worse than that, caused us to assume we didn't have any, justifying her plaint that we were selfish pigs.

At times I felt so much empathy it was excruciating—for blind and homeless men on 57th Street or along Central Park West, for waiters standing forlorn in empty restaurants, clerks in customer-less stores, for Heidi and Black Beauty, Eeyore in the snow, for Rin Tin Tin, for the red token in Sorry! that never got picked; yet never for Jon, even at the end. I had no access to affection when the opportunity was there to embrace him or say "I love you," or to forgive him. Most of the time I felt like a freak and a prankster—"a miserable waste of a human being," as my mother so eloquently put it.

Even when I took to hugging him in the later years, I felt an emptiness in the sensation of body on bony body, as I traveled the sad distance from the vestige of Jon, the anathema, to his actual trembling being. My childhood enemy was in truth sympathetic and unabashed. He was a wonderful, tragic, playful guy, and I recognized in embracing the noble giant and holding him close that I loved him, had always loved him. Why had I never known that? Why was he such an asshole when we were kids? Why was I such a prig? Why couldn't we have been boys together in the fray, accepting each other's camaraderie and fidelity, engaging in horseplay? Why couldn't the sight of him have made me happy rather than steeled and ugly? He was finally such a sweet, beautiful person, crying out for our lost childhood.

Full reconciliation would have taken a long time, but I know that we would have gotten there if he hadn't cut short our time together in this world. I would have found his real body, realized who he was, and wept unsparingly, in reprieve and regret. Once, in 1991, we cried together.

I am still traveling toward my brother's body. When I feel benevolence toward someone even now, my first instinct is to mistrust my motives and imagine myself as devious as she thought I was; that is, as devious as she was (because I am her blood).

It seems then as though I am forever a winsome sociopath, trying to get my way.

And the antidote isn't easy. It calls for a journey through bottomless sorrow, across a sixty-year desert, to the source of my tears. That is the only place at which my intellectual concept of good will, my intent to be generous, meets the pumping of my actual heart muscle, which sends a current of grace and charity through my body. Then I finally feel legitimate and whole.

Yes, Jon had twisted fantasies—they slipped out blushingly at times—but they really were not so horrible. If "love" is not love, then what can desire be? Every possibility would seem either depraved or perverse in some way because there is no compass for not only sex, but friendship, fantasy, empathy, physical closeness. His desires and imagination of them got twisted inside him because he dangled in the wind so long with so many mandates from our mother's regime, her banal injunctions clabbered into imperatives. He assumed that whatever he wanted was bad— real bad—and so he kept torquing it into himself, and that made it worse, so he torqued it more and more, like a hand on a hot bulb.

He could never see the bawdy humor in our animal bumbling, the okayness of just about anything the imagination pulls out of its amoral cornucopia, the ritual teasing that defuses sexual content, the promiscuity of our monkey minds.

Of course thoughts are not acts. But our mother not only never taught us that; she rigged it so that the opposite seemed true. That served her purposes best. Jon took his fantasies way too seriously, and he ultimately managed to turn them into something wanton and unbearable—into a disease he imagined in his gut.

That "disease" became everyone's excuse to abandon him. The lawyer managing his father's estate, representing the cousin-heirs, assumed that Jon was dying of cancer, so they didn't want to throw good money after bad.

And I had no voice in the matter because my stepfather, following in the steps of my mother, disenfranchised as well as disinherited me. Even though he raised me and Jon as brothers—at the crossroads when the sisters came calling on a dying man, he agreed to sign a new will so that nothing could ever, under the law of New York State, end up going to my children rather than theirs.

Attempts by the dead to control the living always backfire in some unthinkable way. Bob put so much energy into making sure that his money would never end up someday with *my* children that he disenfranchised his own in the process. Once he was dead, his beneficiaries took the ball and ran with it. They didn't care that he slaved his entire life at Robert Towers Advertising to create a small nest egg to protect his son and daughter. It was theirs now, and they weren't going to waste it on a hippie mongrel or a luncheonette waitress. So it went into the kitty for anonymous nieces and nephews, and I couldn't free a penny of it to hospitalize Jon at one of the few sanctuaries that knew how to treat his sacred madness. He would have gone too; he promised me that. But the lawyer for the estate said, "It's not his money; he shares the interest with his sister; that's it. He's not a beneficiary."

"But what about the clause that gives you discretion to tap the principal in a health emergency?"

"My only job is to protect the principal for the remainder heirs."

The Turetsky* clan won out over love, honor, justice, or any chance Bob's son wouldn't die on the floor of a boarding house with a knife in him. What he left me, by default, was a landlord's call to the police and paperwork for a crematorium in Hartford. The estate paid the bill but blew off Levy's last charge, blaming him for bad psychotherapy.

---

*Reuben Turetsky anglicized his Russian Jewish name to become known as Robert Towers.

Yes, my stepfather Bob loved me, he just hated the idea of me—that is, of my mother's other lovers and husbands—and I came from both, for she had me by an affair with a *bon vivant* while married to my legal father, Paul, something I didn't learn until after her suicide in my thirtieth year. Bob hated (and unrequitedly loved) Grossinger's, the hotel at which he was the impresario, and my father's best friend, until he had an affair with his wife and was forced into exile because you can't sleep with the empress and be pardoned by the emperor. It was a primal myth we lived out in the diaspora of eternal return.

Neither my mother nor stepfather forgave me for Grossinger's, though a babe hardly is responsible for the actions of his forebears. Nor did they forgive me for my genetic father, Bingo, whoever he really was, a supposed slicko porn-theater operator and Shylock later known as the "pinky-ringed piranha of Forty-Second Street."* One business associate said of him, "That's not a man. That's an animal."†

I have also heard that he was a devoted family man, a legendary prankster, and a generous benefactor. I never met him. He never wanted to meet me.

"A schnorrer who used to bribe the rabbi," my stepfather snorted. "I never liked him." But that's also what he shrieked hysterically in his various bombasts about my father Paul, his old buddy ("a bum," "a crook," "an idiot," "a show-off," "a degenerate pimp"), and then he adored him again after my mother's death.

I have mused about whether my genetic father was the reason why my mother cast in the role of the "bad seed"—I was the

---

*Jimmy McDonough, *The Sex-Gore Netherworld of Filmmaker Andy Milligan*, Chicago Review Press, 2003, p. 94.
†ibid., p. 118.

child of an ostensibly disreputable man. However, I have concluded that Bingo was at most a bit of corroborating evidence.
The Grossinger myth encompassed me, no matter who my real
father was, but, more to the point, I think she and I took one
look at each other at my birth and knew we had been adversaries
for a long time.

Upon leaving Grossinger's, Bob became the advertising man
and promoter for many of its chief competitors. He used to joke
about putting Paul out of business. He liked to tell me that especially after I got back from a visit to my father's resort.

In the end he more or less succeeded.

If he had sided with the family of his household, despite everything, he would have at least left me in charge of Jon's fate
because I was the only who truly cared for and could tolerate the
bearded, marijuana-addicted vagabond, who saw the sad short-
stop and poet in him. By putting his son in the hands of his sisters, Jon's aunts, whose motives behind the rewriting of his will I
justifiably mistrust, he ultimately left the final call to well-mean-
ing cousins who were in over their heads and had their own children and careers. He made Jon dispensable.

The lawyer for the heirs, who was also the hireling who rewrote
the will on Bob's deathbed, the one Jon fondly called Jaggers, was
the lead zealot projecting terminal illness onto him. Fed up with
his feral charge, with his antics and bills, he let him die like a dog,
unwilling to write a check for hospitalization. "He was going to
die anyway," he sneered later. "He probably had colon cancer."

No, he had another disease deep in his guts, and that is why
he took a knife to himself and tried to cut it out, so that the
crematorium could immolate all of it—the disease, the rape, the
evil thoughts, the guilt, the insomnia, the constipation, and turn
it into mute and ignorant ashes to be scattered to the winds at

last. So he could become the ghost he always was, the ghost that was the only part his mother left him.

Jon didn't understand—couldn't understand—that at the core of his fantasies was simply thwarted compassion, beauty, desire, the wish to be touched. That is the price that my mother's combination of prissiness and persecution, her unabated sarcasm and tortures exacted. It may have begun as her own self-hatred, self-revulsion once upon a time, disgust for anything that came out of her body, including us, but in the end, there was no way for her child to cry for help, no one to call to, no tool but a knife, no act but violence, no direction, but in, and in, and in.

Emile and his son Joe meet us at the Teapot in Northampton. Though Emile was my brother Jon's best friend at Horace Mann, I haven't seen him since 1960, some forty-six years ago. Jon's suicide put us back in touch, also reminding both of us of a trauma shared, for Emile's older brother, Harry, a year ahead of me at Amherst, hanged himself in 1972, a year before Jon, then twenty-three, entered Sheppard Pratt. After Amherst, Harry became a student at the London School of Economics where his colleagues included Bill Clinton and R. D. Laing.

Emile is now a psychiatrist in New Jersey, on a road trip with a fidgety but amiable eighteen-year-old.

I remember two things about Harry that defined him silently for me: One, we were in the same Abnormal Psych seminar at Amherst, and the class visited the Northampton Mental Hospital, a tableau out of Hieronymus Bosch. We circumambulated its halls and grottos like Dante and Vergil (1964), ghosts of the damned importuning us to rescue them.

I wonder what could have happened to that *magna cum laude* man about campus. "Too many drugs and too much Vietnam-era politics," Emile admits. "He never recovered from R. D. Laing and LSD. He got angry and then he got paranoid."

The second is an older image of Emile and Harry, fixed in my mind in search of an explanation. I see them walking down 83rd Street, the much taller Harry holding one finger on the center of Emile's cranium, Emile rotating round and round as they moved.

"My god, I forgot!" Emile exclaimed, "We were twirling. That was something Harry and I used to do. We twirled."

The most innocently profound feelings lurk in our hearts and make us who we are. At times they come up and dance with us and we are totally alive and okay with everything forever as it is, as long as it lasts, even if it doesn't last. A mysterious light shines from within, as radiant as the night is dark, touching everyone with soul grace, *"illuminating my mind,"* as Harry Chapin once put it, though, unbeknownst to himself, he had little time left to enjoy his taxi-man moment. I think it is wonderful. I also think it is terrible.

As we travel from the outside in, peeling the orange, we are being lived inside out. The sensations are as pagan, inscrutable, and wild as a being we don't even know—or the only being we do know. Yes, *"I've got something inside me…."* (Chapin, 1972).

I feel a rush of exhilaration, rattling my '92 Ford Ranger down Route 198—Hadlock Pond flaunting its lily pads and blossoms like a tangka painting to my left, WDEA oldies out of Ellsworth: Tony Orlando and Dawn belting, *"Knock three times on the ceiling…."*; then the Vogues, *"You're the one that I'm dreaming of …";*

and Lou Christie, "*… the gypsy cri-ii-ii-ied …*": almost an embarrassment of riches. Goddamn, is this complex—profound, elusive beyond calculation! Everything else has to be for us to be. It is that kind of a universe.

As I doo-wop along, these canticles call up a tenderness and a wonder that have nowhere to go, yet are unconfinable, know no bounds of time or space. That is, I don't know where to put the feelings, how to take care of them—or what should be done with any of this under the rude circumscription of mortality and time.

There is ultimately not enough space in this big old world for all its elation/euphoria, its horror and rage—tempers flaring, bullets firing, women weeping, suicide bombers tearing the skin off the orange and blowing the ultimate shards of meaning and light out of the system. The "streets of Baghdad" or "Lebanon as hell" is all the context I need to keep my joy confined to a minor chord on 198 … passing reverie of a morning.

"*Twice on the pipe/if the answer is no.…*"

Billowing clouds crown Norumbega Mountain afore the junky black truck I bought from a teenager in Somesville last year.

And everything in this world runs out eventually. Everything turns plaintive and sad. Somewhere, sometime, we will be transported into a different realm, and this passion and fuel will be sublimated into something that has a way to go, to be synopsized and sublimated. Yes, West Side Story, *there's a place for us,/a time and a place for us.* For no other reason than because we were *happy once.*

But damn, is this display compelling or what? It has a tempo and a duration, a sparkle and a depth, a lilt and a tune, and most of all, there is nothing to replace it. I came to that perception initially about a year ago: Even if we leverage reality a micromillimeter off and peer through a temporary rip, it slides back instantly because there is no underlying gap to sustain the opening.

The set-up here caulks everything, pretty much on call.

I take it that advanced yogis and Zen meditators cultivate a lever with which to pry a slit in *maya*, and that is why they do their practices so assiduously, with poise and humor under duress.

The reward is, they get to see where they are. They get to distribute every one of their raptures and sorrows and flights of empathy into a bounteous domain where everything rolls and conforms like fog, becoming only what it is. They get to be happy without diminution of loss. They get to sound the bell, to clear their minds.

If they peer through the fissure long enough, then the world is no more and never was; they become real.

But the Kinks, circa 1973: *"All that I see/is so unreal to me...."*

Either we are frauds and none of this amounts to a hill of beans, or we are time-lapse angels, tuned to an extremely fine frequency, then calibrated to the next frequency or something else when this body annuls and the marvelous paradisal world with its shanties is no more. When we cross the river.... *"Oh, Shenandoh,/I love your daughter...."* and *Away,/I'm bound away,/'cross the wide Miz-zour-i."*

There is nothing, not even residue, at the surcease of a dream.

But *"Is it a dream/or is it the real reality?"*

Well-put, apemen. Worlds within worlds, lives within lives are driven by an incredible karma, an exquisite ordination, a quantum and divine engine that only ever tenders the minimum that needs be remitted on each platform—but that minimum turns out to be so much, and all this—and forks over the most necessary forms to take on form. Flowers and ballads and gypsy arias and boundless mains—all absolute to a condition in which they are rooted and which is their undiluted source.

Now Jimmie Rodgers: "*Wish we didn't have to meet ... seee-cret-leee.*" Kudos to this disk jockey. Damn it, he's on fire.

The whole purpose of a universe is to seize up the unconscious elements at its core and render them vivid across its tundra. We are figments of a protean and primal design of anything at all within multidimensional waves that distribute it into sunflowering meadows and hiphop poetry jams. And these cheap oldies are part of it, of trying to sing the core out. Under that proxy they are as good as Homer's *Odyssey* or Machu Picchu or Bach's organ works: "*Optical illusions as far as the eye can see....*"

We are drawing an unfigured figure, giving the shapeless void a spool—"*wish we didn't have to kiss ... seee-cret-leee.*" That too.

And yes, "*you're the one that I really miss ... /Baby, you're the one that I love ...*"

Though our reveries and revelations are great, while they last—and preferable to ennui or despair—they are followed by other, duller things that are just as central to existence. Even though many moments are downbeat, sad, gloomy, stupid, their moods are necessary to thatch a place like this.

Homesickness for nothing in particular is the broken memory that drives life.

The pivotal line from Gillo Pontecorvo's *Burn!* serves as an epigraph for all indigenes who have been dragged into the modern world as slaves to inexplicable economies and technologies generating unspeakably useless wealth: "Better to know where you are and not know how than to know how but not where you are."

The wings of the hummingbird, flapping so fast they cannot be seen, carry its body close enough to me that we share a brief glance. Writhing like an electric field, it inserts a needle and alchemizes a florid echinacea.

Dusk at Seawall

Ocean churns and crashes onto rocks. In the sky is a single star, a planet, maybe Venus, or Jupiter. Either way, waves fission violently upon its mantle—hot sulphuric acid or frigid methane.

Three separate, connected worlds: here and there, each joined to the others by gravity like silk, each splashing sinusoidal designs on its shoals.

We inhabit the orb of watery seas and tidepools, while globes of pure fire and ice bob in our sky on gravity's gradient, suspended apart, such that, as we smell the marrow of the local kombu, we appreciate the greater movement of light through darkness through light.

That eerie glow on the trees was no phantom car but a meteorite, a stone in its last cohesive seconds, having traveled a billion billion miles to splatter this ray onto consciousness.

Today at yoga class I tipped too far back across the giant exercise ball and plunged into nausea: *dwipada viparita dandasana*. I suddenly felt where I am rooted, all the way past my false bottoms. It imposed its own yoga, a more ancient and wounded posture, corkscrewing beyond grasp or breath.

During a brief leniency in my plunge, I spanned new terrain and felt my mind come open. Then the spiral overwhelmed me, the feeling of there being no bottom or container for me, no rung to grasp, nothing to keep prostration and chaos at bay. I was on a roller coaster for which there is no track.

I bolted onto my knees, hung my head, closed my eyes, and offered my body to anything that would hold it. Patricia set me on a mat with gentle weights on me to tie down the vertigo; she gave me time to it work through. It was still yoga, but a more lenient form.

For an instant I experienced a flicker of birth trauma, not as some profound forgotten coloration but a distinct ping that imparted my seam, a chink at which the pebble hit the pool, from which ripples are still spreading.

The sole reason that the many random events and coalesced objects in the universe hold together is the karma driving them. Karma creates all necessity and also all chance. It determines which way a piece of soot drifts and whether a child runs drugs. It is presently uncoiling the destinies of every man and woman and hedgehog in every relegation and household across the universe.

Gravity is a subset of karma. So are magnetism and electricity. Karma is a far more meticulous and profound force than the lot of them. Gravity does little more than juggle ballasts and hurl weights; it is a bowler in a saga of dwarves, smashing balls of indeterminate size and mass against one another to make thunder and nebulae. Though of uncertain pedigree and exerting mysterious influence at a distance, gravity adheres to karmic rules.

Even heat is chaperoned by karma.

Karma is vast; it arranges whatever occurs anywhere and knits it to its manifestation/occurrence, setting its course and exploring its nature as it unfolds through circumstance.

Karma is "situation" at the same time that it is "conditionality."

Karma is weightless, invisible, taciturn, has no signature, leaves no mark; yet holds the power to get everything in the universe from one moment to the next, one station to the next—a power that exceeds gravity by a factor of trillions. While gravity requires mass, karma requires nothing except that there be a universe because a universe itself is a statement of karma, constantly sprouting, maturing, and fading, replaced by fresh karma, all of it so tightly annealed to events that you couldn't squeeze a quark between them.

Karma has no story to tell, no destiny to write. Yet it is the sole cause whereby attributes occur, whereby everything in existence has, not so much a meaning or a rationale, as a proximal source and an outcome.

The story of creation blazes before us, undifferentiated, unrevealed. We are pupae all. What flights, dimensions, apocalypses, apotheoses lie ahead we cannot imagine, dumb as we have been, gullible as we are, greedy for this one life, from the pellicled zooid propelled by ciliated filaments to the consumer of words.

Creatures dwell in realms yet to be disclosed.

Odd as this may seem, George Bush II has made Saddam Hussein look like a genius or at least a skilled bureaucrat. The late sociopathic dictator kept order in the streets of Baghdad, successfully banned roadside incendiary devices, kept potential suicide bombers out of the markets, enforced a Sunni-Shi'ite armistice, shut the Kurds out of Turkey, ran the oil industry efficiently, quarantined al-Qaeda, imposed secular rules on Islamic society, drove the religious fanatics underground, and neutralized Iran, all things we can't begin to do and desperately need. Saddam is exactly the leader whom the Americans would like to elect under some alias or other: "a rose was a rose is still a rose." American policy in Mesopotamia has come full circle, back to the Sunni imperative that the nation itself arrived at after generations of fractiousness before Mr. Know-It-All decided he understood the joint better than the locals or the skilled diplomats of his time and, on an adolescent whim, smashed it all.

The result of Bush's rash invasion is exactly what Colin Powell and other military pundits warned him it would be before he decided to exercise executive privilege and set the bull loose: "Break it and you own it."

W didn't care that he was vandalizing a delicately interlocking operating system, a geopolitics too complex for him to grok. Left to their own ceaseless squabbles by the British, the contentious tribes had been held in stasis by the delicate fiction of Iraq until they were gratuitously tossed back into strife and chaos by neo-con ideologues wanting to play war games.

Iraq was even less than a fiction to them; it was a *tabula rasa* on which they thought they could append any lame-brained agenda or slogan. It takes a special brand of inanity to think that you can write over history with salutations and parables, as if Baghdad were Boise.

W's mixture of spoiled brat, yahoo, wannabe general, blithe zealot, and Twelve Step turkey hurled a royal "fuck you" of Pentecostal chutzpah at all the liberal intellectuals and statesmen. He dispatched the army into the china shop, with no plans at all, let alone contingent ones, to deal with the perturbation or its half-lives; he had only a petty vendetta against two authorities: his father and Saddam. He was neurotic enough not to know the difference between political abstractions and facts on the ground, and provincial enough not to reflect on his own patrician optimism. And then there was Dickboy Cheney leading him around like a pig with a ring.

Saddam may have known by then that he had a losing hand but that history would rehabilitate him as an aspect of Saladin. He may have smiled, presuming he had a smile in him, at having lured the dragon into the labyrinth. His life was forfeit, but he would be vindicated in other ways.

The subsequent burlesque—from finding the dictator hiding in a hole to counting his teeth like a goat to taunting him on the gallows—was a second "trial of Charles II." Each day Saddam looked more like a comedic Lear, a tragic anti-hero, a protector of Arabs and Sunnis, even a martyr, than the thug who magisterially gassed the Kurds and cut out the tongues of accused traitors. Bush rehabilitated the guy at the cost of his own honor. There's no better spin to put on it. In fact, Bush has refurbished many of the jerk despots in the world by hectoring them and making them martyrs of superpower intimidation.

Of course Saddam was a remorseless butcher, a rabid sadist who tortured and mangled and gassed his own citizens. But, despite the commotion, he kept the electricity on, the vendor stalls safe, and the Sunnis and Shi'ites at home—not that Mussolini didn't also get the trains to the dot. It is just that, in what was recently a modern city, George W and crew can't achieve 1940s-level utilities or security approaching East L.A. level outside their own sprawling Green Zone. These five-star bumblers and inflated proconsuls couldn't keep the looters out of the Baghdad museum because, evangelists and philistines that they are, they enjoyed the animal-house scene, conflating it with celebrations of free people. They also reveled in shutting down the hospitals and chastising the doctors because it could be construed as a slash against socialized medicine.

Because they didn't understand basic civics, they disbanded the army and police, drove the professionals out of the country, and unleashed brigands, hit-men, and terrorists onto the boulevards. They couldn't have summoned al-Qaeda more effectively if they had rolled out a red carpet. And don't think for a moment that Osama's operatives were in Basra or Baghdad before "Shock and Awe." Saddam would have rounded them up and had them shot.

He was not the one, finally, with weapons of mass devastation. That gig was left to us to enact by carpet-bombs and tank barrages, by "smart" missiles, no less brutal for their digitalization and anonymity, and tons of risk-assessment-approved* explosives that took out whole families as a by-product of assassination attempts

---

*They allowed themselves up to 29 innocent victims per quality target and thereby slaughtered about 300 men, women, and children during the initial invasion, liquidating not a single "enemy" in the process. Did you hear that, when the long American convoys of tanks ran over civilian vehicles, they didn't even stop to get the corpses and crushed chassis out of their way, mashing them into the ground like squirrels on macadam?

on top Baath officials, leading to the systematic destruction of neighborhoods and infrastructure. Then we put on our exclamation point with the roundup of innocents on the streets and in their homes, right into torture chambers of Abu Ghraib.

We took to creative coercion like a duck to water. I mean, has anyone checked out the constabulary of the Michigan and West Virginia prison systems for degrees of humanity surpassing those of Baath goons? But that's who we convoyed over there to represent us, along with criminals and skanks. And Rumsfeld and Cheney up the chain of command, sending them love.

Whether Saddam's stranglings and beheadings were more gruesome and depraved than our foaming pit bulls and jackbooted muggings, enforced fellatios and human pyramids, is something for Iraqis to judge. I think I know which ones they consider more humiliating and dishonorable.

In truth, our leadership shares more with Baath contempt and expediency than voters usually give them credit for, misled as the American electorate is by W's blood feud with Saddam and his pinning 9/11 on him like some bully kid in the playground pointing to the wrong perpetrator and looking to see how many adults salute. I am not even sure that Saddam has more corpses on his pelt than W, as these men display opposite kinds of savagery. Saddam was a vulgar beast who hacked and blasted and bombed away. W is a corporate killer who does it with insolent command and euphemisms of democracy. He managed to wipe out the heart of the middle class in both America and Iraq and to increase both countries' homelessness five-hundredfold. Now *that's* an achievement for the ages. His main attitude after things went downhill was, "The loss of this war is not going to be pinned on my ass. I'm gonna keep the troops rotating and hold my successor accountable, no matter how many Americans and Iraqis have to die. My reputation is more important, and I'm the only one who counts. Plus, God's on my side—so you never know!"

Saddam and W are in a dead heat as regards lack of compassion or concern for other sentient beings, though W knows how to mask his arrogance in sound bites promoting liberation and democracy. He does the crocodile-tears bit and plays possum with aplomb. Both autocrats ruled from the viewpoint that their kind of people (Sunni loyalists for Saddam; wealthy conservative Republicans for George II) are the only ones whose lives are worth saving. Everyone else is a potential mercenary, enemy, customer, or sorry: collateral damage.

I'll add this: rarely has a modern nation paid such a high price for the hubris of a son. At least George W answered the $64-trillion-dollar question: why didn't Dad drive all the way to Baghdad when he had the chance? Now we know, punk, but the answer didn't come cheap. W would have been better off leaving that leaf unturned and continuing to grandstand like some hardass patriot to the old fool's Polonius. Yet this guy was bonkers enough to think he could go over his father's head to God. Oedipal chutzpah indeed!

The West has bloated into a giant Potemkin village, with the rest of the planet obligated to conduct business and pleasure under its yoke:

Sweatshop Earth. Democracy and free trade are mere slogans; the only game is extortion and control of resources, especially human ones. Now the chimneys of the West are burning off waterholes and drying up rivers along the Equator, melting the habitats of Eskimos and penguins.

The neocons have, by the most generous interpretation, the same sincere illusion as Spain's conquistadors, kidding themselves that conquest and colonization are really liberation, that markets and value conversions are tantamount to life, liberty, and the pursuit of good times. Our rulers have valorized consumer choice and monetization of content to such a degree that they have lost any perspective. The truth is, the blind acceptance of these values as absolute homilies is almost psychotic. The "prerogative to SUV," the right to patent and exploit genes—try selling that in the Sirian star system as anything less than a planet gone mad.

The delusion has become extreme enough that Bush and company think that the Iraqis are ungrateful and should be thanking us for bombing and occupying their homeland, just because we whacked Saddam and brought in Big Daddy Halliburton.

If you were Palestinian, Iraqi, or Pakistani and had seen your family and friends, your people, treated like human phlegm, your honor casually dismissed, if you had experienced humiliation, poverty, and theft of your lands from waking to troubled sleep while others flaunted luxury and occupation (and called it freedom), you too might join up with the suicide brigade and turn your body into a weapon against the oppressors. When language is totally corrupted, diplomacy becomes impossible; violence is all that is left.

Get these things right: 1. The Muslims didn't start this war. It's the Americans who occupied Mecca, not the jihadists who invaded Cincinnati. 2. It may be called Islamofascism or jihadi terrorism, but it is also a "return to sender" of the terrorism the West has routinely visited on the so-called Developing World, e.g. the world. Bin Laden is the same guy we backed in Afghanistan, and his mujahadeen are still the mujahadeen: "It is impossible for me to humor any of you in the arrogance and indifference you show for the lives of humans outside America." Case closed.

Imagine yourself born and growing up in the autonomous, unfederated regions of Pakistan among loyal kin—noble, salt-of-the-earth men and women committed to the Prophet. You too would survey the evil empire across oceans and want to see it blown it to bits. Your supreme goal from early childhood would be to pierce the armor of the Great Satan, to live to see the lewd transnational corporation die. (A lot of Americans have come to feel the same way. We, folks, are no longer just Donald Duck and Elvis, Dylan, and Ali. We are now officially the bad guys.)

Capitalism is not the sanest or most humanitarian system and certainly not the only possible one for running economies and societies. In fact, our bondage to currency and commodity at the expense of every other ethic or value is as cowardly as it is shameful. It is poisoning and suffocating the ecosphere in order to make the wealthy even wealthier. It is "trickle up" instead of "trickle down": Subprime Heaven. Or Hell, depending on your position in the game.

The suicide bomber has established that there is another angle on this whole affair; the world is not just markets, products, and hedge funds. While jihadists are detonating explosives on the West, most of all they are planting another meaning, another interpretation of day and night.

Life is not life, and death is not death to them.

They are demanding that materialist idolators wake up and see where this whole planet, us and them both, sits in the greater zodiac. It is not about shareholders or job security; it is about the rude phenomenology of existence, as final in a Gaza refugee camp as at a Texas barbecue. We are all alive, and we are all free, to act. The Sun and Moon don't hedge and don't play favorites and, even if they did, the stars surely don't. This whole affair is a gambit of destiny not privilege—stone and dust and water, not stock markets and bank accounts.

As is so often the case, our enemy is the only teacher motivated to teach us what we need to know.

I used to believe that my work was really special, getting at big stuff in the universe. I had hopes for recognition, though now that I think about it, what was I contemplating? The front page of *The New York Times Book Review?* Translation into other languages? Discussion of my themes in *The New York Review of Books?* A movie of my memoirs? A regular slot in college curricula?

Daydreams and vanities all, long since forgotten. What would any of these have amounted to anyway, against the greater darkness and actual battles of our time?

I suppose my pinnacle came early, with the publication of my first book, *Solar Journal,* by Black Sparrow Press when I was barely twenty-five. A year later (1971) I stood with Robert Duncan and Allen Ginsberg onstage at Kent State University, reading to two thousand fans on the anniversary of the first State slaying of civilians on a college campus.

Duncan introduced me to the mostly youthful audience as one of theirs and then, extending a palm in my direction, added, "After that I hope he doesn't blow it." I was petrified, but I soon heard my voice ringing with hope and conviction. I knew I had the calling. I would have been astonished to learn that night that it would be all downhill from there.

In his preface to *Solar Journal,* Duncan had more or less anointed me the heir to Olson and voice of a new generation, which is why I was even invited to Kent with him and Ginzo. Yet in memory my words that night were already whispers fading into the wind. I didn't just blow it—I didn't even attempt the journey proposed by Duncan. I went somewhere else entirely. I didn't belong there, and time would prove that.

At the moment of Kent I had a two-year-old son; my daughter wasn't born. Now both kids are well into their thirties, and I look back in disbelief: "What was I doing on that stage? Why did Duncan think to baptize me publicly?" I was first and foremost a homebody, not a literary adventurer, not a budding star like Anne Waldman who should have been there in my place.

At the time, *Solar Journal* was regarded as a radical vision and widely praised in avant-garde circles—as were my texts that followed, three of them from Black Sparrow and then one (*Book of the Cranberry Islands*) from Harper & Row in 1975. Soon thereafter my work was featured in the *Whole Earth Catalogue, The Canadian Whole Earth Almanac, The Chicago Review, Caterpillar,* etc., and I was invited to read my literary prose at dozens of colleges, coffee houses, and poetry festivals. I even headlined the 1975 Chicago Poetry Festival with John Ashberry. By then I could claim a growing cadre of several thousand committed readers.

Though the song inside me continued to be true, I never felt remotely comfortable on stage, not at Kent, not in Berkeley or Chicago or Toronto or Los Angeles. I was relieved when the invitations stopped coming—relieved at one level, disappointed at another—so I went on with my life and continued to take down the hermetic text.

Long after—thirty years after, more than thirty books later—it has become obvious that, despite the precocious start, I have been speaking to almost no one for a very long time. I now have maybe a hundred loyal readers and no publisher except myself. Even to those who fancy literary cosmology, I don't exist.

For a decade or two beyond Kent I still thought, in those ceaseless self-reassessments one does in their head, that the precision of my writing, its "no punches pulled" gumption, transcended its commercial dud. To my mind I was composing one of the more significant works of my time, proceeding undauntedly and without attachment, despite the fact that I was working in a forest where no one heard the trees.

I considered myself lucky—and still do—to have founded a publishing company, so there is no obstacle to my getting my books out, even if most of them sit at Durkee Drayage, our overstock facility, in Richmond, California. Mine would be a totally unpublished opus otherwise, manuscripts in dusty boxes, files in old programs and on unreadable floppies. Yet, one by one, my writings have appeared publicly in sparkling new tomes, packaged and designed with a care and integrity usually accorded to bestsellers—that is, as if someone were actually reading them.

Well, of course someone is. I value regulars of the caliber of Pir Zia Inayat Khan, Mary Stark, Paul Weiss, David Ulansey, Bill Kotzwinkle, Rob Brezsny, Bill Stranger, Anne Marie Molnar, John Upledger, Phil Wohlstetter, and others I don't know. I appreciate old literary friends like Paul Auster, Jonathan Lethem, Ishmael Reed, and Robert Kelly, successful novelists and poets, supporting me in print. But in terms of an audience at large, my score is functionally zero. I have composed a library of thirty-five-plus ambitious books with no takers. I think this may stand alone in contemporary American letters. Or is that just more narcissism and false humility hiding wounded pride?

The majority of people who avidly consumed *Solar Journal* and *Book of the Earth and Sky* and Lindy's and my journal *Io* during the '70s have moved on to other matters. Some, I know, are doctors, librarians, or curators, Buddhist teachers and English teachers; others remain artists and activists but my writing no longer interests them. Ken Warren's tiny stapled *House Organ* is the only paper-and-ink literary mag left from our one-time renaissance of tabloids, from *Yugen* and *Poems for the Floating World* to *Truck, Coherences, Tansy*, and the like. Though I occasionally appear in *House Organ*, my only real venue these days is *Elixir*, the publication launched by Pir Zia, grandson of Hazrat Inayat Khan, the Sufi teacher whose yellow-jacketed hardcovers I discovered in Weiser's Basement of the Occult at the time in high school that I bought my first tarot.

I don't think it is entirely bitchy to note that a good deal of the best stuff being written now garners little actual attention, and most poets and literary novelists toil in anonymity and are frustrated with their public apportionment. A "winner take all" lottery prevails over any baseline of text. Artistic success has become a high-stakes tournament with a marked deck.

Well, that pique aside, either my stuff is not in fashion, or it really was never as good as I thought it was. Those are both real possibilities.

Now Olson is long gone, Duncan is long gone, Dorn is gone, Brakhage is gone, even Creeley is gone. It is not just that they are gone, but the waters have closed over them as if they never existed, as if they were not all that much to begin with.

In his time Olson was as major to me as Shakespeare, Duncan as fundamental as Keats or Da Vinci. Brakhage was a Kurosawa. Dorn was as funny as Richard Pryor, with a game face as grim as Jonathan Edwards'. They are now antiquarians' relics, while I who was once their acolyte, their pretender—though never more than a footnote to the Black Mountain logos—am a footnote to something that never even happened, buried under an avalanche of other screeds to the same or different ends.

Duncan's imprimatur wasn't exactly like "Bruce Springsteen, the future of rock 'n' roll"; it was a requiem about his recently deceased friend (Olson), plus a shot-in-the-dark prophecy for a neophyte. He offered a challenge in the form of an enconium. But either I wasn't up to it, or he wasn't as prescient as reputed—or, more likely, the era I was supposed to open never came.

Instead Lindy and I had a far happier fate. We raised our kids in anonymity while inventing North Atlantic Books—a riveting engagement for twenty-two years. I was the parent at home. Returning from grade school, Robin and Miranda looked forward to tallying the day's receipts and conveying the checks to the bank (where the manager supplied a changing platter of cookies), then hauling boxes and mailers to the post office. In high-school years we graduated to Chinese food, comic books, and *The Sporting News*.

I hoped that our children would be creative, happy adults— and they are. But it never occurred to me that they would see the whole journey we shared through Maine, Vermont, and Berkeley as a privation that they now need to remedy, an indulgence of hippie parents who were self-aggrandizing and just plain weird.*

In the prime of their own literary and scientific careers, they not so much don't read me (because whose kids do while their

---

*This piece is of a day and a mood. My kids are wonderful human beings—talented and compassionate, gracious and kind. One is a brilliant, internationally recognized artist and the other a biologist and Earth steward. However, the sentiments expressed here are also real; they are true in the way that things and their irreconcilable opposites create a dialectic. Personal relationships are never simple, and families generate their own chaos and internal contradictions.

dads are alive?), but have come to regard the fact of Lindy's and my writing as self-delusion and affectation, something to get angry at us about insofar as it inflicts our narcissism on them and draws energy and attention away from their own accomplishments. Mainly what they will tolerate is gushing over their achievements, along with *mea culpas*, thank you. They even worry that I will embarrass them by giving a book I wrote to one of their friends or colleagues. ("Read it?" Robin retorted not long ago when asked in my presence by a peer about a tome. "No, I *lived* it.")

I imagined all through the Seventies and Eighties that we were initiating our children into a hermetic work, that their wandering spirits chose us for that task—and that we shared a wonderful, daffy time together, adventuring through Maine and Vermont and between coasts before settling in Bezerkeley.

All through their growing up they behaved as though our family was fun and the place to be. Our son was our wise collaborator and compatriot, quick to irony and drollery; he never spent time away from home till college. His younger sister was his sidekick, house psychic and gleeful sprite; she had Mommyitis, a condition she exultantly proclaimed, hanging on Lindy's reentry when she was out, greeting her return with theatrical dances. Together they were each other's protectors and inseparable friends.

People used to ask us what our secret was, how we managed to raise such wonderful, bright, and loving kids.

But was their behavior mere compliance with the family regime? Did we run a cult as pernicious as any Moonie?

I used to flatter myself that "recovered memories" were other people's problems; I never envisaged that I too would be subject to unflattering revision. Now I learn that we were fatuous, preoccupied adults who had no boundaries,* that we dropped them off howling at daycare centers, that we were blasé about their crises, that we didn't see them for who they were, that we turned them into workaholics, that we confided to them our adult crises before they had any emotional basis to deal with them (guilty as charged there, a Seventies hazard for sure), that we put stuff in their heads they now can't get out (guilty on that one too, I suppose).

The jig is up. We are full-fledged relics of a bygone age, the stage having been cleared, different props in place.

Forget the crack in the cosmic egg through which Bruno gazed, the lyrics of Lawrence and Williams. Our solidarity with the Australian Aboriginal dreamer and Sioux shaman now read as myopic hippie vanities. We were "playing Indian," Gnostic bard and bueno parent too.

I am a marginal affair, left over from what they pejoratively call the "me generation." They identify that as the Sixties and Seventies. I thought of us then as awakening from a long cultural sleep—our elders' beguilement with playthings, bromides, a "Leave it to Beaver"/Beetle Bailey/Archie world. We felt as

---

*A few months after I wrote this piece, my daughter told an interviewer, "My parents loved me, but they had no boundaries." This is both dead-on and grandstanding at our expense. Our ostensible lack of boundaries is, to my mind, a euphemism for our being process-oriented rather than accepting traditional roles. We were Rich and Lindy, not Mama and Papa. Like many parents of our era we made up the game as we went along, following the muse and invoking candor and emotional honesty, no matter the consequences. Our kids are trying to restore a measure of the boundaries we took down. The intimacy we sought and were denied by our parents, hence gave unwarily to our children in hopes of turning society around, is of no interest to them.

though we were pioneers glimpsing a mysterious and magical cosmos, the so-called dawning of the Age of Aquarius.

In their revisionist history we are indulgent, half-assed flower children, wannabe beatniks, rather than poet-sages or even responsible guardians. Alternately we are aristocratic Ivy League intellectuals with mean, critical, politically incorrect writer friends. The caricatures contradict each other, but then so does everything else.

Lindy and I began writing our poetic texts during the early counterculture, in dialogue with the Black Mountain avant-garde, and we continue to write forty years later more or less under the same aegis. But, despite their one-time allegiance to the enterprise of our writing and North Atlantic Books, our kids now regard the whole shebang as elitist bullshit and treat our present efforts much as they would the hobbies of parents who putter around the shop or crochet all day. 'What is wrong with you?' is the repeated query. 'Why are you guys so fucking retro?'

As to Jon's suicide: "So sorry to hear about your brother, Rich, but we're here to celebrate new life." "Sorry…?"—wow, that was a quick Hallmark moment; I almost didn't catch the sympathy part. Usually insincere condolences hang around a little longer—this one, from my daughter-in-law's sister, two months after Jon's death and a month before the birth of my grandson Leo. I wonder if she fretted half a second that I might think she *didn't* care. As I said to Lindy at the time, one day it will be, "Gee Robin, too bad your parents died, pass the tamari."

But if sarcasm is the trope of our generation, sanctimonious platitude is theirs. If we are Sixties anti-materialistic, they mean to restore the good life with its high-end, well-crafted merchandise and urbane get-togethers—and they portray us as misers and skinflints for not helping to underwrite their affairs.

We are too ardent; they are too cool. Except when it's the opposite.

They are literalists, avowedly so, in both their professional and personal lives, even when they are being hiphop and improvisational. We are the apostles of 'nothing is literal, nothing is as it seems,' to the point of driving them up the wall: "Yeah, Rich, we know. We're being simplistic. It's more complex than that! It's always more complex."

Literalism is not literal to them; it's a way to practice anything without unconscious conflicts or undone homework; it's a tactic posing as an epistemology.

Our kids want us to sidle off gracefully into the oblivion of "here's your Grandpa Rich and Grandma Lindy," our time over, our song hushed. "Out with the old, in with the new—so long, br'er Jon."

They want far gushier grandparents than us, like the endlessly cited confectioned parents of friends, who can't ever log sufficient gran'chile time or cluck dulcetly enough: prototype sweet seniors. They want to use the generational game to reduce us to Ma and Pa Kettle, a charade whereby everyone smiles condescendingly while we get to play the fools. After all, by their own declaration, we not they are in charge now.

It is amazing how love can turn into punishment, meniality and subservience supplant play. But that's why we were process-oriented. When there are only roles, relationship becomes aggression. Imperious and casual dismissal of the elders is as old as the primate band but a new genre in our family.*

---

*A character in a *New Yorker* story by our daughter wonders whether she would murder her parents if asked by some attractive guy and decides she would. But, as I explained to a friend who asked how that felt, "Hey, it's fiction."

I feel as though we are being asked, not for love, not for authenticity, but for submission, gifts, salaams. We are feeding a hungry bird that can never be sated or lauded enough.

Is that all it has come down to, what I once thought of as magical children, karmic compatriots, just a handful of years ago?

"But you don't understand what you did," my stepmother commented some years ago. "You created a sanctuary and a paradise, and they will never forgive you for letting them find out it doesn't exist."

Maybe at the level of subconscious mythodrama this is true and will always be true, but at an Oedipal level where patriarchs, from the alpha orangutan to Socrates to Joe DiMaggio, are overthrown like clockwork (no biggie!), they recall it differently, not as a paradise but a state of regression.

I thought we were giving our son and daughter freedom and power, but we were giving them only our own freedom and power. I fancied myself beneficent and liberal but, like my own parents, I was merely furthering my generation's narcissistic mythology, empowering my children solely to serve my agendas, agendas too commonplace for me even to be aware of. It was all carried out under the cover of things I thought more "important"—avant-garde and profound enough to merit clan loyalty and set against other agendas and lives.

I so feared for myself and them, our tenuous existences, that I deprived us of our individualities, and them of their own mythologies. I used a theater of intimacy to prevent a more dangerous intimacy. I empowered them at the expense of *seeing* them, which stuck them with the burden of being compadres in a magnificent mission, of helping me carry the equivalent of the ring through Mordor.

I mean, how could they jilt such an offer, in good conscience turn down my invitation? Such fealty, such homage, so much power from their own father! Only it was *my* ring and *my* Mordor, and it was the way I tried to entrap them in my world, even as my parents tried to entrap me in theirs.

The visions and utopian fantasies of the Sixties make absolutely no sense any more, so our kids have to destroy them, at least metaphorically. They have to remake our family by the logic of their time, the gender politics, pop psychology, prescribed speech, and attachment parenting of their peers; they have to ally vicariously with punk and rap and bling to smash our obsolete pieties and inflated myths. They have to convert us in their equation to our antithesis, to chill and live.

As for my writing, I have come to satisfy myself with passing the candle to unknown tribes. Surely that is a grander ambition anyway than "fifteen minutes" of throwaway culture.

I have convinced myself that readers beyond my lifetime will exist, whether they discover my work or not. In fact, I enjoy inventing them and the tricks of fate by which my writing might or might not survive. It really doesn't matter which, as long as they are somewhere, because, after all, the words are ultimately more theirs than mine.

I believe, as Blake did, in readers of a future time and have begun to address them, in my mind's eye.

That too seems absurdly grandiose. After all, I'm a privileged white male in the "First World." The real poets of my time scriven among the underclasses across Africa and South America. Many of them will never put words on paper or hard drives. Muslim and Chinese minstrels have far greater claim than I on the pulse of the Earth.

I have lost the faith and surety that my kind of readers will exist—not after a few more degrees of global warming and pole-melt, after decades of superstorms dwarfing Katrina, after the

8.1 earthquake on the Hayward Fault, after thousands of terror-ist attacks on the West and its institutional infrastructure and distracted populaces, after the bird flu and supervolcano and nuclear winter, after the collapse of the system of commerce and reward within which I composed my bleat, after the blowout of money and machines, major urban centers and factories—whether any of these disasters ensue or not. Whether they befall us or whether the West somehow blunders through, the force of the future is already a hurricane obliterating all logic, all deed.

My work will not survive in any form. The few printed books, their ephemeral pages and inks, will be pulped or drowned in seasalts. All digital records will be scorched, incinerated by bombs or wiped from the planet in a great file-burning after the triumph of global jihad, a fire that will consume the "satanic vers-es" of my old colleagues Banks and Lethem and Auster too—as the next world age and its sanctioned art takes hold. To them we will all be blasphemers and heathens. Maybe a few volumes or silicon files will endure somehow in the odd antique shop after the impending dark ages, and those in the future will know some of us existed … if they even ply the Roman alphabet.

None of it will survive a planetoid hit, an explosion of the Earth itself, or a nova of the Sun, so what's the point anyway? Why carefully craft and hone epiphanies upon the void?

The syllables I call forth are already frivolous and ephemer-al, their meanings to be replaced by other dialects and tongues, their phonemes already tattering like dead leaves in autumn. A quack or a caw means as much to the night sky or the fishermen of Vega as American English.

More to the point, late August, seated on a bench outside the Ellsworth library, the day our kids departed from a two-week family get-together in Downeast Maine, I can no longer indulge my old idealisms about us or pretend to be innocent. I waited all summer—and several summers before that—for them to come to visit the magical land of Maine; but we raised them in California, and they are West Coast kids. They didn't want to be here. They are moving at a different speed; they cruise right through the place without seeing it. They are not even that interested in us. Big surprise, they honor the mores and aesthetics of their colleagues and friends.

I have to let them go—the ideals and memories of so many years—let them move on. I have to consider too that *they* are right. Lindy's and my art is quaint compared to the cuttings of their generation. My readers who have never been will never be.

I am willing to die. I am willing to have my work expunged.

But I am not willing to expunge it myself like a doddering, frightened elder vilified and called to answer for my crimes. I am not willing to profess my errors and renounce myself before Red Guards. When they ask that of me, they ask too much.

And for whom are these agitated words intended this very moment such that I am compelled to scribble with a failing pen in a yard-sale binder while Lindy checks out a thrift shop down Main Street?

I am imprinting the Akashic Record, which doesn't require words anyway because our lives etch it. As we stumble, outspoken or unspoken, through the great labyrinth, we inscribe our existence on the part of the cosmos that is indelible and immemorial.

The reason, obviously, that I don't have to use words to write into the Akashic Record is that the record does not accrue or preserve itself in language; else how could future humans and sentient beings on other planets in other planes contribute to the same text as us and draw their own lessons and karmic destinies from it? How could it be transmitted and known in the boundless unconscious mindedness of creation if it were penned only in provincial dialects?

These are words on the surface only; the deep-syntax strings generating them are not only deeper than Romance or Indo-European, but deeper than *Homo sapiens* or Milky Way. Their dictation comes from beyond language. I am merely the translation device.

I am writing to the mute presence of all those dimensions within creation that string theory tells us must thrive somewhere, untapped, unreleased, raveled into stuff, atom by atom (but dormant and null in this bardo)—as many as eight of them. Esoteric legend promises far more.

If they exist, I am permitted to write. *Because* they exist, I am supported in carrying the phonetic equivalent of the *chi* ball. Because they exist, I can be gullible and deluded. Nothing of that sort is judged; nothing of that sort matters. Writing the Akashic Record is my only job.

This text confirms only the space I occupy, makes me feel whole beneath Orion and the Dipper, a swain who is turning up an ace. I murmur gaily as though in dialogue with an unknown intelligence that courts me with its refrains, relaying them through my bare existence to intelligences in realms I cannot reach.

Coming out of me is a *daven* not unlike the trill of the gull or crow who cries for words before words are possible. Emitting from wetsuits in squawks and howls, what they began in stymied curiosity or involuntary bestial frustration, I am finishing in syllables of twenty-first-century English, a parlance of a mere millisecond in the corridors of space-time. I am turning their stridulations into semantics, without a smidgen of their authenticity. I postulate in overeducated caw. Neither of us is satisfied, but neither of us is particularly unhappy either.

Though I am not writing into the Akashic Record as directly as they are, I express a kinship with their chirping and silently breathing onto cosmic tablets, whether these tablets exist or not. I am like other birds, other frogs, crying in the face of all that stands against us, in chorus with all that might stand for us, if it could only one day exist.

If I have lost the way, I am in a migration of lemmings who have collectively lost the way, though luckily Ellsworth is peaceful this afternoon and the light this far into Vinland is luminous and holy. There are bees yet in the flowers, hundreds of them. We get to go on another day.

These pages will be obliterated sooner or later, but there are hidden dimensions, muttering silently in the most obscure of places, muttering though no one can hear them. And the Akashic scribe gets, in fact, everything.

We are now in the reign of a king every bit as mad in his own way as Caligula, as ruthless as Henry VIII, as nepotistically investitured as Kim Jong-il—rumored as well (in underground buzz) to be possessed by the Dark Priesthood and in liege to the Secret Government.

As if things were not fragile and dangerous enough, the whole American dreamworks is splintering from massive stress, about to crumble under entitlement programs, farm subsidies, corporate handouts, and foreign debt. We inhabit a republic that was once a democracy, now governed by ignorant and gluttonous racketeers who wield nothing but inherited machinery and deeded privilege, aggregate resources bled from two-plus centuries of sacrifice and dreams, a collaborative melting pot of craft and industry squandered on a maudlin orgy of schemes, thieveries, calumnies, and Halliburtonesque pillages.

They impose corporate Guernicas on every idea or creature or thing that gets in their way. But in the way of what? Some sterile conquest of the planet by a mafia of talking heads in suits? A capitulation of the Earth to the Lucifer Rebellion and the alien Greys? A takeover by Illuminati, Skull and Bones, or Sonz of Babylon?

Guys, what's the game that makes it worth destroying the planet, the lodges of all its creatures, the sentient-being network that has been in-sourcing itself for over a billion years?

Greed is greed, any way you slice it. It means many die so that a few can pig out in behemoth vehicles, consumerized tanks, and 25,000-square-foot homes. It means jails packed with political and cultural prisoners, addicts, and the mad and homeless. It means no responsibility to the ancient human enterprise or Gaian species-web. It means locusts with human personae and adminstrative power.

Some hundred thousand suicide bombers are training and being born to train, in the West too, to take revenge, maneuvering outside the global economy where this entire pompous affair unfolds. They aren't shamans or Buddhists or even good old-fashioned Marxists, Mau Maus, and Maoists. We have earned much badder enemies than that. We've got an entire neo-fascist brigade of patriarchal clerics and their feudal assassins and holy terrorists. We are fighting orcs and mantises who don't speak our language and will not allow us to surrender.

The West is going to lose the Crusades this time. So much softer and more pampered than the Sunni/Shi'ite jihad, it boasts a cowardly arsenal of smart bombs and mercenary armies made up of small-town yokels and gang-bangers, crank covens and street hooligans.

The new war pits Coca-Cola dreams and Wal-Mart mercados against the Talibanistan outback and jihad.com. Having abandoned any self-discipline, any moral basis for the consumption of the planet, having forfeited any role in funding creative consciousness and sustaining perhaps the last best hope of mankind, America is now without friends and without its former moral shield.

Just as Hitler could not alone build concentration camps and slaughter six million Jews along with assorted Gypsies, homosexuals, and other "undesirables," so George W. Bush didn't invade Iraq or create extraordinary rendition and wiretapping all by himself. America is as responsible for Bush's carnage as Greater Germania was for Hitler's.

Vietnam could be a mistake, Mr. Rumsfeld, but Iraq and Guantanamo make it a policy. The reelection of George W, after everything that went down in his first term, stamps it "made in America" and not just a stolen election. These aren't my words; they are right out of bin Laden's September 2007 State of the World address.

We have nothing left worth preserving or selling. We have no basis, no reason why those not feeding out of the corporate trough should be grateful any longer or care.

Forget the brave soldiers of "Over There." Forget the Marshall Plan. Forget Frank Sinatra singing *"The house I live in, a plot of earth, a street...."* Forget the Constitution and Bill of Rights. The present toady regime has rendered those as vapid and hollow as Andrew Jackson's treaties with Indian tribes or Stalin's post-war pacts with Latvia and Lithuania.

What do we have to be proud for in the universe or even the planet? Las Vegas? Hunting ranches and jeep-riding cowboys? Kiddieporn and blood-and-gore cinema? Grand Theft

Auto? Gun shows? NASCAR? Reality TV? Britney Spears and Michael Jackson? American Idol? The saga of O. J. Simpson and Scott Peterson and JonBenet Ramsey and Terri Schiavo and Anna Nicole Smith and Paris Hilton while millions die of hunger or work as slaves and indentured peons to support the imperial consortium? The mullahs are right. We have become a malignancy on the Earth.

Whether they were fairly elected or not (at all the levels on which that premise is worth considering), our leaders are trying to kill the dream, kill the planet in the name of Christ (which means kill labor for the benefit and Rapture of capital). Meanwhile our enemies are trying to eradicate the biosphere for Allah (which means to kill capital in the name of tribal monarchy and male privilege). We live under not only the death of the radiant city of Jefferson and Hawthorne but the death of any and all aspirations to restore it.

Oh, how we have allowed the least among us, the most venal and brutal and stupid and compassionless to lead, to lead us over the cliff.

When only violence can be done, in word and deed and by order of moguls and transnational bosses, there are no words, no useful actions, only explosions and increasingly bad weather.

What Is an Archetype?

It is our task to find the inside of the universe. The outside of the universe is already identified—rock and fire and water and physiognomy.

From the first trail in the forest to the chert handaxe to the rock circle to Mesolithic stilt house to the Neolithic village to the walled Mediaeval city to the shopping mall, the human primate scratches the mark of the inside on the outside, cuneiforms onto a husk.

We take runes from an unknown source and hammer them on the garment. Without a world, nothing would get ciphered.

The waters contaminated, the permafrost melting, entire species dying off, self-righteous armies preparing for at least a century or two of battle, genocide a no-brainer in their handbooks—the spirits of many plants and animals are departing this zone: good riddance, man!—or so report reliable witnesses. Yet others say that creatures previously unknown on Sol/Planet Three are streaming here from all dimensions, to aid our birth process, to observe its grief-stricken pangs, to witness an event that happens only once or twice in a universe, to pray with the star seedlings until we know who we are.

This is no accident. This is no mere battlefield. This has never been wagered before, been dared, in any galaxy. This is the game we were born to play.

We are getting to experience how messy things become on worlds, how hopeless the plight of living. We get to be here, with our destiny and planet at stake, in a civilization sinking into mire. We are confronted with saving our entire Pleistocene legacy, with redeeming creation, beyond big bangs and white dwarfs and any and all apocalypses. We are being offered the only way to understand *what a universe is.* The real universe, the one that beats in our hearts, that casts its luminations across our dreams....

Having gone this far into the demise, when the moment comes in a billion years or so, we will know exactly how deep we have to go to reclaim everything and turn it around. Because we will have already done it by proxy.

Otherwise, for the level of consciousness we now are, we are in way over our heads. This was never a crisis we could resolve or repair.

Predation was the first precept of business on this planet, an axiom implanted by unseen gods in subcellular life. It was the only way to spawn a living entity, to jumpstart both ontogeny and phylogeny.

Life is a lesson in being consumed, in being made and then dismembered, in getting our innards—stomach and lungs and entrails—twined into mind-nerves, elegantly and remorselessly, and then having them ripped back out of us, if not by talons, claws, or incisors, then by viruses and bacteria.

The dharma is conducted fish by fish, lizard by lizard, hyena by hyena, cells synergized to waves of hunger that sweep this planet with a greater force than hurricanes. We are as ravenous as wolves, but we pay mercenaries to kill for us. It's all the same on a cellular level.

In our dimension, yes the maiden horror is that creatures have stomodea, rapacious openings to swallow other life forms, internal tracts to absorb them. Energy must be stolen in order for anything to survive. This makes peace impossible from the get-go. The primal despair of the hunt, quilled into animal psyches, transposed into arrows and bolos, hemorrhages into electronic weaponry. The primal imperative is to ravage before getting ravaged. No wonder we are at an impasse in an imbroglio; it is our own impasse, who we are.

I don't think that carnivorousness either has a moral purpose or is amoral. I also don't think it is malign.* Consciousness arose out of a slumbering universe—a universe in a trance so profound it didn't know it existed or that existence was even possible.

It had to get at itself. It had been inside a false boundary, unconscious for aeons of timeless time.

From those bearings, there weren't a whole lot of options for how to get consciousness going—how to make something out of *zéro*, how to hatch and individuate creatures that feel and do things.

Acts need fuel; they need differentiation and context; they need desire; they need purpose and boundaries. The first, blunt dialectic breeds contention. To get enough friction, life must rub against itself right away, harshly and for keeps. Bionts are not hibernating dream-bundles but vortices with portals. They love their bodies and those of others, love them enough to tear them apart and devour them. They love them as if they were themselves, for life is primordially the act of turning other into self and self into other.

That is the origin of psyche—sweet pretty psyche, lullaby psyche and psyche of the war dance, dakini of glamour, voracious hag—stepping like Aphrodite out of her own bloody sea. She's the beginning of fire, and language; the origin of the knife and the wheel and the sign.

---

*I am guessing that, if not on other worlds among the stars, then in other dimensions of creation, animals feed off light, sugars and carbohydrates of pure radiance, or what passes for sugars and photons. Creatures of light need only to swallow vibrations of light to survive and be radiant and happy. Places where sentient beings kill and consume other sentient beings are low on the cosmic totem pole. It is hardly an efficient way to run a planet.

Time was created long ago, by movement, clouds ripping through other clouds. Creatures propagated out of the mutant seeds of prior creatures, swallowing their DNA kinsfolk. Cells can arise only from cells, feed off cells alone—mind likewise, psyche too.

Predation is not adversarial; it is simply logistic. Something has to be stalked in order to stalk, some aspect of consciousness has chase in order for another to flee, has to gobble and be gobbled to get the attention of the universe as it spars to put its flickering ember onto a wick, to breathe its flame sentient, to become alert—something has to bid matter give itself a notion of becoming alive.

Eating is thinking; it is the primordial act of thought and movement.

That is why souls from so many planets and dimensions have come great distances to watch the morality play here. Their outcomes as well as ours hang in the offing. To their taste we are singing a beautiful song.

The riddle the universe is trying to solve through consciousness is the old one—being and nothingness, darkness and light, love and the abeyance of love, terror and epiphany, greed and compassion, eater and eaten, war and truce, but most of all, primevally, inside and outside.

The payoff is not the endless petty exercises and skirmishes here in this theater, regal and epic though they seem to its players—but the big one, before and beyond worlds, out of which all worlds and landscapes arise, and through the enactment and traction of which this will eventually be transformed into something unimaginable (but something that assuredly follows).

The mystery alone makes it worthwhile, makes it something rather than a big nothing.

We must place a medium-sized rock, greenish-gray perhaps and somewhat round, to mark this site in creation, a place-holder. The existence of a pebble assures us that we exist too. HERE WE MADE OUR STAND. HERE WE BOWED TO UNKNOWN GODS AND ACCEPTED OUR MISSION.

Carriers of the banner of the sacred Eel, we have wept her tears, puked her innards, and marched in her catacombs, armored and barefoot, in herds and solo. We have fled a million times and scavenged likewise but always returned, crown chakra bowed, loyal to the end.

We are in fact the only loyal soldiers the universe has, through all its bottomless transparency and damnable mirages too. At this threshold we make our claim:

WE KNOW IN OUR HEARTS THAT IT WILL BE OKAY BECAUSE WE WILL MAKE IT OKAY.

If you wonder how it is reasonable to have faith in outrageous notions like reincarnation, multiple lives, bardo realms, karma, and transmigration you first have to recollect that an ancient advanced civilization encompassing India, Tibet, China, Mongolia, Japan, and much of Southeast Asia contemplated these issues for millennia and gleaned a sophisticated science out of them, an inquiry they preserved in rigorous practices and texts. Long, long ago they posed the only question worth its breath: "Who are we?" Then, over ensuing centuries and generations, they kept asking it, more precisely and persistently than their Western counterparts. They milked their pedigrees in schools more austere than any the West has accredited; more meticulous, for being without abstraction or metaphor, than those of physics and algebra.

Yes, they could be wrong, dead wrong, hopelessly deluded, deluding others, for they were dealing solely in paradoxes and absent machineries. But again, remember, they analyzed these matters far longer than the West has analyzed molecules and thermodynamics. Their conclusions are empirical and pragmatic, refined through lifetimes of meditation, centuries of ascetic practice, some of it in caves and on barren hills where the view is long and deep and obstructions few.

They were not measuring or counting motes while salesmen in the West were setting up shop; they were not inspecting carcasses or sticking flags in peripheral topographies. As corpses were tossed onto public pyres, they were dead-reckoning the account from inside themselves, consulting transpersonal entities, extrapolating from direct experience of auras, life energy, and pure mind.

They were neither veracious nor conjectural. They did not invent methods in order to support a case; they did not even cultivate techniques qua skills; they simply moved into the proximal space that our situation allows, in which everything (and anything) is both indisputable and ordinary. Generation after generation, they stayed on topic, stayed the course, consistently enough to grasp the lay of the land. Their transmissions, teacher to student, monk to novice, were almost impeccable. Until reincarnation became inescapable fact.

It takes a rigidly cultivated benightedness and obtuseness—a collective civilizational denial—for us in the West not to see the universe, not to recognize the vectors that rule our lives. In homage to technocracy and linear time, we have dulled our imaginal organs. Having rendered ourselves myopic and insensible, we do not experience or even intuit bardo realms. We simply work the heavy machinery and sigh—sixteen tons of number-nine coal, and *"another day older and deeper in debt."**

The West now lacks any context but wealth and material progress—that is why its nations have lost their way and can proffer no ontological defense against the equally linear, apocalyptic army of radicalized Islam with its vantage of a different chess match on another planet. The fatwa-crazy madrasas are not ashrams or zendos, or even affiliate Sufi lodges; they are psychic military schools that have arisen almost solely as a counterattack on runaway consumerism and the soap opera of Western history. The political arm of Islam freely adapts the tools and habiliments of the West, presuming, by cargo-cult logic, that Allah meant those portions—planes and explosives and seas of underground oil—as manna, spiritualizable swords for believers.

We are being crushed between Muslim fundamentalism and Christian fundamentalism, with Science no better than a referee with an outdated rulebook. All three parties honor the same materialistic heresy, leaving us truly strangers in a strange land.

Why such a perverse choice for so many of the habitants of a sacred planet? We desperately need to know.

Karl Marx called religion the opiate of the masses, but I think it is simpler than that: our state of existence is excruciating, our situation of unknowing unbearable.

A religion like Buddhism converts unknowing and suffering into something tolerable and explicable, a foothold in creation.

Fundamentalist Muslims and Christians, on the other hand, tell themselves elaborate back stories because, finding

---

*As sung by Tennessee Ernie Ford—and don't forget the moonlight gambler himself, Frankie Laine, because *"if you haven't gambled for love in the moonlight,/then you haven't gambled at all."*

the spaciousness of the open road, the open mind, inadmissible, they want a drama to explain what they are doing here and what is going to happen. And sadly, they want a set of rules whereby they can win.

Opiate of the masses, for sure!

Indian pundits dismiss all sides: worlds come, worlds go, they say; species are born; species die; civilizations rise, fall; universes extrude, balloon, and collapse. No big deal.

A friend who is a skilled martial artist, a thirty-year practitioner of the aiki, from t'ai chi and hsing-i to capoeira and taekwondo, told me that his girlfriend recently saw her young nephew mesmerized in a hand-held martial-arts video game, hour after hour, spurning any human interaction at a family gathering. Finally she could not resist saying to him, "My homeboy does that stuff for real."

The kid looked up and, after a moment's puzzlement, snarled, "Yeah, but can he *do this?*"

For no particular reason her parable reminds me of an event with a similar cadence but an opposite meaning. About twenty-five years ago two friends of ours, a couple who run a large New Age healing center in rural Northern California, were seated with us at lunch on a crowded outdoor patio, talking to some businessmen from Chicago who were considering an investment in their enterprise.

This couple had had a relatively late-in-life son who was about nine at the time, and they made a point of treating him respectfully, as if a reborn lama. The kid in fact was a holy terror, but no matter how many anthills he kicked up, TV wrestling matches he mimicked with grunts and burps, revved-up conversations he conducted in Donald Duck's voice, they were unperturbed, instructing him with mild speech as to what was compassionate and courteous.

On this particular day he came tearing down the road on his Big Wheel, doing pop-a-wheelies, and at exactly the spot where pavement turned to dirt on the patio, he swerved to a stop, showering our table with dust and pebbles and ruining the food.

"Joey," his mother finally spoke in a voice that was only slightly strained, "I think you can find a more appropriate expression for your *prana*."

He looked up, confounded for a second, and then bellowed: *"But I ... LIKE IT!"**

Near a place I shall not name is a marsh. Where the runoff from an ancient mountain worn to its last few hundred feet settles, the muck is fully carpeted, mostly with clubmoss (moss and liverworts too) such that the landscape gleams in lime radiance like a forest orbiting a more emerald star.

Remove your shoes before entering the house. There is no softer rug. You are treading on a giant alive sponge. The water

---

*One additional application here: Comparing the two stories reveals a gap between 1983 and 2007. Joey was at least putting his body on the line. Computer games are mere digitalized skits for the nervous system—a poor initiation for kids who should be skate-boarding, running down fungos, racing kayaks, and the like. Life isn't a database projected onto a screen; it is more like All-Star Baseball's metal spinner rattling onto batters' propensities on cardboard disks.

retained is frigid and tonic as it courses over your toes, sometimes up to your arches. Through your etheric footpads it cleanses your body inside and out and recharges your *chi*.

Walk as gently as you can because you are a big zooid and your paws are forever altering its face.

Mushroom sentinels, orange and brown, lurk among baby translucent caps that tend toward crimson in spots where they have tint. A slim white fungus, delicate and vertical, is a soft nail hammered into dead bark.

Ferns congregate wantonly like casinos, flaunting invitation.

Patches of young horsetails elevate, shoots of deeper green sprouting from their joints.

Pitcher plants here and there decoy as gas stations.

Very small wood frogs travel along the mat. Where one halts, it becomes a dead leaf, the canary yellow mascara around its mouth leaflike as well.

Occasional bigger frogs are their precise replicas.

A freshet from underground trickles through the sponge in such stillness and blackness that it is transporting dust on glue without apparent motion. Water that is flowing yet still, mirror-like and diaphanous, suspends rocks and sticks, timeless coins in amber. Surface motes drift, oblivious to destination or haste.

The creek winds sinuously through the tapestry, going under it in spots, reemerging in ebony pools before regathering in a cohesive stream. Its inkiness suggests tar but is actually as sanitary as an aquifer. Nectar passes under root hairs and is filtered through cleft trunks, their bark lemmas so charcoal-like that the clubmoss appears almost a lunar reflection.

In spots the rill flows through pudgy clumps of soil held together by tiny plants and old root systems. These aerodynamic tunnels are as cindered as imploded volcanos, their grip on the soil a mere feather. They snap loose in clods.

Elsewhere rivulets tunnel through quartz-impregnated stone. Giant boulders coated with plants, mostly clubmoss, dam and redirect the ichor. Up close their fur looks like lilliputian ferns.

Above this stygian grotto, the distant headdresses of the trees flow inebriated in sunlight. Their leaves play percussion, as a breeze strafes their isobar.

That bird gliding over us is not a crow or even a hawk. Dig the white tail feathers and brown wingspread! That is a bald eagle, thinking eagle thoughts while scanning for mammal and reptile bundles.

We are in a sanctified place.

The stream continues to curve capriciously, arcing bayou-like and sculpting Arthur Tress dreamscapes on its moebius course. The water not only suggests the unconscious mind; it *is* unconscious, for it transmits a deep, elemental cosmology.

Now the topocline slopes to a massive wort-covered outcropping, favoring channels its runoff has been cutting for centuries. The water slides across the stone table's edge, down its face in membranes with gushers of Pan-like music. Vegetating vertically on the rock, club moss and fronds break the curtain in ways so subtle that myriad tributaries with ingeniously diverse outcomes comprise a waterfall in multiple strands. Near the top, shrubbery catches liquid for an instant and then releases it in dotted lines. These become staccato series of bubbles, as droplets percolate out of the fabric in the manner of blood from cardiac tissue.

The transmission of fluid down the wall is not just a drumroll over rocks; it is a pipe at such perfect pitch, with so many irregular stops, that the output is both Peruvian and Beethoven. I hear the chorale of a Tuvan throat singer, complicated but primitive.

These are the lungs of the troll; its plants, its bronchii. They are exhaling the stream such that, at their bottom, oxygenated water collects in a black pool and then finds its way down new waterfalls.

Without beginning or end, the scroll modulates from quietude to turbulence; then at splashpoint occupies something in between, becoming a foam-filled tarn from which it is reconstituted and curls away toward the beaver pond.

In this boundaryless laboratory the planet concocts its sweetest, most bitter medicines, synthesizing humus, succussing mountain wash and light. Few spots on the planet are this potent, this moist and, at the same time, so dry and alchemical— plump with water and yet navigable.

This is a watch in a totemic vigil, homebase to osprey, eagle, and pitcher plant.

You brush against the Earth shaman's very robes. Show gratitude for this herbal bath.

Albeit so, the marsh rings with this unbroken message:

You should not be here, you should not be here.

This is mine; this is not human.

Enter and be served.

Enter as a dream.

You will never understand.

Earlier this summer I awoke each day with an inexplicable joy, a hopefulness transcending all evidence, embracing everything and everyone. I wrote for an hour or more before breakfast. Three times a week I drove to chi gung or yoga.

Nothing could go wrong, not in the final count, not in the end. The sky was blue, branches fluctuated gracefully in offshore breezes. The birds were so many and cheerful and on my side, the side of hope. The clouds were pure shape-shifting artistry.

Now that same life seems reversed—grim and paranoid. I feel omnipresent doom. Everything seems brittle and flat.

When I was happy, I didn't ever want to leave this world, aggrieved that my time here was limited. There was not enough life in which to do it, feel it, explore it, get enough of it into me.

Now I am so terrified and discouraged by this situation that I think life is too long an exile in such a harsh and uncompromising place.

On some level I intuit that these are the same thing, different pitches of the same song. I am experiencing wavelengths of one state. Bottomless grief is a form of joy. Total despair is in fact what makes hope and courage possible.

Three and a half weeks into my dark arisings, I hit upon a clue, a way out. It is guided by my breath. Each in-breath takes fresh energy from the cosmos—stars, plants, mountains, wind-gliding birds, and all the abundant light and dew and sensation and spirits alive on this world, and all worlds, all the way out to the farthest-most imaginable galaxies and beyond.

Each out-breath flushes stale, dead energy from my cells, pushing it through every pore of me back into the universe, to be recharged by the vast anonymous engine, to be replaced with stuff that has traveled across space, fresh and wholesome, and is now bathing the Earth. Old molecules will be reconstituted, as they are breathed in and out by others of many species and by stones; they will be remitted too as wind and rain and fog.

This is an exercise that twice a week Paul Weiss teaches in his 7:30 chi gung class. Make a mudra torch with your hand and point it beyond the outer Solar System, through Andromeda toward titanic starfields at the edge of time and space. Feed yourself their fluvium. Draw in their spume and spunk. Savor every cell of your body sucking in and absorbing this elixir. Imagine fine quarks of *chi* originating beyond space; traveling light years in an instant; zooming through the Oort Cloud, past Sedna and Eris, past scattered comets and Plutinos, past gas giants and the asteroid belt; creasing this planet's ionosphere and stratosphere, down through clouds over the Atlantic, onto the Maine Coast, into this room on Gilbert Farm Road. It is no doubt *something*, something else, but imagine it as this.

The freshet melts my grief; it lifts me out of torpor—though the outcome is not automatic. I arrive in Town Hill barely awake: grumpy, sullen, a muddle of paralysis. At first, *chi* doesn't even dribble; any movement by me aggravates, hurts. Dry as dust, I shut off on a dime. Breathing through this state is like shaking cobwebs that are taut nerve-impregnated fibers into my liver, kidneys, and, ouch!, heart. I flat-out balk; I stand there in a brown study and have to will myself to carry out the meagerest instruction: "Dancing palms, fuck you!"

I don't have to exist at all, but I am even too irritable to go away.

Then I do it, and the world gradually gets very very large, or my shell melts, and the world always was this large. The blue jays at the window, the squirrel balancing on the line to get at the bird-food, the faces of my cohorts in the class—all are delightfully and absurdly beautiful again. I am among The Eight Brocades.

On Patricia Fox's yoga days I let the weight of everything that is me hang and tug my vectors. I feel the mass and disposition of my body—body-mind—such that its bare reality cracks the scab of my mood, converting discomfort and awareness of stiffness into light catharsis, a hint of tears.

My own weight and attention literally pull on my fibers, enhancing their sensations and letting me sense how thick and basic they are, how much stuff they are carrying in them, including lost emotions, and how it is my not-feeling them, rather than their lesions, that aches so persistently. They actually taste good. And they chafe almost unbearably.

I am at the gate.

I will carry this memory back into the secular world and move in a slightly different way. There will be tissue memory to contend against habit as I sprawl through the sprawling terrain.

Breathing in, I experience pain from all over the Earth, not only agonies of war, disease, desolation, loneliness, separation, but the suffering of every creature terrified or dying. It is a single, homogenous generic pain.

What hurts is the Earth itself hurting—a big and terrible pang every moment. Sucked into my sinews, it is released. On its way out, it is worth celebrating, rejoicing, redeeming by an expanded heart meridian/cardiac muscle.

Inhale.

Breathe out compassion and empathy for everyone—imagined, beyond imagination.

Breathe in the reality of bodily existence; feel how broad and profound its fact is.

Breathe out.

Breathe out the willingness to support and comfort, even if it is not selflessly realized.

Breathe out unabashed desire to be part of only what will heal and forgive and redeem.

Breathe out solidarity of sadness, of camaraderie in this strange and beautiful incomprehensible place.

Breathe in how fragile and unbearable and exquisitely poignant it is.

Breathe out that I will not forget you, fail you ever.

Breathe in stellar wind.

Breathe in self.

Breathe out that I grow closer to you with each exhalation, closer to comprehension of our shared plight.

Breathe directly into the gravitational flame that lights galaxies throughout space-time.

Breathe in the life thump and silk of consciousness in a universe.

Breathe out that I can keep from making it bad for others, that I can find us a way out of here.

If every creature were fanning this mantra at once, it occurs to me, the world would tremble and then change in a single breath.

Breathe in clear mind, *only* witnessing, *always* in attention, ever wondering, never not open to revision or revelation, always willing to give everything away, knowing that it can never (and doesn't want to ever) fathom what it will get back.

The intention to clear one's mind and heart is three beats. The cosmic mystery is a single long release, not only from a state of pure ignorance, but admitting and submitting to it, kicking up sparks of enlightenment that catch at the onset of the next breath.

Breathe out the mystery—I don't know shit from shinola.

Yes, it is work, but no one said it was going to be handed to us on a silver platter.

Fourth Cycle

A pro basketball player explaining why he refused to be baited by an official:

"You don't want to get into a fight with a pig because you both get dirty and the pig likes it."

Life is not life, and death is not death. Those who would scam us about anything scam us about everything and scam us big-time about this.

I do not discover my own mortality; I simply rediscover it as something else in this realm. Immortality is "something else" too.

Attitudes toward death have nothing to do with the personal phenomenology of death; they are cultural indoctrinations, funereal melodramas, shadows of the psyche, *danses macabres.* When someone "dies," s/he leaves the social order, the polity, its rules, and that is shocking to those who remain—to lose the trajectory of a friend, a parent, a colleague, forever.

To have the slate wiped clean in an instant, to have everything that counted suddenly not count. To have any claim to property or service expunged. To lose your seat at the table, your number in the census, your place at the party, your right to wake with the new day and breathe the Earth's air like everybody else....

"It's hard to jump in. Like cold water."

"Once you get used to it, it's not so bad. You could even stay there forever."

We are modes of consciousness only—only.

When this condition ceases, a new one begins, new rules, new terms. Even if there is no situation, one goes elsewhere in the matrix. Even if elsewhere is nowhere.... Like electrons, we follow choiceless destiny.

A dead person communicates to the living, if at all, through mediums and circuit boards, as ghosts (at best) or more often as stray motes of consciousness and innuendos, in conundrums and enigmas and soupçons only—he or she has little choice in the matter. If an entity exists anywhere, it has to use what is available for transmission: the local equivalents of compasses and theodolites and wireless.

Meanings are different in the other world. Indirection is *the only way in which the dead can speak at all;* that is, the only way in which we can understand what they are telling because they aren't actually embodied, say with pharynx, lips, tongue. They don't have a brain or a language center. As you know, they left those accoutrements behind, dust to dust. They must rely on telepathy and mutual intention, yours and theirs. They are broadcasting, if they bother to declare at all with so many other pressing things to do, in bursts and drools against gale-force winds. They push letters of a sacred alphabet through blankets of radiation and infinitudes. Now and then they may displace objects on bureaus, but not many and not very far. Attend to what they push and ask yourself why. Query it as you would a symbol in a dream.

What does it impart about their locale and its relation to here? They've no ballast, no leverage, no calibration. They cannot move mountains; they can only shift paradoxes; they can only allude.

⟡

When my son Robin was young and we went places on planes, he loved the adventure—staring out the window at tiny vehicles loading suitcases and then rising like a winged sled and bumping among clouds. He told me once, around age ten, he got it that this was real—that our safe arrival was not guaranteed—and suddenly it became more scary than fun.

The statistics might be on our side, vastly so, but each plane has to fly the route correctly, and its engineering has to work throughout that flight. The pilots can't fall asleep.

"Real" and "not real" are relative notions, and we have a long dormancy in childhood, protected from the "real" before we know how to handle the way in which we are here. We need to gestate in a life before we understand that it is actually real in a whole other way.

Then, by the time you are used to everything and have the routine down, you must get used to the fact that everything is actually something else.

Ah, what fools these mortals be! Can you believe people are involved in things like "focus groups"? God, is life ever wasted on the living!

When I was awakened for the first day of Horace Mann School by my sister's nurse Bridey (6 AM, September X, 1956, age eleven), I felt the sheer strangeness of existence. The day was a raw lemon. My body throbbed with intimations of other places, other times. There was a meadow of blackeyed susans yellow with yellowjackets. I stood alongside our long-forgotten pineapple Olds.

I could not get myself fully alert. I didn't want a new school with its catechism—but P.S. 6 had ended and there wasn't anywhere else to go. I was fated to ride the subway to this distant academy for the next six years, an eternity then.

I wished Bridey did not have the radio blaring its bristly all-news beacon, warning mankind, while she merrily dropped pancake batter (for which I had no appetite) onto a griddle. That radio would warn and warn and warn for the next six years, right through Quemoy and Matsu to the Cuban Crisis. By then I was a college freshman, living in a dorm.

I would get used to the pale awakening. It would come to seem ordinary.

Now and then a reminder is delivered: suddenly the universe gets really really big—and it is all bardo realms.

Emma's Revolution is two women, Pat Humphries and Sandy Opatow, life as well as singing partners. Pat is a folk-music veteran who joined up with the younger Sandy a few years ago to create the duo named after activist Emma Goldman.

I first heard Emma's Revolution by accident, which is how one often discovers music. Lindy and I were checking out a Saturday yard sale by Salsbury Cove; I was toting a highchair for our soon-to-be-visiting grandson when I decided to park the car a little closer to where Lindy was still poking through stuff. The radio, which had been on WERU, returned with the engine just as "Peace, Salaam, Shalom" was beginning.

I now know that Pat composed this chant during sleepless nights following 9/11. With new violence crescendoing across the planet, a prayer came to her as three words in sync—"peace" in English, Arabic, and Hebrew. It quickly became an anthem for peace groups.

The song goes simply: *"We believe in peace,/we will work for peace,/we can live in peace,/Jerusalem, Ramallah,/in Tel Aviv, in Washington,/in Hebron, in Baghdad,/in Lebanon, in New York City ... /Peace, Salaam, Shalom...."*

The effect is magical, the words varying slightly in spacing and pitch so that the meaning intensifies with each cycle. On October 7, 2001, the day the American military began bombing Afghanistan, a chorus of ten thousand people streamed through the streets of Manhattan from Union Square to Times Square with Pat and Sandy, singing, *"Peace, Salaam, Shalom...."*

As is sometimes the case with a song I adopt, I initially am unsure if I like or dislike it. "Peace, Salaam, Shalom" is unconventional, rising and falling antiphonically, suggesting melodies it doesn't quite complete. At first the tune feels slightly off and intrusive. For the same reason, after a number of listenings it becomes perfect. Its perfection lies in its imperfection, it sounds like nothing else, like a biblical hymn of anger and joy. While it has a simple, some might say "simplistic" message, the words are not the deal. They are mantras to be chanted, to activate the chakra where real peace resides.

Another lyric expresses this sentiment literally: *"If all the world were peaceful now/and forever more,/peaceful at the surface and/peaceful at the core,/all the joy within my heart/would be so free to soar...."**

---

*I had assumed for a long time that these were Pat's lyrics, but they aren't. They come from her friend Jay Mankita who remarked at the time, "I just wrote a Pat Humphries song."

That too could sound facile, but what makes it profound is its dichotomy: *"peaceful at the surface … peaceful at the core."* Most discussions of pacificism don't explore the violence that lurks even in the gentlest person's soul. In truth, we are all addicts who need to stand up each day like Alcoholics Anonymous members and proclaim, "I am human and I am violent." A typical peace song doesn't nearly get there, doesn't recognize how deep that core and how painfully far we have to go for it to get actualized.

"… and we're living on a living planet,/circling a living star.…"

Which is why we can. *"We can change the universe/by being who we are."* Truistic, yet profound.

WERU was giving airtime to Emma's Revolution because it had scheduled them for the Full Circle Fair in Blue Hill three weeks hence. We had planned to attend anyway so, after their song got into my head, I circled the group on the calendar.

As it turned out, we didn't go in the pouring rain on Saturday because we thought Emma's Revolution was also performing the following afternoon. By sunny Sunday, Pat and Sandy were gone. A friend described how the two women played at the peak of the downpour with the thundering percussion of the rain on the rooftops of the stands and bleachers almost drowning them out … a living planet circling (with local thunderstorms) a living star.

By luck, a single copy of their CD remained at the concession stand.

One X 1,000,000 offers a coda of love songs and underclass politics: a young woman who worked as an illegal immigrant on the 80th floor of the Trade Center, torn from her partner by 9/11; lesbian commitment under societal censure; a "silent spring" testimonial to Rachel Carson; a refrain for the Refugee and Woman's Network; a ballad for global warming: *"What has been for 11,000 years/ancient ice and snow/is melting like 11,000 tears/down the face of Kilimanjaro."*

The CD's opening lyric, "Bound for Freedom," has a prologue of conventional activist lines (*"I will organize for justice,/I will raise my voice in song...."*), but their concordance builds to an epiphany: *"With our conscience as our weapon/we are witness to the fall,/we are simple, we are brilliant,/we are one and we are all."*

Transcending naïve shibboleths, this catharsis synergizes all such tired and trite slogans and mutates them into a psalm.

The song "One by One" opens with strums of a folk guitar and quickly matures into an ingot of rage and solidarity. It was written to be group-sung during annual November protests in Fort Benning, Georgia, at the Orwellian-renamed School of the Americas (now the Western Hemispheric Institute for Security Cooperation AKA School of the Assassins). Throughout Central and South America graduates of the SOA have been responsible, directly or indirectly, for the torturing and killing of clergy, labor organizers, and civilians who aid the poor, as if these were their graduate theses. That's the kind of college SOA is; it makes West Point and the Air Force Academy look like Quaker seminaries.

After fiery speeches and songs and puppet shows and Catholic Mass and other prayers and chants, Pat and Sandy rise each year to lead an assembly of habitants of North and South America, protestors of all ages and nationalities: Indians and mestizos, priests and shamans, old lefties and young libertarians, who fall into ragged unison with them. The opening line strikes like an anti-bullet:

"We have come to this place/to renounce this disgrace ..."

Then the ballad states its metaphorical and magical intent:

"Brick by brick, wall by wall,/we will make/this building fall."

Separate indictments against the school are issued under the burgeoning swell of *"one by one."* The ritual escalates on site, the actual academy of torture behind a chain-link fence surrounded by guards, while unarmed sentient beings chant for its ritual and vibrational dismantling.

"... this school, drenched in shame/cannot hide/behind a name ..."

While one chorus is imputing, the other is counting the bricks of its crumbling walls—defiant yet contained, progressing by equal parts fury and compassion: *"We have paid,/ ... One by one ... /Against our will,/ ... One by one ... /While men torture,/ ... One by one ... /Maim and kill,/ ... One by one...."*

And then: *"In one voice/we will stand;/We will sing, we will demand ..." "... One by one...." "Close the school,/cross the line."*

The gathering thunder of the song makes the performance an apotheosis: protest at the surface—transformation at the core. Pat and Sandy's genius is to generate landscapes like these. Incantations like "Peace, Salaam, Shalom" and "One by One" evoke the archetypal melody and aria of life on Earth—there is fish-song and tiger-song in them.

After we got back to California in October, I began checking out "gigs" on emmasrevolution.com, hoping to recoup the summer's loss. To my delight, early November dates were scheduled around Northern California. Not only that, but the singers asked their fans to try to arrange more concerts for them, targeting the East Bay where we lived.

I began an email correspondence with Sandy, trying to line up something at local venues like Freight & Salvage and Café Trieste. But there wasn't much lead time and, as "harridans of social justice" rather than makers of commercial music, the women weren't "Dixie Chicks" enough for short notice. I was about to give up when Pat pointed out that not only did they do house concerts but preferred them to clubs for last-minute bookings. If we could put together a small group, she said, they could supplement it by sending out an email to their list, and we could probably get enough of a turnout for them to perform at our home. Everyone would pay at the door, just as at a public concert, but the setting would be a living room rather than a club or theater.

Over the next two weeks I managed to collect an audience: fans from their trusty list, curious neighbors, friends, plus our son and daughter-in-law with their baby.

Pat and Sandy arrived a couple of hours early with guitars. Their album pictures hadn't really betrayed their personalities. Dreamy and conventionally coed in her photograph, Sandy is actually incisive, androgynous, and lefty intellectual. Pat's photograph is utterly concealed and impenetrable; she looks like an old Indian or lady golfer. Soft-spoken and super-articulate, she is charismatic, even shamanic in presence.

After an hour of chatting and living-room logistics and the arrival of our farmer friend Richard Firme to contrive an organic soup from twenty or so different turnips, daikons, cabbages, kales, onions, and herbs, the place filled up with paying customers around 7:30. Soon afterward the women startled us by entering from the kitchen as if from a stage door, immediately hitting their guitars and intoning in big voices. What we had missed in the Blue Hill rain was unfolding before our eyes in the East Bay hills.

For almost two hours they put on a full musical, narrating their activist adventures and then singing their associated ballads.

In one familiar fable, Bush and bin Laden are identified allies in the Carlyle Group, and bin Laden himself—Pat and Sandy reminded us—is a product of the CIA: our boy. After providing

conspiracy theory 1A, "*They say code War,/we say codePINK....*
CodePINK for freedom,/codePINK for peace,/codePINK till hun-
ger and war have ceased." Justice and revolution blend with melody and linguistic suspense, even as the great ones do it: Dylan,
Woody, Robeson, Baez.

After the concert I got into a conversation with Pat. While com-
plimenting her on her craft, I also tried to articulate something
else—how the haunting lilt and emotional transparency of their
songs commuted their ideologies into something more moving
and profound.

"I had to work real hard for a very long time to get there," she
told me. "I started off as your typical folksinger. I thought all I
had to do was put the ideas out there—peace, justice, feeding
the hungry, helping the marginalized, saving the planet—but it
didn't work. It felt empty, like rhetoric. So I dropped the whole
thing for a number of years and just went out and met the people
I was singing about, shared their lives. When I started up again,
I found I was at the heart. The politics weren't automatic anymore; they came from empathy and understanding. The words
were suddenly real, not just slogans."

Ten months later I saw Emma's Revolution again in concert
in Maine, at the Unitarian Church in Ellsworth. What struck
me was how much energy and spirit Pat puts out in song. She
stands or bounces in place, throws her head back, and howls with
the fervor of a wolf singing to sisters faraway on another planet.
Her fingers hit her guitar so hard that you'd think something
other than music would rise from that deep in the box. Yet it is a
controlled passion, shaped by and shaping language, cosseted in
melody, its outrage shining with an irrepressible and contagious
joy. She is changing the universe by being who she is. It rocked
the church like gospel, so that members of the audience stood

and swung, clapped in rhythm and snaked their arms in the air like comatose shamans awakening.

"We Are One" is my favorite song of theirs. Pat composed it on June 16, 2000, the day after the leaders of North and South Korea met with each other for the first time in decades. Three years later Emma's Revolution was singing it at reunification events in the DMZ and Seoul.

The lyrics of "We Are One" start by proposing personal disarmament through self-recognition and regret, and go from there, with the eloquence of understatement, toward healing the breach between the two halves of Korea, between North Korea and the world, between North Korea and its own people, and between us and the cosmos. It starts quietly like a lullaby:

"Smiling face, outstretched hand,/through disputes small and grand/we will lay down our guns./We are one."

"We Are One" is more than a modern peace ballad; it is a reincarnational, science-fiction hymn from combatants in another galaxy who have finally learned, after many more battles than we've had, what they feel about themselves and their enemy: *"In the rage/through the war/we have shared pain before./In our grief, when it's done...."* But it is also us, for 100,000 years and more, from the brutalities of the Palaeolithic tribes through Persia and Rome to the Khmer Rouge, Hutus, Tamil Tigers, and U.S. Marines, slaughtering our brothers and sisters, our children and fathers, ourselves; arriving at a transcendent sorrow and recognition, breaking through finally to grief and reconciliation.

The second time around the title phrase *"We are one"* changes to Korean: *"Urinin hana,/Urinin hana."* Either way, the antagonists see themselves in each other, get a hint of the depth of the universe.

"*By the moon/by the sun/we are one, we are one./Where the earth touches sky,/we are born, we all die,/where the clear waters run/Urinin hana,/Urinin hana.*"

The Korean comes unexpectedly where the meter and rhyme call for English. Phoneme and cell equally begin and end as one:

And there is finally no war or peace, just birth and death, the shriek of a hyena, the call of a falcon, cosmic silence and cosmic judgment eternal.

Can you picture "We Are One" being sung by Americans and Koreans standing side by side beside the guns and turrets of the so-called demilitarized zone, renouncing the battle, laying out the only direction in which we can go now as a species, as a planet; the only way we can remember who we are, where we have come from, and how much we have lost and lament along the way?

In their own crude way the North Koreans and Taliban are already reaching out to us:

"*In the birth of a child,/through the fierce and the mild,/through our daughters and sons/ Urinin hana, Urinin hana.*"

The imperative could not be any clearer if Gregorian monks chanted it at St. Patrick's Cathedral.

At the end of the evening, Pat left me some CDs of her own early work. Her old political stuff is playful and smart: "*Bye bye this American car,/buy this American car ... /The steel was all made in Japan,/impressed into shape in Botswana./For the engine they paid/ twenty pesos a day/to a worker in south Tijuana./The ignition Korean,/the tires are French,/the bumper's from Botany Bay....*"

But it is her songs of eternal love and loss that tell who she really is and what Emma's Revolution, in just a young woman's dream, would become:

*"Let her go,/let her go,/as the tears and sorrow flow./Restore the soul within me./Free my heart and let her go."**

Don't you consider it bizarre that so many people profess allegiance to the life and teachings of someone they don't particularly like and whose lifestyle they don't admire? The most vocal Christians in America today live in complete contempt of Christ, in spiteful opposition to his teaching. This is a guy whom they would kick out of their church group for his smell alone, to say nothing of the glow in his eyes and rabbinical ancestry. Anyone who approached their congregation acting and talking like Jesus they would ridicule, boot out, and dismiss, and might do bodily harm to. Gives you an idea how screwed up they are: they would vilify the actual Christ as anti-Christian, e.g. gay or wimpish, because they have turned his alias into a war god and hanging judge.

Just look at who many of the self-professed Christians are and how they posture. They worship guns, adore vicarious combat, hold grudges, despise the poor, admire or drive Stingers, and support ("hell, yes, fry the bastard!") capital punishment. They share far more with Christ's enemies and crucifiers. They may be playing a homeboy/homegirl game, but they've got the wrong sponsor: Christians my ass—more like Christ-shuns. Christ is Evangelical Christianity's victim, not its passion.

The dark church of Satan has actually succeeded in obliterating the living Christ, the radiance of divinity, and replacing him, under his own name, with a stooge god, a petty magistrate in whose kingdom poor farmhands and unemployed ethnics are

*Written by Charlie King.

herded in shackles down Dead Man Walking Alley, and wealthy moguls lure the youth of the underclass into futile wars while repressed priests molest kiddies. This is hardly the offspring of the holy fire of Kether (The Crown), Hesed (Mercy), and Tifaret (Beauty). This is Beezlebub's church. But then, as the Bible tells it, Satan is not only a great deceiver; his specialty is masquerading as all three, Father, Son, and Ghost.

In America, Christianity is merely a smokescreen for ruling-class law and its sacred prerogatives, the sanctimonious anointing of the red, white, and blue.

If George Bush had been alive at the time of Jesus, could you really picture him among the apostles rather than the Roman soldiers? Or maybe he would have found himself a desk job, even then. He would have dispatched Christ to the Cross along with the other paperwork that came across his portico, just as he vouched Texas convicts, innocent and guilty alike, to the executioner. On his watch men, women, and children were crucified in record numbers, even for Texas.

Had he been among the street rabble, as perhaps he was in some past life in Israel, do you think he would have cheered for Christ over Barrabas? No way—not when he chooses Barrabas again every day. Forget the Lord of love and peace—Bush doesn't even have a consul or working senate; he has unplugged his State Department and diplomatic corps; he ignores the real generals and listens only to yessir and toadie brass, his so-called "men in the field." It is for Barrabas he shouts again and again. *Barrabas alone for everything.* Barrabas to whom he has entrusted his entire plan.

To him Barrabas is not only a warrior and a soldier; he is the slave class of a volunteer military, the aristocracy's chauffeur and bodyguard, commissioned to die again, and again, in the name of the emperor. Like Kim Jong-il with his Italian chefs, Bush could care less about the starving poor, the honorable troops, though he will invoke Christ and the men in uniform at auspicious moments to tuneful effect.

This is not only unutterable sin. It is blasphemy of the most reckless sort.

In last night's dream I found myself on a mission to Mars. I know it was Mars from our dramatic entry into the Red Planet's gravity zone, its vast alien face bracketed with Lowell's canals.

Equipped with spacesuits, we were climbing on buttes, seeking the remnants of a million-year-old vanished culture, afraid that yetis or humanoid locusts might pop up suddenly from behind rocks. If such creatures existed at all, they would not have not been part of us since the pinwheel of fiery dust in which the Solar System began or at best the Octantis Mons microbes that seeded the anaerobic Earth by stowaway on meteorite. It would be a spooky meeting. We are relatives only in the most remote sense.

Afterwards I went to sleep inside a crude fortress with the rest of the crew, still clad in my spacesuit. In the morning in my dream I awoke to find myself in ordinary clothes, and there were trees and people and all sorts of things happening, clearly unrelated to Earth. Mars was alive and bustling—it could have been a village on some continent back home, though it wasn't. Everyone was involved with his or her own stuff and didn't even seem to notice us; they were speaking and acting Martian, which was far stranger than Hopi or Hungarian. They may even have been communicating telepathically, though I imagined I could hear words.

This was an efficient planet in an entirely different circumstance.

I opened the windows to let in air. I carted our junk to a furnace and ignited it behind a metal door. Some crew members were patching holes in the wall of what had become our dormitory.

It was okay to be on Mars, our presence exposing a fraud perpetrated by outfitting us in masks, sending us so far away, telling us that the Martians weren't like us and we would not be able to breathe.

It comes down to little more than the Golden Rule. That doesn't sound like much, but I think it is one of the keys to the universe, even before the might and awe of stars and demons. We have so few reliable clues to guide us.

Treating others with dignity and compassion brokers a way for the universe to treat us likewise, with care and grace, for even its most horrid entities to treat us that way.

In fact, the devouring wraiths that cannibalize our souls in the afterworlds of Dante and Don Juan may be twisted projections of our own hostility and greed. We can assuage them only where they arise, can make ourselves safe only by mitigating our actions and cancelling our stern insurance policies against the actions of others.

I am coming to think that our paranoid fantasy of the universe defaults as our destiny, so more and more these days I am careful about what I intend because, when I scan myself honestly, I see someone who, despite all resolutions and avowals, has been grabby, indulgent, heedless. I have excused myself for no good reason and in ways that leave me stuck in a cycle of no wisdom/no growth. I have to dig deeper.

My acts create the type of universe I'd like to be in, but more than that, they determine if I am to have anywhere to live, any viable path through shadows, any reliable source of love.

I do not want to concede the macrocosm to a power struggle of merciless beasts.

"Do unto others as you would...." is that simple; there's nothing more.

Even if you agree with George W. Bush's policies and accept his Weltanschauung, you would have to admit that just about every action of his has been a total failure, yielding a result diametrically opposite to what he purportedly intended.

If W wanted to decrease the threat of terrorism to Americans and protect the homeland, he has exponentially elevated the danger, gratuitously spreading hatred and mistrust of the U.S. across the Muslim world from Indonesia to Somalia and making sure a whole coming-of-age generation is stoked to go after us. He is breeding and motivating armies of fresh terrorists, all younger and nastier than their predecessors. He put a big fat bull's-eye on America for them, establishing us as a callous bully, an occupying power threatening the *Ummah Wahida*,* which it is every Muslim's sacred duty to defend at any cost and by any means. He has kicked the hornet's nest big-time with the usual results.

If he wanted to strengthen the U.S. military, he has shattered it to the point of collapse; he has chewed our vast defense capacity down to a nubbin. He grandiosely threw almost all his troops into a battle of immeasurable depth with no plan, no explicit foe, boundaryless in both space and time. And he so little understood what he was doing, the consequences of his attack on a sovereign nation, that he was playing the victory march fifteen minutes before the war began. A bad mistake in war: to underestimate the

*One [Islamic] Community.

enemy* (in W's case, he forgot to account for its existence or retaliatory capacity). Now even the National Guards and emergency equipment from most of the fifty states are in Iraq; there is no one left to handle floods, fires, or riots, or protect our borders from Guam and Alaska to El Paso and the Keys, let alone to invade Pakistan and protect the nukes from anarchy (except maybe bank guards and mall cops).

W sapped and vexed regiments of American militia, supporting them by unwieldy or second-rate technologies and armchair generals who got automatic promotions for failure and disgrace. Then he saved money by giving them third-rate medical care.

It is clear now that his priority was to enrich the defense contractors and allied capitalists who supported his campaign, not to wage effective war or deter terrorism—that was merely a pretext. In fact, he so took victory for granted he was scheming on behalf of Halliburton instead of thinking how to win. He was booting out useful diplomats and policy grunts just because they were Democrats, as if he could afford that kind of frivolity.

New soldiers are trained in ten days and airlifted to the battleground. When their tours are over, they are cooled down for a month or so and then dispatched right back to the red slayer, sometimes to the same deteriorating Iraqi neighborhood. Morale is a thing of the past—desertion, fragging, and suicide on the rise. And this is a volunteer military!

The Commander has no deterrent left to bluff Iran. So maybe he'll just go Air Force with a three-day blitzkrieg and regret the collateral damage—a routine he's got down cold by now. (Or as his sidekick McCain joked with typical Republican vulgarity, "Bar-bar-bar. Bar-Bomb Iran." Lighten up, you say, John? Well, do you know any good jokes about Hiroshima or Darfur? In

---

*I know I just said there was none, but he created it by invading.

case you forgot, people, most of them innocent—no, all of them innocent—die miserably when explosives are dropped from the sky. But if you think it's funny....)

If W wanted to impress the rest of the world with America's might, its capacity for "shock and awe," instead he exposed it as a paper tiger. Uncle Sam can't fight a guerrilla war in an Islamic homeland any better than France or Russia or India could. Our military is incapable of imposing its will on even a demilitarized and fractured Iraq. If it can't defeat hooded brigades of mostly civilians with old guns and roadside bombs, how is it going to stop a Talibanized Pakistan or North Korea pouring over the DMZ? What about China and India and even Putin's new Russia?

If our fear and respect factors around the world before the Iraq invasion were 9.5 out of a possible 10, they are now at 4.5 and melting faster than Greenland.

If he wanted other countries to heed America's voice out of what—idealism, dread of consequences, self-interest?—he actually made America irrelevant for the first time in over a century. Who would give the time of day to a government that can't waddle two steps without tripping over demagoguery and red tape; that sneers at treaties; fucks international law; spurns codes of civilized behavior for itself but enforces them for others; asserts itself above the order of nations; and can't spend a dollar without siphoning off fifty more into graft and fraud?

We are no longer the big bad wolf. We are more like the fat guy who just got mugged. He was strolling down the avenue with his oversized wallet. He'll go home, re-stuff the wallet, and get mugged again, by warlords in Karachi or Baghdad or Mogadishu, as not just millions but billions of smackeroos disappear into the underbrush along with arsenals big enough to topple any puppet we set on the local throne. The world's fear and respect go now to the guys doing the mugging.

If W wanted to boost America's image while enhancing its prestige among Islamic countries, he had a funny way of going about it. If introducing an occupying force on the Iraqi streets wasn't bad enough, he sent degenerates who—no surprise—ended up torturing, murdering, and raping. "Leading naked Iraqi males around on dog leashes and covering their heads with women's underwear ... imprinted an indelible image of American depravity on the entire Islam world."* What a job of promoting America and getting the animosity quotient down!

Didn't anyone tell Bush that this was how the Soviet Union became so popular during the last century? Didn't anyone explain what the ethical, humane behavior of America was worth on the international market and how it tamed the beast over the last two hundred years? Does the President really want to suspend the rules of civilization and go jungle? Because, frankly, they've got people in the bush much nastier than our worst—we lose big-time there....

If his goal was to check that so-called Axis of Evil (Iraq, Iran, North Korea), he strengthened and emboldened it; he unleashed chaos and civil war in the first nation and gave the club's two remaining members excuses to develop nuclear weapons, something he was powerless to halt and had no diplomatic skills to adjudicate.† He brought North Korea and Iran into collaboration and brokered a Syrian-Iranian détente.

If he wanted to project American power into the Middle East and stem Iranian influence, he accomplished quite the opposite.

---

*Need any more be said? John Gray, from "Power and Vainglory" in *Abu Ghraib: The Politics of Torture*, Terra Nova Series, North Atlantic Books, Berkeley, California, 2004.

†To get rid of those nukes he finally had to swallow his pride and meet North Korea's negotiating precondition. He went right back to where Bill Clinton and team left off, with mega waste and ado in the interim.

Iran was the biggest winner of his invasion, al-Qaeda second, the Iraqi Shi'ites third—the U.S. and the Sunnis were the top losers. Didn't he think any of this through for, like, five seconds beforehand? Why was he so hot-headed and war-happy that he started a costly fight before weighing the diverse other strategic options he had in 2001 (and no longer has)? Sadly we spent our entire budget many times over on a boondoggle. Yes, haste makes waste, and a stitch in time....

But then that was always Bin Laden's long-term plan: no all-out frontal assaults. Just prick and goad the bully and see if you get a rise or, even better, an all-out over-reaction. Provoke the superpower to bankrupt itself. Then sit back and enjoy the show.

Bush got suckered right into this one as though Aesop wrote the fable for him. We are bombing Iraqi bridges and rebuilding them six months later, as our domestic infrastructure crumbles and our nest egg is drained off to other lands.

Great strategic move, George: you played right into the enemy's hands!

Didn't someone explain the whole thing of Sunnis and Shi'ites to W beforehand? Wasn't it made clear that, if he overthrew Saddam, Shi'ites loyal to Iran would take over and take payback against the Sunnis? Didn't he understand that the Sunnis would fight for survival in a civil war? Couldn't someone have given him a dumbed-down synopsis of the last thousand years? After all, he was President; he could afford a decent tutor. Or did old tin-ears just not care to register?

If W wanted cheap oil out of the Middle East, he managed instead to shock its supply and triple its still-rising price. He threw the Iraqi petrochemical industry into dysfunction and set up the whole Middle East for hydrocarbon sabotage.

By the way, here's a thought: if you don't want Muslims to think that this is the Crusades all over again, then don't (for a starter) use that word; don't keep quoting the Bible, and don't keep talking about your own nation as singularly blessed by God while vilifying others as spokes in an Axis of Evil. I mean, even if they are "evil," why provoke them? Why inflate them; why give them an excuse? From a diplomatic standpoint, this is infantile rhetoric.

Any fool can say, "I'm on God's side; you're evil." Hasn't every king and petty dictator since Babylonia played that card?

Plus, what does "evil" mean? Sunni, Shi'ite, and al-Qaeda militants may incinerate marketplaces and schoolyards with car bombs, and that's certainly evil; but it's "hot evil" by comparison to George W's "cold evil." He holds up clean hands and spouts pieties while bombing civilians for purely ideological reasons too.

Against the advice of soldiers and diplomats, Mr. I Listen to My Generals allowed the disbanding Saddam's military and civil service, leaving Iraq with no enforcers of basic law or order. Did he think that the entire Iraqi army was responsible for Baath policies?

But that's what ideologues do: they punish the wrong people for the wrong things. They actually just punish everyone without regard for evidence. They care more about doctrinal purity than what is really happening.

The problem is that the neocons are up against a much smarter ideologue in al-Qaeda, on its homefield. Of course, they are overmatched. Of course, they are playing right into the enemy's hands. Anyone who doesn't get it that Bush-Cheney is an al-Qaeda dream ticket is not watching the game.

At a time when we are facing an unprecedentedly ruthless enemy, one without any limits, conventional morality, or compassion for man or woman, child or animal—an enemy who would destroy the planet, literally leave the Earth lifeless because it believes in abstract morality and satanic verses—we need someone really lucid and wise at the helm, resourceful and also good, a samurai. Instead we have Bluster and Braggadocio, Beavis & Butthead and Scrooge McDuck wrapped up in one, or as Bill Maher put it, "Shit for Brains." We're being led by Jubilation T. Cornpone.

If W wanted to replace the Afghan government and its "guests" —who after all were the ones who hijacked our airliners and bombed our cities—he got so goosed by Iraq and diverted so many of his resources there that he left most of Afghanistan naked and ripe for an Osama escape, social chaos, and a Taliban comeback.

If he wanted to dry up the narco trade out of Talibanistan, look again: our hero underwrote a bumper crop, historic yields, flooding the world with opiates.

If he aimed to be fiscally conservative and reduce the national debt, that's the biggest laugh of all; this guy was the most reckless and irrelevant spender in Planet Earth history, shooting the American deficit through the ionosphere. What he accomplished was windfalls for his wealthy friends, the Republican Party, and the military-industrial complex. Maybe that's what he meant by "fiscally conservative" and "mission accomplished."

If he wanted to model religious values and spirituality—and I question whether he did—he managed instead to undermine charity, ethics, and even God himself with senseless, fatuous killing and destruction and aggrandizement of secular power and wealth. It is more that W wanted the evangelical votes, so he took those naifs with a bumpkin "man of God" routine that shouldn't have cozened a goat. He is not even a churchgoer, preferring Sunday brush-clearing. I don't even believe it was Jesus who got him off the bottle. Texas scuttlebutt has it that Laura said: "Jack Daniels or me and the kids, big boy. Choose." And then we elected the dufus President?

I could go on for another hour or two here, but you get the idea. So what do I think is actually transpiring? Is this guy mega-crafty and an adept liar or just a know-nothing idiot, a callow pawn of archfiend Cheney? Or a bit of both?

Doubtless W was way undereducated and underprepared for the job—I mean, at the get-go he thought Slovenia was Slovakia, didn't know where Kosovo was, was even vague on the distinction between Austria and Australia, and it's unclear whether he never heard of Sunni and Shia or just thought it was sort of like Baptists and Episcopalians. A long-time sap for pop politics, pop psychology, pop economics, and pop religion, he applied these flummeries to complex problems and issues and the fates of real people, and then acted surprised when things didn't work the "Stand on the Carrier in My Flight Suit While the Troops Cheer" way they do in comics. I take that to be mostly provinciality and craven stupidity, along with the black-and-white moralism and arrogance of the untreated alcoholic who has merely stopped drinking, the cocaine addict who has repudiated—in fact, blackballed—the drug but not the habit. By provinciality, I mean a class myopia that causes him to see the world in terms of fairy tales rather than the kind of stuff he must have at least overheard at Yale and Harvard, unless he was too busy kicking ass and partying at DEKE.

According to psychiatrist Justin A. Frank, Bush has a mare's nest of symptoms: an inability to manage anxiety or distinguish between reality and fantasy; a combination of paranoia, Oedipal fury, and omnipotence delusions; hyperactivity, conversion re-actions, and Tourette's Syndrome (always bouncing around, touching people, making inappropriate jokes, mixing Freudian slips into stutters and malaprops), as well has his afore-noted uncured alcoholism—a deadly cocktail. Among other things, these deficits left him a pushover for Cheney, Libby, and the neocons, a willing puppet of them and his own unresolved rage.

He actually belongs at the 19th Hole, a beloved bartender spouting off, no real danger to himself or anyone else. That's more or less where he would be if he hadn't been born into the Bush clan, son of a President.

I also think he was intentionally devious. He rigged evidence and prevaricated about Iraq for a variety of reasons, not all of them clear even yet.* Perhaps he wanted to take his war machine for a drive and show the world that Uncle Sam couldn't be pushed around ("No one can now doubt the word of America!"). He needed a milksop opponent (we know who got the last laugh there, Mr. Mission Accomplished). He wanted to nail Saddam's ass to the wall; after all, given that Uncle Sam had set him up in business in the first place, this ungrateful SOB flouted American corporate interests and then tried to assassinate his father.

The meta-Oedipal drama could play out on multiple levels: W could both surpass and avenge his father by actually driving all the way to Baghdad and capturing one-time American collaborator Saddam, thereby committing double patricide, and he could displace his undifferentiated wrath and anxiety from America onto Iraq, thereby assuaging and valorizing his revenge fantasies and his guilt and latent fears. He found a perfect way subconsciously to stave off his own terror, by reversing it and attacking terror itself.

Buddy Rove no doubt told W that a war was the perfect energizer for his base; it gave him a chance to express his presidency on a big stage. The neocons figured that a splashy victory

---

*The MIHOP crowd believes the war in Iraq was, in part, a ruse to distract attention from the *real* attacks on the World Trade Center and Pentagon.

would reap limitless benefits that would allow them to continue making the rich richer and keep Republicans in office and, since they figured we'd ace the battlefield, he'd be a heroic war-time president with accolades and unlimited political capital to pursue a pro-business, anti-labor, anti-environment agenda.

By the way, you don't take people's lives and wreck a whole country for abject political goals. Just by the way....

I imagine W also assumed he could gain control over oilfields, establish an American base in the Middle East, and get to hobnob with Israeli bigwigs in the process, but those were bonuses. As it is, he managed to fight a war for oil and realize none in the bargain, and even the shamefully sprawling Potemkin Green Zone isn't safe from Shi'ite attacks.

And while we're at it, his throwaway line—"if we leave, they'll follow us home"—has got to be one of the more ridiculous slogans for a war launched and sustained on high-grade bullshit. Exactly who will follow whom where? If what he means is that terrorists will try to attack the United States, how does he figure that our being in Iraq is going to lead to fewer jihadists or less resolve among them to hit the homeland? The real worry should be that they are already here, and they are us, Americans, American Muslim youth and prison gangs radicalized by his presidency. Those are the ones he and his cronies should be concerned about because they are not illegal anythings and don't have to slip over borders.

Oh, I forgot; it's just a line.

W entered a war that he didn't need and couldn't win. He couldn't win it because, guess what?, he had no definition of victory beyond jingoism—his geopolitics had no relationship to any real situation on the ground. He invaded a cartoon image of an imaginary place and then found himself in a real war. (Who exactly are we fighting even today? When there are three or four or five different factions, each with its own agendas and long-term strategies, how do we know if we win or when the battle is over? Abu Musab al-Zarqawi showed a snippet of droll Islamic humor when he taunted Bush by video, "Hey, while you're at it, why surge thirty thousand; why not just send all your troops for us to slaughter?")

War is an unconditional ceremony that should be performed with care and as a last resort. George, you don't try to clear a pond with a putter or go three inches along a green with a wood. You don't use war when other methods might get you the same result. War creates reservoirs of karma. War cannot be controlled (as in "the fog of"). War brutalizes civilians, makes scads of new enemies, starts millennial feuds, and ignites spiraling cycles of violence. In the face of such a powerful god, one is cautious, modest, cogent. But, yes, fools rush in, always.

We could give George W the benefit of the doubt and say he chose war consciously and intelligently, aware of its consequences and ramifications, having considered all options with due diligence. I don't think so. I believe he chose "shock and awe" from long-standing ignorance of what war actually is and sheer lack of imagination and diplomatic skills. And Cheny was masterfully goading him. W allowed his evangelical dualism to supplant any reasoned analysis of the situation, so his palette quickly got reduced to good and evil, war or appeasement, them or us. Plus he was not exactly a battlefield guy himself, nor was Cheney. They were classic wannabe soldiers—idea guys, money guys, Yale freshman drunks and good old boys, chicken hawks who preferred to keep their hands clean and their guts inside their skins. They knew mainly how to delegate others to get blown up for their bacchanal. Let the slaves bludgeon each other while you sit safely in the stadium, getting off on the death-and-power trip.

The President liked "shock and awe" because he presumed the outcome was rigged and he owned all the expensive war toys. It was like hunting big cats on a Texas ranch. No, it was a giant three-dimensional video game with real lasers, real noise, real buildings, and human blood. That George is rumored to have let out a loud whoop at the onset of Iraq Battlezone II tells you all you need to know about him.

What W was really about—has always been about—is the transfer of wealth from the social-service sector and middle class to corporations and wealthy investors, those in his and Cheney's circle (certainly not Hollywood or Silicon Valley). He also apparently wanted to sink the Federal Government by creating such a huge service on the national debt—even if it meant handing over the treasury to foreigners—that there would never be anything resembling compassionate socialism or a New Deal again. He wanted to set the clock back to Herbert Hoover—and an educated, vocal middle class was in the way. I think he won that one. Just look at the rising cost of college tuition, of owning a home. But it was a stupid, mean ambition.

I mostly see him as a small-minded guy with petty conquests in his brain, the big picture nowhere in that noggin, viewing the world in terms of sporting events and watered-down biblical metaphors. His father at least had a sense of duty, a range of compassion that, if limited, was authentic. George W seems to have the personality of a deceptively affable sociopath and undiagnosed bipolar patient: no empathy, no sense of shame, no real comprehension of the damage he is doing. His words sound robotic and ring false; everything is over-pronounced for effect. His so-called straight-shooting is perjury and snake oil. He may preach about sacrifice and honor and declare how much he appreciates those who are making the ultimate sacrifice, but I don't get the sense that he actually thinks about where the rubber meets the road—the deaths of real sons and daughters and men and women with prosthetic limbs—or feels anything for those whose lives have been devastated or cut short by his reckless gambits. He says he cries in private, in fact oceans of tears, but don't they all?

I suspect that to the day he dies George W. Bush will feel no real grief or remorse for what he did to the world. His sense of privilege is dumb and impenetrable.

He delivers mountains of garbage, propaganda, clichés, and deceptions, and then strides off as if he just gave a combination Gettysburg Address/Sermon on the Mount. His signature look is something like "What, me worry?" surprise with a dash of outrage and the smirk of a cat who swallowed a canary but can't quite get it down.*

I think that not only does W fail to understand diplomacy; he doesn't believe that such a puppy exists. Because he has no talent for it and lacks the temperament to do it, he pretends that it is a mere affectation or a façade to parley weakness. Thus we get his parody of diplomacy—to bluff, scold, threaten, badger, withhold. His diplomatic arsenal consists of bullying others to get them to flinch, twisting their arms into seeing things his way, and then giving them a Texas back slap. The rest of the world is hip to this by now.

Perhaps W convinced himself that diplomacy only mollycoddles dictatorships and terrorists. He does not see that in the absence of real compromise and leadership by example, there is no world order, only Hobbesian brutality. In a state of lawlessness and escalating chaos, an assortment of gangs, jihadists, ca-

---

*Bill Maher describes him as bumbling through a mass of mangled English and fake oratory and then flashing a "nailed it!" mug at the audience as, "Hail to the Chief," he departs.

marillas, and drug cartels rule, not the joint with five percent (and dropping) of the world's population and the noble institutions.

Diplomacy is a subtle art, a means of plying both your power and vulnerability strategically—and it is unavoidable because even the most powerful are vulnerable in some way. Every act is a diplomatic act, or not. W is carrying out incompetent and counterproductive diplomacy by other means. He does not comprehend that military might is transitory and inherently limited. In other words, because he does not recognize or appreciate the tenets that allow him and his clan their prerogatives and prosperity, he mindlessly blows them off and now has left the world without its old order and no new one to replace it.

Diplomacy is an animal dance of respect and grace and the feigned enactment of rapport, even when all you feel is antipathy, horror, and outrage. Watch two aggravated cheetahs or crabs. They know how to get down with each other and be cool. If nations can't play at that, they can't deal with allies, let alone enemies; there is no way to arrive at common understandings or policies. War is the only option.

The inverse of diplomacy is contempt; you get contempt back while gaining nothing in the exchange. Yeats was right: when the least among us lead, mere anarchy will be loosed upon the world.

In response to an iPod blast of Frankie Valli and the Four Seasons doing their neglected classic, "Alone," Ed Mondazzi comments, "If he sang any louder, only the dogs could hear him."

It was quite a scene last night at the Russian River Brewing Company, Santa Rosa. Leaving work early on a rainy Tuesday afternoon, we drove an hour north and took a room at old Hotel La Rose on Wilson Street. We hiked to a Chinese restaurant for dinner. Afterwards we grabbed a table along the wall of the nearby brew-pub and hung out till Dave Insley and his Careless Smokers arrived and took the stage.

Well, it was more a temporary platform by the door.

With his wise, wise-guy baritone, Insley was great, and he brought along a riveting genre-splicing, anti-Nashville, honky-tonk band. I'm not sure how the economics go, but he had four people playing, and there were maybe a dozen or so fans on hand, plus another twenty bystanders gandering from the bar. Still, this crew of Texans plays Santa Rosa every three months or so as part of their Nevada City-Reno-Sacramento swing.

They were loud but classically melodic Country & Western— two guitars, steel bass, drums. One guy wore a cowboy hat; another was Tex-Mex with Spanish on his t-shirt.

Later I got the names and instruments: Dave Zirbel (filling in for Bobby Snell)—steel guitar; Dale Allen—electric guitar and backing vocals; Daniel Jones—drums; Vance Hazen—bass guitar.

Despite the northern California setting, the couples hitting the dance floor were pure Texas: two shake-rattle-and-roll middle-aged ladies; a huge man blobbed over a tiny lady wearing felt antlers but sexy; a little cowboy with a toothpick and a tall, sad gal.

The Careless Smokers have signatures. Among things they do is stop on a dime in the middle of a song and then pick it up in a blast. Sometimes they all freeze in position with their instruments, like gunfighters waiting to draw. They throw out regular Texas homeboy lines like "y'all havin' a good time?"

One of the songs is about a limerick that Insley's dad had to provide in order to bum a cigarette from his friend. Speak that and he got a smoke; say anything else and he was refused: *"Roy Boy with the Floy Joy with the Killroy with the Frank Buck,/How your cigarettes holding out?"*

Insley is somewhere north of forty. He's a hell of a writer, and the performance was all his own work except one Conrad Twitty. While taking breaks he mingled with the audience, so we got to chat with him a bit. A sweet cowboy ("Bless your heart" is his favorite expression), he is also a funny man on and off stage and should draw bigger crowds. To one of my questions he replied that lots of bands incorporate stops like that: "We are showmen and have plenty o' little tricks and moves, but we can't take credit for inventing hardly any of them."

"Are you all cigarette smokers?"

"Only two in the band, including me, but we all smoke reefer."

I told him how we had heard him first in Maine on WERU, and he said that he knows they play his stuff, "bless their hearts," but he's never been to Maine and would love to go.

"Well, our publishing company gave WERU a big donation," I began to conspire right there at the table. "Maybe we can get them to invite you to their Full Circle Fair."

Three hours is a long time to nurse one beer, but we closed the doors at midnight. As we hit the street, Dave called out, "You know I play the Starry Plough; see ya'all in Berkeley."

Consider these lines from "Other Trails to Ride"; it starts: *"Put me on my favorite pony/Point us toward the settin' sun./Please make sure my hat's tipped right/And there's bullets in my gun...."* Then: *"Give my weary mind a rest and let my spirit sleep."* The death song only gets more awesome: *"When this ol' paint comes back alone/Give him oats and give him hay./Brush him down and turn him out/and put my tack away."*

Step aside; the man is on a song-writing roll: "*Know how much I loved the road that I've been down with you/and all them pretty sunflowers and all the hard miles too …*" and "*I loved you in your waking hours,/Now I'll love you in your dreams.*"

Then he tosses out the magic invocation, the hope and wish, the terror and haunting too, for life on Earth since the Ice Age shaman found the planetary mind inside himself and peered into the darkness, from where he heard an answer coming back that we still hear, listen or not: "*Even though you can't see me,/I'm still here by your side.*"

The following summer, July 28th, Lindy and I arranged for Dave and the Smokers to play at Full Circle. They were just as delightful, bringing their Texas foot-stomping to the Blue Hill Fairgrounds—but rain clouds hovered and the crowd was sparse, only about forty for headliners on an evening when a thousand people trekked through the concessions before sunset. Three times their number watched the amateur reggae histrionics that preceded Dave, a garage band of Sudanese and locals from Waterville shouting pat political slogans, making taxi-cab confessions, and parading about the stage as if they had just taken the heavyweight title from Joe Frazier.

"We're not a hippie band, and this is a kind of hippie setting for us," noted Vance nonjudgmentally, as I was lamenting the turnout afterward.

"It just seemed sad for such a special group that came a long way."

"Special? You like us, come to Austin. We're a dime a dozen there."

"Maybe, maybe not. But I think you should have drawn more. I know it had nothing to do with me, but I couldn't help feeling responsible for the crowd."

"Let it go. We had a great time, the people there were into it. Don't internalize, man."

Now, Vance, that's a bass player.

"If I lived before," you ask, "why can't I remember it?" And, you may add, astutely, "If the answer is that my past lives really happened but are no longer in my memory, then they aren't really my lives, are they? It wasn't me. By what measure do the events of lives I can't remember have anything to do with me? How are they different from the lives of other people? Aren't you just saying that all consciousness is one?"

I am saying that, yes; consciousness is one the way electricity is one. But I am saying something else too. I am saying you lived before and will live again.

"You" are not your memory. You are something else, something you don't even begin to know how to name. Inside the cozy and not-so-cozy coverlets of yourself, inside the dreams and nightmares and fantasies and obscure desires, inside the terrors and greeds and narcissisms and memoranda and furtive reckonings is another self entirely, a tiny diamond—your ineradicable core. That alone keeps you honest, keeps you real, creates your personalities, connects you to the source; it is the template of you, whenever, wherever, whatever. It makes you you.

"You" don't need a single specific recollection from this or any previous lifetime except maybe a faint intimation that it *did* happen plus its collective lesion upon your—for lack of a better word—soul.

Consider the myriad details, large and small, crucial at the time and incidental, that you have already forgotten about this life: most of its minutiae and even some of its momentous occasions, for instance, your trip down the birth canal—gone pretty much forever. Your birthday cakes and favorite toys, no matter how wonderful at the time, blur together; you may not be able to locate or disentangle all your old friends and lovers. Consider also how many of your so-called "reliable" memories you have altered by internal dialogue to make a consistent and attractive tale (and sob story) to tell yourself who you are.

Your so-called memory is a partial reconstruction of packaged and revised moments, idiosyncratic details, a selective, discontinuous, changing narrative burned into transient neurons. It is not you, not who you are. Even if you forgot it all, as you will, you would still know.

So what is it that you know?

How can you claim the life you are living if you can't remember most of its details? How do they define you anyway in collective amnesia?

You exist as an entity not because you archive cumulative interactions and photographs, a sound track, etc., but because a thread holds your beads together, forgotten ones along with those yet remembered. What "you" are is not the beads but the thread. And its skein is not silk or wire but energy.

Take away body, take away language, take away each and every experience and event—there is still a thread. That thread binds any one life and multiple lives together.

From lifetime to lifetime you may have names and identities, characters you play with enthusiasm, but that's hardly who you are—Geoffrey Sable or Sergei Schinkel or Tatanka Iyotanka.* Think about it. Are you your name even now? Are you one and the same as the person, the persona within

---

*Sitting Bull.

whose orbit you enact a role? No, that is your dharma, your day job.

In the bardos between lives the many beads on your thread illumine equally. It is no longer one very urgent, immediate life and the others mere faint keepsakes and idle speculations. Your existences in other epochs, perhaps on other worlds, fall coequal to this proximate term. You are all of them not just linearly, in fact not chronologically at all, but as the crucible of what you are.

Between lives you soon enough have access to your entire repertoire. You know everyone and everything: births and deaths, partners and protagonists, parents and offspring. Your destiny—what it is, what it was, what it portends, what options you still have—becomes lucent without language or thought.

Beyond the sights and sounds of your last life, you experience yourself utterly, a fact within memory but opaque to memory. Your most recent life meets the existentiality of all lives through which your essence has passed. More than that, you get an inkling of the greater ambience that kindles lives at all, the odeum in which scripts are ignited, in which meanings ignite in eros before they can be exported and appareled, before there is any possibility of being or ego.

Through a mode that precedes sight and sound and touch and in fact provides their algebra, you get a glimpse of the amphitheater containing all proscenia, all players and plays.

This is not enlightenment, but it is profound, very intense, an epiphany while it lasts.

I believe that the purpose of the universe *is* consciousness: to produce multiple foci and expressions for all creatures, who are in effect one creature, One Consciousness—a Monad, experiencing itself as self and itself as other—simultaneously, alternately, inextricably.

For instance, the notion that you yourself are intrinsically good or godly while another is inherently bad or condemned to some hell is ludicrous when, over time, you are both and get to embody the consciousness of both. That asshole you are deploring is also you, somewhere among the layers of your own subconscious knowing, as much as you try to suppress the annoying qualms. That is why you are irritable and ambivalent. He is too close for comfort. He has been you and will be you yet again. Too bad! But also too good!

The state of any one man or woman or entity—isolated, dualistic, perspectiveless "I"—is not a life; it is a view. Real lives are compilations of many such views until the single ground source of their projection becomes obvious. That is why the goal of consciousness is to end ancient battles between idols: you have been fighting yourself all along, as the multidimensional layers of your mega-being transit through one another. Only in extending legitimacy to others—compassion, compassion, compassion—do you become who you are, do you acquire your greater life, do you *see*.

Paradoxically, no life, even the most deprived or dolorous, is unchosen. A karma underlies it, as you become who you need to be each time in order to complete your configuration. It is not a matter of winning the Darwinian lottery or a providence being joyous or tragic, privileged or destitute. There is no treasure to win, ladder to climb 'cept this: lasting happiness is finding your core and becoming whole.

In the bardo between lives, death appears differently from the dread specter that smothers out any one lifetime.

Even without contemplative mind, creatures know and fear the Grim Reaper and his approach, rear and bolt, quake and

appease, turn and hiss, or couch and hide. He has the same pur-
port everywhere, among frightened flocks on provincial planets,
an absolute terminus of what they are doing and what they are.
He will take it all away, and there is nothing else. Equally ant
and zebra turn tail and flee, flee the anteater and the lion, flee
their own hunger and thirst, flee their diseased bodies, flee the
zero point and terror of non-being, until they are changed into
something else.

Death becomes less an ultimate extinction of ego or an exile from pack members, family, and favorite haunts, and more
a gate—a molten gateway or tunnel of gateways—between
realms. (The word "passing" is appropriate, but so is the word
"haunt.")

Once having "passed," you get all the beads on your thread: long
lives and short lives, lives of grace and charity, lives of villainy and
combat, lives of professional fulfillment, lives gloomy and forlorn,
free lives and indentured lives, lothario lives and leper lives, high-
waymen and voodoo men, maidens and lads, lovers of maidens,
lovers of lads, seduced by different genders and creature embodi-
ments on countless worlds, giving birth and getting born, killing
and getting killed. You are male and female, androgyne and clone,
Mr. Prosperity and Miss Beggar, healthy and deformed, mammoth and minute, whole and mutilated, idiot and genius. You get
to be proud and intact; you get to be eaten alive. You get to experience each talent and the absence of those same talents—propensities for music and dance, mathematics and acrobatics. No one
is a great mathematician or poet who has not sometime been utterly without number or song. The experience of a skill's absence is
what drives creatures karmically to seek and cultivate and train it,
to reincarnate the aptitude with the necessary genes. The vestige
of self that was deprived of song sings loudest and most exuber-
antly, writes the most compelling melodies. Damn well it does!

Likewise no one can be kind and sincere who has not been utterly without mercy or reprieve. Every lama and nun was once a rodent and fish. Molecules learn only through being, through not being—in exile, even from themselves.

You commit every crime, against nature, and your own nature, and you punish or redeem those same crimes; you avenge and forgive, transgress and are transgressed against. And then you do it again, and again, as different entities.

You grab the gold ring, and the ring eludes you, and you don't even know there is a ring. You go on always, merely, because you have been placed somewhere as *some thing*—a spider in a dusty corner—and there is no choice but to shift and spin. You do it because *it* is and *you* are. Crawling innocent and blind across the contour of infinity. Poor creature. Blessed creature.

You experience your own limitless courage and shriveling cowardice. Adored forever, you will yet be spurned and abandoned forever. You forsake your loved ones. You find her and lose her and find her; you live in times of peace; you are born amid slaughter and mayhem. You are raped and then rape. You hoard and you give away.

The accumulation of all these experiences makes a Great Life—*your* life. Its thread is as long as it is myriad. Along it you recall indelibly brief sparks of insect existences, eternities as dull juicy worms. You taste salty flickers of snail desire and frog ecstasy, not only in the neurons of those animals but as their vestigial resonance through your human cells. You spread your wings again, in your mind, or nonmind, shape-shift over unnamed oceans. You prowl obscure jungles, not knowing the Name or the Word, those grasses so much thicker by scent than the expanse of extinct sky. You burrow into the ground and wrap your body in radiant soil, safe at last. Safe for a moment. Then you are swallowed and mutated into something else.

You don't know what you are. You don't know where you are. You *didn't* know what you were. But, in another sense, you did, always. The lives themselves may be tetherless, open, conditional; yet *you* are cognizant, wise. The thread persists; it cannot be excised or erased. All you can do each go-round is receive the rulebook, your body; execute the plan.

Of course you remember your past lives. You remember them more vividly than the life you are living but in a different way. They are what you are, while the life you are living is what you are forgetting, becoming. The creatures you were define you and give you a crux and identity, inform you moment to moment tacitly of your essence and location like some Cosmic Positioning Device. They are your context. They make it possible to live, now, at all.

Between lifetimes other beings appear to you not as mother or ally or son but as who they have been across many awakenings, who they actually are, which clarifies who *you* actually are. You tend to stay in families and other associations and try out becoming each other's fathers, sisters, lovers, wives, chums, rectors, doyens, assassins. In what seems like an uncanny series of synchroncities and *déjà vus*, you bump into each other in new situations all over again. You hook up with old crewmates.

Grandparents who died when you were young come back as children, younger than you, deepened by the events of their last life and transmuted by their most recent passage through a bardo where they were debriefed and enlisted again. A pet who was run over by a car twenty years ago is no longer cat or dog (or child) but all of them and a luminous spirit too. He will be back. She will be back. You will be back. You will meet again, even if you don't know it at the time. But you suspect it—that is, you suspect something.

After each life and death your situation becomes clear again in the bardo between lives but, in the same fashion, this life is but a bardo between deaths, between other views of the schema and landscape of all existence. We are always in transition between panoramas; life is no different from death or dreaming any other state of being in that regard. As long as we are anything, we are passing. What else could we, in truth, be? Bardos are what there are.

Think about it for a second. What were the other options? Back at the beginning of space and time, what else but this could be compelling, if you have eternity and nothing to do but to create and live in worlds, be used and revealed by them, then forget them entirely and exist as something altogether different? Except that you don't forget them, not at the soul's core.... Drama, romance, love, adventure, revelation, death, all real, all final when they are happening. Can you think of another set-up that makes more sense?

The lights go out. In fact, much more than the lights go out. America dissolves. Amnesia is no longer amnesia. And the sky fills with a billion or more stars, all of them you.

Thoughts on the Virginia Tech Shootings

1. No clarity or usefulness comes from concluding that Cho Seung-Hui was demonic or deranged. Empathy is the sole possibility for insight here. It is not a matter of condoning his acts, but of feeling the agony and ardor that drove them. To begin to understand what happened is the first step toward healing the wound as well as preventing the next such paroxysm.

The pop psychotherapy conducted throughout the media in the aftermath of the shootings—uniformly dreadful—was likely at the level of the bureaucratic psychotherapy enacted in local facilities to which Cho was "committed" for treatment: no thoughtful analysis, no transference, just grad-school taxonomy leading to protocols of behaviorism and requisite drugs. He was juiced with anti-depressants and other factory potions that the medical sector routinely dispenses to people as if they were the pill equivalent of "ideas." Such chemicals are not remedies; they have manifold and unique consequences in each psyche, few of which doctors and pharmacists gauge or comprehend.

Everyone's depression is unique; even the chemistry of everyone's depression is unique. Mix a cocktail of ideas, molecules, and paranoid fantasies and you get the voodoo you deserve.

Therapy succeeds only when there is transference, when the therapist experiences the mad person as himself, not some fucked-up alien. Then they recognize each other, have a minor epiphany, and each evolves. But to name a condition is to dismiss it. To apply one academic vector or another, after the fact, to a mass killer is to deny the bond between his passion and the passion of all of us, to break communion and forfeit the human connection that alone gives our suffering meaning.

Cho's Centreville neighbor, Abdul Shash, was actually a better shrink than all the talking heads. Noting the gunman-to-be's legendary lack of response to greetings, he observed simply, "He was like he had a broken heart." If Cho had been treated with even a morsel of acknowledgment for his broken heart, there would not have been a massacre. As he himself told people posthumously, "You had your chances, more than enough of them."

Looking scrawny and talking funny is invitation for bullies to peck and pummel away until you become a basket case. Being mocked and reviled is no incidental matter. It dominates your imagination. You become tunnel-visioned and pissed off; you mull exotic revenges. Dylan Klebold and Eric Harris set the rules of engagement for the "school daze" of the future in this indulgent, gun-worshipping land.

The Columbine-High Goths wrote the liturgy, and later practitioners of ritual massacre used their precedent and rule-book: "I want to kill and injure as many of you fuckers as I can"; "I'm gonna be famous"; "I'm going out in style"; and "I just want to take a few pieces of shit with me." Forget the contradictions. It's long past logic. If you are taunted and hazed long enough and brutally enough, you are going to make someone pay, whatever the cost to yourself.

The same rules apply on the mean streets of West Oakland or any 'hood: Diss someone, even accidentally, and you get blown away.

2. The ready availability of guns is a part of the problem, yet the crisis is so deep-seated by now that it cannot be fixed by even the most stringent gun-control measures. Weapons, large and small, are imbedded in the American psyche too profoundly to extricate in any simple manner. A self-righteous "gun attitude" has implanted itself in our national character.

The real danger is not even guns' availability; it is their independent role in American consciousness and the fantasies they generate. Guns breed their own imagination: people begin thinking bullets. Revenge fantasies morph into gun fantasies, as these are conducive objects for metastasizing discontent. Shoot, and your problem is gone.

The coronation of guns as transcendent signs above the law generates its own motivations and diacritic events. Weapons become organs and acts rather than responses to acts.

I haven't fired a rifle since around age eleven at the Camp Chipinaw range, but gun imagery floods my mind. When I feel fury at public figures, I picture assassinations of them by long-range snipers or invisible horsemen with pistolas galloping into Washington—my thoughts corroding into proxy attacks by bang! bang!: swift, hard shots. But it is a sterile, headachey compulsion.

When simple linear machines become vehicles for ideation of rage—as well as a chimerical safeguard against class warfare and a figuration for general alienation simmering beneath the surface of society—then wholesome acts of confrontation and transformation are supplanted by automated instrumentalities and displaced operations.

Guns have been elevated into not only icons but wands, fetishes, and oaths. To loyalists, they are extensions of their own flesh, their alter egos and best friends, the basis of their identity and self-worth—the entire Bill of Rights, to boot. No wonder we have the foreign policy we do—"violent and murderous ... bringing death and displacement to millions," in bin Laden's own words, justification for 9/11. "As American as apple pie," Stokely Carmichael called it way back in the Vietnam era: it *is* our way of life. "Shock and awe" is NRA propaganda writ large.

In somewhat the same spirit that India is the cradle of Buddhism, France the birthplace of existentialism, the Soviet Union the laboratory of Marxism, America deeds the world "gunnism," a living philosophy whereby people arm themselves, fear strangers, suspect their own neighbors, imagine every possible home invasion, carjacking, and crazed street attack, and never, despite two oceans and thousands of nuclear weapons, feel safe.

Gunnology is our Maoism: not philosophy from the barrel of a gun but the gun itself as philosophy. That is what is taught with their mother's milk to kids in the projects and 'hoods. When you carry a gun, you carry ontology, meaning; you get respect. You are in the discussion. While your first seminar may be running drugs and muling cash, the gun is thesis and antithesis, the only argument worth having, even in the schoolyard.

I agree, it would be better for all if the youth at risk didn't pack heat (or put on baggy pants and other convict stylings), but that is what they are taught in Gunnology 1. It is not particularly sophisticated, but it doesn't have to be. All it has to do is make a definitive statement about politics, reality, and power—and unfortunately, it does.

What more do you need to know about the American philosophy of gunnism than a guy in Ohio stepping out of his home and shooting dead a teenage neighbor because he is trespassing on his lawn? People dole out "being and nothingness" from their private slot machines like tinhorn Sartres or Ben Franklins.

If guns could have somehow been outlawed here in the European fashion before they were cathected into sacred emblems, the entire NRA culture with its overkill shootings and pointless domestic mishaps might have been averted before it got going. Now far too many people own too many guns for there to be any practical method to start taking them away. The symbolic "gun" is too widespread and familial to eliminate. We have a better chance of resolution at the other end—a national shootout—rather than Congressional prohibition.

Anyway, the present law, or lack thereof, is the worst possible compromise. We might as well enact the logical consequences of the NRA's interpretation of the Second Amendment: Require *everyone* to pack guns. Make it a law that no one goes out the door unarmed, no one keeps a gunless home. All airline passengers shall be checked to make sure they have their weapons with them. That will deter crimes, hijackings, and mass shootings and rid us of the false piety of gun ownership. Compel us all to arm ourselves and then we will be safe from our own fantasies. If the point is to signify anxiety in weaponry, *let's do it.*

3. The gun lobby probably makes the wrong point when it declares its primo reason for allowing law-abiding citizens their sidearms: e.g. if they were deprived, then only criminals and wackos will have guns (since these kinds disobey the law anyway). I don't think that the Cho Seung-Huis of the world arm their apocalyptic fantasies unless we make it super-easy for them. Put a few curves in the way and Cho probably continues to brood darkly, at least for a lot longer, until something distracts him: he harasses the wrong student; he gets kudos from a gracious teacher, is fascinated by programming his iPod, or stumbles into an unlikely romance.

Conversely, advertise guns on billboards, flood the culture with placards of violence and gun art, and you write the textbook for acting out. You encourage loners to brood covetously and then blast away. You valorize malice and reprisal and racism rather than getting into the barnyard with all the other turkeys and bumbling through the problems, ruffled feathers, fat asses, squawking, and all. In the old days, in normal times, people threw themselves into the mix, bumptious as it was, and came away with a life, even with honor. Now there's TV, the Internet, video games, and gunnist isolation.

Citizens are additionally assaulted by informal coolness competitions, sexual provocations, as well as the random violence and permission-to-violence of Bush's international foreign policy. Maudlin death dramas amp up rap music, cinema, television, video games, and nightly news. There is constant enticement to make symbolic acts real. Easily available guns in stores and on the street are the icing on the cake, the explicit permission to turn revenge fantasies into your own reality show.

This culture is goading its marginal people into deeds that vent their frustration while catapulting them onto center stage—higher ratings for a day or two (the O. J. Simpson factor) with any casualties merely incidental under free-market capitalism.

When Cho Seung-Hui used the word "debauchery" to exemplify the mindset he was rebelling against, he was precisely on target. The jihadists refer to us similarly when their suicide bombers outfit themselves. Each party, however exclusive, is making the same point: if America wants to indulge its faux moralism in capitalist prerogative and all-terrain armed adventure, let it expect blowback of the same.

4. Cho Seung-Hui was sleepwalking for most of his twenty-three years. He needed to wake himself somehow, and he knew it. Inside the bubble of his trance, a bizarre fantasia was getting larger and larger. The front-page headline in April 22's Sunday *New York Times* proclaimed: "Before Deadly Rage Erupted, A Lifetime Consumed by a Troubling Silence: A Loner Becomes a Killer." This cliché-ridden nutshell actually understates the situation. Cho wasn't just silent; he was preternaturally silent. His was not a silence of bare shyness and introversion; it was the silence of the wolf-child abandoned by humans, raised by speechless animals—except he was a wolf-child weaned in an urban cacophony of dialects and cultures, social aggressions and oral competitions.

He elected to become the one who wouldn't comply, who wouldn't put his meanings into words, who was struck dumb, who by being rendered profoundly mute, bore divine witness.

Thus he became tinder for all that was exploding around him, taking it inside himself day by mum day, converting mass collective speech into the inarticulate emotions and icons at its source. He didn't need language—language only gets in the way; language dilutes libidinal purity and drive formation.

Cho didn't speak in Korean as a child in Seoul before his natal family moved to the U.S. when the lad was eight. He didn't speak while in Motown or suburban D.C. (Centreville, Virginia) in either Korean or English, both of which were blabbed widely there. Instead he played video games and shot baskets solitaire, responding, if at all, with a requisite ironical "Yessir."

In grade school when he was forced by pedagogical authority to debut his "English as a second language," a sound came out of him, such an unexpected deep-throated chirp that the other kids began hooting. The teacher merely smirked. Then Cho stopped speaking altogether. His lifelong oath became samurai, not just some namby-pamby snit.

But make no mistake: he wasn't speaking from the get-go as a child in Korea or the States; his silence was an epistemological statement on the planet, the world-age he was born into—a statement that many could have made but for which he was inexplicably chosen, or volunteered.

In college it got to the point that he was a complete and utter cipher; his room-mates couldn't recall him saying a single syllable all semester, not one. They remember an Oriental in sunglasses, a baseball cap pulled down over his face. At one point they bet on whether he was a deaf mute, and one of them offered him $10 just to say hello. You can imagine how well that went over.

What those around him should have realized was that this was not just a meek or sullen silence; it was an extraordinary silence, the silence of madness and apocalypse, revelation and vengeance, and its bearer should have been treated with the same caution and deference that you would cede a rabid dog, or a lunatic about to buy two guns. His silence was the antecedent and also the rudiment of a sacred rage that should have been as terrifying and ominous to those who came into contact with him as the actual guns and ammunition into which it vamped and as which it vocalized at last.

The *Times* refers to "the mystery of who he was," adding that his parents hoped that college would "extract him from his suffocating cocoon and make him talk." That it did.

When Cho produced his videos and sent them for posthumous delivery to NBC, it marked the formal end to his silence. Words spewed out in swift, staccato rhythm—the primitive articulations that had been gestating in him in place of language. Their meaning was not what he said but a rough translation of his millennial silence into locution. That is why they didn't sound quite right; they were very strange indeed.

Acquaintances of Cho remarked, variously, that the figure before the camera didn't look like him because they had never heard well-formed, refined sentences coming out of him. "This is someone that I grew up with and loved," said his uncomprehending Princeton-educated sister, an employee of the State Department. "Now I feel like I didn't know this person."

It was like ventriloquism or dubbing except that the voice matched the body and was surreally apropos. In fact, everything that preceded it seemed a terrible hoax, as if a Down's syndrome child were suddenly delivering a sermon on particle physics, e.g. he was never really who he pretended to be. Cho, the double agent, was debriefing himself, coming in from the cold. Initiated and educated all along, he fully understood and spoke English— modern, hip English. Just not aloud.

Cho was no doubt planning his big coming-out party while he was making the videos, which is why they were so imperative to him, important enough that he gunned down thirty-two people for their trailer: to make sure he was heard and heard in the way he intended. The shootings were the gloss—the liner notes. That is why he took two hours between his first two kills and the last thirty—he was crafting a *tour de force* of speech, not murder but language.

In the short life of Seung-Hui Cho, this was the culmination, the single monumental appearance on the big screen (or in fact anywhere), the only trip to the Superbowl. It was his satanic debutante ball—and he rose to its occasion. He had been spawning underground, a feature-length epic, shot over decades but never screened. Then suddenly it was black-tie, gala, the world premiere—the comeuppance and reprisal—and woe to those who had underrated or dismissed him.

If all the eggs are in one basket, it doesn't matter whose eggs they are. If they are *all there and there are none anywhere else,* heaven help those who get in the way.

The networks had it backwards: the tapes weren't the aftermath of the massacre that preceded and followed; they weren't even commentary on it—they *were the deed.* Murder allowed him to use his voice, the scream that was waiting for permission, for circumstance.

Extraordinary silence begets extraordinary speech. Mere signification is not enough to break through today's incredible noise-to-signal din. If you want to be heard big-time, you have to blow important things up or lie in the street blocking consumers and commerce. You have to get in the way of commodities or create something that itself can be marketed. Like Osama, Cho implicitly understood Madison Avenue, appreciated performance art. Deeds are necessary to render words irrevocable—then even assholes and religious fanatics earn prime-time audiences; even couch potatoes and movie stars have to sit up and listen.

It was necessary for Cho to do more than speak his mind because he had to justify and redeem so many years of silence, to convert them into something worth their price: their communion and purgation, his wolf speech. He couldn't risk merely being shrill or anything less than a redeemer in broad daylight: *Mad Max, Payback, Above the Law, Delta Force.* He couldn't unleash just some old angry voice (which might elicit "Hey, shut up, chink!"); it had to be gunnism, bullets, the philosophy of the American ruling and under-classes. He had to fashion the precise correlate of his unique silence. He had to be a boy to take note of, with a gun.

Once he did that, no further considerations of clemency raised obstacles; the god who gave him his childhood mission and the pluck to do it now required him to remit, to let it all hang out, to see it through and honor the fucking oblation for what it was.

No, it was never first about guns and killing or violence and revenge against anonymous classmates; it was about the Word, as "In the Beginning was...." It was about the origin of civil society, the nature of public discourse in America, and the long-incubated desire of the zombie god of speech to force people to actually listen and regard the garbage they are mouthing all day long, everywhere and everyone. Cho was his disciple, and through him he managed to get out a semblance of his message.

Cho said, "You are all speaking and saying nothing." He said, "The words don't mean anything, and anyway here's what you are really saying." He said, "Here I am, Cho. And I mean what I say. I mean."

Listen not to the words themselves, which are stock and random, but the cadences. The words are almost meaningless and often misnomers, dead wrong or delusional. The cadences are always right: "You have vandalized my heart, raped my soul, and torched my conscience.... Your Mercedes wasn't enough, you brats. Your golden necklaces weren't enough, you snobs.... You had everything.... You had a hundred billion chances and ways to have avoided today. But you decided to spill my blood. You forced me into a corner and gave me only one option. The decision was yours. Now you have blood on your hands that will never wash off."

What an incredibly brazen, unabashed rant: flaming clichés set in insipidly mordant singsong, pure bathos and schmaltz! Yet it is as powerful as any Hamlet soliloquy because, in the end, Cho had no Shakespeare to help him; he was the real Korean (or Mexican or Pakistani) émigré, driven out of Costco society, forced to improvise and splice—so he delivered the ultimate crybaby, martyr rant, in the King's eloquent *anglais*, binding the curses of all the wounded and brooding children who lacked his desperation and bravado to sing nakedly to the world. He was talking back for all the twelve-year-old soldiers ("How old are you?" "Old enough to kill a man")—Double Trouble, Death and Destruction, Little Weapon, Bone Thug, and Blood Never Dry. He was the self-anointed Fourth and Fifth World valedictorian.

If Cho had been articulate or merely eloquent, it would have been Hollywood or a poetry-slam out-take. But he was articulately inarticulate; he was so trite that he was brilliantly untrite—it was *The Little Rascals*, *Survivor*, the lost episode of *Seinfeld*.

He *was* Hamlet, the Hamlet of a time out of joint, when kings are imposters, when money-changers own the academies as well as the temples, when drug lords kidnap politicians, when children are recruited into gangs and militias—when *conscience doth truly make cowards of us all*. Out of maudlin banalities Cho authored the collective truth. Out of linguistic bricolage he created an American opera, and it reverberated all the way back to its roots in Seoul: "*O, from this time my thoughts be bloody or nothing worth!*"

The tempo of his sermon is perfect. Yes, there *were* a hundred billion chances to avoid what happened. Far beyond Cho Seung-Hui's own circumstances and fate, to the remote reaches of America's decadence, into the White House itself—attend the music of failed penance, of inconsolable revenge, of "bad boy" atonement, of shameless vindication, of petulant song.

No wonder Cho proclaimed that he did it for his brothers and sisters and children (what brothers? what children?) and cited Columbine, Christ, and the President God himself. If you are composing a requiem, you've got total poetic license; you can speak in metaphor and allusion, Mercedes and golden necklaces and broken hearts. A million potential saints and sinners are significators in Cho's riff.

"You thought it was one pathetic boy's life you were extinguishing. Thanks to you, I die like Jesus Christ, to inspire generations of the weak and the defenseless people."

How many heckled youths have chanted (or wanted to chant) more or less the same raow on global TV and world satellite? How few get to deliver it in blood! But, kiddo, it wasn't Jesus Christ you were running with, just for the record; it was Timothy McVeigh, Mohammed Atta.

"I didn't have to do it. I could have left. I could have fled. But now I am no longer running...." Not the words—the cadences.

Can you hear the song for which the diatribe is pale parrotry?

5. It is not irrelevant that Cho's mother, Kim Hwang-Im, was a refugee from North Korea whose family slipped across the border during the Great War. North Korea is the great subliminal cipher of our planet that "speaks" for the rest of what passes for rational civilization, speaks in its own vast ceremonial silence, e.g. using people as mosaics in military designs on parade grounds. To say what to the world? To shadow what ineffable battlefield, what prophetic war to come?

His father, Seung-Tae Cho, was an oilfield construction worker shuttling back and forth to Saudi Arabia before repairing home finally to an arranged marriage.

God knows what shadows lurk within our shiftless and spiritually vacant global Kali Yuga when time and space begin to

333

collapse and the black holes of astrophysical cosmology come to dwell in human souls.

6. Cho's fantasies, tropes, lies, and inventions were both clues and cries for help. His "girlfriend," a supermodel named Jelly from outer space, visited him by flying saucer. She called her boyfriend Spanky.

He fixated on female students, two of them fiercely and disturbingly enough with unannounced visits and instant messages (under the screen name SpankyJelly) that they reported him to the campus cops.

There was his other name for himself: Question Mark, a signature he used on school forms: ?. Even he didn't know.

He boasted of having a villa on Mars and traveling regularly from there to Jupiter. To communicate that tidbit, he must have spoken, though what he said was the antithesis of speech.

He claimed to have grown up with Vladimir Putin in Moscow and told folks he was meeting him in North Carolina to hang out during Thanksgiving break, a proposition so absurd and unlikely that it could have only been a lucid statement of an entirely different thing.

The hallmarks of his one-act plays *Richard McBeef* and *Mr. Brownstone*, now immortalized in the literature of crime and madness, are incest, sexual violence, domestic brutality, assassination by chainsaw. Yet by all accounts his own family was gentle and intelligent.

Hey, it's not what they didn't know. It's what they didn't dare to know.

7. This wasn't another al-Qaeda strike on our shores, but it was a full-on successful suicide attack, an aggrandized, fuck-you to perceived oppression and powerlessness and also a prudish clout

to the materialism, vulgarity, puerile porn, and gaudy exhibition-ism of the West—I might add, by someone equally ashamed of his own fantasies. Cho was going to obliterate himself and as many of them as he could before he too became one of "them" and lost the virginity of his rage, before he tarnished the purity of his persecution, turning into an asshole too.

He was saying, "I want to. I don't want to. I am. I am not." He legislated by gun as a way of refusing to be humiliated and trivialized. Remember: being and not-being are the essential blade on which every philosophy as well as every murder or sui-cide takes place. Those Palestinians with belts of incendiaries strapped symbolically and actually to their abdomens—albeit most of them saner and more emotionally mature than Cho—must feel pretty much the same thing: "I hate. I love. I won't. I will."

8. If Seung-Hui could have realized that he was truly known to God, or Intelligence, in all his weirdness and differentness and pimpliness or whatever, *and was loved nonetheless,* he might not have had to hide his name even from himself, might not have had to hide his voice from the world until it became a call of death. I don't know how that could have come about except through a metanoia to which he was not open, and which nothing around him pointed the way towards:

"Oh Lord, you have searched me and known me! You know when I sit down and when I rise up; you discern my thoughts from afar.... Even before a word is on my tongue, behold O Lord, you know it altogether.... Where shall I go from your Spirit? Or where shall I flee from your presence? If I ascend to heaven, you are there! If I make my bed in Sheol, you are there! If I take the wings of the morning and dwell in the uttermost part of the sea, even there your hand shall lead me, and your right hand shall hold me....

For you formed my inward parts; you knitted me together in my mother's womb. I praise you, for I am fearfully and wonderfully made. Wonderful are your works; my soul knows it very well. My frame was not hidden from you, while I was being made in secret, intricately woven in the depths of the earth. Your eyes saw my un-formed substance; in your book were written, every one of them, the days that were formed for me, when as yet there was none of them. How precious to me are your thoughts, O God! How vast is the sum of them! If I could count them, they are more than sand. I awake, and I am still with you."

9. It took a poet, Nikki Giovanni, to intuit what was happen-ing, that she had a maniac in her pack, the kind of person who shoots up classrooms. She wanted him out of her seminar or she threatened to resign.

By contrast, the various therapists, police officers, and univer-sity bureaucrats—constrained by "the law is an ass" labyrinth—were unable to distinguish one more harmless alienated student from a time-bomb on its last ticks. They were so used to idle melodrama, hiphop hyperbole, Internet loutishness, computer violence, that they couldn't recognize the real thing if their life depended on it.

And from here on in, it sort of does.

Trillions upon trillions of Buddhafields co-occupy the universe, many of them along selfsame continua, each distinguished by its own modes of thought and levels of attention. All are devoid of true substance, even as all are chockfull—like our one—of earth, air, fire, water, or their correlatives. In fact, dozens of realms with their own native denizens exist in this very room, contentedly going about their business, oblivious to us. None of these other "sentient beings" perceive it as a room, by the same token that we see neither *their* houses nor their firmament. The imaginal canopy that casts a starry night for them does not exist for us. Not only are its constellations foreign but they are comprised of something other than stars—of vibrations native to their locale. What to us is a rock or hill, to them is an elaborate elf-dwelling. So gnomes, yetis, trolls, and huldufolk dwell in our midst; we catch fleeting glimpses of their passage.

Our seemingly barren Solar System is swarming with antonymous creatures. Fiery Venus and volcanic Io, frigid Neptune and primeval Pluto, even the tundras and ice-covered seas of Ceres and Enceladus are as populous, in principle, as Earth. On each of these worlds are casinos and temples, cowboys and clerks, or their equivalents.

Separate realities teem through the octaves and quartiles of all the solar systems in the modern universe, exobionts and cryptozooids galore, only some made of flesh and blood or even atoms.

General Relativity Theory expresses a much greater verity than we credit it: there are innumerable indices linking space-time to distance; they key the speeds of photons to extradimensional particles. For the Einsteins of upper domains, Ultimate Relativity provides a ratio for simultaneity of creations and states of being, as mirages created by mindedness bend under the gravity of dharmic existence.

Don Edwards is king of the cowboy balladeers—the second coming of Gene Autry with a bit of Willie Nelson's existentialism, Marty Robbins' cosmic story-telling, and miscellaneous portions of Tex Ritter, Johnny Horton, and Johnny Cash. As cowboy troubadour and eco-minstrel, Edwards invokes gods, loners, and philosophers of the range. Like a Hebrew cantor or Hindu ghazal singer he makes sounds rich with the mystery of existence.

1. Sage and trickster, he maps the fading of the old West into shopping malls, a spirit becoming more animal than human:

    a. "… *this is no place for an hombre like I am/in this new world of asphalt and steel….*"

    b. "*He said/all that's left now of the old days/is the damn old cay'otes and me….*"

    c. "*That night as the moon crossed the mountains/one more coyote was heard/and he'd go:/hooo-yip,/hooo-yip,/hooo….*"*

2. Totem keeper and ancestral spirit, he speaks for Earth First!, James Fenimore Cooper, and Black Elk. The rabbits, birds, and coyotes are shamanic, as they track us from sky and earth, a vigil:

    a. "… *when a shadow moves out/'cross the ground./It's an eagle that circles above me,/and he screams to his friends on the hill,/'Stay close together,/move not a feather,/man walks among us,/be still, be still….*"

    b. "*I look close and see/God looking at me/through the eyes of/a young cottontail./I see a cay'ote sneakin'/as he crawls through the brush on the hill./And the eagle screams down,/ 'Stay close to the ground.'/Man walks among us,/be still….*"

    c. "*Soon will be gone all the desert,/cities will cover each hill./Today will just be/a fond memory./Man walks among us,/be still.*"†

---

*"Coyotes," written by Bob Mcdill.

† "Man Walks Among Us," written by Marty Robbins.

3. Gnostic ghost-rider, prairie astronomer, and Martian chronicler, Edwards weaves Henry Vaughan, Thomas Hardy, Carl Sagan into one trope. Suddenly we shoot from Where The Buffalo Roam to another planet among blazing stars above a different Prairie Lullaby, a world that is the same as ours, only elsewhere—or maybe it is the Cosmic Witness in us, sighting Earth as a distant planet, its ranges populated by sleepy cowboys, the canyons of all its worlds howling with wolves and other motley beasts:

    a. *"At midnight when the cattle are sleeping,/on my saddle I pillow my head,/and up at the heavens lie peeping,/from out of my cold grassy bed.*

    b. *"And it's often and often/I've wondered/at night while lying alone/if each tiny star way up yonder/is a great peopled world like our own.*

    c. *"In the evening in the bright stars up yonder/do cowboys lie down to their rest?/Do they gaze at this wide world and wonder/if roughriders dash o'er its crest?*

    d. *"Do they listen to the wolves in the canyon?/Do they watch the night owl in its flight?/Are their horses their only companions/while guarding their herds through the night?"**

4. Rebel libertarian and Trail of Tears minstrel, he accompanies Ira Hayes and Clint Eastwood down the Powwow Highway. I enjoy this funky American Indian Movement fable and never tire of the moment when the narrator breaks with the National Anthem to notice Johnny standing there stolid and mum, sitting this one out, committing VFW blasphemy:

    a. *"Johnny was a Cherokee cowboy,/long braids hangin' from his hat ... /he rode with my Uncle Jack.//He sat like a shadow in the saddle,/and wrote po-etry with his rope./He had a light hand for the horses,/and a smile for us little folk...."*

---

*"Cowboy's Meditation," traditional.

b. *"Hale County picnic … /Fourth of July,/they had a big tent/ and a little brass band/box lunches on the lawn./When they raised Old Glory to the top of the pole,/we all sang the freedom song,/'O say can you see—/Johnny, why aren't you singing?/'O say can you see—Johnny, is there something wrong?/ … Johnny, where are you going?/Johnny, won't you stay/and help us sing the freedom song?'"*

c. *" … then his face got soft and he kneeled right down/and he sounded plumb wore out,/when he said, 'Little pardner, it's not my freedom/that they're singing about.'"**

5. Lama and preacher-man cowpoke, he chants a haunting death mantra. I like that his brown girl is a horse and that the crack of the pistol, the wild Irish girls, and the early light of dawn are equally markers of being in a body on a planet soon to be left behind:

a. *"Goodbye to my pals of the prairie,/goodbye to the cattle and trails,/goodbye to the morning's first gleaming…."*

b. *"I'm riding away on life's roundup/where the sun is sinking low./I'm riding away on my brown girl/to the roundup where we all must go.*

c. *Goodbye to the crack of the pistol…,/Goodbye to the Rimrock races,/goodbye to the wild Irish girls…."* †

6. Texas troubadour, he lays down smooth frontier blues. Leroy Carr and Janis Joplin couldn't have grieved a lost lover any more mournfully: *"I'm all right through the day,/but day fades away,/and the long lonely night takes its place…."*§

7. Cattle-puncher and outlaw, he scribes Part One of the Great American Rodeo Novel. The song-inside-the-story-inside-the-

*"Freedom Song," written by Andy Wilkinson.

† "The Dying Cowboy of Rimrock," traditional.

§ "At the End of a Long, Lonely Day," written by Marty Robbins.

song sets up a cinematic moment, Johnny Depp in his first cow-boy role:

   a. *"... moon is shining still and bright,/cattle all are restin' easy,/ but I just can't sleep tonight ... /'less it's Warbling Jim a-singing, 'Annie Laurie' out on guard ... /couldn't sleep now if I tried,/makes the night feel big and lonesome...."*

   b. *"... nights I drove her home from dances/when the east was turnin' gray..../But her folks says I was shiftless,/wild, unsettled,/they was right...."*

   c. *"And she married young Doc Wilkens./My lord, but that was hard./Wish that fool would quit his singing,/'Annie Laurie' out on guard."**

If you like this sort of stuff—and I can't imagine better meta-physical metrics in the saddle—go to iTunes or Amazon, and check out out "Scheduled appearances" at http://www.donedwardsmusic.com.

(This note is little more than a friendly shout to my readers and, yes, a musical backdrop to this sector of my book.)

Real beauty is of course more than skin deep. Just about everyone gets to be young and pretty once, but all such sirens revert into what they actually are: a person. Exquisitely cut features, ephemer-ally alluring, may mask a witch or a lout. Superficial good looks can go ugly fast, a glimpse into the future by the age of thirty or forty, the emerging truth at fifty or sixty. What was ravishing becomes grotesque. Ultimately we see who a man or woman really is.

---

*"Annie Laurie," an old poem by Badger Clarke, set to music by Don Edwards.

It works the other way too. People with real character and depth get more beautiful over time, no matter whether they are conventionally pretty or not. Their natural charisma dawns as their nature shapes their looks from the inside out. Eccentricity or plainness matures into a glamour and charm that are as individual as they are sublime. Beauty at the heart has a mystique transcending ersatz attributes of beauty queens.

Sometimes one gets to view a former lover or infatuation figure again after many decades and is startled by the metamorphosis. What hid or inveigled itself in the bland comeliness of youth now is sculpted in actual tissues and cells—it could be an executioner, a pedophile, a bag lady, or someone inwardly spirited and heartful.

Our romanticized social world would function quite differently if people could view the full series of personae behind each acquaintance, who they were and who they will become over a lifetime: the cute child, the winsome adolescent, the handsome guy or gal, the middle-aged metamorph, the wrinkled androgyne. Suitors would be horrified to see whom they are courting, kissing, clasping to their bodies as if life itself. "Fatal attraction" in spades! They would tear out of there as if from a corpse's grip.

Flirtation is entrapment for predation, as most insects know from birth.

I think people *do* see their partner during romance; it's just that they shut off the descrying mechanism and go for the sexiness. They don't want to glimpse the future; they blind themselves to censor or fret. In the heat of the moment they want to be seduced by the prince or princess of the now.

But no one actually turns into someone else. "We don't change," remarked the poet Charles Olson, "we merely stand more revealed."

This is a maxim not only of personal life. Consider politicians. During a campaign a candidate manufactures allure, doing the equivalent of what a lover does to try to get a prospective partner to adore him or her. Once elected he becomes, as he must, who he is.

I am still astonished that so many voters, especially on the conservative right, found George W. Bush attractive. He always seemed to me what he was: a fake beauty, a femme fatale under a lot of makeup. He couldn't hide his mean-spiritedness, greed, shallow character, or brattiness, no matter the million-dollar suits, the crafted persona, the showtime patriotism and religiosity, the quippy compassion. Yet people bought it. They voted for this mannequin. They also bought Dick Cheney's toughness when he was little more than a vulgar and vengeful drunk.

You can't hide who you are, not behind high office, not behind mascara and lipstick, not behind the military of the "twentieth century's last standing superpower." A coward and bully with an army is still a coward and a bully.

It's the core alone that counts: who you are when the chips are down. That's why I prefer Barack Obama to Hillary Clinton. Her enemies may demonize her unfairly, but they instinctively sense her dull ambition lacking principle as well as the same kind of phony sincerity that got W to the head of the Republican Party. I see someone seeking redemption for public shame, bristling with anger and inconsolable pride, plus a sense of sport and competitive intellect greater than a wish to serve. Hillary is W Bush in a faux liberal package and female couture.* I don't trust her hollow laugh any more than I do his. Under their game faces, these two are buddies and soul-mates, seeking the Presidency

---

*"Dick Cheney in a pant suit" is how columnist Andrew Sullivan (October '07) put it.

"to fulfill some long-held plan or because they think it's owed to them."*

In the case of Barack, I sense the force of his good will and generosity, his sincere passion to minister to the needy and improve the human lot. He has put what charm and intelligence he has at the service of humanity, not his ego. He truly understands that this is not about him; he is merely the latest incarnation of the tribal warrior onto whom everyone can project their own empowerment and hope. He allows others to become the best of who they are—and people love that and are inspired to come together and do impossible things. That is what a President is—not policy wonking, clever distortions, tough put-down lines, and self-importance, but leadership and a capacity to make personal sacrifices that becomes contagious. This is the dharma Barack preaches: "Ask not what your country can do for you …"—a motto being raised in the language of a new generation for the first time since Jack and Bobby. "I have a dream …" is being sounded again at long last.

Obama is "beginner's mind," unjaded, his ambition empathic and humane. If this nation has the guts to elect him, with his African heritage and Muslim name, it would instantly renovate America's rep throughout the Middle East and Talibanistan. We wouldn't be exonerated, but they'd view us differently; we'd get a temporary pass, especially among the young.

I don't think we have that courage. Instead, we are hankering to turn back the clock to the Bill and Hillary dog-and-pony show because we thought we were happier and safer then. Plus she acts as though she's a pretty mean battle-axe who can get payback from the Republicans, which is what a lot of angry Dems want more than a leader for both red and blue America. They want nasty entertainment and revenge.

---

*Obama's words.

Hillary tells us that if she knew then what she does now she wouldn't have voted to authorize the war in Iraq—but that's precisely the point. You don't get to see the future ahead of time; you have to act on your intrinsic clarity, wisdom, and selfless inclination to do the right thing. You have to call the cargo before the ship sails.

That's where Hillary failed utterly in Congress, where she continues to fail every day, and where she will fail as President if that comes to pass. She has no inner rectitude or creed; her "beauty" is skin-deep. No belief system guides her or, more to the point, if her belief system were revealed, she would never get elected. So, like W, she is living off political correctness, staged performances, and popularized myths.

Monday-morning quarterbacks are a dime a dozen. Hillary will miss the next "Iraq," no matter if it is foreign or domestic, because she is trapped by her vanity and tantrum, plus a myopia so trenchant she actually thinks she is worldly and experienced. Barack will respond from his core and effortlessly choose the proper course, speak the right words, behave like a samurai rooted in the earth. What is Hillary rooted in except three decades of melodrama, lobbyist boot-licking, and corporate gamesmanship?

Damn, I mean is America turning into a banana republic with its own Evita Perons and Imelda Marcoses or what? Hillary touts her foreign-policy experience, but she wasn't exactly Secretary of State under Bill Clinton, and her visits to other countries consisted of taxpayer junkets and catered banquets with political celebs, while Obama lived as a child in Indonesia and Africa and experienced what the United States looks like from outside the house.

Talk about Teflon and agitprop: she has magically transformed her public status as cuckolded wife into virtual co-President with Bill, a remarkably unexamined and uncritiqued act of P.R. spin and pure will that seems to have stuck. When Kobe Bryant cheated on his lady, he bought her a $4 million eight-caret, purple diamond ring. Bill Clinton is trying to win back his wife's honor with an even bigger bauble.

And what about this cad anyway? Yes, he was steamrolled and whitewatered and bimboed by bloodthirsty Republicans—and W's crimes and lies were billions of times more exorbitant and serious, but that doesn't mean he didn't desecrate the White House and the nation's honor by getting a blow-job from a young intern in the Oval Office. The fact that he was also puffing a cigar and conducting business with Congress showed that he wasn't even submitting to the mystery of sex or respecting his lover. Add to that the fact that he was ostensibly *in loco parentis*, the responsible and moral adult, *and* the President.

Character is demonstrated by deeds, and somewhere in this porno fantasy of bimbo subjugation and bondage disguised as disingenuous male libido is Hillary, voyeuring as well as standing by her man. How innocent is she of the seduction of Monica Lewinsky? How does this translate into her standing up to lobbyists or conducting international diplomacy with a clear conscience? Is this the cackling face we want on America?

Love and hate are fatuous when applied to politicians, but that proviso aside, I loved this guy Bill once with his sax and his greasy Southern charm and his ribald imagination, all the way back to his bawdy public propositioning of Germaine Greer in the early Seventies in London—America's first Black President, so named by Toni Morrison. I hate him now for his arrogance and narcissism, his attempt to wheedle his bitch into the White House, his betrayal of not only Black America, but his own legacy and the first truly transpolitical, transracial campaign. "Selfish" and "vainglorious" barely scratch the surface.

The self-indulgent melodrama and lurking tragedy of the Clintons that began long before Monica Lewinsky and Kenneth Starr and his attempted impeachment but reached a particular theatrical crescendo then—a tragedy of hubris and appetite—has been in abeyance these last eight disastrous years that were ushered in by that stupid, venal indiscretion which cost Al Gore the White House and the nation a head start on global warming and terrorism. It is headed now for a Lear-like denouement.

When a man cannot, by the Twenty-Second Amendment to the Constitution, seek the Presidency again, do his partisans then conspire, in smug subtext, to get around the law by electing his wife? Do we now worship the consorts of kings? Is this some mediaeval plutocracy or Hollywood sitcom? Are we really going to buy this charade? Hey, Bill, did Jesse Jackson win Alaska too?

I have no stake in being right here. If Hillary gets elected, I would say, "Lady, prove me wrong! I'm just another jerk with an opinion."

Even today a part of me roots for W to turn out to be right about Iraq, for us on the Left to be totally misreading him. You know the line: he's far more intelligent than he seems, a radical seer, years ahead of his time. I would accept that outcome if it really meant peace and freedom in the Middle East and relief *en Estados* for the lost and poor. I want our President to be beautiful and decent. I want to know that he secretly weeps for those whom he has impoverished or killed.

Prove me wrong, George! Prove the selfless courage of your policies. Prove that you alone stand between the Western Gate and Chaos. Prove that this was not just a spectacle on the backs of the poor and powerless. Be our greatest and most unfairly maligned president. I'm game.

If there were going to be nothing rather than something, right from the onset, from the beginning of time and of everything, then there would be nothing, nothing right to the pith and bottom of existence—or existence's negation.

These diametrics are the same, for you can't negate nothing: Nothing prevails forever. There is no way to beat its oxymoron.

"Nothing forever" means nothing changes, nothing interrupts it, nothing knows about nothing; nothing doesn't know either. But these are mere words and not unlike the definition of enlightenment in the *Prajna Paramita Sutra:* no form, no emptiness, no creation or destruction, no increase or diminishment, no eyes or ears, but also *no negation of them.* Enlightenment and Emptiness, mate, are the same thing: Sunyata.

This is quite different from a universe that never existed—or is it? After all, the fact that mind inhabits this clime, in direct violation of the entropy surrounding it, makes it impossible that the negation of existence is anything other than a different form of creation—another state of BEING. The universe simply *can't not be.* Not anymore.

Existence is finally far more virulent and profound than some word describing or excising it, for even its philosophical antithesis is a cornucopia overflowing with maggots and tubers beside the eternal nothingness and unspeakable void that could have been otherwise, that would have been, if that had been the call. Blotto forever. And not even that. Not even void. Not even latency. Not even silence. Not even black on black. Nada. Na. Nnnnn.

The notion that nothing could have elapsed instead of something is of course horrible beyond conception, although nothing would have stirred in the dark to know either the horror of it or anything. Horror of nothing is already something, in fact a lot.

Yet this crisis passed, long long ago. We are here, and something has been happening—turbulent, rippling, self-organizing, self-transforming—just about forever. And now it is in its present state, and we are in the stew. But something happened once and it can never be taken back or revoked, no matter what or how much is annihilated contingently.

No matter what layer of existence and reality we dwell within—now or then or in another time altogether—you should be assured of this much: "Being" established itself once and forever and cannot, even in the worst debacle and the most desperate of circumstances, repeal itself. You can destroy all matter and everything that meaning means, but you cannot wipe out meaning itself. The universe is the universe and, by definition, laughing at its existence, playing with its own paradox, having fun. It can't be otherwise, either then or now or during this interminable yawn, brushing away cobwebs. We are something on the edge of nothing, until our senses clear and we can dead-reckon where we actually are. When the stars and planets of astrology become those in the astronomer's night sky....

Scientists aver, and those same oracles assert, that we can still be squinched or blasted to nothingness, either as individual life forms or so-called souls, or as a whole planet sizzling under greenhouse gasses or a nova sun, or—sorry, no way out—a galaxy in collision with another galaxy, or the entire contracting red-shift universe scouring its wool, rinsing its specks down to the last quarks of informationlessness, of not even knowing how to construct an atom, let alone a thought.

The luster in us, shining and recognizing the Now, is a thing that won't go away. It confirms an ineradicable universe, and that won't vanish or fail, that alone of our stuff. That alone will last forever, changing domains, changing shape, transmogrifying its expression, reemerging from all pyres, all ashes.

The world is of course provisional insofar as it is subject to vagaries of condition and effect, yet it is totally real insofar as it issues from innate radiance and draws a line in the sand that says, *something, something, something,* always, over and over again, even if it doesn't know what that is—*something rather than nothing.*

Good luck, us.

Mirages on the Trail

Not a late huckleberry but a shiny black fly on a huckleberry bush.

Not a red squirrel but a twisted tree root.

Not an old woman, white hair cascading over her robe, but the decayed remains of a tree.

I do okay, bouncing along atop the waves, when suddenly the real complication here gets me and I realize how fathomless and intricate this is and how much danger and revelation I am in. Sometimes a dream during a daytime nap will do this: open my being to the vastness of the universe and the precariousness and awe of my situation in it. I am thrust into the heart of psyche where truth is not only much more profound but real in a different way.

New Mantra for Anxious Moments During Turbulence on Planes

Stay Interested. That's All the Universe Is Asking of You. Stay Interested.

Clouds of intelligence sweep through the maze of matter and set its conditions, physical and karmic. Nothing can be made, no threat arise, that is not chaperoned by the same mind that created us.

Atlantean, Lemurian, and other unnamable worlds that Rudolf Steiner, G. I. Gurdjieff, Immanuel Swedenborg, and others have posited, plus miscellaneous Loch Ness monsters, yetis, UFOs, ghosts, and Seths, synchronicities and Fortean anomalies, exist within the same multi- or trans-dimensional pool which is wetter than water, at deeper singularity than bodies and minds, issuing from innate complication itself.

We are working out the horoscope of the universe on a level beyond encryption—inscription likewise.

Yet, in another sense, worlds and destinies, the outcome of the universe, have already been settled. We are doing something else: we are enacting, experiencing, taking from latency and dreaming into the bright thrush of creation. We are guiding a threadless thread through the eye of the needle, through its internal contradictions, through the paradox of nonexistence.

Self-created and self-creating, we are en route from something less than a microbe to something more than a rat.

Even the most obscure feelings have roots in things. They *are* something, though they pass too quickly to leave a clue.

They establish, unconsciously, who we are and what the universe is. A clump of orange flowers in a clearing, late-afternoon sun—what does it mean? Even on Echo Lake, hearing the loon's cry, I long for the "Echo Lake" of yore, apologies to Matsuo Bashō.

I think I am not as nostalgic for its forerunners as what it reminds me of, what I was looking for, even the first time. And why I want to chase after it, and would, if there weren't always a raging torrent coming right at me.

Grief and Transference

During my months on Mount Desert, the world seeps into a deeper dimension. Some of it is the childhood nostalgia of the Eastern Woodlands: first frog seen in water, original blueberries still clinging like Easter eggs.

Some of it is the months alone with Lindy on our country road. From a meeting of strangers a month or so before the JFK assassination, we have woven two lives together, "like Sherlock Holmes and Doctor Watson," she used to joke.

Some of it is the changing seasons, the early darkness, nights that flirt with frost (woodfires in the stove) bursting into Indian-summer days that are still warm enough to swim in.

Some of it is the quality of light, the salt air and lexicon of breezes. This feels like another planet, a more ancient, gentler one.

Whatever it is, I experience myself so much more poignantly here. This is our seventh consecutive year in Maine, and the same internal shift has occurred every time, as if I were suddenly under a different sky and a more faithful sun. Not every year in the same way. In fact, that is the beauty of it—there are so many different deepenings, unexpected textures.

As we sit down to dinner beside the field, on the edge of forest, I apprehend the long body of existence, as I did when studying Greek conjugations outside Churchill House at Amherst over forty years ago. Those rustling maples, the girl, that blue spring sky, the calligraphy of Plato and Homer—I am staring at the mystery again.

We are pretty isolated on our stretch of road. The twin houses across the street used to be occupied, first by two elderly women who have since both died, then by a teenage couple (Mike, a fisherman, and Becky, the woman who runs the local spring-water company for her parents). Both are now dark and empty. The street light blinks on and off all night, and we have yet to get Bangor Hydro to repair it. When it's off, it's really dark, pitch black, and the heavens are brilliant, as though the Earth is just a feather in a conflagration of supernatural stones. When it's on, the road sits in its gaze.

I have come to enjoy the light's indecision, as though it acts on its own recognizance, trying to get into dialogue with us, using the sole binary code it knows.

This particular summer I've been looking much more closely at my compulsions and phobias, from the standpoint that they are part of me and I have to make peace with them and also from the standpoint that I have to fight for my independence.

I understand that none of what I feel is that unusual—neither the fears nor the sorrows. Everyone feels these things. It is the meanings I give them, the contexts I create out of them that overwhelm me. I am missing something crucial at my core.

It is as though most creatures have a plug in their aura, a plug that holds in their identity. So no matter what bad or scary things happen to them, they're still themselves, they're still free. They may grieve beyond what would seem bearable, they may be frightened out of their wits, they may get lost beyond finding, but their core cannot be harmed—a state as valid for a feral cat or dying possum by the roadside as it is for a human. Without this plug, it would be too terrifying, too lonely, to live.

I sometimes feel I have no plug in me, as though past and future are about to be eradicated and everything I know will disappear. This is an undifferentiated anxiety and a sadness that seems to drench the universe, and there is nothing to do for it. If I feel it, I will drown. If I don't feel it, I will drown anyway, just more slowly.

The response:

"I know about the plug. It has to be put in very early or one must try to survive without it. But how? I suppose only by loving and through that moving out of the anxious position into the sadness that loss inevitably demands. I think it works like this: you think about the loss and, instead of trying to control things, you accept the possibility and the grief that comes with it. It feels like you, yourself, will die if you allow the feeling of sadness to have its way. But slowly, very slowly, it visits you because ... well, I suppose because it is there ... and you survive the emotion. Perhaps in this survival of sadness and loss one begins to realize the beginning of a sense of self. Not a self held together with paranoid vigilance, not a self made safe through control, anxious ritual, or worry, but a self that has come back time and time again from loss.

"Remember that story about faith I told you once? That we have faith because we 'kill' our parents and then discover that they are still there, psychologically intact, and we realize that there is an 'other' who is truly separate from us? Well, maybe the self needs to die of grief and then return for us to create the plug that was never put in place.

"In facing the death of close friends and the illnesses of others, I have seen that I will, that I have to, come through this and that I have to not just grieve, but grieve in the service of coming back to living.

"Isn't that what we all want from each other? To love and to grieve and to live again?"

We are "born to lose," Ray Charles sang, and this is probably because the only way creation can move forward is by losing what is essential, what we loved the most, then finding it again, as something else—altered by loss and recovery. Unless we lose our hearts, even our souls, and reclaim them, we will never know what they are; we will never really have them. And, more to the point, the universe will never wake up. By losing our hearts, by forfeiting all hope, we regain them more deeply and absolutely. And everything becomes real.

If we didn't go into exile, we would never know where we were or what we had. And the universe would slump into sleep and darkness once again, perhaps forever.

The creation is big enough to work all this out, eventually. That's what balances the crisis of consciousness on Earth. The fundamental plight of our planet, from nuclear weapons and global warming to slavery and mechanized slaughter, rests upon the I Ching of night, a lot reckoned against infinity. Everything has happened, and everything is yet to happen. The stars tell us that.

If science misses this fact, it is because it set out to deny it, in its stance as not science but religion, as corporate ideology, in order to forge the golden calf of materialism.

We, we the people, who are composed of mere molecules in algorithms, are not worthy of real existence or dignity; we may only be bursts of electricity imagining a reality that also doesn't exist. Although no scientist conceives himself a mere illusion pod triggered by synapses, that is the icon he serves, the bronze he has cast and hammered to his office wall, the persona he has adopted for purposes of social and professional recognition.

Where we are looking we do not occur.

But if it's not all consciousness, then we're nothing but frauds and robots. And if that's all we are, fergeddit.

Either consciousness is real, or this whole caboodle is puppetry.

But how, Mr. Scientist, can an illusion be conscious of illusionhood?

There just isn't time to work it all out. People get born, have seven or so baker's dozen solar years at best to glimpse a mere fraction of the wonders of this place and decide under the gun what they will have of it and have it be—that is, what they will buy as a cover story.

You have to live, regardless—regardless of your situation or opinion. You have to get up each morning and do it, even though you are going to die, sooner or later. Unless you choose to die this very day, living's your only option.

Questions of science and faith cannot be submitted to "being" each moment. As crucial as they are, they are meaningless. What counts is what you do and what happens, and that makes its own statement—quite profound, quite inextricable.

To meditate or to go on a vision-quest is "life" too, but no more or less than a chipmunk's meditation, a wild stallion's prayer. Each moment, each move, each sniff of the breeze (what breeze? what moon? what world?) is in and of itself an existential response.

Astronomers from Spain design and manufacture a luxuriously gigantic telescope to spy upon and haul to justice the most distant and ancient galaxies. Their French and American counterparts whip "poor" atoms around wider and more extenuating courses in their cyclotrons, trying to beat the truth out of them even as they all but skid out of existence. Atoms play possum; we can't. As the old line, more or less, goes: you can't repair a Swiss watch with a hammer. You don't smash atoms to get at reality.

Science alters belief, belief invents action, and society hatches indoctrinations for children born in solar systems to carry out: tasks that generate other beliefs, other acts.

In the end, what we think the stars are is *who we are*—baseline cosmology—tribe by tribe, civilization by civilization, sun by sun, breath by breath. The stars are our meaning, for no other reason than that they are there.

Astronomy mutates into biology, biology writes its atlas of physiology; the night sky initiates medicine men and doctors. Anyone who doesn't see that is not watching the magician's handkerchiefs.

We are ripping the voice out of the oracle, the shroud off the sybil. We are stripping love off love. And we learn nothing in the process. We learn only what we cannot know—what knows us but will not itself be known. Deconstructing the apple merely takes us one more cardinal zone beyond Eden, sets one more vortex of flaming swords against our return.

For purposes of cosmology the Spanish telescope is aimed into the wrong hemisphere. The real stars, mind you, the ones that count, are down here, with us.

When the doctor's office folds into the magistrate's courtroom, prior to sign and beyond reversal, the safety margin has vanished. The diagnosis becomes the sentence, and the verdict is death, even when it is life.

Doctors in HMOs are looking through the same lens as those damn astrophysicists, and what they see is waste and destruction, profit and loss, tokens in a hydrogen shell game. Once they have bought into entropic nihilism, they play to win, without shame or regret. It is all statistics anyway, and most of the suffering creatures—say, when galaxies collide—are half a universe away.

So, atop its cumbersome mount, the Grand Canary scope winds into the pristine heavens of La Palma and lets its 34-foot-wide mirror illuminate the weakest and most distant celestial objects and interrogate them—the chemical basis of creation, the birth of starlight, war in heaven. It digitalizes the static, the lingering whisper of the Mungo Bang. Or is it a whimper?

We don't have time for this, world enough or time. Or it is the only thing we have time for, time that is no longer on our side.

However far and deep and subtly we gaze, we see only our own mind, our own nature—the labyrinth in which we have wound ourselves. Karma and desire are what we see, though hydrogen and helium, masquerading as the sole representatives of matter. Stars and atoms are doing a fine job fooling us that they are the terms and conditions, ourselves the results, rather than t'other way 'round. I mean, "Do you love me like you kiss me/'cause you kiss me like you love me?"*

The zen monk is peering into the same faint canopy, looking the other way, into mechanism without technology, into spaciousness beyond space, into stars and heavens and a koan that reminds us we are the only universe we will ever know.

---

*This is the title and premise of a McGuire Sisters song from the 1950s.

Best Website Disclaimer

"No trees were cut for this site, but several electrons were inconvenienced."

Best Answering-Machine Message

"I'm either on the other line or out of my mind."

Kayaking on Great Long Pond

Gouged by a two-mile-thick glacier, set in the bow of Mansell and Beech Mountains, Long Pond is an amazing body of water. Four miles from end to end, it is clear and still and deep, a magnet for loons and cormorants.

I have an ongoing dialogue with Long Pond. I query its breezes and currents, its gulls, the water itself, its great depth. I accept by encounter what is impossible to know as idea.

From the kayak I look down at landscapes of rocks like the battlements and cairns of an unformed world, ripples of light traveling over them. Antique dragonflies attach themselves to the prow of my kayak and ride like scarabs.

Matter *is* the unconscious. It is not above consciousness or better than consciousness for being hard and located in space. It is below consciousness for being primordial and stillborn. It cannot know, and it cannot be. But it is. It rests in psyche, upholstering the dream of time. It is all that doesn't have its own psyche—and psyche is the only thing in the universe that can give life.

Our bodies allow us to be conscious, to scoot across unconsciousness in a craft. I think, as I transit here, that the universe lies not on the border of mind and matter, or even of consciousness and unconsciousness, as much as that an infinitesimally small amount of stuff has been internalized by psyche and made into mind while a huge amount is still unformed, inchoate, unwrought—in other words: most of the universe.

When psyche looks at rock cities that drift by, it is gazing at molecules given shape by the same archetypal force that, pouring through cosmic intelligence, created mindedness itself. At another level it is projecting nonexistent underwater fairies and Lemurias, trying to shape cairns into a landscape can look back and acknowledge the dormant mind of its amorphous stone.

There is a reason why Penobscot Indians believed that rocks were wiser than people and hunted for particularly intelligent stones. Like stem cells, stones can yet be anything, know everything for knowing nothing. They may lack individuated psyche, but they have collective unconscious psyche.

A satellite headed to Ceres will find the same creatures of rock, giants and midgets both, awaiting it forever, without eyes or mouths, without arms or legs. And these will stand guard, frozen in space-time, in fact all the way to the bottom of the Cerean ocean if there is one.

Every rock in the universe will one day enjoy the bounties of psyche; every sphinx will awaken; every boulder utter a syllable or two of meaning. That is what I infer—the anguish and wonder that it will take so long to get there. And that is why, as Long Pond is its exoteric name, my kayak glides over the monuments of an unnamed esoteric water.

Along the shore where cobble has tumbled and sprawls artlessly over its own bodies, the deafening cymbals of descent have ceased, though they leave a hush that is louder or at least more prescient than any sound, as lichen has tamed the rocks, and trees protrude through their fractures.

Tablets of moraine collocate. These are the sarsen stones of the only clock that keeps time, even though it was long ago broken and has no gears, for they frame the temporal boundaries of today and tomorrow and tomorrow's tomorrow, as far as sentience can trace the constellations of their zodiac. Because there is no time in dream or in psyche, because only psyche can keep time and find the direction in which the dream is flowing.

I am alone on this lake. No human is anywhere in sight. This is total freedom. Beaching my kayak at the rope swing, I plunge off the igneous shelf into September's water. It gets a little colder each day. The ice doesn't quite leave your body after you dry off.

Beyond the ledge is an abyss that drops more than a hundred feet down, brown-scale contours jaggedly blackening into dark infinity ... speaking of a universe totally outside experience, beyond sanctuary.

I whip my legs, jetting through the buoyancy of water. I feel how my having a body allows me to experience mind, to bathe in it, to wrestle its difference from me. That is the irony of embodiment: without it, the soul doesn't exist.

I glide in the current of the loch, floating on my back in a cradle of clouds, as the wind leaves its occult mark on us all.

We express ourselves on adjacent surfaces, even as molecules depend on their exterior geography, their capacity to taste the environment, to let some things in while keeping others out, thus keep themselves alive.

My body is matter. It is made of the same material as the rocks and reeds and dragonflies. If I sink or go mad, they will find it at the bottom or washed ashore.

My parked kayak drums on the rocks under erratic sloshing of water. This whole bright blue world—gulls bathing, submerging down to their necklines and shaking their feathers clean— this zone sparkling in detail like onyx or embroidered silk and sweetly whipping up white sky froth, sits in the pedestal. The planet is a droplet of reality, not even the size of a marble, and stuffed to its interstices with creation's wonderments, an entire mythology carved into and inside it, embossed and etched as well along its isobars, our lilliputian home.

The microcosm exists only at the bottom of this gravity well, spinning detached in the void: a single precious gem, its crystallography more calligraphic than anything around it.

I come home to a hot bath, then directionless fugues, bottomless dreams.

A round golden spheroid in the sky aka Sun is a serious thing. It is the entire basis, not just a gravity heap, not just any old atomic pile candescing. It will be remembered, somehow. All of this in fact will be remembered, even as none of it will. The sun is that central; it won't go away, though it is already gone, will be forgotten forever. By everyone.

That is why it is such a major object, a big yellow cat, shedding its coat, now.

And we, who could have existed anywhere—on a flat Euclidean projection of space or a turtle's back, for instance— live, actually live, on a toy ball rolling while it spins in space, a muddy pingo lieged by umbilicus to fire.

Yes, the local star-sun will turn nova, blacken, and disappear, snuffing all life in this System—but the real Sun cannot be destroyed, will not burn out or wither. I speak of a Sun teeming with a thousandfold more sentient beings than the historic Earth, a Sun not made of atoms or hydrogen but of the unburning intelligence that lights all stars.

Back-tracing mutations using mitochondrial DNA and Y-chromosome Haplogroups, geneticists have begun to reconstruct the migrational history of man and woman—*Homo sapiens.* Our ancestors, as long presumed, originated in Africa among other hominids and, generation by generation, disseminated across the planet—on foot, on eo-horses, by watercraft, and in wagons.

Some bands kept moving; others, for whatever reason, said, "Here I stay." A skeleton dug up near Wessex recently was compared to the walking DNA of the nearby towns. One British laborer turned out to be kin to this Ice Age chap—a line of his family had lived in the neighborhood for eight thousand years.

The English themselves are old Iberians, more Basque than Frank or Germanic. Merlin's Isles were settled by small bands of Mesolithic and Neolithic nomads, their migrations beginning some twelve thousand years ago when England and Ireland were still part of the Continent. Later, invaders from Norway intermarried with these tribes, long before the Vikings landed. Subsequent clusters of German and Danish women got themselves to York and Norfolk, their arrival nicked indisputably on chromosome yarn.

Sixty thousand years ago, indigenous Mongolian populations began junkets into the Russian Far East, spilling into what would become Korea, Manchuria, then building rafts and giant canoes, tracking constellations and myths, beaching at Polynesia. From there, a few clans went on to Australia, becoming Arrarnta, Walmajarri.

Some of their Haplo-cousins six to eight thousand years ago marched over the Siberian land bridge into the Yukon and Alaska, carrying telltale Mongolian alleles, until they were Na-Déné-speaking peoples of the Pacific Northwest. Lines of their affines bore the changing vowels and DNA, radiating throughout North and South America, depositing acorn-leachers and Red Hawk Kachinas, mound-builders and root-carvers. A few of their descendant bands roamed all the way to Tierra del Fuego, becoming the Yamana.

Tibetans, Japanese, and Andaman Islanders carried a different mutation; no posterity of theirs got to New Zealand or the Americas during Mesolithic or Neolithic times.

Another Haplogroup dispersed throughout Africa, the Middle East, and the Mediterranean. A cousin tribe, originating in the northeast region of Africa, conquered the Middle East, Greece, the Balkans, the Caucasus, and Turkey; its descendants became the old Semites and Mediterranean peoples of the Trojan War.

Southern India, Sri Lanka, and parts of Korea were settled by peripheral cadres of migrating hunters. Another safari terminated in Northern Europe, its lineages branching into Germanic, Goth, Celtic, Iberian, and French kingdoms.

Other late-arriving African families laid claim to Southern Europe and, blending with earlier-arriving tribes, became Turks, Kurds, and Georgians.

Still other Haplogroups dispersed across Eurasia, India, the Mediterranean, Ethiopia, and Somalia.

But there is another, far stranger story, that of the "human beings" who didn't come along, who were supplanted by the packs that became us. They were not *Homo sapiens*, but they were men and women. They had their own runes and cultures, and they vanished or were defeated and exterminated. Various Paranthropoi,

Kenyanthropoi, and other man-ape hominids roamed the savannahs of Africa before Lucy and her kin were born. Revered patriarchs of the late Ice Age, they were not just anonymous gorillas; they had family bands, histories, cultures, as they journeyed north and east under deepening skies and were hunted by the last apemen and first humans, the Australopithecines.

The forensic files are incontestable; we are Cain, not Abel, whether we committed genocide or just stood by while hitmen did it for us. Gone are those science-fiction species, more Mongolian than the Japanese or Sioux, more Palaeolithic than the Norse or Inuit. They shared the Earth with our forebears and parleyed or fought with them on savannahs and at waterholes and caves. Without even shamanic masks, they looked like lynxes, howler monkeys, and bears; martens and wolves with human faces; yetis and ETs. They had their hogans and sun dances (same sun, different minds), their totems and creation myths, their sacred bundles and dreams of the future. They had children and gods and heroes and games with rules; they beat us to the first awakened look at the Moon and stars. They wrote the text on which all others, blindly and discontinuously, were based. It is their epic too that Homer celebrates, that Parmenides and Anaximander fail to recover.

Georgian Man, Peking Man, Heidelberg Man, Neanderthal, *Homo rudolfensis* and *Homo habilis*, *Homo ergaster* and *Homo floresiensis*, *Pithecanthropus*. Their pundits sat around fires and pondered the philosophy of being; they handed down considerations and symbols that are more completely lost than the books in the library at Alexandria, for they were not in Indo-European or any language known to *Homo sapiens*. Some of these species lasted for fifty, a hundred thousand years or longer, spinning liturgy and custom, a much greater longevity than our own or than, looking ahead, we've proven capable of. Imagine that: ten times, twenty times the span from Buddha to 9/11.

They had mystery teachings to transmit, jokes to tell, alphabets aborning, angels and demons, doubts and inklings, all missing, all abolished. They bore the riddle that lies on the cusp of animal and man-being, of call systems and hermeneutics, of naïvité and knowledge. Inhabiting the Earth a good two hundred thousand years before mankind, they were there in the Dreamtime to greet him, to engage with her in the silent war of genetics and survival. Whispering indiscernibly through Vedanta and the pre-pre-Socratic philosophers, they tell of a stunningly beautiful alien world, a civilization we missed, a destiny we have forfeited forever.

We are the last humans on this planet.

Anyone who finds wars interesting or important is missing what is happening on Earth.

The beauty of our situation is that, despite the danger and fragility and outright darkness that lie on all sides of us, we are free. We are free to be something. There is nothing marshalling or supervising the expression of our whims or will. We can find out what's going on, all by ourselves—every sentient creature can. It must explore embodiment beyond precept or precedent.

Ours is not a set dance or a play with choreographed moves and scripted lines—nor is it even quite, for the lobster crab and mayfly.

Our freedom burgeons, a flowerlike thing ghosting, shapeshifting, *sui generis*. Anything can be chosen today; we can take ourselves down any trail or tracery tomorrow. We can try another spoor or a detour the next day. We are free to live, free to die; free to pout, free to disco; free to fast, free to pig out.

Our bodies are algorithms, warranted to function or not, on any given afternoon. They are not even ours. They are pet dogs we wash, we feed, we play with. And yet we have nothing else to rely on, as we awake and set our course anew. Before we sleep and dream, and wake again.

We oversee a torrent of blood and crystalloids and catalytic saps inside out wetsuit, but we are utterly ignorant of how—how it came to be, how it works, what role we play in its maintenance or innate intelligence. We haul around this oasis of proteins and enzymes and genetic molecules, doing stuff that even advanced biochemists and neurologists don't understand. It is no luxury or high-end conveyance, either. It is a crude proletarian beast, yet our *sine qua non. It* has to happen for us to happen. We rely on an invisible helmsman, the indifferent capacity of impersonal systems, and the esoteric command, to continue existing at all.

As long as these carapaces hold us, as long as they mumble mutely to themselves what to do, as long as the secret vessel sends out ciphers day and night, as long as we draw instructions out of some obscure imagination of what we desire, we are practitioners of the shindig of life. And it's not even that we mumble; it is what is done to us while our minds issue other rhetorical and commands—the derivative expendable stuff that is all we know.

Yet gloriously we are free, without a warrant or deadline. Any day we can live; any day is a good day to unravel and die. Now that is slaphappy, foolhardy, goofy, ecstatic freedom.

We become. Simply that. Exposed to novelty and chance and the aberrations of our own mindedness and circumstances, at every moment—nonlinear, linear. We are the perfect unchaperoned dance.

Each being gets to arrive at the same moments, to make the same decisions a wild rabbit does. Each being gets to be a mystery, to itself and the universe, inside another mystery, to come in disguise and go without warning. Every animal lollygags in the mudhole.

You are alone on this pike, the one of moon and stars, and there is no one in charge—fashion what deities and forces of nature you will. It is you, sovereign, unbridled, unfolding. Unless you are strong-armed and subjugated or forcibly imprisoned or indentured, you can do anything you want. Even under the dir-est of restrictions, you have choices.

You could last here a few days or a century. You won't know for sure until it is too late—thank goodness. This visit is not for the faint-hearted, not for a set period: ten years or sixty or four score and ten. You are born by lot. You die when the scythe falls. The Fates use neither fairness nor logic, not precedent either, to cut the thread that makes the cloth of your life. They do it when they do it, without justification or notice, even when there are signs, bad or good, either way. You never know who will get to live or how long, and whether it is you. That is why you are to-tally free, day after day, and not some reckoned beast or robot with an expiration date: "No one (Matthew 24:36) knows the day or the hour."

In the end, you get to report back to the universe what hap-pened. There was a girl once…. There was a tavern…. There was rain. The coverlet was brown or green. I was, once. There was a child, a wheel, a meadow.

You have to be elated. You want to be elated.

Would you rather be granted a guaranteed lifespan at birth and then have to report to the death chamber on your appointed day? Would you rather be the chattle of a genetic clock with a duration and a warranty? Would you rather exist as a centurion

and guard past universes, your finger ever on the trigger? Or inhabit gaps between universes?

If everything changes, even the laws, even the quanta underlying laws, you were this. You played ball. You swam in a lake.
Would you rather have done or been anything else?

This is all anyone has, or will ever have. And it is wide open,
still.

Telemarketers now target retirees, conning them out of their
social-security and bank-account numbers to steal their life savings. One victim won a Purple Heart, sheltering a comrade under a hail of bullets during World War II—doesn't matter; these
reptiles would pimp their own daughters. They call him up; he's
lonely; they flatter, beguile him, then fillet him like a piece of
sirloin. He's not a hero to them; he doesn't merit their empathy;
he's merely a gull in the way of their play. He *is* their play; they
actually enjoy the game or they wouldn't be so mesmerized by it.
His credulity incites them.

The Internet expands the potential for this kind of crime.
Scam kings and phishers from across the globe, petty Albanian
and Nigerian and Italian hoods, descend on their victims with
the faux ingenuousness of jackals stalking hares.

Such behavior long precedes fiber nets and satellites.
Babylonian, Goth, and Mongol marauders ravaged, killed, and
plundered their way across continents, doubting neither their
right, their God-given license to trespass, nor the legitimacy of
their pillage. They acted inherently and incontrovertibly, because
they could.

Lineal descendants of the primeval horde, modern Afghani
militiamen break into a Kabul household, slaughtering the

adults and sodomizing the daughters—one of the intruders bites a finger off a teenager to get her ring.

Are we to accept that this depravity, this sociopathic cruelty *is* the human race, is the planet? *Is* the universe? *Is* Creation?

Maybe. And maybe not. Perhaps it doesn't come or go as easily as it seems. Perhaps none of these acts are as simple or uncontested as, at first glance, they appear.

What plunderers and serial killers don't realize is that it is not only theft and rape as a way of life; it is violation as the destiny of the universe. And this is a universe trying to emerge from not only original sin but a crime and desecration at its heart. It is trying to open a golden age at last, a livable cosmology for its creatures.

The universe wants to toss off its gloom and curse, the violence and violation that saturate its extant fabric. It wants to find even these criminals—to make them happy and make them safe. And that is why it has put us here, like chess pieces on the board, to work it out. The gods can't do it, so they have no choice but to appoint us in their stead.

More and more these days hooligans, murderers, and genocidal bullies push the envelope in order to understand who they are, who *we* are, what we have to do in order to turn this layer over and move to the next, the next proposition of consciousness. This is their deep motivation, whatever they claim or strut otherwise.

Why else would members of the Sierra Leone RUF (Revolutionary United Front) motor into villages, jeeps packed with soldiers; line up the residents, most of them, mow down with machine guns; the rest, mainly children, machete off both hands to the laughter of the troops? Is this to win some bogus war that everyone knows will be lost anyway, once it is won? Or *is* something else going on, obscurely and latently, out of a script that was never composed, cannot be read, even by those acting it as though their lives depended on it?

The whole universe and all its beings are waiting for *us* to do it.

Go ahead, chomp off her finger, bite down with gusto, relish the act. Chop off his hands; make a joke out of it. Chuckle while you can. Take the full, glorious, macho depravity into your cells.

But don't think you are getting away with just a bauble. Don't for a moment imagine that your potential punishment (or clean escape) is what it appears to be. You have to finish the matter, not only for yourself but for all the forms and stages of sentience, once and future, who are witnessing you and praying for your success. You have to enact more than just the doing; you have to see it through until you get to the bottom of it, in yourself.

This is what the universe wants to make possible in order to make *itself* possible, in order to get us born and wash these acts and their motivations out of its sinews forever. Everywhere! What a worthy undertaking!

So the present edict is: Do and be done. Return to the scene of the crime as many times as you have to in order redeem it: "I have no way yet to reach you, for you to reach me; no other measure to make myself whole."

This is why the Dalai Lama wept for the Chinese soldiers and not the nuns they executed. The humble penitents were liberated in a flash; the guards must carry their acts and atrocity inside themselves across a termless desert, through the watches of time, until they solve them, until they deliver them to their source. The nuns have moved on; the soldiers are trapped as what they are.

There is an invisible warp imprinted in the entire cosmos, has to be. That is why things like this are even possible. We must get at the yaw and live it through. In proxy for all of us, executioners, molesters, swindlers, and violators of bodies and minds must guide the warp in the fabric back to where it began, where it began to crimp, which is not its origin any longer but its destiny.

Once you realize that you are acting upon your own recognizance, that you are intentionally opening the universe to debasement, you begin to get it, sort of, if you trust the message. Every so often someone stumbles upon the opposite of his act, is awakened, like a fresh breeze from nowhere, and begins rescuing potential victims from the next transgression, his or yours, and mentors those who would commit depraved acts, liberating them from their own traps, their own suffering and abrogation.

Either way, reformed or not, you and he now have a different mission, a different course—you are going to have to see its transfiguration through, to its very basis in meaning, to the very basis of meaning itself, until you know what the ring is, and why you wanted it and, more than that, why you even want to live, wanted to be here in the first place, to do such things. For yourself, for all sentient beings.

From there you will have to drag that burden across galaxies and lifetimes, even to get back to where you thought, at worst, you might be.

It has to be done. Every creature in the universe knows that now, knows it at its nucleus—unconsciously of course—knows it in every cell of its embodiment, every fluctuation of its unembodied wave; every child and every mouse, every creature watching and not watching, awake and not awake, born and yet-to-be-born.

Just look at those crows overhead, the deer stopping and starting. What else could they be thinking, beyond automated impulses and attentions moment to moment of their situation and conditional existence? What mega-thought disposes all other figments, and steers, not their every (or even slightest) movement, god knows, but the overall signature of their lope, their patterned flight upon the heavens?

Until the crease is found, until its transubstantiation is accomplished, nothing else can be done. Until you do it, you can't move on to the next critical thing. You can't know anything else. You can't be happy. You can't stop pollution or global anything or save the rainforests. You can't build a more ecological or peaceful civilization. You can't pretend to be good, or generous, or innocent, or even nasty and bad. You can't end the war, the one that won't end. You can't be safe. You just continue to move in a shroud of illusion: illusion, disappointment, and despair.

So go ahead. Take your bite. Those vets and old fogies will be dead soon. The money in their accounts is nothing except whispers of make-believe numbers in a giant bunco game. The universe is one big subprime loan without collateral.

That is the first step you must take anyway, toward the salvation of God's creation. And how could you not, with everyone watching and pulling for you, even the most sociopathic criminals and sadistic, shameless executioners and mobsters in the history of all the galaxies? You are working for them too, Mr. Wise Guy.

(BTW I challenge anyone who claims that he or she can "remember" being in, say, a Nazi concentration camp in a previous lifetime to know for sure whether they were a prisoner rather than a commandant, rather than both.)

This all broaches a prior question: Does the universe really want to torture, crucify, and terrify its own creatures throughout its dimensions and realities? Does that make any sense? Does it seem rational or economical, whatever else it may be? How long will it presently allow any of them to suffer before their existence disintegrates into the next identity, the next meaning, beyond consternation or comprehension, into something else entirely, someplace else entirely?

Does death always intercede before unendurable pain? Does death come in the nick of time? If not death, then what? If not time, then what? What are we being taught? And why?

French inquisitioners of the Cathars tried to lacerate, burn, and mutilate their victims, to get at not just their bodies but their souls. They wanted to inflict more than agony. Torturing for them was no incidental infraction. It was a bald attempt to foil the intervention of death, to crack the very souls of their captives before they could escape.

What an ambition for the universe to ply! The twisted minds of these vipers grasped an essential truth and from it gained their dark purpose: if you really want to do damage, you have to scald and maim and terrify the body and mind so thoroughly while a person is still aware of what is happening that you get through all the divine, angelic, and other karmic rings of protection, past the sanctuary of innocence, past the limitations of mind and matter, past God Himself, and ruin the soul. That is the way to effect true harm, to minister demonic possession; it is what is primevally and traditionally called evil—the evil likewise of the serial killer who wants to enjoy his victim's suffering until her mind snaps before him. He hopes it won't snap, ever, because he wants her company to the bottom of his own urgency. He not only wants it; he can't bear the thought of not having it. That's what an atrocity *is*.

The inquisitioners' goal was to impose enough pain to get people to confess, as they were dying, to crimes they didn't commit, so as to graft onto their souls something that didn't belong there. And this wasn't Satan at work; this was the Church of Christ, trying to sever direct access to God, as if it were possible for man to impose such a verdict. What a dread understanding of who God is! And who we are! What abject insolence!

These acts ring convulsively through the minds of all of us today. Not necessarily the acts themselves, or the actual casualties to the soul, but the karmic record of the attempt inside all of us, the fact that people desired to do such things, that they could desire it, that they sought such an outcome. If it is in one person, it is in every person; it is in the bare fiber of creation.

That is the shadow lying across ancient and modern worlds indiscriminately, leading over and again to war and despoliation of Mother Earth, not because the shadow falls and not even because it is a shadow, but because we are unaware that our so-called light is actually darker than interstellar space. We proceed in full and righteous ignorance.

That such depravity can be carried out in the name of the Prince of Peace shows that somewhere, somehow, someone or thing succeeded in grafting evil onto souls in galaxies near to us and far, that the universe has now got this huge gob inside itself, this spreading toxin, and has no choice left but to drive its creatures toward full knowledge, toward complete, last-grain-of-sand disclosure, in order to get it out and begin the long process of healing.

Maybe it is not evil at all but the logistics of Creation—the myth that the biblical myth of a forbidden fruit on a tree in the Dreamtime esoterically hid and, by hiding, foretold.

The inquisitioners ultimately succeeded—because look at the world today; look into your own mind—but they also ultimately failed. Because we are still alive; we are still patrolling and fighting back, in fact with everything we have.

A chicken or pig being dismembered stops knowing and feeling. On Earth as likely on all planets, death does intercede, mercifully they say. But if death didn't intercede, how much torture and agony, bludgeoning and exposure to loss and mayhem and pure pain, days on the rack, minutes in boiling oil, can a creature bear existentially, does the universe make it possible for someone to know? How much of this forbidden kundalini knowledge will it permit, will it initiate frail mortals into? Beyond judgment, beyond torment or pleasure principle, beyond synaptic streams of sensation…?

How much does it need to tell us in order to get the job done? And how much must it withhold to the same end? If there is a limit, what imposes that limit? How is it imposed? From whence do grace and compassion derive if in the beginning was fire and stone only, then the hunger of the eternal beast, shedding virally at every seam? If there is no limit, what imposes that? If there is a meaning, how does one beach upon its shore and get sanctuary from meaningless suffering? Either way, what is the reasoning; what is the cosmic plan?

If you can answer that one, you have found the barest edge of the boundary of space-time and the adumbration of God across the many layers, you have intuited a direction toward the passage out of this entire manifestation, from its source in a fire that is still burning to bring us here. You have saved the only real church left, the pagan communion of dark and deeded passage.

If you can't die, as some entities may not be able to, in some body-mind states on some worlds—insofar as death may not be death—you must then, under termless maximum duress, transform anyway into another state of being, beyond pain, beyond grief, beyond terror, beyond duration itself. Is that the law? Is that the revelation, the way out? Is that the most forbidden of all forbidden knowings? Is that what the universe is trying equally to erase and know, to know so well that knowledge itself erases it? Is that the threshold at which the present sacrament shatters and turns into the next, unknowable insinuation? Is that the mew of the universe in us, trying to talk to us as ourselves?

To apologize? To establish rapport? To end our dormancy and wake us to the magnificent possibility of anything at all? Is that, again, why the Dalai Lama wept for the troops and not the nuns?

This is the central question of consciousness, since it is all only consciousness—one reflection through another through a shadow which is also a mirror—whether real and enduring or will-o'-wisp. The "other" must, by sacred fiat still, sustain its assault on individual identities even if that identity shives and splinters, leaving mad souls in mad houses or wandering naked in Gaza with broken minds, broken hearts. Or something else. Something else entirely. So special we cannot even conceive how we would imagine it if we had that kind of imagination—which we don't. Not yet.

But then, yet again, that is why we are here at all. There is no other rationale, no alternative explanation.

If a particle on Jupiter has consciousness and experiences nausea in its tumbling swirls, and if it cannot shut off its mind, then it is blown in rapid-fire circles and erratic whirlwinds and mega-turbulence for so long it must know its plight; yet it must also get beyond it, find the opening at creation's gate. Its anguish is its price of admission, the grail, the illicit apple too, which it has to find to find itself, to stabilize what is, what it no longer can be. That is the coin Charon seeks as passage, to ferry any molecule across the dark shoals. That is liberation, freedom, the faint out-skirts of enlightenment.

Everything fragments into schizoid personalities untold, shatters into something else, and then cracks and changes again. Every mental disease is an awakening into another sanity. Every seeming stability breaks the edifice of its own obsession and fractures into lunatic shards. That is what we are, consciousness splintering across zones that only seem to be rational and benign or malign. That is why the Nazis had to build their concentration camps on the face of night and carry out their occult deeds, zombie-like, under the devil's swastika, unknowing, in a darkness of which they were not aware, a night transcending day and night. They had nothing better to do, and no one else could do it.

How does the Jovian particle get out of the trap? Lifetime after lifetime.

Wilhelm Reich offered this simple homily, this clue: a worm, if grabbed hard at its center, writhes and, by its body, says no—the ultimate primal NO! Life-giving, illuminated, mercurial free organisms also say yes, always: I love you. I want you. I melt into you. I adore you/us, forever.

Love says yes, always. And the universe is fundamentally a love machine, saying yes, trying to integrate its knowledges, across its squirming body squirming every which way to become what it is, in all its severed creatures and mind-sets, to unwind kinks that have developed so long ago in something forgotten, that is both nothing and anything.

The Afghan brigand will do the deed, as long as it is no longer nothing, as long as embers of anything go flying in the air, as long as anything lives, including you and me—saying yes by saying no, until it is all yes. Then something else happens, likely something unimaginably good.

Fifth Cycle

On the express train out of Brooklyn to Canal Street we are packed together in sweltering heat, sweat running down foreheads and chests, and everyone merely wants to breathe and get cool. Suddenly a young Muslim man, round hat, embroidered robes, scruffy beard, opens his Koran and begins chanting loudly and hypnotically. In his trance he has put on a game face: 'Fuck you all, I'm down with myself, in serious spiritual endeavor. You don't like it? Well, make my day!'

In a moment of horror it dawns on me that I am in the one place I can't be, where I assumed I would never be because I somehow would always be clever enough to avert it, unlike those riders whose viscera were splayed onto the street and detonated across world headlines. None of them, I suddenly understand, planned to be here either, when the augur began singing, when the curtain came up and the suicide act commenced. Those folk imagined they were just as clever as me.

I am wide-eyed, suspended in terror, my heart beating, a cold ping numbing my spine, my mind working overtime. Lindy, seated facing me, catches my eyes. She mouths worriedly, "Are we on the right train?" I nod while saying to myself, 'No, we are on the wrongest train in the world.'

"Did we miss our stop?"

I shake my head.

Then she scans around and gets it—a sober nod. (Later she says, "I wasn't worried because he didn't have a bulge." But suicide bombers don't need bulges these days. Weapons can be digitalized,

379

transistorized. Soon one droplet, ignited by a cellphone a continent away, will be sufficient to take out half a city.)

Of course this might be nothing at all. It usually is. Life goes on.
He is probably not a suicide bomber—but then again, if he were,
this is what he'd be doing now, opening a line to Allah, getting
ready for his launch to Paradise. On the other hand, he has to
pray five times a day, so he might as well get one in while biding
his time on a hot train. I assume he knows where Mecca lies,
curving underground as he rotates with the track.

I reassure myself that maybe he'll at least wait till 42nd
Street—greater crowds, bigger venue. These jihadists are into
performance art.

Luckily we are going to bail for the shuttle at 14th.

No one else seems the least bit concerned, people strap-
hanging with blank looks, perusing newspapers in Spanish, English,
Chinese, Polish, lost in various ear-bud worlds. This is New York;
they've been through it all. I don't think anyone but me even notices
this guy despite the fact he is the one thing alive and activated.

It is such a rush for me. I can't help it. I am picturing the light
of the explosion, imagining what its initial heat and force will
feel like. Will it hurt? How long will I know it's happening before
I cease to exist?

At first I am edging away to the degree that the car's crowd-
edness and reconnaissance with Lindy's position allow, a fool's
errand no doubt, but then I realize I am doing the opposite of
what I should be—no reason at all to scram. I take two, three,
four steps back toward him. I might as well hitch a ride on his
shot to Paradise, better that than ending up convulsed on the
ground without legs or mangled in a hospital.

Even if he isn't a suicide bomber, a searing light is always
breathing down on us, the possibility of excision of the great

nerve net—the fact we are made of binary synapses only. His presence and my fear have merged to teach me again the truth, something approaching the truth he sees, whether he is dressed to kill or not.

There is nothing to do. There was never anything to do. If it is not him, sooner or later it will be him: the djinn of Hiroshima, the Tamil Tigers, the aluminum shower, the snapping of the silver cord that attaches us to a body.

Those caught in a suicide attack are no different from those who aren't, on a bus in Jerusalem or London or Lahore, because something will eventually snap the cord. The moment of reckoning will be a quick flash that then engulfs us. The bomb doesn't say "Enola Gay" or "made in Iran," "courtesy of North Korea" or "minion of al-Qaeda"; it is just more light, brighter and quicker than what we know. Then it ends, the whole charade. And light travels faster than sound.

Ultimately, jihad or not, the cord snaps. And the brightest, most scintillating glow fills time and space with itself.

Today's Long Pond lessons are almost too vast for reckoning. The world is so huge and mute and intentional that I can do nothing but submit. Gulls on high wheel about their business. Sunlight streaming through their flight is vast and brilliant as though they are holograms and might any moment turn transparent into sheets of textured flame.

I see them close-up, as my kayak intrudes on their bird-birth. Rising from the splashdown, they shake off their wetness, casting nimbuses of fizz in the air. So fresh! So messy! So alive!

Waves go about their business, leaving checkerboard patterns in the breeze. Little fish, alive and darting, have no use for me, no evasion either—just flying by my legs on their flicker-flash of awareness.

Now that I am getting old, the creatures about me seem so young. They used to be grandfather birds and squirrels, my seniors. I was the eternal child, even when I wasn't young. Now I am *their* grandfather.

Still-fuzzy ducklings peck my kayak and, after I beach it and go swimming, they paddle to my place, check me out by circling. They flap their wings and come racing across the water at me, first from one direction, then the opposite, splattering me, doing me the honor of not being afraid, of frisking with me, making me part of their game.

Their regard relieves the anonymity of nature—and yet even it is a chimera. For I am as illusory to them as they are to me.

Then in two seconds flat they are gone, halfway across the lake.

Gulls circling and landing are truly indifferent, maybe even contemptuous in a "gull" sort of way, buzzing my kayak as I interrupt their baths. They are the great-great-many-times-great-grandchildren of ones I saw in childhood, or distant cousins of same. Their ancestors are long dead, those molecules swept back into winds of time. The children alone bide—relentless, ingénue, constantly hatched into the bright world.

I understand their cries differently now, for I am not a boy. They are singing a land that will go on when I am no longer here. And that is why the ducklings honor me by their attention and fearlessness. And that is the most amazing thing of all.

Nature is neutral and I can be no more than that, despite my luxuries of thought-making. I am neutral too, another being formed by atoms in matrices. I have a spaciousness of mind I cannot empty enough, as I glide on my back in thoughts, memories, and unnameable static, opening and closing my arms like a ctenophore, as the gulls swoop in the clear-blue space mind of their own intrinsic beings, parading like flocks of black holes through daylight, oblivious to clouds as names.

A late afternoon sun falls on the flowers in the meadow beyond, and all the sorrows of life collect there—a single melancholy mead pouring toward me.

I have always protected myself from knowing, because knowing was not only contraband but unbearable. It is still unbearable. I carry a vibration so profound and absolute that it would take lifetimes to redeem or absolve. And since I love so much of what is here and want to be happy, I let its obscure sensations bathe me, a sprinkle or splash at a time. I carry it behind me and inside me and through me, a tabernacle of colors I can't see, a palette of emotions I never quite contain. It is not the mantra I chant but the mantra my body chants for me. And it has become a global sadness, for not only my ill-starred childhood family but all loss in this magnificent zone. Maybe it was ever this way, even when I was little. Yet if my family hadn't thrown open the gate, I wouldn't have strode blindly through it into such a profound and fearsome ceremony.

I thank them for what they were, and I abhor what they did, and I fear for them even yet, for all of us still. I want it to have been different so I could have known them well, known them even a little; so they could have known me, in better times.

And I want it to have been no other way because here I am.

Joke

Two kids, Johnny and Frank, grew up playing baseball together: Little League, high school, PONY League, college, semi-pro. To wile away the hours between games they used to debate whether there was baseball in the afterlife. Eventually they made a deal. The first one to die would somehow get a message to the other, telling him the answer.

Then Johnny was killed in a car accident. Frank waited to hear from his friend. He waited for weeks and years; no response. He attended to radio static and picked up and read scraps of paper. He didn't know how Johnny would get a message to him, but he was sure he would find a way.

Finally, four years later, Frank returned to his motel room one night from partying after a game, and a voice was whispering his name in the darkness. "Is that you, Johnny?" he asked.

"It is. And I've got good news and bad news. Which do you want first?"

"Tell me the good news," replied Frank.

"The good news is that there's baseball in heaven."

"What could the bad news be?"

"You're pitching tomorrow."

What makes Patricia Fox such a great yoga teacher—beyond the ropes and mats and blocks and Iyengar straps that sort of drive me crazy with their busyness and contraptionhood, beyond even her astute comments like "you may not get that position in this lifetime"—is that she somehow communicates an ongoing yoga of being that continues after the classes. She makes everything yoga and the lesson merely a span of greater attention to the requisites of embodiment.

Inventing each class as we go along, addressing each of us with the compassion of an angel and occasionally the playful slap of a Zen master, she communicates silently that our bodies are her body, that she will take care of us. She invites deepening in a way that cannot be refused. She is always bemused, funny but not ha-ha funny, more a sort of light distraction, in the way that absolute, curious attention can sometimes seem a bit spacey.

When she has to, she holds us up. That is, she holds our actual bodies up or, if necessary, lets us grasp her legs like trees.

I feel myself and my differential weight so much more profoundly. Movement beyond the studio has novel possibility: a stretch or deepening or leaning into some other way, into something I have never done, at least consciously, or have forgotten how to do. Every moment, even the presence of my voice, even the shift of an eye, holds a possible weight, an opportunity for yoga.

She gives me back little lost spaces, like around my sternum and collarbone; she helps me dissolve the deadened shield between my neck and chest. A little becomes a lot. My mind slides into a joint around my clavicle I long ago lost all sensation of. I get a tingle and it lights the way. She restores my sacrum and spine.

She asks a very important question: "What's that hiding behind your knee? Go there. What is it telling you? Let it speak. Have it give up its secrets."

She may not know our secrets, but she knows we are keeping them because she can see us. She knows the value of their surrender. She sells that to us, against its cost and pain.

She makes it possible to grow and expand tenability. And I don't know how she does it because, through the gauntlet of all these postures and paraphernalia, it isn't fun. In fact, I can't wait for the ninety minutes to end. But I feel so much better driving home than coming there.

I guess the class is difficult because I am working against the resistance in my mind. What else could be holding such stiffness and making parts of me inaccessible, what but intractable, manipulative, "let me hide here for just another moment" resistance? By comparison, my body is a pushover.

Afterward, I depart through the oilpaint smell and abstract color squares of her partner Charles' studio into the light—red on tomato plants, yellow-orange tansy buttons. I am buoyant because there is less friction in every direction. I feel thick but spacious. The world is a rainbow.

Swimming the next afternoon in Long Pond, I feel the actuality of my propulsion. I open and close hydra-like. I weigh; I have mass; I convert energy into motion on gravity's trundle.

Driving the car two days later down the Maine Turnpike, I try to release tight neck and shoulders. As I locate them, their placement and mass, I sink into the vehicle such that my foot on the accelerator sets off combustion. As fuel streams out the tailpipe, I shoot ahead: a tin-can rocket. Press down, and I am between Earth and Moon.

Every moment has potential, has depth, has another way to hold it. Every moment is newly promising, once I take stock. Or, more precisely, I have gotten into binding myself in a chassis created by anxiety, habit, fear, cynicism. When I change even an eensil, these other matters change too, and it all moves along. We clean house.

At the end of the class, as we get into corpse pose, *shivasana*, Patricia says, just before she begins to sing to us in Sanskrit, "Forget everything you ever knew, about anything, ever. And feel what's happening, right here, right now."

It is said that spirits like to frequent clans, so I sometimes wonder who my grandson Leo is—if he is even someone I know. It amuses him to call out, "'ello, Rich." He will repeat that phrase again and again as I wheel him in his carriage. He is staring straight ahead, not even looking at me, but all of a sudden, "'ello, Rich." He practices it to himself while playing on the floor in my care, as though to keep our connection. But he doesn't ever greet me with it. He's way coy for that.

I think, he could be his great-uncle on my daughter-in-law's side, Kilton Stewart, the Senoi dream savant, having returned to this dreamworld for another go at theory and practice, playful as ever. Or perhaps a tinge of my brother's wild tormented spirit has hitched a ride on Leo and now and again tumbles a forgotten memory and flicks me a thoughtful glance: "'ello, Rich."

Whoever he is, he doesn't remember and doesn't know, and I can't help him out, but the way he says it, the whole universe is on board.

When I taught college in the Seventies, I liked to tell my students that three neglected figures defined the twentieth century: G. I. Gurdjieff, Aleister Crowley, and Wilhelm Reich. This surprised them insofar as pretty much no one had heard of them.

I mean it wasn't as though I had told them Mahatma Gandhi or Carl Jung or Elvis.

This outsider all-star team had an unexpectedly big impact on a few. One callow student from 1970 at the University of Maine in Portland, years later became the formal executor of the Reich estate. A Goddard kid from 1972 started a Crowleyite school for magic in San Francisco in 1983. A number of others did Reichian therapy or Gurdjieffian exercises.

G, C, and R defined the twentieth century as much by the way in which their work was almost universally rejected as by what they stood for. They each proposed a still-unknown energy loose in the universe. For Reich this was orgone, a cosmic force permeating the galaxies and conferring design, vitality, and life. For Gurdjieff it was a transdimensional stream of octaves that could be cultivated by disjunctive dances and breaks with habitual motion. For Crowley it was Magick, a means of contacting disembodied entities and putting into action "Do What Thou Wilt Is the Whole of the Law."

I believe that these three different propositions are the same and that the energy they prescribe remains substantially unacknowledged and undiscovered. What made these men masters is that, in a century whose attention was directed vehemently elsewhere, they believed unconditionally in their invisible energy's existence and value; they developed complex systems to map and explain it (each as thorough and explicit as James Clerk Maxwell's laws for the volume of gasses). They gave their lives to it, and two of them died for it—Reich in prison, Crowley in an asylum. Reich in fact stubbornly and unnecessarily went to jail as a point of honor in defense of orgone.

Each of these men was a tyrant and ideologue and wreaked havoc on his family and followers.

Other, less grandiose figures also defined the twentieth century: Charles Olson, John Upledger, Peter Ralston, Ellias Lonsdale. They too discerned something absolutely.

For Olson it was a novel force simultaneously of history, time, and syntax, an ontological projective process. For John

Upledger it is pure, self-transforming healing energy, beyond ideology, system, or logic, accessible at the basis and germ of every creature. For Peter Ralston it is a set of principles for effortless power. For Ellias Lonsdale it is the bridge between the living and the dead.

Upledger's healing is as nonlinear as Crowley's summoning of spirits. Ralston's martial movements parallel Gurdjieff's ritual ones. All of these men warranted: "Don't try to explain or prove this stuff. Don't be intimidated by authority or naysayers. Just do it." Their children had to make the best of it.

The convictions of these patriarchs, despite residual damage, should alert the rest of us that we are missing the boat.

The Earth's Major Religions

Hinduism: celebration

Jainism: compassion

Shamanism: transformation

Confucianism: order

Judaism: manifestation

Buddhism: being

Christianity (Catholic): faith

Christianity (Protestant): works

Islam (Sunni): devotion

Islam (Shia): submission

Science: knowledge

Zoroastrianism: creation

Some thoughts on HBO's *Big Love* at the close of its second season

1. The show could not make any clearer that *Mormonism is* de facto *polygamy.* A nonpolygamous Mormon is a dry drunk. When the so-called official Mormon establishment pretends to decry polygamy with public handwashing, it is both ingratiating and disingenuous—ingratiating in an attempt to sell itself to mid America under a decoy of quotidian Christian patriotism and disingenuous insofar as in the highest Mormon councils, polygamy is undoubtedly still considered a sacrament and mainstay of the faith. Church leaders just don't discuss it outside the Tabernacle. They are going to wait out the Government on this one.

2. The "Principle" evoked by Bill, Brenda, Nicki, and Margene— the Henrickson family—is to model the family unit for the next dimension. Life is basically a tryout and rehearsal, albeit an unforgiving one, for later heavenly disposition. A domestic polygam created on Earth, on this plane, is a numinous blueprint, a convention of souls laying the basis for a mirror ensemble in the Afterlife—the real and enduring clan.

A Mormon family is minimally patriarchal, bigamous (but not polyandrous), astral, and eternal; it is constituted by divine law, holy writ, and personal prophecy. By "astral," I mean that its *modus operandi* is manufacturing a celestial replica for a future meta-dimensional phase—similar to the angelic union proposed in Hebrew mysticism whereby the internalized marriage of a man and woman hatches a third body in heaven, fashioned of the souls of both of them.

The awkward distinction between mere lust and true supernal love, which is of both sporadic and more than sporadic interest throughout Western civilization, is crucial in Mormon polygamous society because only a family endorsed by Divine Sanction and authorized by Sacred Notification will survive onto the eternal plane. A wife lured into a grouping by lust will not only *not* make it into the next life but will sabotage the enterprise for the other wives and scatter them and the paterfamilias to the winds.

Esoteric Mormonism uses "tangkas" as compass points somewhat in the way that Tibetan Buddhism does. A Mormon tangka is an internal oracle that discloses the sacred family to the patriarch so that he can "marry" a new wife because God intends it, not because he desires her. Of course, God usually discloses the first through the second, so the ambit where physical desire meets ecstatic theophany is a difficult one for a Mormon householder to navigate.

In that regard, it is interesting to note that the dilemmas of fidelity and jealousy that arise in *Big Love* as well as the legitimacy of each potential wife comprise exotic variants of the same crises in monogamous society. In monogamy, there are two possibilities: fidelity or illicit affairs; under Morman polygamy, there are three: faithfulness, illicit affairs, and courtship of additional wives.

3. Late nineteenth-century America was a hotbed of millenary cults aflame with clairvoyance, clairaudience, and automatic writing. An incomplete sample would include branches of Freemasonry, theosophical and neo-Gnostic covenants, Christian heresies, Swedenborgian denominations, John Ballou Newbrough's 1882 *Oahspe* Jehovan Bible, Mary Baker Eddy's Christian Science, plus a mishmash of ghost dances and extraterrestrial sects. Spilling over into the twentieth century, this unfederated church took a more intellectual and cosmological bent, as evidenced by *The Urantia Book*, 2097 pages dripping wet, received as empyreal

dictation by a group of otherwise skeptical intellectuals in Chicago during the 1920s.

Still Christian in orientation, *Urantia* was Gnostic science fiction with chapters on "The Central and Superuniverses," "The Local Universe," and the home planet: "Earth (Urantia)." It concluded with 77 papers on "The Life and Teachings of Jesus," apocrypha well surpassing The New Testament itself, with a full scoop on Christ's childhood, teenage years, and preaching tours.

Blending many of these elements eclectically, The Church of the Latter-Day Saints (LDS) proved to be the consummation and superstar of millenarianism.

Because the deadline on certified Christian denominations ran out more than a hundred years ago, you could not invent such a faux Christian religion as Mormonism in the late twentieth century and have it be anything other than an object of derision or its own self-fulfilling cataclysm. It wouldn't stick. Corporate Christianity may continue to permit pagan Jesus cults insofar as they are too marginal to be a threat to orthodoxy and offer convenient ecclesiastical whipping boys. But the zero hour has otherwise passed, at least until the Second Coming, be it Christ or anti-Christ. New cults are maligned as imposters and blasphemies out the gate. Those Mormons and other Pentecostals who cleared the nineteenth century are now sitting pretty, fully enfranchised. Joseph Smith simply beat the clock.

Religions founded by individuals and channeling plot-heavy messages tend to have the same hokey otherworldly flavor, like a "Rocky Horror Picture Show" parody of the Catholic Church. These days they may implode apocalyptically: cyanided Kool-Aid or fiery shootout with the feds—e.g. Jim Jones and the People's Temple in Jonestown, David Koresh and the Branch Davidians of Waco.

But the nineteenth century honored theosophical revelations, even erotic creeds with harems. Utah gave Joseph Smith a free pass and, while he wrapped himself in the Bible as artfully as Jerry Falwell, he was far more salaciously occult and Tantric, something like Bhaghwan Shree Rajneesh a hundred years ahead of his time: "For Tantra everything is holy, nothing is unholy," so proclaimed the latter-day guru of Jabalpur, India, and Rajneeshpuram, Wasco County, Oregon. Change Tantra to God and substitute polygamy for Krishna Consciousness, and you've got the short hairs of Mormon epistemology.

L. Ron Hubbard's scientology is the closest modern American parallel to Mormonism and, despite its unlikely éclat (given that it began as overt space opera), without Bible-belt roots it can never acquire the legitimacy that Mormonism fudged into by its nineteenth-century pedigree.

In truth, Mormonism is no more Christian than Dianetics or EST; its Christianity lies solely in the unexamined precepts and indoctrination of its architects. Like other new-fangled Jesus religions, it is pop Christianity. The *Book of Mormon* still reads more like something out of a Robert Heinlein novel (say, *Stranger in a Stranger Land*) than a real Judaeo-Christian testament.

But it had to simulate Christian patriotism in order to get a toehold in American society, in fact to the point of being able to run elders for President. No Rajneeshi or scientologist, not even Tom Cruise or John Travolta, could be elected to high office, but Milt Romney is a legit candidate (as was his father). And even he is disdained by most evangelicals as a trash Christian.

4. LDS is biblical science fiction cum American frontier Christianity, an adaptation of the Bible to the fantasy New World. Anything could elapse there—mermaids, sea monsters, reappearance of the lost tribes of Israel, angels with gold tablets.

Zion and the Bible were as immediate to those folk as a daily newspaper in 1950.

Modern Mormonism is a pasteurized, watered-down version of Joseph Smith's original wild and magical creed with its witchcraft, geomantic astrology, Pennsylvania German alchemy, Amerindian totems, feminine qabalistic God, ritual dowsing, divining rods, homemade talismans, and lamans on the loose (e.g. holy inscribed tablets like those Moses found on Sinai). Smith collected peep stones and seer stones, held séances, spoke in tongues, and went on occult treasure hunts long before Urim and Thummim came courting.

In truth, the Salt Lake establishment is as much an apostasy of basic Mormon shamanism, tantra, and thaumaturgy as the Papacy is of Christ's grass-roots mysticism. Check out *Early Mormonism and the Magical World View* by D. Michael Quinn and *The Reformer's Fire: The Making of Mormon Cosmology* by John L. Brooke.

5. All millenary (apocalyptic) religions share a style and a strategy, a plan of working with God like some sort of jinni or magical supply clerk. Ordinary items become symbolic sacraments and then take on supernatural powers, be they a cargo plane in South Pacific Melanesia, a ghost-dance shirt in Nevada, or the personal relics of Joseph Smith. Cargo cults tend to be "religions of the oppressed": lower classes, peasants, indigenous peoples under occupation.

The reason why *Book of the Hopi*, Frank Waters' millenary conflation of Hopi religion, rings so true to Old Oraibi is that it takes basic Hopi tenets and ceremonies out of the kiva and re-stages them in the context of a Mormon creation myth, e.g. hieroglyphic tablets of Bear, Fire, Spider, and Sun Clans manifested laman-like from cornstacks; annual Coyote-Swallow races like theosophical fairy tales out of Hans Christian Andersen; Two Horn priests and White Buffalo dancers putting on mystery/morality plays, reuniting the Tribes of Dan and Judah with the Tribe of Jesus and Joseph; Blue Kachinas ascending as UFOs in the ceremonial sky over Hotevilla. Even the transition of Tuwaqachi, the present Fourth World, through the smokehole into the Fifth World reverberates with biblical Endtime, as Mormon craw colonizes an ostensibly Pueblo text.

6. Just as *The Sopranos* was about different types of mafia families in the New York metropolitan area, *Big Love* is about hierarchies of polygamous Mormon families in Utah. They range from self-righteous nonpolygamous, Republican-wannabe Mormons; to the exemplar Henricksons trying to live a sexy, ethical polygamy in mainstream America (just like any ordinary law-abiding Utah family); to the corrupt feudal polygamous compound at Juniper Creek with its rampant pedophilia and preacher king, Roman Grant; to the roaming polygamous mafia unit (the Greens), indistinguishable in mob mores and brutality from the Sopranos (in fact, more ruthless and criminal in that they have no mellow suburban side).

7. *"It's a skippedy doo-dah day!"* Thank you, David Byrne, DJ of the series soundtrack. There wasn't a better way to close the third-from-last episode than having Rhonda Volmer sing Lorreta Lynn's "The Happiest Girl in the Whole U.S.A." Irony, yes—the chirping bleat of a bird who was never free, who is sort of free, an ambitious brat/American-Idol waif trying to put her lilt of greedy, ingenue narcissism into every note—as a tableau of characters and situations segues, one after another, across the screen. *"Why did we move that bojangle clock/so far away from the bed?"* For sure!

It may be the fade of a single chapter, but it speaks to the whole epic: an impossible but sacred joy in the face of entrapment and fundamentalist autocracy. After all, this is the fourteen-year-old bride-in-waiting of Roman Grant who already has one hundred and eighty-seven grandchildren, yet she is crooning as though it were "A Closer Walk with Thee, Lord": *"And thank you [Lord] for letting life turn out the way/that I always thought it could be."*

Loretta Lynn, meet Laura Bush. Britney Spears, meet Mata Amritanandamayi. Irony and anything but irony. Love and what stands in the way of love. Innocence forever, innocence stolen forever: *"There once was a time when I could not imagine/how it would feel to say/'I'm the happiest girl in the whole U.S.A.'"*

The Tibetan Buddhist teaching is that life, this life, is an illusion— not a lesser thing, not an irrelevancy, certainly not something expendable—just an illusion.

It lasts as long as the gong is sounding.

Everyone knows how easy, relatively, it is to hypnotize people and how "duck soup" it is to get them to accept chimeras and fabrications, even without formal hypnosis. Life is a passage from one trance state to another, to another, not all of them recollectable from the next that follows: from the tumult of birth to the timeless watch of infancy to the sleigh rides and hard-fought games of childhood; from the infatuations and larks of adolescence to the mature accomplishments of professional life—from being small and out of the loop to the height of one's influence and powers to a decline that began with the first breath. Each definitive trance melds into the next, indistinguishably, inevitably, incredibly yet ordinarily.

The moment you are born, for less than a quarter second you are the newest creature on Earth; then you are nudged along by other creatures coming behind you, pushing you into the trance, deeper and deeper, as they occupy your niche. For a long time you don't even notice that you are getting jostled, that the new ones are all younger than you, that there are more and more of them and fewer elders up ahead. But even in your first month of life, fledglings clambered behind you, filling the zone, shoving hard, as the blossom of your enchantment here spread through your mind and you were suffused by its nectar, its nuances of meaning and difference.

Then the bell stops clanging. The frequency changes. You go back to sleep and awaken to another dream.

In this world, brain tissue establishes landscapes in us by beta, theta, and more obscure waves, as well as hallucinogenic gaps where there is nothing, until there is everything. It dragoons us into simulations of places and things and we respond, like cuckoo birds.

But the brain is just a slab of complex hydrocarbon operating as a tuner. There are so many wave states in the cosmos that no one could map their spectra or geography or calibrate their relative registers because everybody is on some octave or other.

They are all illusion, and none of them are expendable.

I used to think that monastic existences were remarkable, admirable, and beyond my reach. Yet today in yoga class, 7 AM, during an extreme *trikonasana*, I recognized that *all existence is monastic*, and that what a monk or nun does is simply eliminate some of the more obvious static and distractions, riding the trance as trance, so that it suddenly deepens and gives them themselves as they are.

The trance doesn't stop; the desirings don't stop; the longing changes like an open fifth on a Peruvian panpipe or sacred harp—but it never goes, away.

In the flow of habitation through time, in the hurly-burly of galactic space, markets rise and fall, and staged dramas ride on photon fluctuations, all of it virtual anyway—just us and the furniture in the whirlwind.

Far outside consciousness is a beam of papier-maché-like figures, a great wind that shatters forms as it bears forth and forward the whole of reality, juggling crystal worlds in its hum without popping their bubbles.

Call and repeat on any planet: Om.

Inside each of us, even if we don't see it—even if we never see it—is a mandala, a castle that shines with a soft purplish light, sometimes cracklings of orange radiance from its core. It is not a castle in the sense of a building; it is a cathedral only in structure and complexity.

The mandala sustains our existence and supplies us with fortitude, with a mysterious and inexplicable hope, a sense of inviolability, even during the most dire or miserable of circumstances. It is the candle, invisible, indivisible, that is you, the golden flower that makes existence tolerable.

As I wrote earlier, toads and muskrats and even gnats have this mandala inside them too.

I see it sometimes as a gift, but, more than a gift, a surety that things are all right, that the pilot light is still on despite all transgressions and betrayals. This mandala is about as kind and unassuming as anything I know, especially given its drop-dead magnificence in the absence of a hands-on God.

It reminds me of the Palladium of which Matthew Arnold wrote: *"It stood, and sun and moonshine rain'd their light,/On the pure columns of its glen-built hall./Backward and forward roll'd the waves of fight/Round Troy—but while this stood, Troy could not fall."* Nor can *we* waver or concede so long as we harbor this radiance inside us.

But what is a palladium? Arnold's word presently denotes a soft white metal, akin to platinum—but long before that, the Palladium was a legendary statue of Pallas, the attentive goddess who watched over Troy. Its preservation was essential to Troy's safety; she guaranteed asylum, refuge, even while the war raged beneath, even today while the same war still rages: *"... red with blood will Xanthus be;/Hector and Ajax will be there again,/Helen will come upon the wall to see."*

Arnold was *très* blatant; he pronounced the Palladium a metaphor for the Soul: drenched in moonlight, with waters plashing past. He was, of course, not Tibetan Buddhist, so he did not say, "The tangka is within you, but you must reinforce its icon, use it as an alias to summon the real ground-luminosity to your waking mind."

He did not give instructions for how to fabricate it, element by element, by an act of interior visualization. He did not objectively analyze it its etiology, position, and construction the way a naturalist would investigate the body of a flounder; instead, he lyricized it as a traditional myth within the West. He made it metaphorical and moral, decorative more than functional.

The Palladium/tangka is a sacred cinema inside the third eye. Its floating hologram was present for Arnold as it is, right this second, for Tarthang Tulku and Tsoknyi Rinpoche and multifold yogis, priests, and lamas everywhere. It is what binds us to them and grounds all sentient beings in a vast and spacious realm outside of ordinary space and time.

Without this light we could not live at all.

I think everyone glimpses it at least once, but most people, like Hector (whoever he really was) bide their time—it seems like forever—*"in Ilium far below."* Nay, he *"fought, and saw it not—but there it stood."*

Loons keep their breath under Lower Hadlock Pond for breath-takingly long dives, so long I assume they have been swallowed by a Loch Ness monster or turned into a trout. Their heavy prehistoric bones propel swift submarine pursuits. Unrelated to eider ducks, they are in fact older and more primeval. Their hardwired call is to a planet that hasn't existed for some seven hundred thousand years.

We can only attend in awe, not just of them but the majestic habitation of Earth over untold eons. Its billion-orbit vista sits before us on pond and in sky: caterpillar fuzz gnawing maple, snake scooting under granite, chipmunk chittering on spruce, osprey commanding oceans of air.

At Ship's Harbor each tidepool is a medicinal bath, a little eco-system. I bathe my feet, testing temperatures. The hotter pools bake on the seawall in the sun; the colder ones are still getting splashed by the Atlantic. I hopscotch from stone to stone, trying not to cause havoc, but I am a ponderous ape.

Gulls utter resolute notes, as they observe my pastime. Kneeling at an underwater garden, I lap ocean on my face, and then harder, on my hair until it is drooling down my eyes and shirt. I realize that each icy flush opens a specific doorway inside me, deposits a cache of memories; they deepen, splash by splash. Then I travel to another kettle where I cup and douse myself with nectar again. It has its own unique temperature and memories, little crabs scuttling across the zone with local agendas. As water slops along my skin, I intuit the molecular source of all.

Treading on the seawall, my cooled feet feel how hot and dry it is, big flat stones and unsorted round ones. They play a silent piano as I cross their keyboard.

When NASA's *New Horizons* spacecraft arrives at needle-in-the-haystack Pluto sometime in late 2015, I would like it to return video images of boulevards of apartment buildings and shops like midtown Manhattan. I look forward to the attempted explanations by pat scientists. Mostly I would like astronomy's reductionist interpretation of the cosmos to fail at the edge of the Solar System, beyond the gas giants, where things become airless again and cold-cold-cold, where the Sun is but a remote star. I would like Pluto's buoy to point outward to Centauri as much as back to Terra for the golden city.

If photography from Ceres shows the ruins of a great metropolis, that will betray something a bit more ominous: that the asteroid belt is the remnants of a civilized planet that exploded millions of years ago, a world like Krypton of DC Comics fame. The pixels will cry: global warming is not your only problem, Earth!

I fished long ago as a child. I remember catching a small perch with my brother Jon at the Nevele Hotel, using string and a safety pin, snail goo as bait. A year later my stepmother Bunny took me out in a rowboat on Grossinger Lake with a coffee can full of worms, bare-bones fishing rods, and an empty pail for our catch. In eerily deep water I felt the sudden tug of the line, the appearance of a mystery creature out of the void. I was enchanted; the thing was so bright and new and strange. We went only a few times after that, and though I regretted the damage to the poor fishes, I loved the scavenger hunt with its accoutrements and protocols, the sweet drama of the splash. I aimed to go again. Yet it didn't come close to happening for more than fifty years.

There is an idyllic "Trout Fishing in America/River Runs Through It" aura about recreational angling. It is deemed rustic and wholesome Americana. The provocation of fish is ever-present on Mount Desert Island—sportsmen on lakes in outboards and canoes, adults and children casting from town docks, and working boats setting out each morning at dawn into the North Atlantic. In fact (duh!) I wrote my anthropology thesis between 1969 and 1974 on the economics and ecology of fishing out of Bernard and Bass Harbor.

Finally in the summer of 2007 I got enough momentum behind my hankering to take the first step. On a shopping trip to the Ellsworth Wal-Mart, I grabbed a ten-dollar fishing rod and then two two-dollar-fifty-cent lures—each with three nasty hooks in a scrap of fishlike silver—and surprised Lindy by depositing them in our cart. Back home I quickly discovered that I didn't know how to assemble the thing. After I strung the line through the guides and then through the eye of the hook and tied it on, I turned the handle, but the crank ran freely without catching the string on the spool.

My first lesson came from my college buddy Dusty Dowes in the backyard: he put on his reading glasses, threaded the reel properly around the bail, and patiently reattached the hook with an artful fisherman's knot. Then he showed me how the pinion ran off the crank and how to set its anti-reverse. He freed the line from the bail and, as I ducked, cast the lure across the yard. It glided an astonishing distance through the air before getting caught in the grass; the second time he had to unsnare it from a bush. I got the idea.

I had been told by the ladies at the Southwest Harbor town office that, whereas you definitely needed a license for freshwater, you could fish off the Manset or Southwest Harbor town wharf without one. They suggested trying that before laying out $24 for three days: "You'll find plenty of company, and it won't cost you anything."

My second lesson came courtesy of Yosarian; it began as I was standing on the empty Manset dock, wondering what to do next or if I was even in the correct place. Arriving barefoot on his bicycle, Yo was a godsend. After we chatted fifteen minutes of requisite conspiracy theory and AIDS politics and he got to decry my cell phone ("people are frying their brains and leeching nano-bits of plastic into their cells"), I asked him if this was the right spot for fishing.

"Of course. There's no one right now, but people fish here all the time. If the mackerel are still running and you don't catch one, you ain't half trying."

"Where should I stand?"

"Not up here, for god's sake. You've gotta go down to the floating dock." He pointed the way.

"Is it better down there?"

"Of course. It's closer to the water, closer to the fish. You also need to get out deeper."

Yo was headed in that direction, to board a rowboat and check his tourist schooner, the *Annie McGee*. While he debarked by oar across the harbor, I stood on the swaying, rolling slab of wood and, despite my propensity for motion sickness, held the line in the water. Nothing happened. Twenty minutes later Yo came rowing back.

"You're not gonna get much action that way," he shouted. "You've got to cast and pull in the line, jig it, like this." He dropped the oars and jerked his hands in midair. Then, after tying the boat, he came to where I was.

In truth, I had forgotten Dusty's casting lesson. Taking the rod from me, Yo reviewed its essence. He flipped the bail back, squeezed the line against the rod with his thumb at a spot near where it approached the reel, and flicked sharply with his wrist. I ducked again because it sure was a mean trio of flying hooks. I had gotten my finger caught on it while tying the lure, so I knew how sharp and inextricable it could be.

The weight went sailing out, far enough that I exclaimed, "Wow!" Yo forcefully reeled it back in by the crank, tugging sharply every half-second or so, "jigging," as he put it. His uneven yank-and-spin motion was clearly a signature of something he had done many times. "You want to make it look like a wounded fish," he instructed, giving an especially dramatic twist to match the words. After a few such adept if unfruitful casts, he handed the rod back to me and headed off with a patently rehearsed comment, "Fishing is a good way to get a lot done and do nothing."

Yo had given me a skill to work on, separate from the more problemataic issue of catching fish. I found it exhilarating to cast. I would free the bail, hold the loose line against the rod with my thumb, and then time my release like a baseball pitcher. Unreeling the nylon, the lure always landed farther than I imagined possible. I quickly snapped the bail back so that the line came taut, and then I reeled it in.

Fighting off nausea from the dock's pitch, I cast a dozen, two dozen times. On only one did I feel a spine-tingling tug, likely a fish's attack on the decoy. I hastily scrolled back, but it was gone.

A few casts later I realized that nothing was happening when I reeled. I looked down and saw the line all tangled. After diagnosing its path, I unscrewed the large knob, freed the spool, and gradually loosened and rewound the nylon. Two casts later it tangled even worse, getting around and under the mechanism, and no amount of gyrating could undo the maze of string-theory tangles. Instead of improving them, I was turning them into full-fledged knots.

I got more and more motion-sick, for the wind had picked up and was rocking my barge. Finally, in exasperation and nausea, I took out a utility knife and cut the line. I tossed the lure in my pail, but by then I could barely direct my hands or get my sight to adhere to the landscape.

I staggered home.

The residual dizziness having finally worn off, I returned four days later on the sparkling morning of pro football's opening Sunday. A young man and his lady partner were casting off the Manset floating dock and, as soon I reached it, I saw a plastic container full of dead fish, long, thin pointy ones with a bluish-silver tint like giant herring. At the time that Yo spoke of mackerel, I didn't know how I would recognize one if I saw it. Now it was obvious: our friend Sergei had been frying these things and calling them mackerel at his Full Circle Fair party earlier in the summer. "

Are those mackerel?" I asked, by way of introduction.

"That they are."

I silently counted seven of them. Then I stood aside and watched him cast. His line had about eight different lures and hooks plus a float. It was like a child's bracelet of doodads and charms. He was determined to catch stuff and obviously on a roll.

"Not quite two hours" was his response when I asked how long it took to score that many.

I picked a spot as far away as I could get myself on the dock and began casting gingerly. He turned to look and propose right away, "There's space between us if you'd like." Accepting, I was still extra careful with my flings.

Yet it was impossible to stay completely clear of their lines. The wind was blowing so hard that my casts which started off in one direction were tossed in midair to the completely other side of the dock. Though our lines regularly overlapped, we never tangled.

They both smoked, but gusts blew most of the tars away, so it wasn't an issue. In fact, the scent gave the air a World Series nip.

His name was Eugene. He was just out of the army, back from Iraq. His wife was Asian, and she wasn't so much fishing as leaving her rod handle in a hole in the dock to fish by itself while she enjoyed her tobacco and prepped the mackerel. They were from Albany, New York, on a camping and fishing vacation.

The wind was brisk and the movement of the dock pretty rough. Eugene offered that my motion sickness was a physical-fitness problem: "You should work on it, you know—train." He pondered a bit more. "Now I can tell the dock is moving, but I don't think about it, or if I do, I enjoy it, kind of like a roller-coaster. I mostly don't think about it. If I did, I'd probably get sick too. You have to be disciplined in your mind. Otherwise the world'll make you crazy." I listened attentively. Real lessons come from unlikely sources, often when unexpected, and this guy had been there; he would know.

After about five minutes I felt a tug, a real thump; my rod bent so far I thought it would snap. "You've got something," Eugene called out. As I wound the handle, I saw it—a silvery

streak active at the surface, tossing and wriggling in violent outrage on my line. I reeled it closer until he shouted, "No more!
Now lift it up." Even as I did, he was sidestepping quickly, for
he had snared a fish too. Because he was more adroit, our twin
mackerels lifted simultaneously out of the water, side by side at
the ends of our lines. Wriggling frantically as if about to become
flying fish, they were almost too real and three-dimensional to
believe.

What a sight! Flopping on the dock, the nasty hooks in its
mouth. Such a horrible thing I had done—tricking it, hasping its
flesh by its bite, dragging it in. So much pain needlessly caused.
But I am in the middle of the action, and there is no leisure to
stop.

Eugene offers to remove the hook, so I accept. Holding the
fish down, he gently slides the metal from around bone and torn
flesh.

It is flip-flopping loose on the dock. I catch it, keep it from
sliding out of my grasp and, holding tight with both hands, put
my catch into my pail of water. But that's no good because it almost leaps out. Holding it in the pail, I carefully pour the water
into the sea.

"You want me to clean it for you?" Eugene asks. I am stunned,
compliant. He doesn't bother to kill it, just slices it open with his
knife, removes its organs, and tosses them in the ocean. It is still
flopping around in the pail.

"I feel bad for the fish," I finally say.

A look of surprise crosses his face. "Really?"

"Yeah. It's a painful death."

"You get hungry, you won't feel so bad for it. You get hungry, you
want something to eat. I'm catching these guys to bring to my army
buddies back home." He is thoughtful for a moment, then adds, "I
know what you mean, though. I don't like hunting for that reason."

All the rest of the day I regret what I have done; I think long and hard about it. The football game I was looking forward to is remote and meaningless.

To catch and kill is what fishing is. No amount of spin can change that. I don't know what made me think it was romantic. The image of fresh-caught trout in a pan over a campfire is not that far off human corpses tossed onto a pyre in India. The line between cuisine and mortuary is a thin one. Even as a boy, I knew it was wrong to dig worms out of the ground, snails out of shells, break them apart, and attach them to hooks, but I didn't *know I knew*, so I persisted, sometimes just to see fish come in numbers to loose bait. The child amusing himself was disquieted but resolved to do it anyway; he is now addressed by the man he has become five decades later. The act has come full circle.

In my mind I find myself reciting Robert Kelly's old stanza: *"When we take life/what do we give?"* And I realize that I have experienced but a mite of the killing and pain that humans are imposing every second on the creatures of the planet. So much of my fodder this lifetime began in an act like today's, though I neither saw nor imagined the cruelty with which it occurred.

And that does not even address what animals routinely visit on each other, including what my mackerel was intending to do to the wounded fish it thought it was attacking. But animals hunt unconsciously and do not know what it is they are, let alone what they are meaning. That is the difference: *we know*. Or at least we think we know, who we are and what we are doing. Everyone somewhere inside him, even Eugene and his buddies, has a conscience, an identity, an emergent psyche beyond fishhood or moosehood.

Yes, I succeeded. I caught a free and mysterious one. But in the aftermath my act feels cheap, mindless, dishonorable compared to what a fish is. I have done nothing to earn it. In a most underhanded way I have deluded it into swallowing a harsh metal.

Then, like a thoughtless bully, I ignored its suffering for an idle act of sport. I watched it grieve and stood by and passively contributed. It was still flopping in the pail in its own blood as I brought it home, sliced almost in two. This wasn't a frolic; it was a funeral.

What stays with me most of all is that I struck down Beauty, defaced and mutilated it. I turned dancing brilliant life, an iridescent map of tens of thousands of skies and marbled labyrinths of creation, into a dead blue parchment, and I forfeited everything that made it what it was. It lies there fading, its flesh a painting of another universe, a primordial rendition of hundreds of millions of molecular gyrations under the ocean—now a coin of dead meat.

I prepare my mackerel for dinner, but it is overkill. We already have corn and eggplant, rice and beans.

It still seems to be flopping in the boiling olive oil. The garlic and soy sauce are an affectation, an insult.

What are we doing?

Cuisine like fashion is denial of murder.

I didn't need a mackerel for this meal. There was no reason for it to have to die, to not get to swim on and be what it is, what it was born to be, today and tomorrow and tomorrow.

How much human food and clothing is superfluous? How many hapless flying spirits have been torn from the sea in devious ways to be ground into pet food or tossed into garbage cans as restaurant waste?

The larger holocaust does not excuse my part.

Suddenly everything in this book seems academic. All the philosophizing and preaching and speculating and wit. All of it! Everything!

Life is so beautiful and vibrant and free. To capture and destroy a feral thing is horrific.

The fish was so much more than these words.

Two days later Lindy and I walked to the Manset wharf at twilight where we saw a family casting lines and pulling up mackerel so fast that fish were flopping and dead all over the main pier. Their little girl was jumping on the still-alive fish, such that her mother told her to stop, commenting, "I'd rather suffocate than have my belly crushed."

I grieved for all these dying fish, but it wasn't the same as my own mackerel. That was personal, between me and him: eye to eye, *mano a mano*—"You are catching *me* and dragging *me* with a hook in my mouth." I can still feel his reproach in my bones.

I took his life, and I ate him. And he will not forget. In the taste of his flesh he was still talking to me, exploring our ongoing relationship, asking me if I liked him enough to justify what I did to him, to warrant ripping him out of the water.

Like him? Even though I had eaten mackerel happily in the past, I could barely swallow him. Yet I would not waste his body on top of having stolen his life.

In the end we simply *are* in the world. No rules; no evasion; no escape. No subpoena. No verdict. No redemption, likewise. And, as Don Juan told Carlos, someday we too will be prey for a creature that will snare us as incidentally as I caught that fish.

I understand now what I intuited dimly while fishing as a child: every cut we make into the universe we are making directly on ourselves.

My life is a sorry mannerism beside the pure and wild thing I have violated.

Hearing about my brother's suicide, Dusty remarks, "It doesn't matter how much horsepower you have if you've got no traction."

Notes on *Rescue Dawn*, a film by Werner Herzog

✦This film could also be called *First Blood—The Revenge of the Sith*. Yes, Sly, the greatest fighting weapon known to the world *is* the mind of man.

✦*Rescue Dawn* has characters, but it is more profoundly a movie about sky and earth and the difference between them. Beings who operate only from the sky don't understand the earth. Especially when they ascend tens of thousands of feet up inside cabins jetted from gaunt battleships, carrying compartments full of bombs. The quadrants and forests and fields beneath them on which they plant their explosions float by like a time-delayed dream, inhabited by cartoon characters, not real men and women with families and farms, not bands trekking through the jungle with swinging censers and tall netted sticks, catching and roasting large insects and small birds.

Those on the earth cannot comprehend the corporate agenda of the sky. When fighter pilot Dieter Dengler crashes and finds himself a captive of the jungle and then the earth people, he cannot fathom at first why they are treating him so roughly and disrespectfully. "Stop that!" he screams, as though he has any moral authority or leverage, as though he can say anything that they might honor if they even could understand his words. That he deposits death and destruction upon them from the sky is all they know about him, and he has oddly forgotten that (if he ever really knew).

After a while "the man who fell to earth" realizes that there is no returning to the sky. Even his fellow sky beings won't acknowledge him. They are blind and foolish, as he once was, discharging their guns into foliage; they know nothing of the complications and labyrinths below.

This is a Gnostic fable. "The man who fell from the sky" can get back to the macrocosm only by evolving into a magician.

✦The grunts, the American soldiers, the ones in actual life-and-death combat, share an existential truth with the Pathet Lao and Vietcong whom they are ostensibly fighting. They are equally oppressed by the Idea, though neither knows it or wants to know. All of them are under a spell and cannot go home. They are jointly commanded by the Men in Black, those Secret Ops with extra-legal prerogatives and intellectual battlefields who move pawns between squares as if they were the rulers of this planet and everyone else was their vassal.

All Dieter Dengler wanted was his wings. And the Americans were more than willing to give him those.

✦I recall words that Utah Phillips imparted to his son under a lilac hedge in Spokane just after the latter's high-school graduation, what the folksinger called "the only real lesson I learned from my military service in Korea: I will never again abdicate to someone else my right and my ability to decide who the enemy is. It might be I wouldn't have to go thousands of miles to find him either."

The boy enlisted anyway.

Yes, Sky and Earth remain separated by an abstraction equally deadly to both.

A crow landing suddenly in the maple leaves at twilight caws, looks about, and is gone. The universe winks a billion eyes at us and itself, inside itself. This crow is responsible only for its single neuromuscular package of fluvia and pinnae, that mysterious spark of ego-being within it.

Who lit him, Blake? Who fashioned him from energy and debris, to fly and fall from flying?

What does a falcon think it is as it awakens from egg? What does an ant know about anthood or anything? Existentially there must be a spark of reflection in him, of irony, even if it weighs less than one electron. Otherwise he could not be. What does the beaver know about worlds, about the one he is or the beaver body he got? What does he *not* know, that is also knowing?

Every moment things live—even in the way of birds or fish or mice—the stories they tell themselves about who they are make them who they are. Their commentary frames their becoming.

Yes, animals have stories and excuses, though of course they don't call them that. Their days have plotlines; their actions, goals; their fates rise and fall on skirmishes as dramatic, to them anyway, as a Shakespearean play. They know themselves in terms of unrealized tropes. Without a subliminal story, a fly could not be a fly.

We are a link between the universe's innate complication and the eternal void. We have lives, strange though they be, and, even stranger, after a while they no longer seem strange.

Do not rotely correct the body or its breathing! Do not meditate upon the deity! Do not ask!

The sole lasting enterprise is to locate and become the self—not the ego, not the instinct body, not *prana*, not the thing you do best or want most, not even empty mind, though those are part of it. The self is indelible, an unaccountable thing that represents the stopping point, the intrinsic vanishing site, like the North Pole, from which a movement in any direction is south.

Absolute existence is what lives in you but does not manifest otherwise. The self instills, even in a paramecium or worm, an intrumentation and a limit, a doctrine and lore: "authentic, natural condition," even in a marsh marigold or rock rose. I call it the "self" (*selber, soi-même, sí mismo*) rather than the "soul" (*seele, âme, ánimo, ψυχη*) because I mean to set it beyond metaphysical identity. Like gravity it is everywhere and nowhere. It has a shape, a cathexis, and an aura. It is just "oh," and then the next thing is obvious, always. It is why this whole creation doesn't have a meaning, doesn't tell a story, offers no climax or clue. Do not ask!

It is self-evident, not just sort of, but precisely.

We might not have been born; we might not have come. But, despite all other issues big and small, apart from every accoutrement, cosmic and local, this is the one irrefutable happenstance, without riders, without codicils. Elected, though by whom or how we know not, we *must* serve.

Life interceded—it alone—and here we are, doing it instead of some other thing. Hares are called to the task as well, to be hares. Wasps arise as wasps.

Migrants between worlds, we are couriers, discussions of cells, post-graduate seminars in universe-invention.

As objects in a dream, we are driven by the intelligence of dream formation.

But then Elvis: "*How many, how many/ I wonder,/but I really don't want to know.*"

No, we don't.

I don't understand it really, any of it. I don't know why we are who we are, do what we do. I don't understand what I have written. I can't gauge whether it even carries the weight I feel I have loaded into it. I can't tell whether I have pushed out beyond some real edge or am merely thrashing around in an indulgent, delusional reverie.

There's not a whole lot of space between the edge of this book and my greatest hopes and fears about *everything*.

I have written myself very far out on some limb. Discounting my own myopia and the innate limits of the act of production, I sense I am approaching something radical, naming a landscape that, quite apart from my role as chronicler, cries out for description, elucidation—that "da man" seems to be missing.

I have been writing for decades about ostensibly occult and esoteric topics, but I feel as though in the early years, until fairly recently in fact, I was earnest and wistful (and overly literary) and did not address the bigger issue of a pagan, secular universe with its incontrovertible waterfall of logic and explicit landscape. To what real end does any—does all or any of this exist? What is context of "being"? What is the nature of the Word?

Is there an actual "root karma," a true "supreme source"? Is pure or total consciousness attainable by sentient beings anywhere: clear essence of self? Even in the best of circumstances, does the goal of "enlightenment" make any more than interim or provisional sense? Was our crisis inevitable? How far can we go toward overcoming a spiritual impasse on a secular level? If there is only one creation, isn't all activity ultimately spiritual?

If there is an unaltered condition, how and why did our natural condition, the condition of our conditional existence and clouded consciousness, become conditioned?

I think that the point of this book is to confront the big riddles of life and consciousness in the universe: origin, meaning, predation, love, violence, evil—to put out there questions that respect the level of depth at which the universe is asking those same questions of us, asking them by creating us and giving us minds and bodies and situations. It isn't worth it merely to gab about nonviolence or compassion or not eating meat or King God and his court or even to talk smack because the universe hasn't set it up that way. There *are no* contingent solutions.

Dig this most basic, disturbing piece of news: *It is not necessary to behave well to have a life. It is not a precondition of existence, or in fact anything, to be a good person.*

Karmically, it is the best news of all.

Viewed from partway up Mansell Mountain, Long Pond is an inscrutable papyrus of ultramarine furrows in a late-September breeze. Gulls cushion their glides against the pillow of air, circling with the precision of a silent alphabet. Great-winged crows leap from branch to branch, contemptuous of scale. A red squirrel dashes from a moss-covered stone to a decaying log. As a single loon paddles its way into the far cove, Lindy wonders how any creature selects one act over another, takes a detour on its own. What is that loon looking for, if anything? What does it think it is doing? Why does a lone gull choose such a divergent arc and head for splashdown outside the bathing party? To what semblance or memento do animals respond; what emblazonry, what herald summons them? How do they bow to the gods that made their bodies?

The fact that nature is indifferent to us makes the world far more interesting and complex than if it responded to our presence, either in some mother tongue or through general telepathic brogue. We cannot talk to nature, and it cannot talk to us,

Socratically anyway. This barrier forces us to develop another way of being, something deep enough to interact with the universe beyond its indifference, beyond dialects that arose from the call systems of hominids and were arranged in linear sets by Stone Age poets and madmen, a lingua franca in which we now think, in which Parmenides and Hobbes and Cro Magnon pondered our state long before us.

It is not about thought; not even actions count. There is a caesura between us and any creature or event in nature such that our separation ceases at our disjunction, to create a basis for meaning in the wave that forms it. Nothing will ever happen in that chasm; yet everything that happens is disposed by its existence.

The bardo of waking life was projected by a far deeper hiatus than that between nature and man but a contiguous one. Once mindedness existed and was fated to exist—don't ask me why or how—once it became the background for a Universe of which this galaxy-filled tunnel is a local subset, there was no way thereafter to cross its gap. That forever sets a measure between the vastness and omneity of mind and the creationary force and desire realm it strives to recover. Mind occasioned its own individuation and evolution, its migration of intelligences.

Bardos are all exquisite prisons. Ignited thus, they are domains for the expression of mind's prior claim—a sort of temporal cyberspace in which "being" elaborates its pickle. The perplexity of any one bardo—that is, the perplexity of existence itself—lies at the root of what mind is and the impulse of mind to explore *its* nature. Thus arises karma and, with it (to the West), fate; thus issues the molecular, gravitational, inertial wind, blowing Long Pond and all spirits along, endowing them with creaturehood and making of mere ontological abstraction and surmise actual landscapes of inextricable forms. Chinked and crannied at every point with logic and algebra at the precise degree of discrimination that minded-ness confers, each set is potentiated by a prior one and gives rise to a next. The information highway disguises this savory realm.

"It's all good," a current popular expression, stands more or less in place of "Is this fucked up or what?" Another hip tautology wages the same irony, "It is what it is."

Whatever....

William Burroughs told his readers that he became a junkie not because he liked junk but because he couldn't think of anything better to do.

Neither could mind. Neither could the universe of universes. So here we are, in *le trou à merde*.

The embryogenic phylogenetic process identified by Darwin and Mendel, riding on the heels of Newton, has become totally jacketed in algorithms and paradigms by post-modern bioscience. After all, how could anything worthy and sensible be made by someone other than us? Where could there be a bold intelligence in the void, let alone one rivaling our talent? If it is all random, and we are random too, then we are (hurray, hurrah!) the only creators in the universe, by default and in lieu of our trophy as the originator of evolutionary theory.

We tend to forget that life is neither a machine engineered by nature nor a patented autonomous idea lodged into matter and generating species and persons by trial and error and natural selection. It is, instead, the splash of Great Frog into Great Pond—the multidimensional trajectory/skim-line of cosmic intelligence against the edge of a field in which it is bathing or which it has inherently created and cannot get out of.

Ontogenesis is mindedness at its radix, not only the DNA-based linguistic template for all later ciphers and communications but the stem of the hidden spiral. The grizzlies and hornets and other shapes within this waking life—for that matter within any condition—are merely the shortest path between two points, neither of which we ever see.

Once people pass out of the waking bardo, they become wolf children again. Without language, they can find no identity, no thought-stream, no calendar or clock. Demoted to hungry ghosts, they race through nonexistent fields and jungles, seeking anything familiar, just as they do here.

I used to wonder how the dead spent their time without landscapes, objects, or events to keep them occupied. After all, what does a spirit mean when he tells a medium he is planting a garden or going fishing? What serves as his flower or a fish?

But the dead might likewise wonder how the living can continue posturing emptily in their own chamber of mirages.

All worlds are idioplasmic. The dead are not without events. They, like we, wander with beautiful dreamers, animal and human, their attentions culled into streams. Only a tuning fork separates us—a tuning fork and its chime.

So Caliban charms Sycorax, so Circê beguiles the souls of sailors, although they don't hear her and are no longer in ships.

That the blastula is holographic and each organism is synopsized in every cell, archived identically in snippet after snippet of DNA, betrays pretty much that a single pattern is being magically projected through multiple chrysalides. The internal multiplicity of the embryo shows a round dance, not a blueprint. This is zero cool.

The perfume of pine and huckleberry in the woods as we cross Mansell ridge is why worlds like this were created. And why we wanted bodies in which to visit them.

Quebec Notes

Arriving

As we drive north out of Skowhegan on 201, industrial and agricultural Maine gets sparser and sparser, replaced by frontier towns and tundra panoramas. One village has a dead horse strung up by the neck in front of the grade school, literally. Children and adults mill around. More curious travelers might have stopped to inquire.

We come over a mountain and look down into a valley with a giant lake filled with islands, beyond it more peaks. Mountains and rivers without end rise and fall toward a violet dusk in this corner of America that for most Americans doesn't exist—the signature hump of Maine at the beginning of its jagged ascent above Moosehead and Kennebec toward the St. Lawrence.

Jackman is like a TV stage-set for the Yukon, right down to the bearded loggers taking their smokes on chairs outside the gas station's store. A magnificent stone church anchors the center of town with rugged, spare solemnity, as if dumb glacial rocks long ago organized and were climbing to heaven.

When we cross the border into Quebec, it is sudden culture-shift: clean vistas; gentle, colorful architecture; French signage; farms on hillsides, like Italy; modern architecture for biotech and printing. In urban areas houses are set a block or so off the swift highway (now labeled 173), little access roads so that you see neighborhoods and their habitants and bikes safely to the side, going about their business at their own rates. Settlements are consecrated: St.-Côme-Linière … St.-Georges … St.-Joseph-de-Beauce … Sainte-Marie.

The last fifty miles into Quebec City is superhighway (73). Then suddenly we are in an old-fashioned European city at twilight, trying to recapture logic from MapQuest, which has mutinied—the street cascade ceasing to match its chosen itinerary. When we ask for help at a packed bus stop, either no one speaks English or Free Quebec's partisans are boycotting us. After all, we arrived in town five minutes ago with solely provincial presumptions.

Quebec is a fortress on a hill, the original defended North American settlement, so the gap between its lower and upper sectors is fundamental—and we are in the wrong quadrant; we need to chug up the great rise. Once we do, MapQuest is at home again, though it takes several reconnoiters through the shopping district and gate to find rue d'Aueteil.

Our petite hotel, L'Auberge la Chouette, is Cambodian-owned so has a Cambodian restaurant across the lobby from the front desk—a plus.

Midway through dinner, friends we haven't seen since Ann Arbor days (1968) show up as planned: Andrew Lugg and Lynne Cohen. He is retired after teaching philosophy at the University of Ottawa for thirty-five years. She is a photographer, with books from Routledge and Aperture.* As we gab back and forth across the decades, trying to locate the gist of our lives for each other, the landmarks that matter, Lynne reminds us that Lindy and I oversaw her first publication, in *Io*, the *Mind Memory Psyche* Issue (1974): a series of tacky Midwestern interiors with sofas of all sizes, shapes, and marginalia; odd and elephantine hammocks; garish carpets; TV shrines cluttered with family effigies; and vulgar bar murals with exotic *trompe l'oeil*. "Beautiful in their own way," she muses even as she did back then. Her recent work, pulled up online at the table, is similar, but more industrial and corporate: canonized spaces and inadvertent temples and altars

*Check out www.lynne-cohen.com.

hidden within factories, hospitals, and office landscapes—still ugly, still somehow beautiful (or grand), if you could forget their context.

Andrew and Lynne live full-time now in Montreal, but by amazing luck (else we would have missed them altogether) Lynne is working here these next few days, shooting an exhibit for the 400th Anniversary of Quebec in 2008. We are each on a different journey, but we intersect at the gate to old Quebec.

Quebec City

With Andrew we hike the city all the next afternoon in escalating drizzle and gusts—up and down hills, along old forts and battlements historic with cannons. Winding cobblestone streets are crammed with tourist boutiques (lots of skating animals with hockey sticks and iconic H-embracing red C's, Montreal Canadian emblems, as institutional and profound here as Dodger blue or Red Sox kitsch in their climes). Inuit gift shops* offer diverse and pricey house-brand clothing and souvenirs, lots of fur and leather with petroglyphs.

After an exhausting search through overpriced Parisian junkfood and faux cafés, we find tasty crêpes for lunch at a little hole in the wall among art galleries in lower Vieux Québec: Café Bistro du Cap. As the only customers, we must stir the waitress and chef from their newspapers past 3 PM. But it is a relief to find a destination after rejecting more than a dozen establishments for either the menus or the view in the window. We were running out of actionable town.

What a stiff October gale off the St. Lawrence! You can lean back into it with all your weight and not fall over. Lindy and I are finally wearing our heavy LL Bean coats, purchased

*Not run by Inuit, I learn later.

at the Ellsworth outlet store five years ago for a day like this. The smell of fallen autumn leaves has been long missed, that dank nostalgic incense endemic to the Eastern Woodlands— as deciduous trees are being stripped today in legion. Gray squirrels bound across parks and sidewalks, at work.

Other than the requisite buses, Quebec has a strange mode of public transportation, one that you couldn't imagine without being here to see it in operation. Two funiculaires, overgrown gondolas, descend from the upper cliffs to Basse-Ville and— more important—go back.

Andrew is a Wittgensteinian/Kleinian, so is very droll in his conversation as we hike, dropping minimalist and witty perceptions. Inclined more to housebodying than hiking, in a new city he usually stays in a hotel room and reads and writes while Lynne photographs. Between heavy breaths today he manages, "I never knew being a tourist was such hard work." We are all huffing and puffing and getting cold and wet.

We see a group of grade-schoolers being led along cannonaded ramparts by guides in maid and cat costumes, their faces painted with white grease and whiskers. As one of them climbs a small tree and begins miming a prowling feline, peering this way and that as if Marcel Marceau, Andrew gazes disapprovingly and then turns away. "That is plain embarrassing," he declares.

Four years prior, after I reconnected with him by email following a lapse of decades, I thought that maybe my embryology books might appeal to the philosopher in him—but he quickly responded that, whereas he was intrigued that science interests so many people, it did nothing for him because he figured the universe has to work some way and he could care less which way that was. Recalling that comment, I say with a smile, "But Andrew, they've gotta be doing something."

"Yes, but does it have to be that?"

"We have values here," Lindy adds. "We don't have to like every kind of behavior just because it's happening. We're not relativists."

Politics

Sometime in the 1980s I read a newspaper article in which North America was remapped as seven or eight "meta-nations," defined therein as the continent's true socioeconomic polities, the so-called real power centers of U.S.A./Canada, each with its own "capital." I remember now that the Greater Northeast included New York, Philadelphia, and Boston, its capital at Quebec City, the site at which we now stand. The author explained, "If Réné Lévesque [then the premier of this secessionist province] had the courage of his convictions, he'd close the border and charge what his hydroelectric power was worth."

Here along the Gulf of St. Lawrence at the geography that the natives called Kébec ("where the river narrows") sits the provincial capital of modern Quebec. The thermodynamic, hence commercial, hence military, hence cultural power of New England and New York rests in these waters and the primordial ice north of us, above Montreal, Trois Rivières, Quebec City, Saguenay, and Sept-Îles. The Silicon Valleys and electric cars and shopping malls and wi-fis of the second half of this century are buried there, in the vast sub-Arctic.

Free Quebec is not just a dated slogan; it is a country yet to be born.

(Only one other power center in the article was notable enough for me to remember: Miami. While the other regions each included several states and/or provinces or sections thereof, Miami was itself an entire meta-nation, the capital of a virtual polity encompassing Latin America and the islands: Haiti, Jamaica, Curaçao, Cuba, Bermuda, the Bahamas, *et al.*—that is, the drug trade plus the Havana connection. Alone of the regions, this city-state needed no actual land beyond its airports, ports, alleys, and covens.)

After breakfast I am trying to locate open wireless on the streets, and I stray under a scaffold, four or five stories up, on which a guy is plastering the side of a stone building. When grit falls amid drizzle on my keyboard, I look up to foreign words being shouted down at me. Then, as I jog across the street, folding my laptop for safety, I realize enough high-school French is lodged somewhere in my brain that I understand: "Take your sorry Yankee ass elsewhere!" (*Allez quelque chose!* or something like that.)*

Montreal

Between Quebec City and Montreal, rain blows in sheets across the highway amid patches of fog. This is not an easy three-hour drive. When the sky clears the next morning in Montreal, it is a different climate. Frost has caked the cars overnight, the last colors draining from flowers and trees.

La Basilique Notre-Dame de Montréal is lit with a kind of soft pastel neon, multi-colored like a Christmas tree. Various caches of candlewax in votive holders make separate tangkas, pathways between the human world and the angels. This scrabbled iconography of tincture and stained glass leads to a raised altar, a dais toward which all pews face, on the wall above which Christ is being crucified again, in floating three-dimensional statuary. Or, more precisely, the central emblematic event of the

---

*Of course, that's not a real translation, just a joke I indulge in privately as my reward for understanding, and also in recognition that the debris perhaps had some help in landing on me.

West is displayed flagrantly, with all the drama and awe and sacralization that the architects of the time could summon. It is an effigy not of the visible but of something faraway and long ago, concealed in the blatancy of its representation, which is what it has to be for the world to be the world.

In a small subchapel, people are praying intently, slumped, heedfully extending candles toward shrines. Their sincerity reminds me that the modern West provides few places where our internal life is real, where sorrow and grief and loss can be brought without being professionalized or reduced to commodities and pharmaceutical opportunities. Here is a sanctum where feelings and glimmerings are respected for what they are, a terrain for expressions of hope and thanksgiving, for communion with the Divine through the intercession of the saints. Here the universe is as mysterious and uncertain as it really is, and humans don't know; they simply don't know.

Jesus was just a man, but he did something which perhaps hasn't been done since: for a few years he embodied an aspect of the Christ function here in this dimension, the Christ function which is vibrating at such a high level it would shatter the nervous system of anyone who tried to incarnate it fully on Earth.

And everybody knows it; everybody, whatever else they suspect or are blind to in the universe, intuits that there is a seventh wave somewhere—at least a seventh—and that angels or something, unseen, watches over us, always.

On the secular boulevard an oasis acknowledges and reaches out to this higher order of knowledge, and with the degree of sobriety and gravitas that the occasion calls for.

English overheard on the streets: "old wood-frame construction burned down," "party on Sunday, Monday, Tuesday," "figure out this scarf," "do you want to go get some hot chocolate at Europa?"

The Montreal Biodome is a series of user-friendly habitats—tropical rainforest, Laurentian woods, Mexican desert, Antarctica. Despite the luxury of their dioramas, lynxes, chuckwalla lizards, and rockhopper penguins are trying to claw, poke, and swim their way out of these "Truman Show" paradises, to find the exits in the camouflage. Most of the chuckwallas, for instance, are digging away at their quite ample sandbox, but one is endeavoring to burrow into the Southwestern landscape painted on the exhibit's wall, inventing his own Escher-like psychosis.

The smaller, more active of two Quebec lynxes paces and scans the make-believe sky with ferocious attentiveness, searching for the elusive trail. It would pounce on any or all of us if it could.

Several penguins are certain that egress consists of diving, zooming underwater, and plopping up feet-first on a new shore—only to find themselves back in the same company.

The prairie dogs, on the other hand, are content to tumble and wrestle in the dirt, oblivious to captivity. The puffins please themselves with splashing their feathers over and over in rapids that are pouring out of the wall into a drain. A nearby king penguin cleans itself with rapid full-body vibrations on the approximate principle of an electric toothbrush.

A sluggish capybara, accompanied by two ducks, chews forever on a soggy leaf along the shore of a brief stream.

Meanwhile, giant catfish and piranhas float, suspended in a dream of a dream.

The West Island suburbs of Montreal awake to a raucous serenade of hundreds of Canada geese passing north above the houses in long, undulating V's. Favoring Lac St.-Louis, a touch of wilderness wings through the gray corridor. As workers hustle into their more earthbound commutes, traffic jamming up 20

EST, drivers hear the honking of things rowdy and free.

"Hoo? Hoo?" the geese ask as they wend their way across a twenty-first-century Western sky.

"Hwy? Hwy?" the meadow mice whisper in laboratory cages in birth, suffering, extinction.

"ΩΩΩ?" cries the owl, the universe.

Only love converts evil. Only love melts terror.

Mercy melded with desire.

Only in your ancient animal body will you find the God you have, we have all lost, in this pagan pagan clime.

Quebec to Vermont

Autumn in Quebec is past its peak, most of the trees stripped of leaves—those that are left: deep brownish red with blazes of ochre yellow. After we cross the border into Vermont, we see that a rainbow of shades still resides on the mountainsides, not only red and pink and canary and quince but a spectrum of oranges from orange-yellow through sulphur and cadmium to tangerine, reddened orange, and vermillion. These pepper the mountainsides and hills in intricately detailed relief, grove by grove and even tree by single tree, the dead ones providing a soft three-dimensional brush that paints the distance toward Oz.

On the highway from Burlington to Montpelier we recall that this is where we used to live, amid the hills of Plainfield when gold maples of the Seventies swam in a translucent blue sky. Now, a few blocks from where Robin attended Marshplain Elementary, we stay with friends whose house abuts a section of the longest waterfall in Vermont. All night it sings of things we cannot know but want to hear, the signature rush of atonal chimes against rocks and stars, everywhere and nowhere. In the morning the captive brook is a pure god of time, spooling rapids along rocks, whipping up little pockets of spinning foam, and measuring the opulent thread that connects winters and springs unending.

"There's nowhere to move back to, because if you move back, you're either in the lagoon or in the ocean." Anote Tong, president of Kiribati, to the U.N. climate conference in Bali, Indonesia, December 5, 2007.

It is inconvenient for terrestrials to put a value on the future or the planet itself. This item will be in the background for a while, as we continue to languish in our misplaced dramas and ill-begotten occupations.

Secondhand smoke is a metaphor for our entire failure of logic and cosmic etiquette: "I'm not going to alter my lifestyle for you."

Melting villages in the Arctic and disappearing Pacific Ocean islands will be the result of China's and America's secondhand smoke. Global warming—in fact all pollution and consumption of irreplaceable ecosystems—is: "I'm not going to alter my lifestyle for you (even if it kills both of us)." We are now splat in the SHS century.

Overwriting the Text

Sanity

Throughout my adult life, people have said to me, "It's amazing you turned out so well, considering the family you come from." It's a well-intentioned compliment for sure, but it has a kind of hollow ring for me because I didn't do anything. There was never an alternative; the impulse to be normal overrode everything else.

I simply persisted in my stuff, following some innate compass, keeping an unacknowledged allegiance to something, though I can't tell you what it was. I was born with a sort of ballast, so I poked along. I *assumed* I would be okay.

I didn't understand my actions as strategic at the time. It wasn't a tactic and it certainly wasn't clever. I just didn't want to be a victim. That would have been dishonorable. I knew implicitly it would have cost everything.

My determination on this matter trumped all other factors; it is an obduracy that astonishes me even now whenever I run up against it—a mixture of blind faith and pride. I refuse to concede an inch. My will is a fearful thing to countermand. A Jungian astrologer once told me, "You have the kind of loyalty that doesn't just overthrow tribes or nations; it overthrows civilizations."

In subsequent years, through long sieges of anxiety, verging on almost surreal panics, I refused to take psychiatric drugs—sedatives, Xanaxes, or Prozacs—or for that matter even deem myself "sick." To this day my sole medication is the Western standard of living—a serious addiction, to be sure, but beyond my power to ameliorate. I never visited or helped in Africa, or backpacked across Europe, which is what I think I would like to have done, at least for a while out of college. As it was, I didn't even carry out my anthropology fieldwork in a non-Western culture. As much as I wanted to meet Cuna and Ainu medicine men and test myself in their company, I wasn't ready for a break with American life. I lost that capacity somewhere in childhood and will always regret it. A PhD thesis on Maine fishermen sufficed.

Except when assembling paperwork for the military draft in the late Sixties, I rejected diagnosis. There is no solace or alibi in being labeled obsessive compulsive or paranoid verging on schizophrenic, as my childhood shrink did in a letter to the Selective Service—the *coup de grace* in getting me a 4F. Those are just terms of convenience anyway; they're not concrete diseases like polio or pneumonia. To my reckoning they fall within the purview of personal choice, malleable to resolve, either way. My responsibility, my mission has been to repair the damage, at least incipiently so I could live on my own terms.

I understand genetic predisposition to mental illness. I see it unequivocally on my mother's side of the family, apparently passed down through her father, the Rothkrug clan. In her three brothers, all veterans of World War II, it was a steady-state rage with a short fuse. Perhaps the urgency of the battlefield, converting their anxieties into courage, kept them sane. Their mother, a Rothkrug by marriage only, was a shallow, querulous lady. My mother, on the other hand, was the Inquisition.

The "gene" came into its own in my generation: eight of nine siblings and cousins if you count me, running the gamut from suicide, hospitalization, disability, retardation, and permanent medication (at the high end) to chronic fatigue, mild autism, and steady-state anxiety.

I don't have to extrapolate any of this; I feel the stuff in my own nervous system; that is, I experience what I witness in my relatives: charge, instability, intensity, vigilance, low threshold, superstition. I feel like a camera with its iris set at 1.2 or wider. It is not just the amount of data coming in—it is the incompatibility of levels. So I tend toward introversion and social inappropriateness.

I recognize the sensation the moment I awake; it is there in some form all day. In bad periods it can escalate to fear, all the way to full-blown panic. In good times it is fun, a high-energy ride, making the world new and magical.

The charge has no intrinsic shape or manifestation. It is what you make of it: fury, paralysis, terror, red alert, paranoid fantasies, obsessive compulsion, omnipotent grandiosity, retardation—also sensitivity, psychic awareness, childlike innocence, wonder, delight, a portal to other dimensions.

I used to tell my brother: "We were initiated into a sacred lodge, and we can use our powers for either good or destructive ends. Our mother chose the dark side, but what we inherited from her can be negative or beautiful. It can be lethal, and it can be magnificent, but it can't be neither. There is no middle ground." He believed me, but he also deemed it an intruder to battle and defeat. I thought it was a force to yield to and accept, the sword of a higher power. "Like being knighted," I told him. "You might as well try to vanquish electricity."

My daughter Miranda inherited a variant of it. She engages her own demons and tyrannical fantasies. A few years ago she told me, "I know a terrible thing happened once, but only since I am grown up do I realize that it *didn't happen to me.*"

She indicts me for passing it on to her; that is, for transmitting the vibration of the cataclysm. I would have practiced better hygiene if I had been more astute, but I had no such leeway. I was involved in my own narrow getaway, and the drama was still so vivid that I relived it and kept its latency alive.

I wanted my kids to be not only my playmates and disciples but cohorts in an ideal family. I meant well and was sincere, but I was who I was. I came from the people I came from. My parenting, rooted in love, was a bit radioactive. As my stepmother said once of her own children, "I couldn't give them what I didn't have myself." Plus Miranda was so psychic that she couldn't have been quarantined or inoculated.

She has used her bequest to become a keen observer of human nuance, a gifted performer and writer. The Rothkrug fire is not the only tool in her palette, but it is some of how she catches latencies and subtexts, reads secrets telepathically. An innate empath and medium, she tells other people's quirkiest stories. She is also brutally and cruelly frank.

She has invented a vocation whereby author and text, self and other, actor and audience seamlessly switch places. It is an act of genius on her part to go in a socially improvisational direction rather than a cosmic one like my brother and me. That became her remedy, even her coronation—she is not only an exquisite artist but the kind who wins international prizes.

My recent therapist, the only one I ever had who gets it, has told me that of a hundred people in my situation, ninety-nine don't become functional adults. Most either fight back forever like my brother or hide out and develop evasions. They end up loners, hospitalized or on meds. They rarely stay with one partner. "They sabotage relationships," he said. "I know because I see plenty of them. They think they want partners most of all, except they don't. You are lucky. You may suffer disproportionately, but you have walled off your wounds and lead a charmed life otherwise. By all the rules that should not have happened. But you instinctively found a pretty amazing way to survive."

Another bunch of accolades ... but I decline them on the same basis. They belong to the universe. All I did was follow my stars and let the invisible source lead me. When everyone else in the family armed themselves, storming around, I was instinctively self-effacing and did totally fucked-up stuff. They were all such bigshots and tyrants; they never understood how I could let myself be so pathetic, such a spaz. I took the hit for them; I became the local defective and lunatic.

I cried for us when no one else cried for us. I will accept credit for that much. I was willing to be flawed, to be lonely and sad. I was following some sort of guardian star like the Fleetwoods singing, *"I'm Mr. Blue."* When my brother insisted that the point of life was fun and I was losing because I was so sad, I went to our sister's Irish Catholic nurse and put the matter to her: "Isn't the point of life to find your faith?" Somehow I thought to say that at twelve. It wasn't show-offy or faux adult, nor was it an idle piety. In fact, it was so much true to something big and faraway and crucial that tears welled up in me; I felt like someone coming home at last.

She looked at him and then at me, as we restated our respective cases, and then, totally flummoxed, said, "Get out of here, the both a' you with your nonsense." But a twinkle in her eye betrayed where her loyalty lay.

Although I wimped out on many things, I was counterphobic when it counted, charging right at the stuff I had to have, going to battle, as Charles Olson wrote of Enyalion, with my nakedness my only weapon. I presumed survival, I presumed love, I presumed success, I presumed the angels' blessings, despite ghosts that accompanied me all my hours. I made friends with them, as best as either of us could stand. In their company I learned humility; I learned to stay put.

I owe my sanity in large part to Lindy, her presence in my life, her support through the hard times. But then something in me recognized and chose her when I was only nineteen. Something also got me to nineteen, out of my mother's household, pretty much unscathed, at least as far as the big things went: dignity, faith, imagination, joy.

Lindy wasn't obvious. We are hardly peas in a pod, so the decision wasn't a no-brainer. I could have missed her. I could have ended up with someone else or suffered a string of relational disasters from my over-eagerness to have a girlfriend—break-ups with the sorts of terminal regrets that make it hard to get out of bed in the morning.

Lindy is a vivid and dramatic figure, emotionally complicated, unexpected and strong-spoken: a riveting, almost cinematic presence. Much like my mother, she commands attention when she enters a room, but her hauteur is guileless and her heart pure. She has a charisma that is alternately flirtatious and transparent. The merry comedian and cut-up among the three girls in her family, she keeps things light. At the same time, she is earnest and dead serious, with perfectionist standards, and carries almost too much gravitas for her lithe personality and spirit. As someone who looks out for other people, she is the kind of soul that holds families and institutions together. I sometimes joke that she is the most cheerful depressive I know.

I take nothing for granted. For all the complication I generate in my writing, my assignment has been far simpler and more basic: vulnerability, permission to grief, human contact, emotional innocence—the best antidotes to madness, to complexity, to terror and rage. I may invoke strange and spooky worlds, but I don't let them mess with daily life or make me Bohemian. I am supremely ordinary. My Goddard students of the Seventies called me Chard, their gut-reaction nickname for a guy who mixed intellectual web-spinning and academic prerogative with spaced-out malaprops and goofy cosmic monologues. It started as "Reee-chard" and then became just the vegetable. "You may have gone to Amherst," one of them told me, "and have some PhD, but you're as weird and loopy as us."

I enjoy running North Atlantic Books with its financial pressures, vendor bankruptcies, employee meltdowns, wrongful-termination snits and lawsuits, workman's-comp scams, and occasional over-the-top predatory authors; it provides a perfect

arena for conciliating ghosts. Without knowing what I was doing, I turned *Io*, a small literary magazine I started with Lindy in
college, stage by stage into a business now employing twenty-five
people and publishing eighty books a year. I avoided most of the
pitfalls that capsized smarter colleagues and wealthier rivals.

I used the same logic on the publishing that I did on myself:
keep it simple and spare. I learned many of my initial business
methods while doing ethnography with Maine fishermen: "One
for you, one for me, and one for the boat" is a great one for divvy-
ing up revenues. Avoid confrontation; offset other parties' scams
tacitly without either person having to admit a thing. And cut
traps when necessary, your own as well as theirs.

I charted a course like some hedge-fund manager juggling
huge, insane gambles with one another to effect a surprisingly
smooth curve. Pragmatic action in a public sphere is a great
antidote for madness. Practical details are the universe's most
grounding practice. Equanimity is contagious, for external success can be internalized and tapped for courage in confronting
demons within.

When I am overwhelmed, what I draw on for solace is the
notion of "limits." Don't try to defeat those monsters or pretend that they aren't there. Graze inside them. Submit, always
submit.

That is why I stayed close to home. I haven't traveled worth a
damn on my own since I met Lindy forty-four years ago. While
I journeyed a bit in my thirties and forties, I always felt like
an undersea diver with limited oxygen, a homing pigeon sniff-
ing the breeze. Some of this was circumstantial after we moved
to California in 1977, the difference between my comfy native
Northeast and the vast, wide-open West.

Once around 1981 I set out from our home in Richmond,
California, on a three-day road-trip to see Paul Pitchford, my t'ai

chi and meditation teacher at the time, in Moscow, Idaho, where he had recently moved. I crossed the Siskiyous into Oregon at night, took a motel room in Medford—but I couldn't sleep. I couldn't bear the thought of getting up in the morning and continuing into an unknown calculus. The landscape and sky were too big, the road too barren and droll, the distances too great. So I got dressed, threw my pack in the car, and made it back to my own bed before dawn, startling Lindy and surprising the kids at breakfast.

"You got to the middle ford," Paul mused later, "but not the 'pitch ford.'" I never did, but I have to believe there are other ways.

I have sealed off the damage inside me like a moth infestation inside a pod, contained it so that it does not eke into the rest of my life and wreck it. I usually tend to forget that it exists. I drift into minimizing or downgrading the shadow. But every now and then I fall into it or awake to its realm within a dream—utterly vivid and solely real. Its imprimatur, stark figurines and cosmic judgments, are horrific but irrefutable. That's when I know that I am sitting atop a volcano. I think, one way or another, we all are; this entire planet is, not just a geological or meteorological one, but voodoo, big-time. Look at how most creatures behave. Take a step back and appraise the reaction to life. Everyone is possessed and haunted. And only some are antidoting it with a poem or a prayer.

In one recent dream a malefic doctor reamed me open from the inside and condemned me to something more ancient and terrible than death. In another, repeating dream, I am wandering lost on the streets of an unfamiliar city at the edge of an ocean or bay, not knowing who I am. In yet another I am in a courtroom, charged with a murder I don't remember committing, sentenced to "life" by a dour judge, then shackled and taken away by guards, thrown into a cell. And the dream lasts forever. Until I awake.

Even these descriptions do not give a hint of the horror. It seems more real, deeper in some way, than the life I am living. In its nightmare I am told the most alarming, hideous things about myself and the universe. It is not even a nightmare but a nightmare inside a nightmare that ordinary nightmares protect us from. There is no escape, for I contain it all.

Are these dreams from past lives; are they traumas cathected from the time before I had language?

I shall never know or have reason to know.

When I awake, I am amazed to find myself Richard again, safe.

I realize too that the dreams are medicines. For dreaming them, each time I become more, not less, whole.

I understand implicitly that the deep nightmare is what we embrace before we pass out of darkness into a different order of things, till we become ourselves. But no one wants to go there, however wonderful in the end. People try to make it go away, with drugs, alcohol, even shock treatment, lobotomy. Yet it's not excisable like some part of the brain in *Eternal Sunshine of the Spotless Mind*. Memory is not a place; trauma is not a thing. They are implicit. That is, when they occur one place, they occur everywhere: in every hologram radiating forever from a source. They recreate themselves in every experience, changing shape, changing frame of reference, to fit perfectly, subliminally. You can't oblate what you are. And anyway it's your only map home.

I also have never used entheogens. I know what a "bad trip" is, I've had plenty of them unbidden and out of the blue. Maybe someday I will take that journey. For now I am happy, in fact ecstatic, to be sane and of this world. A soft breeze. A starry night. Sunflowers. Lindy, even when we are quarreling. Each day, frankly, is a gift.

Literature

During high school and college I read novelists like Robert Penn Warren, William Faulkner, Claude Bernard, Fyodor Dostoevsky, Saul Bellow. Their stories were wonderful, but the things I marked on the page were the great cosmic passages, epiphanies that seemed to rise above the text (or its fictional narrator) to declare the human mystery.

I gathered these lyricisms and elegies, compositions of words and rhythms that turned into flights of eloquence so rhapsodic they might have been whispered by spirits into ears of mortals. These had the feeling of rock 'n' roll songs amidst highbrow literature, as if Alyosha Karamazov suddenly began to croon "Teenager in Love" to his brother Ivan, or Darl Bundren started snapping his fingers Bobby Darin-like and then broke into "Dream Lover" and "Beyond the Sea."

These flights of ecstatic revelation (see Melville's *Moby Dick* and Faulkner's *Absalom, Absalom!*) and stands of unflinching courage in the face of apocalypse (see Arch Oboler's *Night of the Auk* and Jean-Paul Sartre's *Troubled Sleep*) make up a meta-text beyond all individual books, a ballad sung by life on Earth to the universe.

A neophyte collector of these passages, I tried to emulate them in my own writing. My adolescent novel fragments—*Salty and Sandy*, *The Moon*, *The Cloud*, and *Why Do You Want Me So Quickly?*—are packed with such salvos, some of them magical, most of them overwrought and pretentious. A few of (I hope) the former were transposed into books like *Mars: A Science Fiction Vision* and *New Moon*. Of course, some readers, like my English professors and Catherine Carver from back in my college days, would think all the extracts were wordy and exorbitant—even this text were she alive and persuaded to read it.

My romantic predilections completely frustrated poor Miss Carver, an editor at Viking Press whom I miraculously acquired when I was eighteen—Saul Bellow's editor at the time too—but we came to no good end because of my loyalty to ornate soliloquies over her plots. By valorizing poetry in place of social drama, I never composed the book she wanted, a book she could in good conscience present to her board, let alone publish under the prestigious Viking imprint.

Although I didn't realize it at the time, I was not even trying to write what she was pleading with me to do, what she was sure I could pull off if only I would put my mind to it and stop reading obscure madmen and marginal poets.

I thought I wanted to succeed with her; she was my savior and patron. Instead I ended up spurning Viking and Saul Bellow, hitching my star to those dismissed bards, Charles Olson, Robert Duncan, Diane Wakoski, Gerrit Lansing, Robert Kelly. Their work harbored no serial dramas, no social gossip, only tarot cards, sacred objects, epiphanies. They were reaching for the stars, and love, and the boundaries of Western thought—and that was what I wanted.

This book, my current offering, is not a novel, though it is literary in the fashion of the novels I enjoy. I have written only the panpipes and minor chords, pretty much the sorts of extracts I adored as a boy. I have laid it out stark and plotless. Or the plot is transparent to plot. I have not only written a novel without a story, but I have finally written the entire book, the one that Catherine Carver pleaded with me not to write, all but forbade me.

Fiction is a great form. I remain a devoted reader of it: Nadine Gordimer, Russell Banks, Anita Shreve, Annie Proulx,

Susan Minot, Maryse Condé, Pat Conroy, Don DeLillo among my present favorites. I admire the suspense and riddles, the entangling complications of well-told tales, but I have no talent (or patience) to invent people or paint and furnish their rooms.

Enthusiasms

The accoutrements may get fancier, but the acts don't change, nor do the core passions that drove them. As a teenager I would put a stack of 45s on my victrola and let them drop one by one while I lay on the floor in reverie. In my twenties I made compilation reel-to-reels of my favorite songs for long trips in the car. Now I drag bands from CDs, download from iTunes, and copy my old records onto an iPod, then click on the "shuffle angel" while I prepare dinner or drive to work.

The same obscure 45s into which I snapped plastic yellow adaptors, then transferred to cassettes—"First Anniversary," "Don't Go Home," "Forget Me Not," "Applegreen," "Are You Really Mine"—are now MP3-ed along with Buddhist and Australian chants, Bach and Mozart, reggae and country & western. Yes, I am as much an enthusiast and proselytizer as ever. I want everyone to hear all the songs, all my friends to meet one another. I despise the word "networker," but I am an excessive and shameless practitioner. I keep introducing people to one another, just like at summer camp and then at Phi Psi, our Amherst anti-fraternity, even if I create awkward situations by doing so.

And my heart still beats faster each time my team rallies in the eighth inning or the fourth quarter, even as it did when I was eight, just as it does for those eight-year-olds clapping in the stands, holding their hands over their eyes.

Being Jewish

Being Jewish is the least useful thing about me. It is like being no one. Always has been. Around age nine I charged headlong into a wall and knocked myself unconscious to escape one more day of Hebrew school at Ramaz. I didn't want to be conscripted, by anything. After all, my Hebrew teachers (first at Ramaz, then at Park Avenue Synagogue) had me praying for God to smite the Arabs, and at Purim fair they hung posters of Gamal Nasser and other Egyptian caricatures for dart throwing.* Even a nine-year-old knows there is something wrong with passing this off as religious activity.

The yarmulkes and tallits of my childhood never felt to me like the sacred objects they are: power suits of magicians and shamans. They were more like clown costumes wherein others could ostracize us and laugh. They were yolks to the neuroticism of my family, in fact the entire intense Manhattan subculture, and I wanted to throw them off with the fury of a horse bucking its gaucho. Our Hebrew names likewise condemned us to some sort of kinky Park Avenue exclusivity—mine was Reuven until it was changed to Selig for my Bar Mitzvah.

I never wrapped my body with the tfilim that the rabbi deeded me as his gift (I hid them in the back of the closet until they disappeared). So I lost not only initiation in my own lodge but manhood in any lodge—as I would later learn—in Hopi and Aranda lodges too, for entry to them was not my birthright.

The elders never told me that these totem objects conferred a special view of the universe, a divine cosmos; they never spoke

---

*This was the Fifties. I'd like to think that such activity has stopped. Its blatancy probably has, but I am sure that the attitudes are still there, probably even worse, probably much worse.

of the Alcheringa or sefira, Jewish or otherwise. They never said anything, about anything. Being Jewish was simply an honor and an obligation, but for me those straps of fancy wood were surplus baubles from the shul, a house that already attacked with Proustian waves of garish perfumes and suffocation, with unspeakably dark desires and their repressions.

Likewise, I renounce those pandemic social-event seders that Jewish as well as non-Jewish friends perform like little home musicals with a folk-art theme. I find faux Passover ceremonies unbearable, both for the way in which they remind me of the clannish rituals of my childhood *and* the way in which they are themselves profane parodies of the real service. As little as I appreciate the script assigned to the table by the self-righteous American Haggadah, the boy who sat up on the dais for Pesach at Grossinger's and attended the orthodox seders of the Turetsky clan, cries out, "If you're going to put on the show, at least do the goddamn thing right!"

I don't like the story. I don't like the fact that a mystical devotion to God's creation, to cosmic exile, to suffering in the universe, has been converted into a patriotic opera which is then used as biblical allegory to sell modern-day Israeli politics. Overly precious, desacralized Passover rites load Zionist messages into otherwise humanist rites, so that even liberals end up unintentionally mouthing fascist slogans and intoning war prayers.

The trouble with being Jewish is that you can't just be any old thing; you either have to be better than everyone or uniquely singled out for persecution, or usually—and this is the problem—both. You are God's Chosen People and you are also a hebe and kike, branded with a yellow star by the Nazis, by Hamas, Hezbollah, and neo-Nazi thugs in Idaho and Brooklyn, charged with the entire forged "Protocols of the Elders of Zion" by most of the Muslim world. You are accused of being in league with bogus bankers who spread poverty and modernity, and usur and disinherit innocent children of the Third World. How do you renounce all this *at both levels*, the accusation as well as the complicity? Then you are framed for 9/11, as if you bear collective guilt for behind-the-scenes machinations of some malevolent nerd-king concoction of Woody Allen, Nathan Rothschild, and Henry Kissinger. You can never earn back your honor from the mob, as Daniel Pearl tragically proved—and he did about as well as you can in paying homage to the other guys, their culture and language and causes, right or wrong.

As Jewboy, you get credit for being smart, financially savvy, an automatic bigshot, illustrious beyond your numbers, but you also are automatically a lover of coin, a shylock, a miser, a pornographer, a closet predator (especially of gentiles): the moneychanger in the temple, the one who voted for the crucifixion. You have no street cred whatsoever. That is, you're assumed to have endless dough or access to it, intelligence you never earned, power stolen from others. You owe the world something, and the world owes you everything.

The love-hate relationship between Jews and Blacks, kikes and niggers, tells it all—and *there is* true love and deep animosity on both sides. Mos Def, meet Moishe Pippick. I know—Maccabi, meet Algonquin J. Calhoun.

It is hard enough to be alive without having to be self-consciously Jewish too. It is hard enough to find truths without having to garb them first and foremost in Jewish symbols and decorations, in superstitious ethnic pride. It is hard enough to touch your own humanity without it having to be forever confused with your intrinsic Jewishness. And it's all but impossible to be cool when the only way to stop being uncool is to join Kahane-like gangs and cheer for warplanes with the Star of David on them. It's hard enough to come up with a big-game pitcher without it having to be Sandy Koufax or Alan Greenspan.

"A self-hating Jew" is what an eighty-five-year-old woman from Bethesda called me several years ago. She went through the trouble of tracking me down and phoning me from her retirement home after she selected *Out of Babylon* from its library cart. A lifelong secretary on Wall Street, she was provoked enough by my text to give me an earful: "You're a self-hating Jew, Mr. Grossinger; that's what you are."

But I am proud of Qabalism and the Jewish influences on tarot, Gnosticism, and shamanic alchemy. If we are the chosen people, which we aren't any more than Tibetans or Maoris or Xhosas in their own diasporas, then we should be committing ourselves first to deciphering the esoteric blueprint of the universe, as we have been from those ancient coda leading to the Talmud and Zohar to rabbis like Gershon Scholem, Albert Einstein, and Stan Tenen. Our estate runs the gamut from the ministry of Jesus Christ to Madonna wearing her sefira pins.

I love that a Hebrew Jesus has become the planet's Messiah, that the Zohar leads to Thelemite magic, that Yahweh is also Jehovah and rasta Jah. We are all that—bad-ass and crunk too. I can even live with the fascistically narcissistic plaudits from the Rapture crowd, but only insofar as they get us out of the American pop-culture ghetto and onto the battlefield with the other players.

But forget the Temple Mount and funding for the Occupation of Palestine and so-called Battle of Gog and Magog. The Evangelicals have no more real use for Jews than mediaeval Spaniards did—cannon fodder for their Rapture.

I honor the Yiddish of Isaac Singer and the vaudeville theater. I am forever haunted by those primordial Middle Eastern dirges turned into Irish show-tunes by Yip Harburg and Al Jolson. I understand that Irving Berlin's melodies and Bing Crosby's dreams of a white Christmas are really about neither Yuletide nor snow but something that happened long ago in another place, something that we have totally forgotten and recall now in sentimental kitsch. I claim my Jewish heritage by making this book my own Qabalistic commentary. I rejoice inwardly that Hebes can be minstrels like Bob Dylan and Paul Simon, and I wish I could write such music instead of prose.

I'm just another messed-up whiteboy.

You know the routine, we either transcend our ethnic stereotype or become it.

Being American

The fact that I am an American puts a discount on everything I do. I have not been present at the wars and holocausts or abject poverty of our time. I have not seen relatives and friends raped and slaughtered or had them arrested and disappear. I have not had to collect body parts or bury the dead. I have not had to scrap for food and shelter or freedom. I won the lottery at the get-go. As an American, I have led a privileged, sheltered existence.

So my claim to big words and universal ideas sometimes feels hollow to me, like so much arrogance and imperialism under protective tariff. I have the bogus surety of someone who was brought up in a safe environment, made safe at the expense of just about everyone else, and indoctrinated to succeed. My temerity can lead only to counterfeit masterpieces.

For any of the stuff that I say to mean anything, any of it at all, my privilege and advantage and entitlement have to be handicapped and siphoned off as so much blather obscuring my real message, the part of it I actually live. My articulation otherwise is a pampered luxury.

After all, my craft falls well inside the vast planetary fraud imposed by the West with its elaborate engines of propaganda.

For all my experimentalism and rebellion, at the level of economic and literary prerogative I am an obedient employee. We are all commodity chefs in America, producers of bite-size cultural hegemonies and psychospiritualized tidbits, seasoned for export, preening for international esteem and victory. None of us make art from the bowels and catacombs of the real Earth. We all want to eat the good meals, sleep in the warm, fancy huts, use the technology of dominion, and still charm the beggar and the refugee. We try to be lords and landsmen both. Might as well try to shove that camel through the needle!

The real question is whether I have said anything that can survive the necessary housecleaning and purgation: a dram of heart, a glimmer of spirit. I suppose those who inherit the Earth will tell me, probably not to my face and probably not any time soon. If I have written one song that can be sung honorably by them or in their company, then I am a poet, I have earned my keep.

Spiritual Practice

I have never taken a spiritual teacher or pledged myself to a formal lineage or path. I have learned morsels of t'ai chi, chi gung, craniosacral therapy, Reiki, yoga, and the like, and I have sat meditation on and off, including a few evenings a week for a couple of years in the early Nineties at Empty Gate, a Korean Zendo in Berkeley—but my devoir to any of these regimes is miniscule compared to that of many of my contemporaries, some of whom have committed their lives to guru yoga with the likes of Chögyam Trungpa, Adi Da, Seung Sa Nim, and Chögyal Namkhai Norbu, or at least done Goenka's ten-day Vipassana retreats, or regularly attend workshops in Barre, Massachusetts, or at Spirit Rock.

The writing of stuff like this book fills my head in such a way that practices instantly create text. This is a defect in me, but it is my own church, my charm against the darkness.

I sometimes feel that, whenever life is made into a game with rules—a "right think" that leads to a "right way"—at some profound and intrinsic level I don't buy it. My moment-to-moment awareness is so vibrant, so unpredictable, and shifts so profoundly from one latency to another, I tend to follow it rather than "the method," even though either way all phenomena are beyond explanation or definition. I just don't do any practice long enough for it encompass my experience and transform it *at every level* into ritual and faith.

I should be able to stay silent and patient and listen and take instruction, because these teachers have powerful and profound things to say and do, things that change people's universes. But text continues to distract me from practices and rituals. It imposes an obligation like my need to know the scores of my teams when their games are in play.

Maybe it's also that I sat in classrooms too long, so any imposed situation, no matter how spiritually instructive and benign, feels like confinement. That has sadly become just as true of seminars in craniosacral therapy and Buddhist retreats.

Everything not in the room suddenly seems delicious. I know the drill: make friends with uncomfortable sensations, breathe into them, become whole through experiencing them fully; stop entertaining whims and attitudes and worries. Don't let the monkey mind win. Tame the fucker.

Occasionally I break through into a bigger universe. More often at sessions of spiritual teaching I get antsy, mark the time if a clock is in sight, quarter hour by quarter hour, doling out my attention, playing mind games. I am happy to fly out of there, back on my own recognizance again. Ah, the ecstasy of just the plain old street and its noise and traffic, secular hubbub!

I don't return. Or I do—same difference.

Often I fear I am missing, just about everything.

Number

A friend recently attended a seminar at which he was asked to name his biggest unacknowledged fault and its consequence. He said, "Dishonesty. The result: lack of spiritual growth and real compassion for other people." I began to think about what I would have said, and I realized that a startling amount of my own deceitful and insensitive behavior came from my continual involvement in number games. The more I thought about it during the following days, the more instances came to mind. I was shocked to realize, from little more than auditing my behavior, how absurdly wrong-headed and wrong-hearted I had been in my service to inane and inexplicable computations.

Though I am hardly a big-time player in the usual sense, number has had an odd fascination and tyranny over me. I order too much of my activity by compulsive rooting for the twists and turns of sums, retention of objects for no other reason that to extend their informal, private measurement. I have measured time, distance, money, phone minutes, shelf life; botanical growth, scraps of firewood, bottles of shampoo, bars of soap, miles on cars, pages in books, drying time of liquids and surfaces—anything that can be counted and waged. I keep such tallies idly in my mind—all trivial; all pennywise, poundfoolish. It's like—find me a way to give it a number and apportionment and I am quickly inventing a contest and am frustrated when someone interrupts or interferes. It's a travesty even of real measurement.

Because of such games I find it hard to discard a battery from a TV remote, flashlight, or car; or thoroughly worn windshield-wiper blades, toothbrushes, or old tires; or a pair of shoes with holes and a loose sole; or even paper with one side blank. Discarding something is like losing points, though there is no referee and no final score.

When logged and inventoried, these sterile devotions to mathematical operations turn out to be of startlingly diverse nature and application. I find all sizes and shapes of games, calculi, ledgers, and computations, imposing idle quantifications and fastidious operations on my world, making me hyperconscious and distracting me from more useful activity.

After learning from a local shoe salesman that his computer showed I bought a new pair every thirteen months, I decided to beat my profile. But there is no limit to my inning or closure to my poll. With a good cobbler and a tube of Barge Original All-Purpose Cement I am now at six years and counting. The relatively new pair of vegan Earth shoes I am wearing is one I traded for, so it doesn't count.

This is not a totally conscious, heavy-duty pursuit, just a quiet, contrary predilection. I would toss away my ratty shoes in a second (and the thoughts along with them) if I had to, but the sheer fact that I have sported ripped footwear at work with a sense of accomplishment tells me I am addicted to deeds that, although ecologically justifiable and helpful on my carbon footprint, are not rational, are even absurd.

Once, when the odometer of our newer Subaru approached identical mileage to our older Honda (handed down from Lindy's mother), I took to selecting my vehicle for driving on the basis of getting the numbers even. I tried in a low-grade sort of way (and furtively) to manipulate use and even got mildly upset whenever Lindy took the "wrong" car, though I could never admit my real reason. It was a relief finally to give the Honda to our daughter.

It was also a deliverance a few weeks ago when I found a dish of rubber bands melted in the sun, so I could throw them out.

Recently Maine passed Vermont as the number-three state in terms of my lifetime days spent in it, after California and New York, ahead of Massachusetts and Michigan. Of course, none of this is "official"; none of it can really be tallied—so there is always a reason for another recount. By the time I get to number ten, somewhere around Washington or Pennsylvania or Texas, I am parsing weeks. At number twenty, Alaska or Louisiana or Nebraska, I am trying to count single days decades ago.

This endless undeclared low-grade puzzle recalls a high-school diversion among a bunch of us—getting a bus transfer and racing each other to link the consecutive numerals on it by addition, subtraction, multiplication, and division to come out to ten. But why ten and why care?

In fact I don't care about any of this, but that doesn't mean I don't do it. I do it and then I drop it. I play the game and forget it, or maybe I don't forget it, but it loses its hold. There is no hall of records, no spreadsheet of wins and loss, no bottom line. I'm not anywhere close to the Dustin Hoffman character in *Rain Man*, who kept detailed scoresheets of random events, but he marks the general territory—beware!

These days I have a formula for when I want something to be over, like a long plane flight. I have calculated that each minute can count double because it is a minute consumed as well as a minute less in the future. For instance, if I arrive at the airport at eleven, take off at one PM, and, if the flight is scheduled to land at seven (in the time zone in which I started), then two hours into the flight, it will be as long to get there as it is from checking in my baggage to the present. An hour later I will have gained two whole hours; it will be as long to get there as it is, looking back, to taking off. An hour after that, looking forward to landing will be the same as looking back to a point two hours into the flight.

During boring classes in college and graduate school, I enacted tournaments with page numbers in books, using even and odd sides as home and away fields, and divisibility into my lucky-number twelve as the means of drafting two teams—all supposedly to make the time go faster. There were great streaks by my "1, 2, 3, 4, 6" team, but I have forgotten all of them.

There were also innumerable matches between "l" and "t" based on their relative frequency on a page or document like a menu, playbill, or ad. "T" is far and away the more frequent letter in English, so it almost always won big; in fact, the "goal" became to keep the margin at less than by two to one. But "l" is the twelfth letter in the alphabet and the underdog, hence my rooting favorite, and there were the occasional menus with enough lemons and melons or "cold jellied fishballs" and the like, or casts with sufficient "Williams," Llewellyns," and "Lillies," to make for a stirring "l" victory. "L" could never win on a standard document because of the copious "the's" and "to's," but it stood a fighting chance on any sort of list.

In the Seventies when my father's hotel was still in business and I had access to its unmetered company pump, I used to almost run out of gas getting there from Vermont, so as to come closest to the maximum amount of free gas. Why enter "free-gas land" with anything more than a dribble in the tank?

I even began taking a gas can on our return so as to get bonus points. I was shocked out of this farce when the cylinder leaked into the slot around its rim and Lindy lit a cigarette while driving. The fact that she was smoking shows how long ago it was—so you know how few cents gas cost. The fumes could have ignited; we could have been blown up—I was risking our lives and our kids' lives over, say, five dollars. But it wasn't five dollars; it was some damnable abstract magnitude beyond boundary or quota. It was the mellow glow of triumph over entropy and its neg algebra, a trophy that was as vapid as it was ephemeral, yet pleasurable and reassuring nonetheless.

It is now mostly a knee-jerk reaction, an empty, niggling habit I can't quite shake:

Are you going to another second-hand store? You already have too many clothes you never wear.

Don't buy any more butter (or eggs or bread or whatever); we won't use it up before it goes bad (or before we leave town).

Don't buy wine for the party. No one drinks it anyway. Plus people will bring wine; they always do. We'll just have lots of half-drunk bottles to dump.

Don't start the car before you put your seat belt on. You're wasting gas.

Don't speed up when you're coming to a red light.

Don't turn on the outside lights; it wastes electricity.

Who cares about any of this? I certainly don't. Yet for some reason I'm the one keeping score and hoarding points. The money is scant beyond meaningless and, by comparison, squandered in ludicrously larger amounts elsewhere. Meanwhile the cost in good will and good feeling is immeasurable. Lindy tells me that she and Miranda snuck department-store bags into the house during M's childhood so that I wouldn't see them. I am mortified to learn this now, like having some presumedly private vice aired on national television. I didn't mind what they bought; in fact, I loved that they enjoyed getting stuff— yet I still did the dance of the grinch. Why? Why, damnit, why?

Why get every last can lid into the recycling containers? Why squeeze every last globule out of the toothpaste tube, use the same razor blade for months, wear shirts and pants down to bare thread until I am an embarrassment? Why feel a squiggle of excitement when a houseguest polishes off a neglected jar of nut butter or jam that we have tired of, such that it resounds like a goal or a run-scoring double? What's wrong with simply having food available that might not get eaten? Relax, baby. If some of it goes bad, it is not a sin or a tragedy. Why should it mean that I lose?

Who am I serving? Who enlisted me? Where's the game? What's the payoff?

Why ever—ever!—set this compulsion above human decency or considerateness or make the score more important than how other people feel and whether they consider me someone who has the right priorities and can be relied on? Why lose the bigger picture over attachment to some arbitrary system? I'm not that obtuse or dumb. Yet, as I said, I have been a player—a small-time fussy, beady-eyed player, grasping my endless cards as they shuffle in daily algorithms, outwitting my imaginary opponent, throwing phantom dice.

Two opposite moods bracketed my childhood: the game and its antipode. One was sordid and fatuous; the other generous and expansive. The first was a prison, albeit self-imposed; the second was my slaphappy, elating jailbreaks.

I remember during eighth grade keeping a running ledger of how much money I had, writing the new amount on a line under the old one, such that, for instance, if I found a penny on the sidewalk, I got to cross out $30.16 and write in $30.17. This became such a ritual that, when I needed to pick up booklets for a school project at the Philippine embassy on Broadway, I decided to walk instead of take the subway. Only after some forty blocks did I realize I was nowhere close, so I stopped at my stepfather's office and got change for the bus. I had taken none along because I didn't want to go backward on my sheet.

Conversely, I would abdicate with gleeful defiance. In sixth grade, moments after completing a bubble-gum card set, I dashed ahead of my friends, dropping single cards like crumbs for pigeons, for them to pick up and keep as they followed in astonishment. After I had spent a year collecting it, I gave the whole series away in fifteen minutes.

I would also suddenly crumple my financial tally-sheet, shoot it at the far trash can, and splurge on cupcake and ice-cream parties for my brother and sister.

Once, I deposited my whole cache in a blind beggar's cup. And started over the next day.

Those are the gestures that made a difference, that still make a difference.

Smash the compulsion! Be totally lavish! I don't need the money. I don't need your stupid zero-sum game.

I'm pretty good at the grandiose gestures, not so good on the menial daily stuff. I am still always surveying or gauging something: bananas turning brown, pears getting soft, water-filter life, bits of foil and bottlecaps in the mulch pile, dollops of vegetable matter from plates (each morsel a potential grain of soil). I am plucking individual grains of rice, quinoa, and even tinier ones of amaranth into jars when they spill during the transfer from bags and yet scraping cooked gobs of them off plates into the mulch pail.

The stuff I am trying to hoard, at the same time I am trying to give it away, so it becomes crazy-making.

But I will say this in my defense: I don't *ever* gamble or play for real, and in the end I renounce the game in the nick of time, barely. I divert most of my obsessive thought these days into the teams I root for: the Mets, the Jets, the Nets, and the

Ottawa Senators.* Agreed: it would be better if I didn't play. Much better! Just think of all the stuff I could do with the time and energy. Just imagine how much nicer a person I'd be.

The realization that none of it really matters lies at the heart of my business strategy. I will make a ridiculous, imbalanced book contract if that's what the other person is insisting on! I break the tyranny of number and renounce the competition at its highest stakes. Some people take advantage of me, but that's on their karma, just like even making this comment is on my karma now.

Self-important as this might sound, I want a publishing company that serves the consciousness from which the books arise, that returns the surplus to its constituency instead churning it into the coffers of owners and shareholders. I want to cast my lot finally with the kid who tossed his cards in the air. This is North Atlantic's legacy.

---

*There used to be a whole piece in this book about rooting for teams, but I took it out to comprise the last chapter ("The Ultimate Game," pp. 289–292) of another book, *The New York Mets: Ethnography, Myth, and Subtext*, North Atlantic Books, 2007. Here I will borrow back its key conceit: "As much as a vehicle of ancient tribal loyalty, games are for me a container for the primitive rage of my childhood, gestated in a family that was only *against* things, never for anyone, that hated more than loved, that wished ill on others routinely. They experienced clandestine joy at another's failure or demise, precisely what a fan does every day. They competed so hard that they cannibalized their own members without knowing it.... The radiation of that has to go somewhere, be stored in some form, has to be kept smoldering in a safe vessel through its half-life, because otherwise it would get out and contaminate everything, namely the rest of my life."

I am not there yet, but I am trying and I know the difference between that and not. I have friends who hoard big-time and for real. It's apparently not just a game to them because they never quit, never relent, and are decent only when they want to appear generous and magnanimous.

They must imagine they are keeping these acts secret, but they ring out as blatantly as their vocal sounds and styles of clothing. I see the collective price that greed exacts, in faces and bodies, different in each case but static and humorless always. Control freaks, these people can't take a joke. They do not know how to put a limit on their own acquisitiveness and opportunism. They don't need the money, but they need the game. They are desperate to be rescued from it, and they are just as stubborn to play it to the death. They have complicated, self-justifying rationales. They have forgotten that it is just a game.

They are no longer friends. (But, hey bigshot, while you're at it, heal thyself!)

I have other friends, like the guy who told the story of the workshop that opens this piece, who once played for keeps, somehow got the message, and broke free. Are they ever happy and beautiful now!

Marriage

My marriage to Lindy is the central event of my life, and it has been with me so long that I tend to forget its origins or even that it has an origin. I forget that Lindy has been with me as long as I have been with her.

We were an unlikely couple at nineteen. She was a sophisticated Colorado beauty, generally acknowledged prettiest girl in the Smith freshman picture book of our year. Her portrait beamed clear eyes, self-confidence, and a sophisticated smile. I had barely dated in high school and was younger than my

age. If she was number one in her class book, I was hypothetically near the bottom of the Amherst folio, a bashful kid from
New York City, trying to make myself invisible to the camera
(though I doubt that girls ranked our "pinups" the way we did
theirs).

By the rules of the game we never should have met. It was
a Freddie Prinze, Jr./Rachael Leigh Cook high-school movie, a
Steve Buscemi/Thora Birch romance: "Back to the Future," com-
moner and prom queen. We had our first date early sophomore
year, orchestrated by a "lady's man" kind of guy with whom she
went out during freshman year. He lived across the hall from me
and was using me to reconnect with her, though I didn't grok
his motive at the time. He picked me as his unsuspecting go-
between because she and I were both writers.

Once we began hanging out, we bonded. For some inexplicable reason that was not obvious on the surface we were an
emotional and intellectual match from the beginning—partners,
adversaries, interlocking puzzle pieces—though we split and re-
united numerous times before finally sticking senior year. Even
if we had wanted—and we didn't but almost did—we couldn't
shake free of each other. Beyond roles and appearances, we grew
into a couple.

I still remember how unlikely we were at the beginning.
Neither of our parents wanted the marriage. Both sets assumed
they could easily block us or talk their ward out of it, or, failing that, we would fall apart in a matter of months. My father
wanted me to marry someone Jewish, on principle; her parents
wanted someone Protestant, more conventional, no long, messy
hair, and most of all, with financial prospects.

During our second Thanksgiving Lindy and I traveled to visit
her godfather, the poet John Ciardi, in New Jersey and, as we

came in the door, he said something like, "Well, my faith is restored in the hearts of men."

But what did that mean? Lindy was hardly lacking in suitors, quite the opposite. And I was just her Platonic companion then.

In his eyes somehow I was an appropriate-looking boyfriend. I passed as a partner for his lovely god-daughter. The comment stays with me because it didn't quite fit back then and, in not fitting, contained a prophecy.

This notion of Lindy and me as an implausible couple has taken on fresh drama after forty-four years. Seeing us through outsider's eyes anew, I supply the imaginary lines of the time, "Those two'll go to dinner once and never see each other again. She'll marry a wealthy Denver lawyer, and he'll become a hippie poet."

So what happened? How did I get here, live this life as her partner? Am I experiencing an alternate reality, the parallel universe in which Lindy and Rich found each other and made it work?

The truth is, we *were* alike even then, pulling each other across the divide on either side of which we were born. It wasn't just Denver and New York, Episcopalian and Jewish. Her "modern jazz quartet"/Simone de Beauvoir *savoir faire* notwithstanding, she didn't want to lose her connection to her girlhood and, as much as I was drawn to staying boyish, I also wanted to be a man. While I reinforced her rebellious, artistic side, the avant-garde poet under the would-be debutante, she reinforced my straight side, the guy who wanted to be an ordinary householder and citizen despite his nonconformist, anti-social style.

When I rehearsed a mild version of this for our son Robin one evening on the way out the door after babysitting Leo— "Isn't it amazing Lindy and I actually got together, we were so improbable a couple?"—his response was blasé: "Yeah, but it worked out." Even more than blasé—I realize that for his whole life we are the parents, the dyad that was there, Lindy and Rich, at the beginning of time. That's the way the world looked to him and our daughter, not like two people from different universes and picture books but an archetypal pairing like Adam and Eve. They trusted us implicitly and with touching innocence. We weren't imposters. We were family.

I see our event annealed into fact in their bodies and faces. It is longer guesswork or speculation. As Robert Kelly said, "Miranda somehow manages to look exactly like both of you, you who don't the least bit look like each other. Looking at her face is like that gestalt trick—sometimes I see R, sometimes L. But from the back of the auditorium one Annandale afternoon I saw you both, your alchemical blend." He named it: marriage is alchemy.

Esoterica

I am struck by the esoteric nature of just about everything.

Lately, as I do my final passes over this text, I see the many streams in it: the asking and re-asking of the cosmic riddle, the exploration into the nature of biological existence (e.g. "waking life"), my reconciliation with existence in the shadow of death, the epistemology of creation itself, outrage at the present political hubris, and the overwriting of my own metachronology.

By "overwriting the text," I mean finding and interrogating a baseline—the things I do and am, routines and explanations that have been indoctrinated so thoroughly that I know them automatically and comply without considering their source, let alone their implications, let alone whether their claim is legitimate. They are what I accept as autobiography instead of renouncing as subversive narrative. I can only guess at the reasons, but the guesses are part of the machinery of obedience. My confessional storyline with its neo-Lacanian denouements not only masquerades as "life" but, by imitating, becomes.

First-order motives resist smoking out because, in their most explicit form—the only one that matters—they embarrass me, they throw down my pride. In their place I have grafted a false candor, a disingenuous anti-heroic, heroic caper. The goal of overwriting it is to break its cycle of narcissism and justification. By telling stories, I turn them into different stories.

Everyone knows, without it being stated, that a literary text depends on another narrative of which it is the hieroglyph. Every day I write toward an unknowable "real" while I obscure another real, the conventional activity of my American dossier. The "overwritten" plot, which I have to sift out of the drone of internal monologue, is my testimony, the "bardo" book its orphic summary and imaginal transformation.

For all of us, the exercise of unbosoming mundane history disguises cosmic life. Our psychiatric transcript may be exhaustive to a fault, even guileless, but it is just collected gossip.

The idiosyncrasy of my voice, the nuances of style and rhythm that will not fit into ordinary reference, leave their own trail. At the end of the day—every day and all days—only the hermetic text has integrity; only it outlives my life as time outlives me. The rest is slander.

Yet it is that text I am now trying to overwrite—but here is the rub: I am trying to overwrite it not to inflate my faux honesty as if some *real* true story, but to make a disclosure that itself is delphic. In order to incriminate myself, of course first I have to find a crime. But I don't want to confess some grandiose trespass or string of foibles and gaffes with disingenuous humility; I want to bear witness, even in such trite psychobabble, to the galactic picture, beyond America, beyond Earth: our compass and statute of "being."

This might also be "overwriting" of the other, banal sort—not truly forthright but cloying and narcissistic. I worry about that;

I do, every word of the way. In "writing over" the text, am I also overwriting it? Should I have called it "hypertext" instead? Or would that have been further solipsism and inflation? Isn't it really "hypotext"?

The other thing I see in *Bardo*, after the fact, is that I have imbedded the perennial discourse regarding "good and evil." Without installing it as my central theme, I have come back to it, consciously and unconsciously, overtly and subliminally, again and again. I have spoken to issues that Thomas Aquinas and Saint Augustine raised initially in Western literature, though their *summa theological*, their city of God and nomenclature of original sin hearken back to the Bible and Genesis. What exactly was the object Adam ate, metaphorically deemed an apple; what constituted its forbidden knowledge and, most crucially, is it still under interdict?

The answer to the last item has got to be yes and no both for, while we have scored much forbidden knowledge, we cannot *ever know what is forbidden for us to know*. That is the real mystery of the arbor in Eden, and it was the mystery that Patricia Fox taught in our yoga class when she asked us to look behind our knees, e.g. in the concealed nodes and slots of our own body-minds.

The tantric secret of our bodies is the clue to morality in the universe, to purity and impurity, cruelty and compassion, to the *quinquae viae* of man and beast. Hegel and Kant, Kierkegaard and Nietzsche (as well as Hannah Arendt, Martin Buber, and Peter Singer latterly) continue to address Aquinas and Augustine in a timeless seminar, as Western civilization oversees a backdoor discussion of good and evil and their implicit dualism, leading (by the way) to its strident and inevitable clashes with both Communism and Islam.

With Hinduism and Buddhism are now in the mix, we are conducting an East-West inquiry into the nature of God and his creation—infinity, omniscience, grace, freedom, but also divine revelation, karma, and the Tao.

I am in the middle of that not because I am a scholar of these things (I haven't read Aquinas since high school) but because the conflict of good and evil and of karma versus dualism is everywhere, like the background vibration of the universe itself. What was forbidden in the Garden and behind our knees is spuriously revealed in the media at large, as well as by yogis, zen masters, and Dzogchen teachers, only to be concealed in a different way. Because it cannot be revealed, because the more it is divulged and exposed and made blatant in instruction manuals and five-star headlines, the less explicit and available it actually is. It knows how to hide within its name and shape. Yet it is the only thing worth our time and trouble, even now.

Beyond Manichaean and Gnostic and Albigensian and Waldensian heresies, there is the question anew—always anew—of the existence of God, of the role of faith, in a universe that is coming asunder from colliding galaxies to genocides and shelling of civilians to sodomy and torture and the march of child armies.

What is the indivisible secret we are being led away from and to?

The root of evil? The possibility of knowing and thereby refuting Satan and finally driving him out of creation? Disembodied consciousness? Discourse with the dead? The motive behind creation?

My story is a little one, dwarfed many times over by these vast philosophies and concerns. And yet I am in the midst of them by dint of my birth and time in the world and its global culture, and I have come to feel that I am being led on a pilgrimage by forces far beyond my ken. From the vulgar, violent family I got born into, by choice or by lot, and my New York City heritage with its baseball teams and psychoanalysts, to my first tarot deck and early prose, to my throwing in with Lindy and our literary and professional collaboration, something else has been in control.

There were so many crossroads for North Atlantic Books at which I almost stopped, at which I meant to stop, especially in the early years: after the first issue of *Io*, after graduating from college, after the third issue when the money ran out (but then Robert Kelly submitted his "Alchemical Journal," so we had to go on), after moving to California, after the grant funding switched to "presses of color" only.

Since then, innumerable other events have brought us amazing authors and editors and workers but also imbroglios, sociopaths, and epic betrayals, each of which has leapfrogged us into the unforeseeable next phase of evolution, our apostate authors and staff as much as true-blue ones. Even the single worst disaster in our history—the bankruptcy of our distributor and main vendor, Publishers Group West, last December (2006), at a time when it owed us almost $2 million—turned out to be a karmic blessing that overshadowed the debt.

On the same dark Friday (December 29) that Chapter 11 was declared by Advanced Marketing Systems, PGW's parent company, I received Mark Borax's manuscript *2012*. At the time, I thought it was the last thing I wanted to see, since I had not liked it the first time and had given him a near impossible protocol for its rehabilitation—plus we were now without cashflow. But *2012* was the esoteric guise of the bankruptcy, its shadow ushering us into a new literature of planetary reincarnation. That playbill would soon feature the late Richard Ireland, Cullen Dorn with his twice-born son, Mark Ireland with his "soul shift," Robert Phoenix with his renegade soundwaves, David "Avocado" Wolfe with his galactic cliffhanger and "best day ever," Patricia Cori with her *Cosmos of Soul* and *No More Secrets, No More*

Lies. It would be a "reunion on the rainbow bridge," an "angel at Auschwitz," a "hierophant on 100th Street."

The bankruptcy opened a fresh path, as it led to a wave of systemic changes but, most of all, it issued the blatant warning that this whole thing could be taken away in an instant—so do what has to be done, now!

No matter the crisis and quagmire it seemed to be at the time, the default was an incalculable gift. Here is the amazing part: even when it happened, I actually considered the possibility it was more karmic than catastrophic, and I preached that lesson to our authors and staff; yet I didn't believe it. I lapsed into martyrdom. I whined and vexed and griped. I looked for saviors and white knights instead of keeping the faith.

Even though I preached affirmations and hailed the "karmic opportunity," I didn't honor the bankruptcy. Only a tiny part of me saw the flower in the marsh, until it was too lotusy to ignore.

Ten months later we ended up selling our debt to a liquidity firm for most of its face value. Wow, can the gods be nice when they want to!

I am reminded of a day in 1999, September 25th, the day our son got married. Lindy and I had different errands in San Francisco that afternoon, so we drove separately to the wedding, and each of us had the same experience.

Headed west through San Francisco, I encountered a setting sun so bright and directly in my eyes that I had to pull over. Many other cars did the same, the movement of traffic all but ceasing for about twenty minutes. I was never so blinded while driving, and not again until today's sun above the Berkeley Farmer's Market jogged my memory.

Back then I didn't consider the wedding-day episode in esoteric terms, but now I do: When you are raising kids, you cannot see their real lives or what will become of them. You are blinded by the future, but it is not the blinding of a bright light; it is the blinding of an invisible screen such that you stare right at what you cannot see. You see your children; yet their secular figures and actions mask everything.

The sun on the day of Robin and Erica's wedding was a cosmic beacon at the cusp, 1999 itself a mystery date, the end of the millennium, telling us that the sphinx was unraveling and, though I was—we all were, and are—driving right into it, we could not see any of it. It is the crypt of what we have done by living, by requiring a world beyond us; it is what will happen despite and because of us.

The sun said, "You are blinded, but you were always blinded. I am here to stop you, to remind you, that what you are going to, this wedding, you will not understand and will not be able to see. But fear not. What cannot be revealed is what must not be revealed, for it *has to happen*. It is the edge along which your life and your generation and your brief universe forms. By living, you are revealing. Everything is wrong—and everything is as it should be."

That day the sun was so bright and impassable it was shocking. I simply couldn't see over the hill. I was halted right there, a brilliant occult obstacle set before me, like a migraine aura of the whole world.

I sat in the car alone, imagining that, of all absurd things, because of the sun I was going to miss the wedding of our son.

The writing is on the wall, but that is exactly the point: only when it is too late finally is it not too late.

Eight years later, I begin to see.

Life

"Bardo of Waking Life" contains an implicit proposition. I am asking: what do I—or any of us—do? What makes this real?

When I inventory my days on Earth, a medley of simple but profound activities rules the roost: grocery shopping, brushing my teeth, eating because I am hungry, peeing, shitting, washing, exploring thoughts and bodily sensations, morphing from private to public life and back, strategizing the publishing and selling of books, following my sports teams, watching their games on TV, lying down in bed when it is late or I am tired, sleeping, watching movies, consuming sweets, cleaning and tidying the house, hanging out with Lindy, running the wash, driving cars, taking cars to be serviced, sprinting (just for the hell of it), napping, getting dressed, getting undressed, waiting on line, waiting idly, talking on the phone, daydreaming, being outraged at others' behavior, scanning political and cultural terrains, rooting, reading and skimming (books, newspapers, magazines, online), checking out the weather and dressing for it, planting in soil, handling and managing money, thinking about money, listening to music, singing or making noise like singing, facing my mortality, recalling the past, writing letters (emails these days), reading the mail in my inbox, contemplating great literature and films, rehashing plots of movies and novels, looking at art, witnessing the natural aesthetics of the world, feeling nostalgia, going into forest, weeding the garden, getting lost and trying to find my way, taking a hot bath or shower, shopping for clothes, shopping for groceries, shopping for utensils, owning machines, owning fancy objects, operating electronic gadgets, eating at restaurants, trying to fix what is broken or run-down, planning road trips and plane trips, being in transit and traveling, hanging out with friends and family, taking a subway (or monorail or tram), going by taxi, riding the bus, getting my hair cut, attending social events, paying bills, doing taxes, taking care of my body, writing, pontificating, regaling with stories, recounting the day, catching up with an acquaintance, looking at the sky, dealing with illness (seeing an MD, acupuncturist, cranial therapist, or herbalist), riding my bike, being in the audience at concerts or plays, finding a trail and hiking (in Maine), kayaking and swimming (in Maine), and so on.

There are other things I used to do: sitting in classrooms (grade school, high school, Amherst, University of Michigan), studying, memorizing, writing papers, taking tests, playing baseball, playing tennis, playing hockey, learning to dance, speedskating, going to parties, dating, doing the fox trot and lindy hop, playing board games, playing pranks, playing cards, throwing darts, shoveling snow, hiding, making a snowman, throwing snowballs, shepherding around my kids, playing with my kids, relating obligatorily to elders, applying for teaching jobs, teaching courses.

Some things just end and are seamlessly replaced, as we cross the watches of time.

While public and private rosters go on indefinitely, the point is not the items; it is, as my friend Andrew put it, that we have to be doing something. And these are not real acts anyway, just tags. What stands out, as I compile their index, is how each of the purported activities is automatic and taken for granted because it is metabolic or part of the symbolic maze into which I was born. Either way, there is nothing to replace it but raw time.

Bland and self-evident, each act comes right out of the operating manual and is cultural even when unadulterated because there is no wilderness we can broach without imposing our symbology. Even what is raw is cooked. Even the unspeakable is spoken, and the unthinkable is somehow proposed and undertaken.

Every act, though practical or recreational, has a subtle aspect too, an internalizing characteristic that makes it a bottomlessly complex phenomenology. Strung together in aggregate chains, our deeds compose a body-mind in space-time. Their reality and *raison* are not individual but collective; each derives its rationale from its integration with the rest and the emergent belief system that gathers and attaches them. That alone turns animals into people, sounds into language, dinner into culture, action into style. Outside such a network, we spill ridiculous gestures into an empty universe.

Other primal Earth acts are for all intent and purposes absent from my ledger: hunting for food, engaging in intensive agriculture, doing blue-collar labor, working manually hours at a time, toiling in a sweatshop, cutting down rain forest, patriarching a big family, getting tattoos, deserting a household, servicing large machines, going to sea, fighting for survival, making clothing, soldiering, being forced into prostitution, engaging in weapons training, dissenting violently from the government, being incarcerated, drinking hard liquor, shooting up, sleeping on the street, fleeing warfare, painting my face, living in makeshift structures in refugee camps, dealing with the murder of loved ones, enduring tropical heat, starving, enduring Arctic cold, gambling, dieting, being physically handicapped, having malaria or dysentery.

Yet these acts engage and dominate much of the world's population. Not only are they more fundamental to life on Earth than just about all of what I do, they provide the majority of civilizational rubrics and coercions in whose furlough I exist and by whose privilege alone I have leisure and leeway to do my things.

My life is not entirely grounded, or is grounded in semblance and guise. Other people's lives, and in many cases their suffering, make my activities possible. They form the real arena, the one that cannot be evaded in the end, the one that lurks over all my flimsy sanctuaries and triumphs.

This basis cannot be minimized or overlooked. I am floating above a harsh planet in some gratis metaphorical realm and, for all my earnestness and commitment to the real, my posturing and rogering back, I am buffered from the conditions here; thus have the leisure to write this book.

A white native of Zimbabwe describes flight from his beleaguered country: "As we soar away into a crisp, cloudless sky, I feel the profound guilt of those who can escape.... The marchers for democracy are being shot at and teargassed, and I am flying away from it all. A nation is bleeding while I sit here cosseted with my baked trout and crispy bacon, my flute of Laurent-Perrier champagne, my choice of movies and my hot face towel...."*

It is a mystery how lived and unlived milieus card and separate. What thin lens of destiny or decision sunders one lifestream from another? What grants us happiness or misery? How do disparate grids, orchestrated by our relative attentions and inattentions, go together to become precisely who we are?

Other activities break with the reigning cultural matrix, or at least blow it off: running with a gang, raiding with an irregular army, committing genocide from a camel, selling crack, demanding protection money from shopkeepers, committing body and mind to jihad, dueling with guns, shooting random victims, detonating belts of explosives on buses or in markets, planning guerrilla missions, planting improvised explosive devices, talking shit, plotting murder, killing someone or other, robbing, torturing, kidnapping.

Some people intend to get out of the box, prove that the box is a sham and can be smashed; that they can do what they want,

---

*Peter Godwin, *When a Crocodile Eats the Sun: A Memoir of Africa*, Little, Brown, 2007.

whatever that is. Gangstas and hardcore rappers, al-Qaeda faithful and suicide bombers at large are not held in check by language or precedent or standard ethics. The whole point for them is *not* to obey, anything … in order to see what is hard and real and what is a convention and a scarecrow. Much of civilization is façade, so it's "fuck you, bitch!"; so it's "strap on those nitrates and good to go."

Would they marry and make domestic lives and raise children and die in peace if they could? Are they radicalized solely by foreign occupation and economic oppression? Or are their whole purpose and reason to bust the neon zodiac and expose a world that is flaunt and show?

They do not want education, they do not want reconciliation, and they do not want friendship; they do not want love. They would not even use our words or currency if they didn't have to. It is too late for half measures, and anyway that's not their job. Their lives are forfeit, so why even bother to obey those lame-ass red and green signals, except that, if you don't, you might crash on your way to a performance.

Then there are oligarchs and movie stars who carry out large-scale corporate, industrial, military, and political operations whereby they impose their requisites on neighborhoods and control the circumstances of millions. So far as we know, there is no limit on the exponent of goods or authority or adulation they covet.

Guys and gals, at grand and petty levels, stockpile objects and opportunities. They maximize property, wealth, power, fame, charisma, position, prestige, skills, awards, wit, sarcasm, fun, sex, martyrdom. Opportunism pleads the status of an instinct or primary drive; yet unexamined accumulation is duly parodied by the 1980s bumpersticker "He Who Dies With the Most Toys Wins." The rule is actually the opposite: Toys and victories undermine, not enhance bliss. Anything that we want too much or struggle too desperately to hold on to, is already our demise.

Remember Lord Acton's homily: "Power tends to corrupt, and absolute power corrupts absolutely." This is true of everything: property corrupts; charisma corrupts; humor corrupts; fun corrupts—absolute stuff corrupts absolutely.

We live in a hierarchy of domains like concentric rings setting our priorities. Before anything else can happen, we must secure physical life—food, clothing, shelter, security from attack—a short list that is the sole mission of animal life on Earth and was the reigning agenda of our species until recently. Creatures can't take the next, more abstract step before they are convinced that they will survive another nightdrop, wake to another glorious sunburst.

For most, the emotional realm is second. We are made up of powerfully felt responses—some of them quite desperate and extreme—as well as attempts to bring instincts and emotions under control. A human usually has to establish a stable emotional paradigm before professional, artistic, and spiritual enterprises can be initiated. If one's feelings are in turmoil, that maelstrom dominates everything. Disturbances like fear, despair, rage, and loneliness swamp subtler moods and abort or erode thoughts and acts. You can't do *anything* while afraid or depressed, while yearning for something that's not happening. Stuff that usually brings a modicum of pleasure becomes dreary or barren. Everything vitiates and flattens out.

Yet when we float in a serene emotional sea, the merest dollop can be ecstatic. That is the covert goal of all human activity: calm and pleasure. Most things people do belie the ostensible docket.

472

We exist, like any creature in the universe, to sustain the simple vibration of our body, the high-frequency background hum of our existence—the flow of sentience through our neurons, consciousness through our ganglia.

We are the sheer pleasure or discomfort of existence, amounting in the end to pleasure because the alternative is nonexistence, the end of mind-body activity. The myriad deeds and games and meals and accomplishments and material objects and tasks add up finally to proprioception of existence, the mega-act of making ourselves credible.

And it occurs during the shockingly brief time in which we are stuffed into this vivid hologram, as portentous input is loaded—not only loaded but loaded continuously—into an unsuspecting and naïve egoic system.

In 1977 somatic therapist Stanley Keleman told me, "The shape of my life emerges, it is not something I plan.... The human being is a process, a series of biological events that have learned and transmitted very circumscribed things, to translate into action, translations which then reflect the quality and quantity of the process by which we create a life, a bodily life, a lifestyle, and perpetuate it, or not."

I say "told me" because I was taking dictation from him for a series of articles he was compiling into book form. I was helping him articulate his arguments. It was a freelance job before our publishing company was viable enough to pay even one salary. He said, "The human condition is situational or relativistic. The human being is capable of perceiving many levels of reality, many levels of his internal environment, his body, depending on where he's located in his life.... The continuum of existence we experience has no discrete beginning."

Everything, from flossing teeth to walking nowhere to simply looking and feeling and hearing, go together to shape this minded and embodied cellular state. It is its own fact, its own reason for being, even for those involved in gloomy things or placed in painful and grievous circumstances.

Life makes its own explanation. Each of us is a biological unfolding, like an amoeba, whatever spiritual and metaphysical aspects lurk under the manifestation and its expression. Keleman stated a core truth, a mantra that still echoes:

"The act of living is a reward itself. Does that seem strange? Ask people why they like being alive. They just like it. If not, people die like prisoners of war die; they just lay down and die. Young and strong, yet you couldn't wake them up.

"It is an important thing I am saying—most people do not recognize *that the sheer fact of their existence is satisfying; there is nothing to look for, even though they may be in an existential pain situation.*"

All of the activities itemized above have this characteristic: they synergize, they all but metastasize into "being"—so existence itself, whatever its success or failures, joys or miseries, roars its own weight and justification. The world scuffing against our bodies—as air, as light, as water, as mind electricity—*is* us. The rest is required to run runic systems, big machines; keep the liner cruising through time, to create the chimera of purpose, of progress and goals, for our individual lives, for the national patriotic life, the civilizational and species life. That is why people build factories, write constitutions, invent cars and the Internet, prepare for trips to the Moon and Mars. The ecological karma, the tax on the planet is incredible, but that's another story. I mean, the United Nations is already issuing its *final* five-year environmental report to the species, but it doesn't even make the back pages of America.

I watch how people fill their time and am often astonished it can hold their interest and keep them occupied without going mad. Then I think about Keleman's premise; it's not worthy acts and projects that sustain men and women, because most of these don't hold water under scrutiny. It is the mere estate of being alive.

We are in a constant crisis of meaninglessness anyway, especially as all this is impermanent and there will be no local record of any of it. It is one thing not to know what to do—that is healthy, a zen response like a fast. It is another thing not to know what to *think*. That is terror. It is what a terrorist seeks beyond massacre or destruction—the nullification of possibility.

In the end, whatever you do and think, you are reliant on a core to hold life and limb and meaning together. The core is probed and tested across panoramas of bardos, life and death among them. Sanity is merely a phase, insanity likewise.

Making love or engaging in erotic foreplay is so sought and valorized because it deepens the biological trance, the buzz of aliveness. It changes consciousness and sensation, shifting internal and external barriers, breaking down the armor between personality as self and personality as other. Seduction is seduction by the world and creates novelty. It fills time in such a way that we all but forget its passage and become timeless things. It allows intimacy between different characters, each ontologically separate but unexplorably congruent. It contains a recognition that desire, like existence, is mutual, and that a private, forbidden identity can be momentarily suspended and transferred in the service of free and curious people.

You can make a gift of yourself. You can receive another person's gift, his or her beguilement and enchantment.

Life's inventory also includes breathing, deep or shallow; dreaming, waking from dream; kindling romantic infatuations, nursing erotic fantasies; transiting the moment-to-moment strangeness of a foreign country; being in a spell; meditating, working on koans, praying, doing yoga and chi gung; languaging; individuating (creating a self by acts and thoughts and their simultaneous internalizations); accounting a personal history and being responsible to it, its interpretations and consequences; having insights, intuitions, and theophanies; loving selflessly and dispassionately; praying; being sick; dying. Each of these spellbinds us and, though they be single chords in a physical and phenomenological whole, they point to its deceptively unruffled profundity, its majesty and mystery.

So what is this book?

Writing is forever what I do and no longer do, what I never did, what I will always do; it is a part of what makes my life something to me, since I was sixteen years old. I am addressing deities, disembodied entities, past and future scribes, and the principle of intelligence underlying the universe.

The late twentieth century introduced "body snatchers" and "mind parasites," creatures known in earlier epochs by other, more traditional names. The twenty-first century, which has barely begun, will be defined by the fact that the body snatchers *are* the mind parasites, and neither is the half of it. We are moving toward the Bridge, faster than we think, synchronicities cawing about, in trees and sky, like so many crows we can't imagine how they could all just suddenly exist. And who takes a census of crows?

We are not who we thought we were.

Thank goodness for the synchronicities. Anything but business as usual here is a welcome sign.

2012 will arrive, whether it does or not, because we are beginning to make a mirror of our existence. Does anyone yet understand the parities and covert collaborations of the lately completed Cold War—all those nukes to what end, those annihilated cities never annihilated, those clandestine Cuban arsenals in full view, those Strangelove armageddons parodied but never delivered to marching orders? No last headline, no world funeral; no first strike, no retaliatory strike, no claxons and hounds of doom. Now it's unchecked violence and proliferation and raw sewage, species extinction and spewing carbon, offhand massacres and suicide attacks, funny money and Talibanization.

Yes, we are making a mirror, even though its components are pretty much everything you wouldn't use for reflection. That's why, when we see ourselves in it, it will be someone we have never been: half a spade, a feather, soot, dull paper wrap, broken axles, jagged tin parts from anonymous machinery, illicit radiations, unspeakable bodies of dead birds and fish. The ghost in the machine sits at the interstices of commerce and civilization. We have not been laboring so long and hard and barrenly to hatch a monstrosity without unleashing a golem too. We could not have raised a city so stark and empty and soul-less without establishing the sash-weight of a soul.

A giant bird is awakening in our midst. A quiver of a wing here, a spasm of a claw there, a beak that vanishes the moment we see it—psychic and weird and profanely unscientific. Seeping through four dimensions like some global Loch Ness thing. Watch out, boys and girls, Santa Claus *is* coming to town!

Only when reality becomes virtual and prophetic and ghost-busted, infiltrated by nonlinear voices that are neither past nor future, living nor dead, do we begin to understand the approaching landscape. And it's nothing like Mars.

Life is a thought, but it cannot be just a thought. The extrinsic world is the jackpot and prize of creation. We use space and landscape to dispel dangerous and primitive fantasies, to contact and console psychic forces and dakinis that probably existed before matter itself. Geography arises not to overwhelm or betray spirit but to reconcile it. Space is not superficiality or distraction but vista—perspective for spiritual unwrapping.

Inside my body I dream a succession of multiple unimageable and improper shapes, a projection of a teratology I can't see but imagine always part of me, like an alternate self *no one ever sees.*

Last night an extremely tangled tree stump grew on my thigh, multiple roots all twisted around each other and attached to my flesh by tendrils and rootlets, too complex a geometry to excise. It is more real in some ways than I am.

How could such an object be on me without anyone noticing it, without it showing up during my physical exam?

It is an energy placed inside me long ago, made symbolic, and then somaticized.

Standard AMA medicine, aside from everything else it does or doesn't do, presents an implicit quandary: If you deliver your body to experts for diagnosis, preemption, and prevention you are engaging in an act of discursion and dissociation. Earlier in this book, I discussed medicine as healing. Here I am talking about medical ontology as "being." Under medical gaze, a body is a chart as rigorously decisive and omnipotent as any horoscope.

When one submits to the status of a diagnosable object with a laboratory destiny, one is also—like it or not, admit it or not—being incarcerated, being put into a biological jacket, a map without parole. A medical object has to be reclaimed on another level, has to redeem its existential "self" and wrench freedom back from histology and genome.

Technological objectification is clearly beneficial and, by extrapolating the future, alleviates suffering and premature death. But descending series of numbers and demographic abstractions—the data of blood and cells and antibodies—also push us toward oblivion. Just imagine the coming scientistic "utopia" in which each person, analyzed at birth as to genetic predilections, is given an astrology that cannot be dismissed or overridden. Where can such a person go? What can he or she be?

It has nothing to do with Islam. The attack on the West had to come from somewhere.

It has everything to do with Islam. Submission to God—God is great!

New Global Snacks and Lost Crops

Goji berries (pink dried candy drupes from Himalayan vines), young Thai coconut juice (essential syrup of Mounds, vanilla milk shakes, and coconut cream pies, but a clean-burning fuel), Inca goldenberries (tart metallic jujubes with tiny hard seeds, packed with carotene and phosphorus), overripe hachiya persimmons (a natural crème brûlée/mousse), West Indian raw cacao (the bitter chocolate core, ripe in sulphur and magnesium, unsweetened).

That Charles Frazier's *Cold Mountain* beat out Don DeLillo's *Underworld* for the 1997 National Book Award is akin to *Forrest Gump* nabbing the 1994 Academy Award over *Pulp Fiction*. The past, dead on arrival and primping for the prom, somehow stole the future because no one could see where we were headed. Five minutes later we were there. By 9/11 *Gump* was so far over the horizon it could have been a Bing Crosby movie, and the fraudulent, entrepreneurial *Cold Mountain* was several cutting edges short of James Fenimore Cooper's *The Prairie* or *The Last of the Mohicans* for missing its own time, either then or now. When the planes hit the WTC, *Underworld* was prophetically born, and *Pulp Fiction*, once a tad obscure, made sudden total, blinding sense. Even Cooper remained in play.

Herman Melville's *Moby Dick* almost didn't make it out of the nineteenth century, yet we still look toward it from the past.

Artistic and spiritual development—individuation—requires engaging the shadows that attend even the happiest and most successful situations. In fact, those who struggle single-mindedly to impose their schemes—who drive themselves to achieve and perform flawlessly, to get "on the map" and in the network, as if there were no deficit or cost to their avidities—routinely sabotage their own conduct. Refusing their frailties and fragmentation, they subconsciously manufacture alternate versions, pratfall simulacra of their renounced emotional pain, inexplicable mistakes as they bumble along, injury-prone, ill-starred, obliging themselves to keep up with their flagrant self-images, bummed by what they consider continual accidents or bad luck. Over-ambition, over-achievement, and perfectionism *must* be compensated by the dark goddess and her sorrows. Acts are *per se* futile and absurd. Our only lasting capability is negative. Our failures and flubs, even our indulgences, are not mere symptoms or inconveniences; they are the last invitations to becoming human.

Culture is convention. The further afield from a shared reference point a particular artifact or action gets, the more the very logic of creation proves commutable, fickle in its application to matter and life—and the more our own customs seem hopelessly parochial and sectarian, as though we will *never know.* Try playing an Australian Aborigine blow-fly totem to a Beethoven adagio, or rap to a Bach fugue. They violate; they plain don't understand or even recognize each other. At least two foreigners would have a basis of rapport if they bumped into each other in the Gobi Desert or crossing an airport lounge; they have been separated a few hundred thousand years at most. It is enough time for their languages to become uninterintelligible, not enough for their genes and gestures. A vessel of voyagers from Alpha Centauri poses a thornier issue.

The universe is vast and God is disguised, not to flummox, but to inspire us (meaning all creatures) to wonder, to search, to evolve.

It doesn't look like it, I know. At the height of the hyena's kill, her bloody feast at the quivering zebra, on the human battlefield when ingenious tools of the ages are being used to blow off limbs and immolate brethren, it doesn't look like it one bit. It looks like anything but.

Yet behold more closely. Even these events contain irony and possibility. Even these scenes are moving slowly enough that you can feel the unseen hand coaxing the players toward a different outcome, because the present dance is the only way to get there. The field of play exists for a different reason.

What else could it be? Certainly not to feed molecules to other molecules, in ephemeral packages soon to expire, despite the ferocity of their attachment to immediate pursuits. The universe exists for a far grander purpose than to arouse acts, beautiful or ugly, to naught, as impalpable waves suture over, leaving no trace, as none of the participants share in the spoils or survive to tell the tale, ever.

The universe is a machine of love that says Earn Me.

Well, we're getting there, slowly. Slowly. From the Crucifixion to 9/11, from the chalkings at Lascaux to YouTube.... It's not what it seems; it's never what it seems. From a pulse of light on a photosensitive vacuole to a rush of photons along optic fibers, love is the only binding force of matter—pure emptiness, pure charm. There is no other outcome, no better or worse place. And I say that despite the fact that Satan now brazenly walks on high, from Congo to Colombia to the South Side. He sits on every board of every major corporation. He is an existential pretext, a rehabilitation of himself, because at the end of the highway, where everything dwindles into nothing, there may be no difference between good and evil. It might just be one dead star here, one green-blue fish-pond there, mostly gas giants and novas, pterodactyls and bacteria and priests, all the same to Nietzsche or Genentech, all the same to Pan.

Yes, the movement of feathers where there is no bird; yes, the hint of grace at the heart of darkness; a sound like music where there is nothing to make music; the imposition of two unlikely events in the hollow of matter; the dire confluence of souls: all indicia of love.

The operant cosmos is pretty large in order to conceal space in time, real space, that is—the kind of space that lights Pawnee and Hopi totems, blossoms into Aranda and Dogon Dreamtime, floods Tibetan dark meditations, the kind of space that positions sefira on the Tree of Life. Spaciousness, sacred to the gills and at core, is spilling across vulgar and vapid and violent time.

Not a waste, not a sacrilege, not even a diabolism. It simply is. It is what it is about: us, you, them, the others too.

How would we find ourselves except by being forced to look for what's not there?

Despite its occasional lightness and play and patent absurdity, I can tell you that life is basically a serious proposition. I can't tell you how I know that. Well yes, I can. First of all, it is a rude awakening. Awakening from what? I said, "rude": abrupt, unexpected. It is hard getting in, hard getting out. The world is a school; all residential schools are modeled on it.

And then there are the stars.

In the end, whatever that means, it does no good to have even one single person unconscious, one last jerk vandalizing or making trouble, one sentient being bewildered or oppressed, because then the whole universe will be in danger, will be susceptible to falling back into exile and chaos. Any activity at any level by anything, even a mosquito, keeps this universe lit and going, even after all other consciousness has vacated. And one stray or renegade bacterium can breathe the whole thing back to life.

I have heard that erstwhile UFO abductee and horror novelist Whitley Strieber has proposed, with perverse apocalyptic exuberance, that we face a huge imminent "human die-off." He is not alone. Assorted pissed-off environmentalists, climatologists, and ecological activists welcome the disaster looming, as our comeuppance. No species can overbreed and pummel and poison its habitat indefinitely before a tipping point is crossed and its life niche turns against it and slams shut.

Green Earth is a narrow proposition from the get-go. The universe is teeming with Jupiters, Marses, and Venuses but very few moist, temperate gardens. And even this benign and habitable world can turn violent and inhospitable at the drop of a hat. From Katrina-like superstorms to sub-Saharan droughts to Indonesian tsunamis to cholera and malaria, we dwell within a delicate truce of forces and molecules. Our entire civilization is a cocoon inside the crushing mathematics of chaos systems. Oft-placid, benign Gaia is a wild lady at heart.

Christian Fundamentalists are equally grim and dire in their prognoses: Armageddon and its Four Horsemen are now on the main track. But this pessimism, within the flock, is really "optimism," as believers fully expect to be raptured and catapulted into a paradise at the chime of planetary doom. Once in heaven, after World War III and the unleashing of chemical and nuclear arsenals, they presume that their own circumstances will be dramatically improved; they will be happier and more appreciated by the universe.

Flower of Life devotees hone breathing and visualization exercises, practices designed to incarnate personal transdimensional vehicles in which to ride out of an overheated, irradiated Earth into higher octaves of the cosmos. Other New Age schools and cults have their own trademarked mechanisms and esoteric vessels for lifeboats and arks. There is no lack these days of hermetic escape cosmologies and magian science-fiction scenarios.

The same person who told me about Strieber's dread forecast added that, in a radio debate, Mr. Ensign from the cattle-mutilating Greys was challenged by psychedelic shamanist Daniel Pinchbeck who accused Strieber explicitly of *hexing the human race*.

I have thought long and hard about this issue. I was thinking about it as a teenager, back in the Fifties, the bomb-shelter era, and I continued to dwell on it through the Sixties and Seventies when Nostradamus and the doomsayers of the Aquarian counterculture issued their warnings, as the Comet Kohoutek manifested at the edge of Western history in the vicinity of Jupiter, dragging an astral mass the size of our karmic debt—a major portent. It was followed by malefic planetary conjunctions of the sort that occur only every several thousand years.

New Age Cassandras then and since have made their prophesies on the basis of factors ranging from sociopolitical and ecological endgames to magical and astrological denouements. It has been the children of light against the children of darkness for a long time, a battle which even now, as I finish this book, is rekindled at the core of the Barack Obama-Hillary Clinton debate and the prospective clash between Obama and someone like Mitt Romney and the neocon evangelicals (which may never come to pass if Bill and Hillary get their sorry-ass way and have electoral retribution). Strieber and Dick Cheney are on different wavelengths of the same cosmic beam; it is just a matter of who constitutes the agents and foils of evil: alien Zeta Reticullans or Commies and Islamofascists. Now an outsider post-partisan spiritual progressive is challenging a quasi-Marxian policy-wonking cynic. It is not just the Tao itself versus ancient battles that can only be lost or won, but the mystery-we-are versus the grim, maudlin bigots by default we have become.

I have always felt that there were qualities of rage, envy, revenge, egotism, ambition, and covert sadism in the raps of doomsayers. They have rarely seemed neutral in their sorry assessments of our situation. They have some element of "fuck you" and "take that, you assholes." They are, in some sense, fundamentalists and jihadists or maybe just depressives off their meds. With their outrage and hawkish despair they want to take down the house.

I am no model of hope; I don't practice the politics of ecstasy either. Anyone who has read this book knows that I go from paralysis and terror—personal and cosmic—to blind faith and euphoria, equally cosmic, equally singular. It is hard for me to sustain the attacks of fatalists without becoming sullen and listless myself. Suddenly nothing seems worth doing, and I have trouble dragging myself from moment to moment. I believe in human verity and grace, though sometimes I'm not so sure. But how could I not believe? To breathe is to hope. "I believe" is the same as "I am."

Maybe the only answer is to say "fuck you" back: "You arrogant sons of witches, you pimpmobile priests, get a life. You are attacking the mystery. You are undermining God and creation itself. You don't understand that, whatever the outcome, we are warriors in an incredible epic," superheroes in a galactic cliffhanger.

We have been accoutered in bodies by brave paranormal forces, by transpersonal intelligences, to do something that has never been done, anywhere or at any time, in the history of consciousness. We have been woven into suits made of ourselves, every thread and microfilament in their composition a material version of our karma and very soul. We are here for experience, whatever that means, whatever it turns out to be. And it is inalterably and irreproachably sacred—a real rapture, a *bona fide* epiphany.

You may fear the worst—I may fear the worst—as we head pellmell toward the cusp and 2012 and omega points beyond; but don't put a curse on yourself and the rest of us. Don't undermine and sabotage or underestimate consciousness. Let it happen. Let it be what it is. Live out your mission for chrissakes.

No matter how biological it seems, the ecological crisis is merely the physical manifestation of a spiritual crisis. But don't take it personally. Look at every person you pass on the street. I mean, look at them carefully. They are in this with you, intimately and incognitio. Imagine all the people in cities and villages and outbacks across the planet—and there are more than you can imagine, believe me. We are all working on the problem together, privately, silently. We are all serving and awaiting the consciousness shift, even those who are not serving or awaiting it, because anything else is not worth the price or price of admission, and the price now is everything. We are ready to recant all and everything, even our apostasies and betrayals, even our cynicism, even our hope, even apocalypse and our vindication of apocalypse, if only we could still be together, if only someone would instruct us and lead the charge.

I have said this all before, and I will say it again: I feel that the only possibilities from here on in, and in fact forever and yore, are good, because we are awake and incarnate. We are headed for the darkness, for sure, but that is the only path into a different kind of light. We are headed for extinction but nonsectarian rebirth, a radical manifestation of the same karmic-marmic thing.

We are headed toward the universe's truly forbidden knowledge, one way or the other. And we can prophesize doom if we want and hit others over the head with it in rage and outrage likewise, but finally we can only focus on the single pinpoint of being that our personal existence discloses to us. It is destiny.

Life is something that just is. Less a flash between abysses than a sustained radiance resembling a flash, life can neither be solved nor resolved. It has no market value, even as the chemicals that make it up are worth no more than a few dollars on the open market, though a fully formed eye or kidney is priceless; in India, a value equal to another life, or more. And this is where class, belief, and education enter, for a suicide bomber attempts to cash in one entire flash for another, converting hydrogen, carbon, oxygen, and will into the politics of difference among lives formerly of unequal weight.

Life, while measured in time, cannot be measured in time. All lives are the same length—be they fireflies, mice, or people. From the next bardo this life, no matter how sinuous or complex, will seem as if about fifteen minutes.

"Life" is the word most used when someone says what he/she is doing or trying to put together, as in "How's your life going?" or "Tell me about your life." But life is also what is happening, now and anywhere, to anything.

The notion of an authoritarian egoic God-creator, popular in evangelical circles, is as foolish as it is blasphemous. "God" (subject) "created" (verb) "us" (object) makes no sense. The universe is self-creating and self-organizing. Its God-originator is us; that is, our starting point is the same as the universe's starting point and identical as well to divinity's starting point. God didn't make us by separating something from his own being or image. He found us mysteriously in himself/herself, found himself in us, already there. We have raveled and unraveled, folded and unfolded together, and we are still in the muddle, a single cascade of everything, emerging out of everything else in chaos-complexity; integrating, disintegrating, reintegrating, making strange and novel stuff always, out of prior babble and bricolage. Gnostics and Pantheists were true to the living God; they were heretics only to the State and the Church, each of which meant to establish its own lasting authority through annexation of all cosmic power into a private, exclusive Idea.

But the universe is a mode of consciousness, not an Idea or an Architecture. Its psyche is the same as its prairies and oceans and stars, their unplumbed depths and profundity a single thing, their destinies imbedded in one another's. If innate intelligence is the grand source, consciousness is its only expression, and psyche its transaction: the process of bringing grasslands and temples out of the void, out of the bottomless unconscious in which they were thoroughly imbedded and unrealized—utterly, transparently real.

People who claim that they don't care about this world and are just waiting for enlightenment miss the point. What do they think the world is doing here exactly? Where do they think the notion of enlightenment comes from?

The fact that life and a world seem arbitrary and we ourselves in a circumstance without resolution with no way out makes everything not less *but more* enlightened, more real and eternal. If timelessness and joyful eternity were themselves the landscape, the universe would have no shape, no process; we wouldn't even exist.

This, friends and neighbors, is what we are.

No way out. But every way in.

Those who try to work around secular reality or who tell themselves that this world is a mere staging area in order to get to nirvana or revelation or the real stuff beyond it are confabulating an event that doesn't exist. They are distorting the only world we have, overtly and implicitly, making heaven remote and impossible.

If you aren't willing to dig into this as totally real, then there is no point in going through all this trouble to get here or, for that matter, creating a world in the first place.

The path to heaven is through worlds; there is in fact no other path. And it doesn't matter if it is the path to heaven or the path *back* to heaven because these are the same things.

This world and its life forms were created not merely by natural selection through algorithms such that we are slave critters, unwilling participants in a shoddy, lesser affair. It was fashioned by an intelligence, our own in fact, but in a state much older and wiser than us. We made this thing, including how to gestate in cells, how to get born and die. We invented primacy and impregnation, the intimacy of the fetus in the womb; we chose the judgment of the hunt, the reckoning of the kill.

To think of skipping all this now and going straight to enlightenment, aside from the fact that that is the sure way *not* to be enlightened, is to miss the clarity and subtlety of incarnation. More than that, it is to shirk the exceedingly fine stuff of which the soul or self is made, its explicit fiber.

Sorry, but we are snatched in the winds of karma. We have bought a ticket for bardo travel. There is no enlightenment short of the whole trip, however many trillions of universes it takes.

MANSET, MAINE, AND KENSINGTON, CALIFORNIA
AUGUST, 2005–FEBRUARY, 2008

Notes

This book began in the aftermath of my previous collection, *On the Integration of Nature: Post-9/11 Biopolitical Notes*. At the time, it had no title, and I could not predict where it would go. I named it late in the game, about a year and a half in. "The Bardo of Waking Life" captures its main drift, though, as my editor Mary Stark complains, there's stuff in the book that doesn't fit—like those huckleberries at the beginning. But as we all know, everything I could possibly talk about falls somewhere in "the bardo of waking life," even as everything is also part of "the integration of nature": these are nonexclusionary titles.

The material runs chronologically from August 2005 through the beginning of 2008, but I have rearranged some sections to bring thematic elements together and avoid repetition. During parts of each summer and early fall I wrote in Maine. During the rest of the year I wrote in Northern California.

This is a literary work, more in the genre of a novel or poetry collection than expository writing, so I have elected not to have formal endnotes and references. Many notes already appear in the body of the text. In this section I am providing additional considerations, stray and incomplete citations insofar as I have them, and references to other books of mine for those who would like to read more on a particular topic. The publisher, date, and subtitle are given only at the first mention of each book. North Atlantic Books and Frog, Ltd. are our own company imprints and published in Berkeley, California, except where otherwise noted.

Pages 3 and 6–7. For more on biomachines, see *Embryos, Galaxies, and Sentient Beings: How the Universe Makes Life*, North Atlantic Books, 2003, pp. 139–150.

Page 5. See the 2003 documentary *Rivers and Tides: Andy Goldsworthy Working with Time* by Thomas Riedelshelmer.

Page 8. The Long Pond about which I write in this book is also called Great Pond or Great Long Pond to distinguish it from other "Long Ponds" in Eastern Maine.

Pages 11–12. The Skatalites appeared at the American Folk Festival, Bangor, Maine, 2005.

Page 16. Steve Perrin is the author of *Acadia: The Soul of a National Park*, North Atlantic Books, 2003.

Page 18. Dusty Dowes is the source of the "Guinness stout" line. Huckleberry is also one of the flavors in "Lollipop" by the Chordettes: "*huckleberry, cherry, or lime.*" The lyricist probably needed four syllables.

Page 20. Albert Einstein, *The World as I See It*, Citadel, 2001, originally published in 1934.

Pages 23–24. *The Book of Love*, formerly *Jack in the Box*, Houghton Mifflin, 1980, p. 29. The review of *Fan Man* can be found at http://www.epinions.com/content_5699853069

Page 44. "… young black men in a New York State prison yard …" shown on "Sixty Minutes" in 2007. This academic program is administered by Bard College, Annandale-on-Hudson, New York.

Pages 48–50. I have written extensively on the theme of mind in matter (panpsychism); see my books *Planet Medicine: Modalities* (Revised Edition), North Atlantic Books, 2003, pp. 21–22, 533–537; *Out of Babylon: Ghosts of Grossinger's*, Frog, Ltd., 1997, pp. 570–571; and *Embryos, Galaxies, and Sentient Beings*, pp. 308–313 and 421–423. The earliest appearance of this notion was probably in 1979 in my essay, "Alchemy: pre-Egyptian Legacy, Millennial Promise," which was reprinted in *The Alchemical Tradition in the Late Twentieth Century*, edited by Richard Grossinger, North Atlantic Books, 1991, pp. 245–246, 250–253.

Pages 52–53. For my more complete description of Damanhur, see "A Visit to the Temples of Humankind," *Elixir: Consciousness, Conscience, and Culture,* Issue 4, Spring 2007, New Lebanon, New York, pp. 40–47.

Pages 54–58. My "communication with the dead" approximates astrologer Ellias Lonsdale's version as depicted by Mark Borax in his book *2012: Crossing the Bridge to the Future,* Frog, Ltd., 2008.

Pages 64–68. The source for the quotes and information on Bob Dylan is Martin Scorsese's 2005 documentary film, *No Direction Home: Bob Dylan.*

Page 69. The Charles Olson quote about "the universalization of the present" and the lines in the Extracts were transcribed from a tape of his 1962 poetry reading and lecture at Goddard College in Vermont. I published them in *Io/16, Earth Geography Booklet Number 4, Anima Mundi,* Plainfield, Vermont, 1973, p. 83.

Page 70. "Hail and beware the dead ..." is from "A Newly Discovered Homeric Hymn," in *The Distances,* Grove Press, New York, 1950, p. 72.

Page 71. Benjamin Lee Whorf, "The Punctual and Segmentative Aspects of Verbs in Hopi," in *Language, Thought, and Reality: Selected Writings,* MIT Press, 1956.

Page 83. This is Pir Zia's actual response to the piece.

Pages 84–87. For an earlier version of these ideas, see my essay "The Dream Work" in *Dreams Are Wiser Than Men,* edited by Richard A. Russo, North Atlantic Books, 1987, pp. 191–246.

Pages 98–100. For the development of the notion that "the embryo is the universe writing itself on its own body," see *Embryogenesis: Species, Gender, Identity,* North Atlantic Books, 2000, pp. xiv-xix, 720–722, 774; and *Embryos, Galaxies, and Sentient Beings,* pp. 369–379.

Pages 107–117. "On Sexuality" discusses themes that occur also in *Planet Medicine: Modalities* (pp. 116–122), *Embryogenesis* (pp. 575–590, 649–674), and *Embryos, Galaxies, and Sentient Beings* (pp. 177–181).

Pages 112–113. *Capturing the Friedmans*, directed by Andrew Jarecki, 2003; *Mysterious Skin* by Scott Heim, Harper Collins, 1995.

Pages 120–121. Justin A. Frank, M.D., *Bush on the Couch: Inside the Mind of the President*, Harper Collins Publishers, New York, 2004.

Page 126. Werner Herzog's own words from the film.

Pages 133–136, Thanks to Alexandra Grief for her account of the Yi Factor.

Pages 142–144. This initiation into the tarot is described in *New Moon*, Frog, Ltd., 1996, pp. 248–250, 399–401.

Page 152. For a fuller story of the visit to Stan Brakhage, see *New Moon*, pp. 440–442.

Page 153. The image of the latent universe appears first in *On the Integration of Nature: Post-9/11 Biopolitical Notes*, North Atlantic Books, 2005, pp. 264–265.

Pages 158–161. My personal Slaid Cleaves discography also includes "For The Brave," "Careful," "Brother's Keeper," "New Year's Day," "You Don't Have to Tell Me," "Ramblers," "Another Man's Wealth," "Desert Dreams," "The Ballad of Nick and Betty," "Borderline," "You're a Mean One, Mr. Grinch," "Below," "Another Kind of Blue," "Oh Roberta," and "Devil's Lullaby." The last three were written by friends of his; to my knowledge he wrote the others.

Pages 172–176. Here is a critique of this piece from a colleague— far more radical than my viewpoint but worth entertaining if for no other reason than a) the seriousness of the charge and b) the consequences if it is right:

"This is in response to your 9/11 responsibility musings. I don't think you should publish that section as you've written it because it is the product of inadequate research. This is too damned important a topic for casual musings. This is not a topic I ever want to be quoted on, but I think any clear-minded review of the evidence makes an overwhelming case that Cheney *et al.* orchestrated the attacks. They mined and blew up three WTC buildings; they put up patsies whose culpability disappears upon examination; they destroyed all the forensic evidence.

"David Ray Griffin's most recent book on the subject, *Debunking 9/11 Debunking*, demolishes the refutations offered by the anti-conspiracists (it was good enough to impress the always skeptical Lewis Lapham). But rather than revisit the arcana of the attack and its immediate aftermath, I'll leave you with three references:

"One is a leading 9/11 website with a list of professionals who think 9/11 was a state-sponsored conspiracy. Start by reading the comments by the military and airline pilots: http://patriotsquestion911. com. The second is a book by a British national security academic, Nafeez Ahmed, called *The War On Truth: 9/11, Disinformation, and the Anatomy of Terrorism*. It details direct American sponsorship of al-Qaeda paramilitary and terrorist operations as recently as the early summer of 2001. The third is to an Internet video by the unfortunately hyperbolic Alex Jones of www.prisonplanet. Go tohttp:// www.youtube.com/watch?v=1GwJvximahs and drag the play button to eighteen minutes in. Watch for five minutes. Now you tell me that you believe that it's just a coincidence the very same three tube stations that were bombed on Britain's 7/7 happened to be scheduled for mock terrorist attacks on the same morning at almost the identical time.

"America is in the grip of a fascist take-over and unless the 9/11 conspiracy is exposed I predict that, before the election next year, another attack will be orchestrated by the same group. That attack will used as the excuse to kill the remnants of our democracy. This is very serious shit, Richard, and it deserves serious study by anyone who presumes to write and publish on the topic."

Pages 176–196. "On Healing" synopsizes a series of themes in *Planet Medicine: Origins*, Revised Edition, North Atlantic Books, 2005, and *Planet Medicine: Modalities*.

Pages 177–178. The Jule Eisenbud quote originally appeared in *Io/14*, *Earth Geography Booklet Number 3, Imago Mundi*, Cape Elizabeth, Maine, 1972, p. 372, and its meanings are summarized in *Planet Medicine: Origins*, pp. 183–184.

Page 193. Max Romeo, "I Chase the Devil."

Pages 193–194. Edward C. Whitmont, *The Alchemy of Healing: Psyche and Soma*, North Atlantic Books, 1996.

Pages 196–197. This is an exchange with an old girlfriend whose whereabouts were unknown to me since sophomore year of college. See *New Moon*, pp. 358–365.

Page 197. This aria (number, quantity, symbol) comes to me from Jacob Klein via Chuck Stein.

Page 198. The "writing elsewhere" is in *Embryos, Galaxies, and Sentient Beings*, pp. 414–415.

Page 199. For "the cities of Antares" et al., see *The Long Body of the Dream*, North Atlantic Books, Plainfield, Vermont, 1974, p. 20.

Page 201f. Robert Kelly, "On a Picture of a Black Bird Given to Me by Arthur Tress," originally written in the 1960s, reprinted in *Ecology and Consciousness: Traditional Wisdom on the Environment*, edited by Richard Grossinger, North Atlantic Books, 1992, p. 31.

Pages 203–231. There are accounts of my brother Jon in *New Moon* and *Out of Babylon*, the latter including sections from his letters and writings. I also wrote about his suicide in *On the Integration of Nature*, pp. 150–158, 177–181. I collected his poetry posthumously in a volume entitled *Westport Poems* (North Atlantic Books, 2007). Tek Young Lin was Jon's high-school English teacher and track coach; the other three are recognized literary authors.

Page 234. For the "leverage of reality" and "temporary rip," see *On the Integration of Nature*, p. 6.

Page 234. The Kinks sang both "Unreal Reality" and "Apeman."

Pages 244–245. This quote is from bin Laden's 9/07 video.

Page 271. The video-game story is from Ron Sieh.

Page 281. Credit the "pig" to Jon Barry.

Page 284. For an account of the Cuban Crisis, see *New Moon*, pp. 298–300.

Page 310. William Butler Yeats, "The Second Coming."

Pages 311–312. To round out my Dave Insley discography, add "Maricopa Mountains," "Cowboy Lullaby," "White Cross," "Open Road," and "You're the One That I Prefer."

Pages 335–336. Psalm 139, verses 1-18.

Pages 352–355. This discussion of grief and "the plug" is a dialogue between me and a therapist friend.

Page 357. For an exegesis of "what we think the stars are is who we are," see *The Night Sky: The Science and Anthropology of the Stars and Planets*, Jeremy P. Tarcher, Inc./St. Martin's Press, 1988, pp. 334–361.

Pages 364–366. This is an informal review of *The Last Human: A Guide to Twenty-Two Species of Extinct Humans* by G. J. Sawyer, Viktor Deak, Esteban Sarmiento, G. I. Sawyer, Richard Milner, Donald C. Johanson, Meave Leakey, and Ian Tattersall, Yale University Press, 2007. See also Haplogroups on www.Wikipedia.com.

Pages 369–370. The incident in Kabul comes from a newspaper interview with novelist Khalid Hosseini about his 2007 book *A Thousand Splendid Suns*.

Page 384. Danny Harper told a version of this joke during his performance at the Acadia Opry in Southwest Harbor, Maine, September 2007.

Pages 384–385. Patricia Fox teaches yoga in Bass Harbor, Maine.

Page 408. The line is from Robert Kelly's "First in an Alphabet of Sacred Animals," reprinted in *Ecology and Consciousness*, p. 60.

Page 411. For Dusty Dowes, see *Embryos, Galaxies, and Sentient Beings*, pp. xvii–xxiii, xxxv–xxxvi.

Page 412. The quote is from Utah Phillips' CD *I've Got To Know*.

Page 414. I also used this Elvis line over thirty-five years ago in *The Long Body of the Dream*, p. 159.

Page 423. For Andrew Lugg's original quote, see *Embryos, Galaxies, and Sentient Beings*, p. 78.

Page 429. This is from a 2007 Associated Press article, "Warming perils tiny island nation" by Charles J. Hanley.

Pages 429–438. This material is more fully summarized in my essay "A Phenomenology of Panic," pp. 95–163, in *Panic: Origins, Insight, and Treatment*, edited by Leonard J. Schmidt and Brooke Warner, North Atlantic Books, 2002.

Page 433. My daughter won four film prizes with her first movie, *Me and You and Everyone We Know*, at Cannes in France, and then the Frank O'Connor Prize with her first book of short stories, *No One Belongs Here More Than You*, in Cork, Ireland.

Page 434. "… Enyalion/who takes off his clothes wherever he is found,/on a hill,/in front of his troops,/in the face of the men of the other side…." This is from Charles Olson's poem "Enyalion" (e.g. "Helios, the Sun God") which appears many places, including *Ecology and Consciousness*, North Atlantic Books, 1992, pp. 214–215.

Page 438. *Eternal Sunshine of the Spotless Mind*, directed by Michael Gondry, starring Jim Carrey and Kate Winslet, 2004—an irritating but accurate parable.

Page 440. For Catherine Carver, see *New Moon*, pp. 307–309, 330–332, 356–358.

Pages 440–441. Here are some remarkable books by these authors that you might not have heard of or read: *Beach Music*, *The Lords of Discipline*, and *The Prince of Tides* by Pat Conroy (he's too flowery for many, and the latter title was overshadowed by the Barbra Streisand-vehicle movie that can't carry its jockstrap); Anita Shreve's *Fortune's Rock* and *The Last Time They Met* (the latter with a surprise ending that rivals the one acted by Bruce Willis at the end of M. Night

Shyamalan's *The Sixth Sense*); *Close Range* by Annie Proulx (forget the overwrought Hollywoodization of *Brokeback Mountain*: this is a writer on a roll, and every unlikely adjective and chord of parenthetical phrasing tells you that); *Rule of the Bone* and *The Darling* by Russell Banks (classics overshadowed by *Continental Drift* and his cinematized books, though I hear *The Darling* is headed for the big screen); *The Pickup* by Nadine Gordimer (the one true 9/11 novel); *Underworld* by Don DeLillo (it captures the Cold War era, from Bobby Thompson's home run to nuclear-radiation meltdowns to the prophecy of the heat death of the universe); and *Segu* by Maryse Condé (a slave-trade novel immersed in African mythology).

Page 442. For Hebrew school incidents, see *New Moon*, pp. 71–72.

Page 455. For the giveaway of cards, see *New Moon*, pp. 136–137.

Pages 457–459. For Lindy's and my college years, see *New Moon*, pp. 339–507.

Page 477. My "nuclear weapons" discussion here is a loose synopsis of a layer of Don DeLillo's *Underworld*.

Index

About the Author

Gullfoss waterfall, Iceland, 2006

A native of New York City, Richard Grossinger graduated from Amherst College and received a Ph.D. in anthropology from the University of Michigan for an ethnography on fishing communities in Maine. He studied craniosacral therapy under Randy Cherner and through the Upledger Institute and t'ai chi ch'uan with Paul Pitchford, Benjamin Lo, Peter Ralston, and Ron Sieh. He is the author of many books, including *Planet Medicine*, *The Night Sky*, *Embryogenesis*, *Migraine Auras*, and *Out of Babylon*. He lives outside Berkeley, California, where he and his wife, Lindy Hough, are the publishers of North Atlantic Books. Their children are Robin Grossinger, an environmental scientist at the San Francisco Estuary Institute, and Miranda July, a performance artist, writer, and film director.